Pronunciation Key

ā   as in fate, age
ă   as in fat, map
â   as in dare, air
ä   as in father, pa, barn
ē   as in be, equal
ĕ   as in bet, ebb
ê   as in mere, near
ī   as in bite, ice, ride
ĭ   as in bit, if
ō   as in note, boat, low

ŏ   as in hot, box
ȯ   as in dog, law, fought
ô   as in more, roar, door, four
oi as in oil, boy
ou as in out, loud
o͞o as in too, rule
o͝o as in book, put
ŭ   as in fun, up
û   as in fur, term

ə stands for the sound of: **a** in ago, Senate; **e** in open, hopeless, fairness; **i** in peril, trellis; **o** in lemon; **u** in minus, argument; **ou** in famous; **ai** in mountain; **oi** in tortoise.

b   as ...
ch as ...
    (b...)
d   as ...
f   as ...
g   as in g...
h   as in hop (hŏp)
hw for "wh" as in what (hwŏt), wheel (hwēl)
j   as in jam (jăm), job (jŏb); and for "g" in gentle (jĕn'təl) and range (rānj)
k   as in kin (kĭn), smoke (smōk); for "c" in coal (kōl); and for "ck" in rack (răk)
l   as in let (lĕt), bell (bĕl)
m   as in men (mĕn), him (hĭm)
n   as in not (nŏt), ran (răn)
ng as in song (sông); and for "n" in think (thĭngk)
p   as in pup (pŭp)
r   as in ride (rīd), very (vĕr'ē)

r   as in fur (fûr), tar (tär) (This r is not pronounced in some sections of the country.)
s   as in sod (sŏd), must (mŭst); and for "c" in cent (sĕnt), price (prīs)
sh as in she (shē), rush (rŭsh)
t   as in tea (tē), hot (hŏt)
th as in thin (thĭn), bath (băth), breath (brĕth)
t̶h̶ as in then (t̶h̶ĕn), bathe (bāt̶h̶), breathe (brēt̶h̶)
v   as in vat (văt), dove (dŭv); and for "f" in of (ŏv)
w   as in we (wē)
y   as in yet (yĕt)
z   as in zero (zêr'ō), buzz (bŭz); and for "s" in wise (wīz)
zh for "s" as in usual (yo͞o'zho͞o-əl), vision (vĭzh'ən); also for some "g's" as in mirage (mə räzh')

Word Wealth

Ward S. Miller

Holt, Rinehart and Winston, Publishers
New York • Toronto • London • Sydney

WARD S. MILLER, a native of Buffalo, New York, taught English and served as adviser of publications in John Marshall High School, Rochester, New York, for more than ten years. After four years as a naval officer in World War II, he completed his doctorate, taught for two decades at the University of Redlands, Redlands, California, and is now Emeritus Professor of English. Dr. Miller was awarded a Fulbright appointment at the University of Helsinki (1962–1963) and a second appointment at the University of Jordan in Amman (1966–1967). He is now Associate Head of the English Department, Hong Kong Baptist College, Kowloon, Hong Kong.

Page iv, Rose Skytta © Jeroboam, Inc.; 1, © Jeroboam, Inc.; 24, Wide World Photos; 40, Lawrence Hedges © Uniphoto; 41, © Raimondo Borea; 74, National Audubon photo, Photo Researchers, Inc.; 77, Taurus Photos © R. D. Ullmann; 78, Picture Collection, New York Public Library; 82, Wide World Photos; 85, Photo Researchers, Inc. © E. Trina Lipton, 1972; 129, Wide World Photos; 131, Chicago Historical Society; 136, U. S. Army Photo; 140, © Jeroboam, Inc.; 172, Black Star; 179, © Raimondo Borea; 192, American Red Cross; 194, CBS; 217, National Park Service; 222, Film Archives, Museum of Modern Art; 242, Greek National Tourist Office; 275, © Raimondo Borea; 308, Port Authority of New York and New Jersey; 315, John Running; 331, Courtesy Air France; 337, *Both:* Metropolitan Museum of Art; 356, Hale Observatories Photograph Collection, Pasadena, California

Acknowledgment:
Material for the twelve problems beginning on page 365 of "Spelling Tricks and Techniques" is from *Word Wealth Junior* by Ward S. Miller, copyright 1950, © 1962, by Holt, Rinehart and Winston, Publishers.

acknowledgments

This book owes its origin to a distinguished head of the English Department of John Marshall High School, Rochester, New York, Elizabeth LeMay Wright, who first encouraged me, the author, to provide word lists for literature assignments. The lists gradually evolved into the first edition of *Word Wealth*.

Each subsequent edition of *Word Wealth* is indebted to teachers and supervisors in various parts of the United States, whose advice and assistance enabled me to produce a completely rewritten book markedly superior to its predecessor every time. Numerous clerical workers, among them two of my children, Katherine Miller Long and Philip Searing Miller, performed well in previous editions.

For very helpful criticism and advice in preparing this fifth edition, I am especially grateful to Glenn Taylor of Pacific High School, San Bernardino, California; to Ruth R. Lewis, now counselor in Cajon High School, also in San Bernardino; to Virginia Baker of West Plains, Missouri; to Barbara Crist of Shippensburg State College, Shippensburg, Pennsylvania; to Alice Hay of Princeton, New Jersey, for materials; to my son Newton Ward Miller of Iowa City, Iowa, for special assistance in research and in the selection of words; and to Buehl M. Ray, Supervisor of Language Arts of the Buffalo Public Schools, Buffalo, New York, who, as consultant, read the manuscript and offered valuable ideas for its improvement.

Special credit goes to Ann Burk of Highland, Maryland, who contributed the crossword exercise that is a valuable feature of the *Word Wealth Testing Program*.

To Dr. Jachin Chan, Head of the English Department here at Hong Kong Baptist College, my appreciation for allowing me the time to complete this project. The assistance of Lillian Lau Tai Tei in preparing the manuscript also proved crucial. Students who helped in tabulating usage studies and transcribing material include Chung Sin-Hin, Wong Yuk-Chin, Edith To Man-Han, Sabrina Leong Shing-Ping, Winifred Tsui Wing-Yin, and Jeanette Young Yuen-Yee.

Finally, I thank Joan Gibbons of Redlands, California, for her work on the manuscript; Ralph and Virginia Westervelt, also of Redlands, for lending me their home and reference books for the summer; Mrs. L. Amidon and daughter Marion Amidon of Rochester, New York, for their assistance; and my wife Phyllis, who repeatedly protected me from distractions and intrusions in California, Rochester, London, and finally Hong Kong while the work went on.

Ward S. Miller
Associate Head of the
English Department
Hong Kong Baptist College

contents

part three

part four

to the student

THE ROLE OF WORDS TODAY

A word count of President Woodrow Wilson's published works shows that he used more than 175,000 different words, whereas William Shakespeare wrote the world's most widely produced plays with a vocabulary of 25,000. The difference between the two figures gives a reliable indication of the expanded role of words in the twentieth century.

There is still no greater playwright in English than Shakespeare. At the same time, knowledge in a hundred areas of which even the scholars of Shakespeare's plays were scarcely conscious has steadily increased. Dictionaries have expanded from a few hundred pages in the seventeenth century to the 3,194 pages and more than 600,000 word entries of Webster's Second Edition of the *New International Dictionary*, including proper names and abbreviations. This Second Edition claims to be the largest dictionary ever compiled. Yet it contains only a fraction of the estimated four million words that are said to exist.

Woodrow Wilson was a college professor of history and political science before he became President. By the standard rule of three to one, his recognition vocabulary may have been more than 500,000, unless one assumes that in his voluminous writings he used most of the words he knew. In his specialized field he probably did, and he certainly had a well-educated layperson's command of many other fields, including the sciences.

Today, even if President Wilson had been a scientist, he would find hundreds of unfamiliar scientific terms in the newspapers and popular magazines. The areas that offer a host of new words include space science, nuclear physics, electronics, medicine, and all of the social sciences. The whole field of computerization is new, with its binary arithmetic and other manifold ramifications. Great advances have occurred in numerous other fields, from astronomy to zoology, including even the well-established subjects of literature and history.

Were President Wilson to return to earth today, would he know what a transistor is? An astronaut? A space walk? A tranquilizer? An antibiotic? Or a catalytic converter? Nuclear fission, nuclear fusion, supersonic speeds, penicillin, DNA, synthetic rubber, jet propulsion, extrasensory perception, hallucinogens, and even nylon (as well as a dozen other synthetic fabrics) would be mysterious and largely unintelligible. Indeed, Woodrow Wilson would scarcely know what a closed-in car or a freeway is, and he would wonder what happened to the millions of Model-T Fords that once roamed the rough primitive highways of the country at speeds of 30–40 miles per hour.

Woodrow Wilson would have one major advantage that most young people today do not have, however. He studied Latin and Greek. In so doing, he became acquainted with most of the roots, prefixes, and other word elements from which almost every new word in the arts and the sciences is derived. He would know, for example, that *television* means seeing something at a great distance. He would suspect that *supersonic* means beyond (the speed of) sound and that an *astronaut* is literally a star sailor.

Like Woodrow Wilson, Shakespeare studied Latin and Greek. He thus enjoyed the advantages such study gives to an understanding of English words. He did not go to college, but he must have had much more than the "little Latin and less Greek" that Ben Jonson credited him with. He used several hundred Latin- and Greek-derived words in his plays at a time when relatively few were in common use. In Shakespeare's time, the English language fell far short of the adequacy it has gradually attained.

Clearly, systematic training in vocabulary and word elements was never more essential than it is right now. It would be easy to demonstrate that word study is *more important than any other aspect* of English courses, especially if it includes the nearly 300 most commonly used roots and prefixes. One researcher found that fifteen of these prefixes account for 82 percent of those found in over 4,000 words containing prefixes in a 20,000-word sample.*

Intelligent young people learn many new words readily enough just by wide reading. They learn new words, too, by watching news and documentary programs of many kinds on television. Still, with Scholastic Aptitude Tests and other such examinations to face, the natural or incidental accumulation of word knowledge is not enough. Something more intensive is essential, something that compensates for the lack of Latin and Greek. In fact, the reluctance of most students to look up the exact meanings of the new or half-familiar words they encounter makes the natural rate of gain far less effective than systematic, accelerated vocabulary work.**

Word Wealth thus provides most of the practical benefits of two years of Latin and perhaps a year of Greek. And it does this without the memorization of all the declensions and conjugations of these two languages. The aforementioned study of roots and prefixes, which grows primarily out of the study of Part Four, is, however, only one of the values that the book offers.

Two facts stand out, then. First, because of the vast influx of new words in almost every field, intensive vocabulary study has never been more necessary. Second, dedicated word study is the only way to compensate for the values that Latin and Greek once provided. Most of the new words that have come into general or technical use in the arts and sciences are derived from Latin and Greek word elements.

THE WORD WEALTH METHOD

The primary purpose of *Word Wealth* is to set up a variety of adventures in word study that are challenging, efficient, and carefully planned. These are organized in a series of forty units. They cover quite adequately

*This research by Russell G. Stauffer is reported in the *Journal of Educational Research* (February 1942), pp. 453–458.

**According to two investigators who made a scientific study of reading efficiency, students who received formal vocabulary instruction achieved greater accuracy in word recognition and, with it, more detailed, more accurate, and more orderly comprehension, with a clearer understanding of the various elements of meaning and their relationships, than those who lacked such formal word study.

the area of general recognition vocabulary between the words an elementary school graduate knows and those a college graduate does not need to know.

The forty units start with entry words in Part One that are generally shorter, more common in occurrence, and less complicated than those in Part Two. Part Two, in turn, offers less difficult words than Part Three. Part Four, however, ranges from the most familiar word elements to the most difficult.

Each entry word in the first three parts was carefully chosen because it is a word of general recognition vocabulary that is widely used. It may be familiar, but it has variant forms and synonyms that are usually not familiar. It has figurative as well as literal uses, and it may be applied to a variety of situations. Students need to be well acquainted with it.

Each unit of *Word Wealth* consists of a teaser pretest, a study guide, three or four practice sets, and a few exercises. A class or individual student should start with the first unit in Part One, or perhaps with Part Four. If a student or class scores 75 percent or above in the pretest, that student or class should go through the unit rapidly, with special emphasis on the supplementary words and synonyms. The student or class should then do the second practice set, go over the study guide again, and take the final test. Thus, even a superior class will do well to cover every unit, even though the easy ones are gone through rapidly.

There are three possible ways to study each entry. The first is to scrutinize the entry word itself—its exact meanings, the example sentences, and variant forms with their examples. Sometimes these variant forms have quite different meanings. Occasionally there are tricky shifts in spelling or pronunciation from what one would expect.

A second phase of word study involves the synonyms of an entry word, if it has any. In studying synonyms, one goes from the simple denotative meaning of a word to the connotative level, which often involves very fine discrimination between the word and its synonyms. Take *coerce, constrain, extort,* and *impel,* for example. If you *coerce* people, you *compel* them. Coercion implies harshness and lack of consideration. To *extort* a promise may imply violence or the threat of it. Thus, *extort* is a strong word, and it is often associated with criminal action to get money from someone, especially when the noun form *extortion* is used. *Constrain* and *impel* are used when mild pressures from within rather than from without are implied. Thus, *constrain* suggests that it is love, concern, or admiration for someone else that produces the inner pressure, whereas *impel* suggests that conscience or a sense of duty is the inner force. Words are known by the company they keep.

A third phase of word study is figurative. Many of the words are figurative in significance or may be used with figurative meanings. Usually these are nouns. *Zephyr,* in the first unit of Part One, may be used this way as the name of a ship or a plane. It suggests cool, refreshing lightness, but it does not connote enough force or violence to be given to a weapon. *Gobbledygook,* in the same unit, is a relatively new word invented to convey the sound and the meaning—to human ears—of the noise a turkey makes when it ''talks.'' This word is used almost wholly in its figurative rather than its literal sense.

Occasionally antonyms are included in the units, and a class may add hundreds more especially by the use of negative prefixes, such as in- or un- in *plausible —implausible, coherent—incoherent, tenable—untenable,* etc.

Another rewarding aspect of word study is derivation or, figuratively, the ancestry of words. Notes about word origins are thus an indispensable feature of a book such as this. Each note on derivation serves to give a word its proper character and thus helps one to remember it as well as to use it intelligently. Often, too, the root meaning of a word is very important in understanding its present usage.

Part Four launches a pupil into the world of word elements (roots and prefixes). In mastering these elements, a person attains immediate insight into the meanings of thousands of words, familiar and unfamiliar, technical and general, year after year, when one meets them. Each word element that one learns helps a person to understand every other word in which it appears. Thus, for example, the meaning of *precognition* is at once apparent if one knows that pre- means before or beforehand and that cogn- is knowing or knowledge.

Photo- (light) provides a good example of a word element that appears in a multitude of words. A college dictionary lists ninety. And the word element psych(o)-, another excellent example, is found in at least eighty words, among them

psyche	psychochemical	psychometry
psychedelic	psychodrama	psychoneurosis
psychiatrist	psychodynamic(s)	psychopathology
psychic	psychogenesis	psychosis
psychoacoustics	psychograph	psychosomatic
psychoactive	psychokinesis	psychosurgery
psychoanalyze	psychologize	psychotherapy
psychobiology	psychology	psychotoxic
	psychometric(s)	

In each of the word containing this element, psych(o)- means mind or mental. A person who studied Part Four will know -genic, -graph-, -meter, -therapy, and several other of the word roots that appear in the psych(o)- and in the photo- words.

Word Wealth achieves a hearteningly strategic simplicity by focusing on some 600 entry words and upwards of 300 word elements. If one adds to each entry word all the variant forms plus all the synonyms and related words introduced, the total number of words presented in a unit runs close to 100 or about 3,000 for the thirty word units in Parts One, Two, and Three. If one adds to this figure the variant forms of the entry words, the synonyms, the negative forms, and the related words not actually included in the units, the total number of words introduced and derivable runs to 300 or more per unit, and 8,000–10,000 for the thirty units.

If one then adds to these the words presented in the study guides of Part Four, together with all of the variant forms that could be listed and also the negative forms, the total per unit will be much larger than the total for Parts One, Two, and Three. A survey of a college-size dictionary indicates a total of at least 1,000 words that begin with one of the number prefixes in Unit Six of Part Four, for example. The total for the prefixes in one of the earlier units must be considerably more than 1,000. Thus, the total number of words derivable from both the prefixes and the stems in Part Four could hardly be fewer than 10,000.

A certain amount of repetition occurs, and this serves as learning reinforcement. Nevertheless, it appears from these estimates that the number of words presented or derivable from the 600 entry words and the 300 prefixes and roots in *Word Wealth* could hardly be below 15,000 and may well run to more than 20,000.

WORDS: THEIR NATURE AND DEVELOPMENT

What is the nature and origin of the bewildering profusion of words and word elements that make up the English language? How did they get their meanings, and why have some of these meanings changed over the years?

The story is a long one, with conflicting or possibly complementary theories. The fact is that hundreds of languages exist, and each has a different word for a given object. A word like *brother* in English cannot be traced back with certainty to its beginning, but it is interesting to compare six forms of the word in three ancient and three modern languages:

Ancient Languages:

Sanskrit (India): *bhrat(a)r*   Greek: *phrater*   Latin: *frater*

Modern Languages:

German: *bruder*   Italian: *fratello*   French: *frère*

To a linguist, the six forms are more alike than they appear at first glance, and the differences are explainable by certain laws of language change that are quite regular and quite universal.

Because of the similarities among them, it was discovered that all six of these languages and dozens of others in Europe, the Americas, and Western Asia belong to what is called the Indo-European family of languages. These, in turn, trace their lineage back to an ancient language known as Primitive Indo–European. Linguists have been able to reconstruct this early language from a comparative study of the languages derived from it.

Experts do not agree on where the Primitive Europeans lived. A study of plant and animal names and of words for climatic and geographical features seems to indicate that it was part of what is now the Ukraine. As these people spread out, each tribe lost contact with the others and gradually drifted into its own ways of speaking the common language. Changes in pronunciation crept in. Each tribe created new words as it needed them and adopted different ways of using the old ones. These differences created dialects that diverged until the various tribes could communicate only through interpreters.

Several of these tribes, including the Angles and the Saxons, lived in the forests of Germany and Scandinavia. They spoke the Indo-European language that we now call Primitive Germanic. As these peoples drifted farther apart and lost contact with each other, they evolved separate languages from which Dutch, German, English, and the Scandinavian languages (except Finnish) have descended. This divergence came about in much the same way that the Romance languages of Southern Europe descended and diverged from Latin.

During the fifth and sixth centuries A.D., bands of Angles, Saxons, and Jutes began to invade and to conquer the island area now called England. They drove the Celtic inhabitants gradually northward into the mountains of what is now Scotland and westward into Wales. Bands of Danes and others also came in, but the Angles and Saxons became dominant. It was their language, now known as Old English or Anglo-Saxon, that became the foundation of modern English. This language absorbed quite a few words, however, especially place names, from the Latin of the Romans. At about the time of Christ, Rome had conquered what is now England, making it a Roman province.

Old English was really a branch or dialect of German, and many of our everyday words in English are still very much like the modern German words that have descended from the same parent language.

In 1066, after several centuries of Anglo-Saxon rule in England, an army of Norman-French adventurers under William the Conqueror crossed the English Channel to invade England. Winning the Battle of Hastings against the Anglo-Saxon defenders, the Normans assumed control of the country. French was the native language of the new ruling class, but the Anglo-Saxons clung tenaciously to their Germanic tongue.

Gradually, the Normans and the Anglo-Saxons intermarried and learned each other's language. English again emerged as the language of the country, but with the incorporation of thousands of French words and spellings. Meanwhile, through the churches and universities, many more Latin words came into English. Latin continued to be the language of learning in Europe and in England, however, well into the seventeenth century.

As time passed, English continued to grow in vocabulary and flexibility. The Renaissance, the rise of science, the exploration of the New World, and British ascendancy on the seas all added new words. Later, the rise of the British Empire and the expansion of the United States accelerated the process. Modern English has thus become what is probably the richest language in the world. In the United States, the importation of innumerable new words from every country represented in our population has expanded the language steadily.

Despite the very close ties that exist between our country and Great Britain, the American language has diverged in many minor ways from the English of England in pronunciation, inflection, and vocabulary. In England, for instance, a truck is a *lorry,* and crackers are *wafers.* Radio is still the *wireless,* television is the *telly,* a hardware store is the *ironmonger's,* and a drugstore or pharmacy is an *apothecary's* shop. Many more such differences exist, largely because old words have acquired new meanings or new words have gained popularity in one country but not in the other.

Enter semantics

As long as a language is alive, it changes steadily, giving new meanings to old words, adding new words, and discarding words that for one reason or another have lost their usefulness. *Astronaut* is a new word; *rheumatism* is an example of an obsolescent word that has been replaced by *arthritis; cavalry* is a word that has changed its meaning in the past fifty years from warriors on horseback to motor-driven troops and vehicles.

The word *semantics* is an example of the process that it studies. Whereas it once could be defined as the study of changes in the meaning of words, it is now the science of meaning in a much broader sense, dealing with the nature of words, the "meaning of meaning," and the sometimes incautious or unscrupulous ways in which words are used "by knaves to make a trap for fools."

The basic principles one needs to keep in mind about the nature of words and the insights of semantics may be summarized as follows:

1. *A word is not an object or a thing.* It is simply a sound or a group of sounds, represented by a pattern of written or printed symbols that bring to mind an object,

a quality, a situation, a feeling, or an idea. The sounds and the symbols have come to be inseparably associated with the object, called the *referent,* and with each other. The same object will be represented in each of a thousand other languages by a different group of sounds and written symbols. Yet many persons become attached to words as such, or to one special pattern of words. They should learn to distinguish more clearly between the object, quality, situation, feeling, or idea that a word denotes (or connotes) and the word as such.

2. *A word is hard to define* because it often has numerous meanings or shades of meaning. Even a simple word like *chair* may denote any one of a hundred different objects, from a broken kindergarten chair to an elaborately upholstered lounge chair. It is difficult to discover precisely what the essence of *chair*-ness really is. If *chair* is hard to define, however, what about *hope, courage,* or *imagination*? At best, words are terribly elusive as well as illusive, especially abstract words.

3. *Many words have more than one level of meaning.* In addition to the referent, or the literal level of the object, two or three levels of abstraction may also exist. The word *litany,* for example, has at least four of these levels.

　　a. One specific prayer to be used by a priest and an audience responsively. This is the literal level—*the* litany of a specific church body.

　　b. Any prayer of this type, with priest and worshipers taking alternate parts—a litany.

　　c. Any joint leader-audience repetition that is a prescribed ceremony or ritual. It does not have to be an act of cooperative worship, but something that resembles such a ceremony. The cheering at a football game is a kind of litany, or worship ceremony, in a figurative "temple" devoted to sports. The fans tend to make their sport a form of worship.

　　d. Any scene that has distinctive elements of a litany—a figurative leader and a mechanical response of some kind: "The litany of the machines goes on." Alfred H. S. Korzybski was a pioneer in the field of semantics. He elaborately analyzed the levels of meaning, using what he called a Structural Differential to illustrate the process of abstraction. Semanticist Samuel I. Hayakawa went on to describe the levels more simply, using a ladder as his symbol.

4. *Words belong to families and have ancestors.* Most words display some of the traits of their families and ancestors. These traits complicate and modify their meaning. The word *subsistence* carries the idea of something standing under or supporting a person, for example. Similarly, *moral* comes from the Latin word *mores* (customs), and this ancestry contributes to its modern meaning of what is right or ethical.

5. *Words are connotative as well as denotative.* Both kinds of meaning are important, denotations for accuracy and connotations for the affective power that they have. The denotative meaning of *lake,* for example, is merely an inland body of standing water. The connotations include swimming, boating, fishing, blueness, storms, and romantic associations, with perhaps a hundred private associative or imaginative meanings.

6. *Words need to be used with great care,* especially words that stand for abstract qualities, represent value judgments, or have great affective power. Affective language has its place in literary efforts and in oratory, but it does a disservice if it obscures one's vision or vitiates one's judgment. This principle is important in practical affairs. If someone says, "Joe ran his father's car off the road and damaged

it badly," the person is presumably making a simple statement of fact. But to say "Joe is a reckless driver" is to offer a value judgment or a clear statement of opinion that often is not well founded. It is wiser and fairer to state facts, wherever possible, rather than opinions.

7. *Words are alive*. English is not a dead language like Latin. It is a living language in which each word grows and changes. The definitions in a dictionary or in this book set up guidelines, not limits, and are not intended to discourage creativity. If one takes undue liberties with the established meanings of words, that person will fail to communicate what he or she has to say. Yet it is possible to use old words in new ways if one does so judiciously. The purpose of this book is to help students understand more clearly what they read. They will communicate more accurately, not by using words no one understands, but by using the most appropriate words responsibly, intelligently, and creatively.

Pronunciation Key

ā   as in fate, age
ă   as in fat, map
â   as in dare, air
ä   as in father, pa, barn
ē   as in be, equal
ĕ   as in bet, ebb
ê   as in mere, near
ī   as in bite, ice, ride
ĭ   as in bit, if
ō   as in note, boat, low

ŏ   as in hot, box
ȯ   as in dog, law, fought
ô   as in more, roar, door, four
oi as in oil, boy
ou as in out, loud
o͞o as in too, rule
o͝o as in book, put
ŭ   as in fun, up
û   as in fur, term

ə stands for the sound of: **a** in ago, Senate; **e** in open, hopeless, fairness; **i** in peril, trellis; **o** in lemon; **u** in minus, argument; **ou** in famous; **ai** in mountain; **oi** in tortoise.

b   as in bed (bĕd), tub (tŭb)
ch as in chill (chĭl), batch (băch)
d   as in deed (dēd)
f   as in fate (fāt), huff (hŭf)
g   as in get (gĕt), leg (lĕg)
h   as in hop (hŏp)
hw for "wh" as in what (hwŏt), wheel (hwēl)
j   as in jam (jăm), job (jŏb); and for "g" in gentle (jĕn'təl) and range (rānj)
k   as in kin (kĭn), smoke (smōk); for "c" in coal (kōl); and for "ck" in rack (răk)
l   as in let (lĕt), bell (bĕl)
m   as in men (mĕn), him (hĭm)
n   as in not (nŏt), ran (răn)
ng as in song (sông); and for "n" in think (thĭngk)
p   as in pup (pŭp)
r   as in ride (rīd), very (vĕr'ē)

r   as in fur (fûr), tar (tär) (This r is not pronounced in some sections of the country.)
s   as in sod (sŏd), must (mŭst); and for "c" in cent (sĕnt), price (prīs)
sh as in she (shē), rush (rŭsh)
t   as in tea (tē), hot (hŏt)
th as in thin (thĭn), bath (băth), breath (brĕth)
t̶h̶ as in then (t̶h̶ĕn), bathe (bāt̶h̶), breathe (brēt̶h̶)
v   as in vat (văt), dove (dŭv); and for "f" in of (ŏv)
w   as in we (wē)
y   as in yet (yĕt)
z   as in zero (zêr'ō), buzz (bŭz); and for "s" in wise (wīz)
zh for "s" as in usual (yo͞o'zho͞o-əl), vision (vĭzh'ən); also for some "g's" as in mirage (mə räzh')

Pronunciation system and pronunciation key used by special permission of the publishers, Holt, Rinehart and Winston, Inc., from THE HOLT INTERMEDIATE DICTIONARY OF AMERICAN ENGLISH, copyright © 1966. All rights reserved.

part one

unit one

WORD CHOICE

Which word from the list at the left offers the best answer to each question?

abolish
ambush
adapt
admonish
curtail
acquire
divulge
implore
coerce
affirm
deplore
extract
defer

1. What do you do with a secret? You _divulge_ it.
2. When you beg urgently, you _implore_
3. When you make something more suitable, you _ADAPT_ it.
4. When you state a fact confidently, you _divulge_ it.
5. When you make a speech shorter, you _curtail_ it.
6. When you get something new, you _acquire_ it.
7. If you compel someone to do something, you _coerce_ that person.
8. If you delay a decision, you _defer_ it.
9. If you warn or advise your friends earnestly about their behavior, you _admonish_ them.
10. If you do away with something, you _abolish_ it.

VERBS

1. abolish   (ə bŏl′ĭsh)   ***to do away with, put an end to***

Will the legislature abolish the state fair?
The people voted for abolition of the sales tax.

Related words:

> *Erase* (writing); *cancel* (an order); *disestablish* (an institution); *dissipate* (energy, a mist); annul (a law or a marriage); *eradicate* (a pest or evil). Look up *expunge*.

2. acquire   (ə kwiər′)   ***to get, procure, obtain***

You will acquire new friends, new possessions, and new skills.
Laboratories exist for the acquisition (ăk′wə zĭsh′ən) of new knowledge.
An acquisitive person has a knack for obtaining property.

3. adapt   (ə dăpt′)   *to make suitable, agreeable, harmonious*

When guests come, you adapt your schedule to please them.
Juanita's play is an adaptation (ăd′əp tā′shən) of a short story by Poe.
Roommates in a dormitory must be adaptable.

4. admonish   (əd mŏn′ĭsh)   *to warn, reprove, advise*

Do your parents admonish you to work harder?
Carobel listened to the admonitions (ăd′mə nĭsh′ənz) of her attorneys.
A cautious driver heeds the admonitory signs along the highway.

Related words:

> *Forewarn* (notify or caution in advance); *forebode* (indicate beforehand or predict, usually something evil).

5. affirm   (ə fŭrm′)   *to declare, assert*

New citizens must affirm their allegiance to the United States.
The mayor's speech was an affirmation (ăf′ər mā′shən) of his faith in the public schools.
In a debate the affirmative team supports the proposition while the negative team argues against it.

Related words:

> To *declare* is to state firmly or emphatically.
> To *avouch* is to declare solemnly the truth of something.
> To *maintain* a belief, statement, or idea is to uphold it.
> To *warrant* an action or idea is to justify it.
> To *advocate* an idea or course of action is to advise or urge it.

> **Antonyms:** *deny, negate, disavow, repudiate* (p. 196).

6. coerce   (kō ûrs′)   *to compel, bring about by force*

"Will you offer to water the lawn or must I coerce you?" Father said.
Laws provide a system of enlightened coercion.
All governments are coercive about taxes.

Related words:

> Love *constrains* (obliges) one to endure much discomfort. *Constraint* is a mild form of pressure.
> A group arrived to *importune* (implore, entreat) the mayor for help in the crisis. One feels an *obligation*.
> The will of the people will *prevail* (triumph).
> One *extorts* (twists forth or wrests) a promise. See -tort- words (p. 290).
> Self-respect or conscience *impels* (drives, forces) one to be honest.
> School attendance is *compulsory*.
> Imprisonment for serious offenses is *mandatory* (required).

7. curtail (kər tāl′) *to cut down, reduce*

Fred must curtail his spending now to save for college.
Unexpected expenses require curtailment of our travel plans.

Related words:

> *Foreshorten, abbreviate, abridge* (p. 86). Look up *truncate, desiccate.*

Antonyms: *lengthen, amplify, expand.*

8. defer (dĭ fûr′) *to delay or postpone*

Defer your visit to a dentist and you may be sorry later.
Payment of a bank loan may be deferred by renewing the loan.
Business conditions required deferment of the company's dividends.

> *Defer* may also mean to yield or show respect to: A child *defers* to a parent's wishes. Their manner toward their teachers is *deferential*. The audience shows *deference* to the honored guest by rising when she enters the room. See *esteem* (p. 11).

> **Note:** *Defer* (postpone) comes from *dis + ferre;* but *defer* (yield, show respect) comes from *de + ferre.* See -fer- (p. 297).

9. divulge (dĭ vŭlj′) *to disclose or reveal*

Houdini would not divulge his secrets.
Divulgence of a client's secrets by a lawyer is unprofessional.
Reporters will not divulge their sources of information.

Related words:

> *Exposure* is often a scandalous disclosure; an *exposé* almost always is.
> A *revelation* is a mystery or secret opened up or revealed.
> Secrets frequently become *manifest* (open, evident) by accident or detection.
> Alert persons *unmask* a fraud. Guilty ones *confess* their crimes.

10. implore   (ĭm plôr′)   **_to beg, plead, entreat_**

Jerry implored his sister to lend him the money to pay the fine.
In a speech, the student leader implored her followers to join her in a peaceful protest.

Related words:

> *Solicit* (ask for funds, goods, business); *entreat* (beg, especially for mercy); *supplicate* (beg, especially in prayer); *importune* (beg in urgent need).

NOUNS

1. ambush   (ăm′boosh′)   **_a lying in wait, or_**
a hiding place for attack

The mischievous twins jumped out from ambush on their unsuspecting friends.
Guerrillas hiding near the road ambushed the artillery platoon.
One reason the Americans won over the British in the Revolution was that they knew how to fight from ambuscade.

> *Camouflage* is a method of disguising buildings, vehicles, or people by making them look like their surroundings.

2. contour   (kŏn′toor)   **_outline or profile_**

The scouts scanned the contour of the High Sierras with binoculars.
They studied the levels on their contour map before starting the climb.

> *Profile* is used especially for the side view of a person's face.
> It is also used for the graph of one's scores in a personality or aptitude test.

3. guile   (gīl)   **_deceit, trickery_**

Always a cautious buyer, Rosalie was bound to discover the swindler's guile.
The guileless look on his brother's face was quite misleading.

> **Note:** *guile* is guilt, but the term is also often used lightly in connection with pranks and harmless mischief.

4. jargon   (jär′gən)   **_lingo, technical language_**

A lifeguard at an ocean beach knows the jargon of surfing enthusiasts.
Legal jargon is hard for many people to understand.

Related words:

> *Gobbledygook* was coined by a member of Congress to convey the sounds a turkey makes. It is often applied to the language of government publications and paperwork.

Cant is insincere speech, stock phrases, or the special language of a trade or profession.

Argot is the slang, used as a special language, of such groups as baseball players, musicians, criminals, etc.

The *vernacular* is the common language that people use every day.

Gibberish, balderdash, bombast, and *fustian* are older words for wordy nonsense or inflated wordiness. See dictionary.

5. labyrinth   (lăb′ə rĭnth′)   *a maze, complicated network or problem*

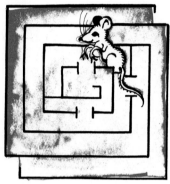

The palace of King Minos on Crete in 1500 B.C. was the original ''labyrinth'' of intricate passageways where one often got lost.

The Pentagon is a modern maze of labyrinthine passages.

    Query: Who were Ariadne and Theseus?

6. medley   (mĕd′lē)   *a mixture or jumble*

Tanya heard a medley of strange noises coming from the zoo.

The orchestra will play a medley of popular songs.

Related words:

    A *miscellaneous* assortment consists of many different items. See misce- (p. 352).

    A *heterogeneous* collection is composed of dissimilar elements.

    An *alloy* or *amalgam* contains more than one kind of metal.

    A *motley* assortment is varied in colors, kinds, and elements.

7. rapture   (răp′chər)   *ecstasy, thrills, keen delight*

Mei-Lee looked with rapture at the award she had won.

To a skier, the last run of the day down the mountain is often the most rapturous.

The two sat enraptured while the orchestra played Gershwin's *Rhapsody in Blue.*

Modes of delight:

    Gusto is zestful enjoyment with an earthy flavor: You eat, swim, paint with great gusto.

    Relish is more refined delight, with a pleasant flavor: You relish good food, good reading.

Enchantment is delight, hinting of witchery, fascination, or charm.
Transport is the delight of feeling uplifted or carried away by strong emotions.
If *entranced,* you are under a spell like a trance.
If *enthralled,* you have a delightful sense of being enslaved.

Note: What is the connection between *rapture* and *rhapsody*? See dictionary.

8. robot   (rō′bət)   *a mechanical creature, an automaton*

The robot is a familiar character in science fiction.
Children enjoy the robotlike actions of the mechanical animals in Disneyland.
A robot pilot is a mechanism that keeps a plane on its course.

> The word *robot* (from Czech *robotnik*—worker) came from a play, *R.U.R.*
> (Rossum's Universal Robots), by Karel Capek. It is about mechanical creatures
> performing manual labor.

9. verge   (vûrj)   *edge or border*

Just minutes before her great discovery, the biologist had been on the verge
of despair.
The old fort in the desert was on the verge of collapsing.
Driving a friend's car without permission verges on theft.

> *Verge,* as a verb, has two related sources. One means *to border on,* the other *to
> bend, turn,* or *incline toward.*

10. zephyr   (zĕf′ər)   *a gentle breeze*

Zephyrs kept swaying the daffodils back and forth.
The fabric was as fragile and light as a zephyr.

> *Zephyr* comes from the Latin and Greek word for west wind.

First practice set

Which entry word in this unit best replaces each *italicized* word or group of words?
Use the plural or a variant form where needed.

1. The article was full of *lingo* about *doing away with* the sales tax.
2. For the story to be *made suitable* for young readers, you would have to *obtain*
   a simpler plot.
3. The *lying in wait* made it necessary to *reduce* the attack.
4. *Gentle breezes* made a *mixture* of soft sounds.
5. Mother *warned* Chris not to touch the *automaton.*
6. The team that took the "yes" position in the debate would not *reveal* its
   sources of secret information.
7. The boy *pleaded with* his father to conceal his *deceit.*
8. Who is trying to *compel* the workers to *delay* the vote?
9. The entrance to the garden *maze* was near the *border* of a shallow pond.
10. With *keen delight,* the hikers studied the *outline* of the hills.

Second practice set

Which depth word from the list at the left best replaces each *italicized* word or group of words?

solicitation
profile
cant
entreat
supplicate
dissipate
warrant
gibberish
exposure
alloy
gobbledygook
constrain
extort
revelation
heterogenous
argot
entranced
camouflage
enchanting
vernacular
importune
enthralled
fustian

1. The people will *beg (in prayers)* their leaders to *do away with* the harsh laws.
2. Fears *oblige* a murderer to *plead* for mercy.
3. The *scandalous disclosure* of their guile was a *mystery opened up* to their friends.
4. The pamphlet is full of *sounds such as a turkey makes* and does not *justify* publication.

5. The *side view of the face* of Nefretete is indeed *bewitching*.
6. A *dissimilar* assortment of citizens gathered to *beg* the mayor to end the crime wave.
7. Speak in the *common language that people use every day* and do not use *wordy nonsense*.
8. He was *infatuated* almost to the point of seeming *under a trance*.
9. Their use of *insincere stock phrases* was a method of *concealing what they were really like*.
10. These coins are made from the same *mixture of metals* found in the jewelry *wrested* from a neighboring people.

Third practice set

Copy the *italicized* words. Beside each, write the letter of the word or group of words which is closest in meaning.

1. *Adaptable* persons: (a) easy-going (b) suitable (c) readily adjustable (d) inclined to say yes (e) tactful
2. *Admonitory* glance: (a) anxious (b) suitable (c) fatherly (d) imploring (e) warning

3. The *zephyr-like* music: (a) windy (b) full of fun (c) western (d) gentle, breezy (e) good-natured
4. Unexpected *annulment:* (a) acquisition (b) cancellation (c) postponement (d) reduction (e) concealment
5. *Labyrinthine* forests: (a) very dense (b) pathless (c) enchanting (d) having intricate paths (e) miscellaneous
6. Demonstrated *guile:* (a) guilt (b) innocence (c) slipperiness (d) deceit (e) lack of frankness
7. To *defer* her departure: (a) disregard (b) delay (c) accept (d) regret (e) permit
8. The *argot* of gangsters: (a) plotting (b) evil thoughts (c) specialized language (d) pay-off or swag (e) ugly speech
9. Eat with *relish:* (a) distaste (b) much taste (c) hesitation (d) refined delight (e) mustard
10. To *avouch* one's faith: (a) mention (b) prove (c) declare (d) explain (e) plead for

Antonyms

Which word comes nearest to being exactly opposite in meaning to the *italicized* word?

1. *Acquire* wealth: (a) waste (b) expend (c) lavish (d) accumulate (e) be greedy for
2. A *rapturous* feeling: (a) downcast (b) bored (c) stifled (d) delighted (e) determined
3. *Affirm* a principle: (a) repeat (b) question (c) deny (d) announce (e) twist
4. *Guileless* as a small child: (a) innocent (b) gentle (c) obedient (d) deceitful (e) faithful
5. *Divulge* one's age: (a) conceal (b) admit (c) falsify (d) apologize for (e) vouch for
6. *Coerce* a guard: (a) importune (b) relieve (c) release (d) punish (e) frighten
7. *Curtail* expenses: (a) report accurately (b) adjust (c) reduce drastically (d) explain (e) increase
8. *Defer* to the coach's judgment: (a) turn to (b) yield to (c) postpone (d) dislike (e) object to
9. Use *jargon:* (a) truth (b) clarity (c) eloquence (d) plain language (e) flowery words
10. Mischievous *zephyr:* (a) tornado (b) north wind (c) breath of air (d) gust (e) south wind

unit two

THE RIGHT WORD

Which of the words from the list at the left offers the best answer to each question?

appall
wrest
counsel
citadel
custody
cherish
deluge
brevity
salvage
obsess
redeem
feign
esteem
chaos

1. Which expresses high regard?
2. Which means to recover lost treasure?
3. Which buys back or makes amends?
4. Which means advice?
5. Which finds you in the care of the police?
6. Which means to horrify?
7. Which describes Noah's stormy experience?
8. Which means to haunt a person?
9. Which expresses both affection and respect?
10. Which indicates confusion or disorder?
11. Which tells how a police officer might take a weapon from a robber's grasp?
12. Which denotes a fortress?

VERBS

1. appall   (ə pȯl')   *to horrify, shock, overcome with fear*

Do pictures of fatal automobile accidents appall you?
Litterbugs show an appalling lack of concern for their environment.

Related words:

> *Dismay* (arouse alarm); *abash* (make ashamed or embarrassed); *overawe* (fill with mild fear and respect); *harrow* (terrify, torment); *petrify* (stiffen with fear—literally, turn to stone).

2. discern   (dĭ sûrn')   *to see clearly, perceive*

If you look closely, you will discern the shack near the top of the mountain.

The differences between a counterfeit and a genuine bill are not readily discernible.

A scholar needs to be a person of unusual discernment.

3. esteem (ĭ stēm′)   *to value highly, regard*

Do you esteem it a privilege to live in a large city?

Will you rise even higher in your parents' esteem as you grow older?

Frankness is usually an estimable (ĕs′tə mə bəl) quality that inspires trust.

Related words:

> *Homage* is stronger than *esteem* and often means active respect or reverence: While you can esteem the pioneers of the Old West by merely thinking of them with respect, you pay homage to them by visiting their graves or speaking of them.
>
> *Deference* is a respectful formality implying esteem. You treat your employer with deference.
>
> To *cherish* something is to have affection as well as respect for it. You cherish (hold dear) your friends and your memories of summer travels.
>
> Compare *estimate* (to put a value on).

4. feign (fān)   *to pretend*

"Feign a virtue if you have it not," said Hamlet.

Jennifer had an unfeigned belief in the existence of flying saucers.

Falstaff feigned death in battle because he was scared.

> A fighter will often make a *feint*, or pretended blow, to mislead his opponent and thus gain an advantage.

5. meditate (mĕd′ə tāt′)   *to think, reflect, intend, or plan*

Francine likes to meditate while she gardens.

The rabbi spent several hours in meditation.

Reading poetry put Gina in a meditative mood.

When injured, do you ever meditate revenge?

Words for mental activity:

> *Contemplate*—think or consider calmly. The word implies intention: You contemplate going to college.

Deliberate—think judiciously, especially in considering various courses of action.
Ponder—weigh an idea thoughtfully. You are puzzled and may not be able to reach a decision.
Conceive—imagine, create, construct mentally. You conceive a plan.
Speculate—imagine what might happen.
Cogitate—think, often in a humorous sense.
Ruminate—reflect upon. The word implies going over a subject repeatedly in the mind.
Retrospection—looking (*i.e., thinking*) backward about what happened or would have happened.

6. obsess   (əb sĕs′)   *to haunt, beset, harass*

Roland began to let the risks of flying his plane obsess him.
A sense of guilt became an obsession for Joseph K. in *The Trial*.
The eighteenth-century English author Samuel Johnson had an obsessive fear of death.

> *Harassment* applies chiefly to physical annoyances and torments, and *obsession* to mental, inward torment verging on the abnormal.

7. redeem   (rĭ dēm′)   *to buy back, make amends*

Aunt Sally promises to redeem the mortgage before it is foreclosed.
Generosity is the spendthrift's redeeming virtue.
The famous Russian writer Dostoevski deals in his works with the redemptive (rĭ dĕmp′tĭv) effects of suffering.
"I know that my Redeemer lives," said the biblical Job.
Government bonds are redeemable at a bank as they mature.

> *Redemption* of a person or of society is the act or process of saving it from the sins, bondage, or evil into which it has fallen.

8. relent   (rĭ lĕnt′)   *to become less severe, soften*

Will you relent and allow the hiking trail to run through your property?
The head of state, relenting, gave a general pardon to all political prisoners.
It takes relentless determination to attain high honors.
The relentlessness of fate is a frequent theme in Greek drama.

> For related words, see *mitigate* (p. 12).

9. salvage   (săl′vĭj)   *to save, restore, recover (part of) the value*

Divers were able to salvage the gold cargo from the sunken ship.
The salvage value of an old car is the value of the recoverable parts minus the cost of the labor involved.
A damaged reputation is sometimes salvageable by hard work and good credit.

> To *rehabilitate* injured or handicapped people is to restore them physically and spiritually.

10. wrest   (rĕst)   ***to take by force, twist from***

Absalom tried to wrest the throne of Israel from his father, David.

A violent group was able to wrest control of the labor union by terrorizing its officers until they resigned.

Wresting a living from the rocky soil was an almost impossible task for the settlers.

NOUNS

1. brevity   (brĕv′ə tē)   ***shortness, conciseness***

In telegrams and classified ads brevity is important.

Brevity in poetry is a quality called compression.

> To *abbreviate* is to shorten. Why are there two *b*'s? What are *briefs* to a lawyer? What do *breviary* and *breve* mean?

2. censure   (sĕn′shər)   ***strong criticism, condemnation***

If the official continues to neglect his duties, the legislature may pass a vote of censure.

Most critics censured the book, which fostered racial prejudice.

The task of a censor (sĕn′sər) is always difficult.

In many areas films are subject to censorship.

> A *censorious* person is harshly critical or faultfinding.
> The ultimate form of political censure is *impeachment*.

3. chaos   (kā′ŏs)   ***confusion, disorder***

A fight will soon reduce a tidy room to chaos.

The owner's mind was in a state of chaos when the business failed.

To a visitor from the country, city life can be chaotic (kā ŏt′ĭk).

Kinds of chaos:

Derangement is a mental chaos, partial or complete.

Disarray is mild chaos, as in one's dress or mental state.

A *tumult* is a noisy, active chaos created by animals, people, or the wind.

Havoc is chaos created by natural forces or by a deliberate human campaign of plunder or destruction. In the Middle Ages, "Cry havoc" was the call permitting an army to engage in plunder and pillage.

Bedlam—from the name of an old insane asylum in London, the Hospital of St. Mary of Bethlehem—is a noisy uproar suggesting insanity.

Pandemonium, the strongest of the chaos words, is literally the place where all the "demons" dwell in howling, screaming disorder: Pandemonium broke loose as the crowds surged onto the field.

Anarchy is political chaos marked by the absence of government and with people doing as they please. See -arch- (p. 314).

4. citadel   (sĭt′ə dəl)   *a fortress or stronghold*

Gibraltar has long been a citadel of British power.
The United States is a citadel of the free world.
We toured the ancient citadel that overlooked the modern city.

An *arsenal* is a factory or storage place for war materiel.

5. counsel   (koun′səl)   *advice, shared knowledge; legal adviser*

A person unjustly accused of theft needs legal counsel.
Doctors counsel their patients about health problems.
One of the camp counselors led the children on a nature walk.
The school provides a counseling service.

A *council* is a group that decides what to do. Its members are called *councilors*.

6. celebrity   (sə lĕb′rə tē)   *a widely known person*

The singer, a national celebrity, was honored today by her hometown.
Can you name a current celebrity who you think will not soon be forgotten?

7. custody   (kŭs′tə dē)   *keeping, care, guarding*

In the divorce action, both parents sought custody of the children.
When police make an arrest, they take the person into custody.
The custodian (kəs tō dē ən) will oversee cleanup of the gym after the game.

8. deluge   (dĕl′yōōj′)   *a great downpour or flood*

Noah built his ark just before the Great Deluge.
Most young people like to be deluged with invitations to parties.

The Nile River *inundates* (floods) its banks every spring.

Though, technically, *antediluvian* means before the Deluge or very ancient, an "antediluvian" (antiquated) car may be only fifteen years old.

9. demeanor (dĭ mē′nər)   *conduct, behavior, manner*

The Scottish chieftain was of haughty demeanor.

Sandra's calm demeanor made the growling dog hesitate.

Related words:

> *Mien* has the same meaning and origin as demeanor: Uncas was a Mohican of proud and silent mien.
> *Deportment* is another word for one's behavior or bearing.

10. epoch (ĕp′ək)   *distinctive age or outstanding period of time*

A long epoch of government administration by the Democratic party began in 1932 under President Franklin D. Roosevelt.

The Supreme Court handed down an epoch-making decision.

The landings on the moon and on Mars were epochal events.

Related words:

> An *era* is usually longer than an epoch: We live in an era of progress.
> A *millennium* lasts a thousand years.
> An *eon* is a very long period of time—thousands of years.

First practice set

Which entry word from this unit best replaces each *italicized* word or group of words?

1. The *widely known person* who will give the address is known for the *shortness* of her speeches.
2. That her friends *highly value* her is shown by the *flood* of mail she receives when away.
3. The secret agent's *advice* to his accomplice was to hide out and *pretend* loss of memory.

4. Try to *see clearly* the difference between courage and rashness, so that no regrets will *beset* you later.
5. The *great confusion* in the gymnasium will *horrify* you.
6. After a *distinctive period* of harsh rule, the government *became less severe*.
7. Claudius deserves our *strong criticism* because he managed to *twist away* the throne from his brother.
8. The queen asked her subjects to *reflect* on what honor should be given the knight for saving the *fortress*.
9. After tripping on the steps, Mr. Bumble tried to *recover* his dignity and regain his usually unruffled *manner*.
10. The bonds will be in her *keeping* until the borrower can *buy back* the signed notes.

Second practice set

On a separate sheet of paper, write the numbers of the *italicized* words. Beside each, place the number of the matching word or group of words from the second column.

A

1. Grandmother's *discernment*
2. Hours of *meditation*
3. An act of *redemption*
4. Financial *obsession*
5. *Bedlam* in the nursery
6. A gangster's *arsenal*
7. The *era* of plastics
8. Bashful *mien*
9. *Inundation* of gifts
10. A *feint* at the enemy

1. pretended blow or strike
2. haunting concern
3. acquisition of purchase
4. behavior, bearing
5. deliverance
6. weapons or ammunition
7. flood
8. reflection
9. period of time
10. uproar
11. concentration
12. perception

B

1. *Antediluvian* relics
2. The *epochal* discovery
3. *Obsessive* dislikes
4. *Redeemable* coupons
5. *Relentless* pursuit
6. *Salvageable* metal
7. An *estimable* gentleman
8. *Ponderous* equipment
9. *Discernible* imperfections
10. *Censorious* decision

1. worthy of respect
2. eligible to be bought back
3. dating from before the Great Flood
4. never slackening
5. capable of being seen
6. capable of being reclaimed
7. distinctive, outstanding
8. harshly critical
9. deceptive
10. crazy or half insane
11. haunting
12. heavy

A word for it

What word from the list at the left best replaces each *italicized* word or group of words?

ponder
conceive
esteem
retrospection
censorious
homage
cherish
harassment
feint
ruminate
rehabilitate
derangement

1. Each year we pay *strong reverence* to the Pilgrims.
2. Collecting antique furniture is a hobby Liz does not *value* very highly.
3. Who is the most *faultfinding* person you know?
4. Instead of truly studying, some students merely *reflect upon the subject over and over again.*
5. You need to *weigh thoughtfully* that major decision.
6. A *pretended move* fooled the other team.
7. The right to vote is a privilege to *hold dear.*
8. *Looking backward* is natural for the elderly.
9. Licensing laws prevent *persistent disturbance* by door-to-door salespersons.
10. Compensation insurance helps *restore* people *to their former state* after an injury on the job.

Shipwrecked

Write a paragraph on this topic. If you describe a large ship with a valuable cargo, and if your imagination is lively, you will find that you can use more than half the words in this unit.

If you prefer, write a description of an earthquake or a tornado. This also will give you an adventure with many words in the unit.

unit three

TRAITS

Which of the choices best matches the *italicized* word?

1. A *dour* look: (a) angry, bitter (b) stern, gloomy (c) ugly, spiteful (d) sick or sickly
2. A *plaintive* note: (a) easy to understand (b) broad and flat (c) legal (d) mournful
3. *Lucid* thoughts: (a) free-flowing (b) honest (c) clear (d) beautiful
4. A *pensive* mood: (a) thoughtful (b) tired (c) heavy (d) grief-stricken
5. A *candid* reply: (a) sweet (b) misleading (c) confident (d) frank
6. *Plausible* schemes: (a) dishonest (b) appearing reasonable (c) fair-minded (d) vexatious
7. *Furtive* actions: (a) clever (b) quick (c) stealthy (d) dishonest
8. *Obese* actor: (a) tiny (b) excessively fat (c) dramatic (d) playful
9. *Nebulous* plans: (a) hazy (b) treacherous (c) ambitious (d) explicit
10. A *potent* drug: (a) deadly (b) poisonous (c) powerful (d) sold by prescription only

ADJECTIVES

1. brusque (brŭsk)   *abrupt, blunt, curt*

Did the teacher's brusque speech frighten the young student?
The guard's brusqueness made the woman angry.
A passerby brusquely ordered the children away from the excavation.

Other ways to be unpleasant:

> Be *uncivil*—impolite.
> Be *tactless*—lacking in skill or grace in dealing with others—easy if one sees only one's own position and fails to put oneself in the other person's place.
> Be *surly*—rude, haughty, bad-tempered, and thus blunt in an unkind way.
> Be *churlish*—boorishly blunt in an ill-natured way.
> Be *blatant*—disagreeably loud, noisy, or gaudy.

Be *obstreperous*—unruly, noisy, and *boisterous*.
Be *abusive*—physically cruel or verbally insulting.
Be *caustic*—cutting, biting, stinging, sarcastic.
Be *impudent*—rash, bold, or insolent in a self-superior way.

Antonyms: *Tactful, civil* (p. 150), *gracious*.

2. candid   (kăn'dĭd)   *frank, honest, truthful*

A candid answer may sound brusque, for truth often has a sharp edge.
Tell the salesclerk candidly that you are not interested in purchasing the product.
Candor can be charming if one speaks kindly.

The Latin root *candidus* means white, whiteness.

3. delinquent   (də lĭng'kwənt)   *wanting, failing, overdue*

You must pay a fine if you are delinquent in returning a book.
Human delinquencies range from forgetting a thank-you to robbing a bank.
Are adult delinquents more numerous than juvenile delinquents?

4. dour   (dour)   *sullen, gloomy, sour*

Years of hardship often make a person dour.
Dourness hinders friendships.
Scrooge frowned dourly when his clerk asked for a holiday.

A *dismal* person is gloomy, cheerless, or woeful; but *dismal*, unlike *dour*, is used
of places and scenes, too. See *melancholy* (pp. 116, 249).

5. obese   (ō bēs')   *fat, stout, corpulent*

Which Shakespearean character is seen as obese?
Obesity often makes a person look important, but such overweight can create
problems.

Obese comes from the Latin verb *obedere,* to devour.
Compare *corpulent, corpulence,* from the Latin word for body.
Adiposity is a less familiar word for obesity and corpulence.

6. furtive (fûr′tĭv)   *sly, stealthy*

The leopard is a furtive hunter.
Several students looked furtively at their class notes.
Furtiveness of behavior often betrays guilt.

> *Furtive* comes from the Latin word *furtivus,* meaning stolen.
> *Surreptitious* is a synonym, stressing secretiveness. Sub -sub- (p. 288).

7. lucid (lōōs′ĭd)   *clear in (and to) the mind*

The most disturbed mental patients may have lucid moments.
Few physics teachers can explain Einstein's theories lucidly.
Portia presented her legal argument with lucidity.

> *Lucid* (from *lux, lucis,* light) sometimes meaning shining, glowing, or transparent.
> See -luc- (p. 357).

Related words:

> A *glib* explanation sounds simple and fluent, but is really careless or shallow.
> A *coherent* explanation holds or sticks together well, thus achieving clearness.
> See *clarity* (p. 38).

8. macabre (mə kä′brə)   *grim, gruesome, death-haunted*

When the battle ended, the field presented a macabre spectacle.
"The Fall of the House of Usher" is one of Poe's macabre short stories.

Related words:

> A *weird* experience is eerie, unearthly, or mildly horrible.
> A *grim* person is firm, relentless, or merely determined, but a *grim* spectacle is
> one that stirs a deep, awesome regret.
> A *ghastly* sight is shocking, harrowing, ghostly, or *spectral*. It leaves you *aghast*
> —as if you had seen a ghost.
> A *gruesome* sight is sickening, unappetizing, or loathsome.
> A *grisly* scene, like the Nazi death camp at Buchenwald, or Dachau, is even more
> revolting and nauseating than a gruesome scene.

9. mature (mə tyōōr′)   *ripe, fully developed*

Too many people marry before they are emotionally mature.
Corn planted in the spring will mature in August.
Family responsibility can change immature young people into adults overnight.
Adults who have reached maturity do not always behave maturely.
Superhighways would have been premature in 1910.

> **Note:** Human maturity implies the stability, resulting from education and experi-
> ence, that makes one less changeable.

10. nebulous (nĕb′yə ləs)   *vague, hazy, indefinite*

Your proposal for a new park is nebulous because it omits details about location and cost.

The nebulousness of the alibi made it questionable.

> *Nebulous* comes from the Latin word *nebula* for mist or cloud. What are the Dark Nebulae? What is the nebular hypothesis?

11. pensive (pĕn'sĭv)   *deeply thoughtful, wistful*

Marilyn looked pensive after reading the letter about her aunt's illness.
Her pensiveness grew after she left college.

> *Pensive* comes from the Latin *pensare,* to think, not from -pend-, -pense- (pay or spend) (p. 289).
> *Wistfulness* is a somewhat sadder state than pensiveness.
> A *reverie* is a state of daydreaming. Compare *ruminate* (p. 12).

12. placid (plăs'ĭd)   *calm, serene, unruffled*

The Swiss are generally thought of as placid people who get along well with their neighbors.
Does high altitude foster placidity (plə sĭd'ə tē)?
Sheep grazed placidly on the hillside.

Forms of calmness:

> A *tranquil* person or scene has the special charm of inner and outer calm.
> A *demure* person is reserved and modest, often falsely so.
> A *sedate* person is calm but with less charm and a hint of being somewhat rigid or complacent.
> A *bovine* person is calm like a cow, unexcitable, and probably imaginative.
> An *imperturbable* person is calm and very difficult to stir up, though often quite rigid or tense.
> A *stoical* person is placid, but such calmness is based on a cultivated, willful indifference to pain and pleasure.

13. plaintive (plān'tĭv)   *sad, mournful*

An owl sounds plaintive, like a child who wants an ice cream cone.
The plaintiveness of ballads like "Sir Patrick Spens" reflects the fear and helplessness which the sea inspired in ancient times.

> The *plaintiff* in a lawsuit is the one who complains (signs a complaint) and thus starts legal proceedings.

14. plausible (plô'zə bəl)   *appearing true or reasonable*

If you do not accept the invitation, you must give a plausible reason.
Plausibility is an important quality in fiction. If a writer can explain a mystery plausibly, people will believe it.

> **Antonyms:** *implausible, incredible, unbelievable.*

15. potent (pō'tənt)   *powerful, very effective*

Both organized labor and big business are often potent factors in national politics.

The potency of the new drug makes it dangerous.

> See the -pot- (power) words (p. 315).
> *Potentate* is a mildly comic word for ruler or monarch.

16. pungent   (pŭn′jənt)   *sharp, stinging, keen*

Do you like pungent wit? It is terse and pointed.
The stifling pungency of ammonia is unpleasant.
Her criticism was worded pungently enough to get the desired results.

> To *pique* one's curiosity is to arouse it sharply.
> *Piquant* remarks are lively and interesting, and at least mildly pungent.
> An *aromatic* odor like that of cinnamon is sweet, spicy, fragrant.

17. rigorous   (rĭg′ər əs)   *rigidly severe, exacting*

Astronauts undergo rigorous training.
Athletes must discipline themselves rigorously.
In her career as a journalist, she had endured the rigors of desert heat and Arctic cold.

Related words:
> A *rigid* schedule is stiff, unbending.
> *Rigor mortis* is the stiffness *(rigidity)* of death.
> An *austere* person is harsh, stern, severe in habits and discipline.
> *Stringent* rules or regulations are strict, very tightly drawn.
> A *scrupulous* person is very exact in following the rules.
> A *punctilious* person is very precise in adhering to rules, but the word *punctilious* implies exactness and discipline as ends in themselves, whereas *scrupulous* implies the presence of ethical motives.

18. wanton   (wŏn′tən)   *senseless, malicious, reckless*

That country has long shown a wanton disregard for human rights.
The waves smashed houses with the wantonness of a small child sweeping away a toy village.

> *Wanton* comes from Old English *wan* (deficient) and *teon* (educate, bring up). Wanton actions are thus ill-advised, and a wind, for example, is wanton because it lacks intelligent direction.

Antonyms: *discreet, cautious, judicious, provident, responsible.*

19. wary (wâr′ē)   *cautious, watchful (in facing danger)*

Pedestrians who are wary in traffic live longer.

The boxers jabbed warily at each other's face.

Wild animals either learn that wariness is vital or they die in the process of learning.

> To be *chary* is to be frugal or cautious in giving: Selfish people are usually chary of praise.

20. wily (wī′lē)   *crafty, cunning*

By charging extremely high prices for their goods, wily traders took advantage of the settlers.

Wiliness was the counterspy's main defense against discovery by the enemy.

First practice set

Which entry word from this unit best replaces each *italicized* word or group of words?

My friend Tom is rather *fat*. Although he is usually *serene* and *deeply thoughtful*, I have known him to be quite *blunt* in his efforts to be *honest*. His ideas are seldom *hazy* and his explanations are always *clear*. Naturally *cautious in facing danger*, he may seem *stealthy* only because he is shy and sensitive.

Tom, an amateur detective, recently set out to discover who committed the *reckless* crime of poisoning the town miser, a *gloomy* old man. He checked every *reasonable* lead and, never *falling short* in his duty, every unreasonable one as well. Tom was determined to track down whoever had done a crime so *gruesome*.

A(n) *exacting* examination of all the evidence supplied by the *mournful* widow turned up a detail missed by the police. A giant flowerpot, filled with herbs of a *sharply stinging* odor, was discovered missing from the miser's home. Nosing about, Tom traced it to a nearby farm, the hideout of a *powerful* mob of *crafty* criminals. Through his *highly developed* investigation, he not only unearthed the murderers but the miser's gold as well. The gold, as you may have guessed, was buried at the bottom of the flowerpot.

Second practice set

Which supplementary word from this unit contained in the list at the left best replaces each *italicized* word or group of words?

grisly
bovine
reverie
obstreperous
piquant
stoical
imperturbable
coherent
sedate
demure
stringent
rigid
credible
impudent
surly
caustic
glib
wistful
aromatic
blatant
chary
weird

1. Though *reserved and modest*, Judy is not *unexcitable (because unimaginative)*.
2. The entrance requirements are *very tightly drawn* and the dormitory rules *unbending*.
3. *Stingingly sarcastic* remarks cost a *fluent and shallow* public official his job.
4. The reporter gave a *well-connected* account of the *more than gruesome* trial.
5. Do memories of childhood make you *sadly thoughtful* and spark a state of *pensive daydreaming*?
6. Her *mildly pungent* wit was never *rash, bold, insolent*.
7. The coach is *indifferent to pain and pleasure* when we lose a game, but our team captain becomes *rude, haughty, and bad-tempered*.
8. The *spicy, fragrant* odor coming from the factory is *eerie* when you pass by at night.
9. Some people are *cautious* about accepting even the most *believable* explanations.
10. Seldom *loud and noisy*, the islanders make a virtue out of being so *calm you could never upset them*.

Language, the tool of diplomacy.

Third practice set

Write the numbers of the *italicized* words. Beside each, place the number of the matching word or group of words from the second column.

A

1. A *plausible* theory
2. A *candid* criticism
3. *Wanton* mischief
4. A *furtive* search
5. *Macabre* scene
6. *Pungent* quips
7. *Lucid* explanation
8. *Mature* plans
9. *Rigorous* control
10. *Placid* lake

1. sharp, keen
2. fully developed
3. cheerful, pleasant
4. exacting
5. appearing reasonable
6. calm, serene
7. reckless
8. grim, death-haunted
9. frank, truthful
10. sly, stealthy
11. angry, irritable
12. clear (to the mind)

B

1. A *brusque* admission
2. A *nebulous* dream
3. *Pensive*-looking cows
4. A *dour* storekeeper
5. *Wary* bluejays
6. *Delinquent* payments
7. *Plaintive* meows
8. *Obese* workers
9. *Potent* mischief
10. *Wily* fox

1. sad, mournful
2. mysterious, puzzling
3. corpulent, fat
4. wistful, thoughtful
5. abrupt, blunt
6. crafty, cunning
7. watchful, cautious
8. vague, hazy
9. overdue
10. sullen, gloomy
11. stupid, ignorant
12. very effective

Write a paragraph

Invent a short tale about an animal, a dream you have had, or a movie you have seen, using as many of the words in this unit as you can without overloading the story. Bring in two or three words from earlier units if possible. Underline each word taken from a unit.

unit four

CHOICES

Which of the choices best defines the *italicized* word?

1. *Purge* one's thoughts: (a) change   (b) cleanse   (c) burn   (d) twist
2. The old *derelict:*   (a) tired sailor   (b) widow   (c) kind of car   (d) outcast
3. *Cite* the guidebook: (a) examine carefully   (b) disregard   (c) refer to as example   (c) hunt it up
4. *Satiate* one's appetite: (a) whet   (b) satisfy to excess   (c) share with another   (d) overcome
5. *Pervade* the air: (a) infect   (b) rise into   (c) spread through   (d) stir up
6. A *harbinger* of joy: (a) messenger   (b) symbol   (c) embodiment   (d) haven
7. A clever *epithet:*   (a) disguise   (b) performance   (c) token or gift   (d) descriptive title
8. A small *aperture:*   (a) opening   (b) change   (c) tool   (d) camera
9. An effective *anecdote:*   (a) remedy   (b) paragraph   (c) proverb   (d) brief story
10. *Resent* a suggestion: (a) retort   (b) take offense at   (c) deny   (d) offer

VERBS

1. abate   (ə bāt′)   *to lessen, decrease*

Storms and floods at length abate.
Not until autumn did any noticeable abatement of the epidemic occur.
Scientific research requires unabating zeal.

Ebb words:

> Tides, passions, seasons, and one's fortunes all rise to a flood stage, or flow, only to *ebb* (decrease, fall off).
> All *diminish*, too: *Ebb* is poetic, *diminish* a factual word.

Floods, passions, tempest, and tensions at length *subside* (die down).
The long day *wanes* (fades). *Wane* is poetic, used more with qualities like courage and nonmaterial factors like fortune.
Ebb has similar uses.

Antonym: *wax*—The moon *waxes* before it wanes.

2. cite   (sīt)   **to mention, refer to, quote (for proof or example)**

Can you cite an instance in which a dog saved a child's life?
Do you know anyone who has been officially cited for bravery?
Citations (sī tā′shəns) from the atlas show that Texas is not the largest state in the union.

> To *cite* persons for a traffic offense is to summon them to appear in court.
> To *incite* argument is to arouse it or stir it up. Compare *recite, excite.*

3. entice   (ĕn tīs′)   **to allure, attract, or beguile**

Ad writers know how to entice consumers into buying their products.
A higher salary was one of the enticements of the new job.
Fresh ripe fruit is very enticing.

Modes of inducement:

> *Lure,* unlike *allure,* implies a temptation to something harmful. You lure animals or fish.
> *Inveigle* implies trickery as well as clever persuasion: You inveigle a person into applying for a job or serving on a committee.
> *Cajole* implies coaxing, wheedling, flattery: You cajole your friend into telling a secret.
> *Beguile* can mean to deceive by guile, or merely to charm. The word has a hint of magic in it. The sailor beguiled us with stories of mysterious lands.
> *Seduce* is mostly evil: Does a TV program ever seduce you from your homework? See -duce- (p. 296).

4. frustrate   (frŭs′trāt′)   **to thwart, foil, defeat**

In real life the hero does not always frustrate the villain.
A common form of teen-age frustration is to be turned down by the college of one's choice.
Ray found courses like physics or trigonometry very frustrating.

Other ways to frustrate:

> You *foil* (thwart) a criminal by locking your car.
> You *balk* at a plan by refusing to accept it.
> You *circumvent* a plot by outflanking, sidestepping, or going around it (p. 299).

5. manifest (măn′ə fĕst′)   *show plainly, reveal, display, evince*

Children normally manifest a great affection for their pets.
Caroling is one of the many manifestations of Christmas joy each year.
The manifest destiny of the United States in the early 1800s was to expand all the way to the Pacific Coast.
The Communist Manifesto by Marx and Engels is the formal declaration of Marxist views.

6. pervade (pər vād′)   *spread through, permeate*

On Mother's Day, the aroma of fresh roses pervades the house.
The Christmas spirit is pervasive in December.
The pervasiveness of the smoke in the burning house made rescue difficult.

> **Synonyms:** *permeate, saturate, diffuse;* see per- (p. 277) and -fus(e)- (p. 280).

7. purge (pûrj)   *cleanse, clear of impurity or guilt*

The Great Fire of London in 1666 served to purge the city of the bubonic plague, which had killed thousands the year before.
The dictator ordered a purge of certain members of the army.

> *Purging* often implies heat, fire, medicines, or suffering.
> A *purgative* is a cleansing agent, cathartic, or other means to eliminate waste or infection.
> *Purgatory* for Roman Catholics is a place where souls, not damned but also not ready for paradise, are refined, purged, purified. A prison may be regarded as a purgatory, since it functions as a place of usually temporary banishment, punishment, or suffering.
> An *expurgated* edition of a book is one in which offensive phrases and passages have been changed or removed.

8. reproach (rĭ prōch′)   *to blame, upbraid*

No one will reproach you if you do your best.
Proud persons find reproach especially hard to bear.
A reproachful look is often all the punishment a person needs.
Abraham Lincoln and Robert E. Lee led almost irreproachable lives.

Blame words:

> To *chide* is to scold mildly, especially a child or a friend.

To *upbraid* is to scold strongly for some specific fault.
To *reprimand* is to rebuke rather formally for something specific.
To *impugn* is to call in question someone's motives or qualities.
To *reprehend* is to find fault with, take to task.
Compare *rebuke, reprove, condemn, censure* (p. 13), impeach.

9. resent (rĭ zĕnt′)   *to take offense at*

Do most artists resent criticism or suggestions?
Joe acted resentful when he did not get the part he wanted in the play.
Unjust laws breed deep resentment.

Anger words to study:

Wrath, ire, vexation, exasperation (p. 54), *indignation* (p. 54), *animosity* (pp. 54, 360).

10. satiate (sā′shē āt)   *to satisfy to excess*

There was enough food at the picnic to satiate a football team.
All but a few reached the point of satiety (sə tī′ə tē).
Salty food makes one insatiably (ĭn sā′shə blē) thirsty.

Related words:

To *sate* one's appetite is to satisfy it to the full.
To *glut* the market is to flood it. What is a *glutton*?
A *surfeit* is an excess of something ordinarily pleasing.
Cloying sweetness is so excessive that it no longer pleases.

NOUNS

1. abyss (ə bĭs′)   *a deep or bottomless chasm*

From our mountain perch, we looked down into an abyss a thousand feet deep.
Time is an abyss which has swallowed up many nations.
My ignorance of that science is abysmal (ə bĭz′məl).

Figuratively, an *abyss* is anything profound or immeasurable. The Greek root *abyssos* means "without bottom."
A *fissure* is merely a narrow opening or *cleft* in the earth.

2. anecdote (ăn′ək dōt′)   *a brief story or incident*

A magazine article often starts with an anecdote.
Most jokes are the anecdotal type.

What does it mean to say that people are in their "anecdotage"?
Look up *dotage* (p. 91).
What is the word for something to counter the effect of a poison?

3. aperture (ap'ər chər)   *a small opening*

Narrow apertures in the castle wall permitted the defenders to shoot their arrows with little danger of being hit in return.
The aperture in a camera is the adjustable opening which lets in the light to make the picture.

4. derelict (dĕr'ə lĭkt')   *an abandoned ship, an outcast*

The derelict that had stayed afloat for months finally sank in a wild storm.
A hobo is a human derelict, usually a wanderer, with no home and no job.
Drunk driving is a foolhardy dereliction of responsibility.

> What is the derivation of *derelict*? Compare *relict*.
> *Derelict* is a good example of a word having a basic meaning and a metaphoric level of abstraction. The word is applicable to anything that is like an abandoned ship.

5. epithet (ĕp'ə thĕt')   *a descriptive title*

"Stonewall" was an epithet applied to General Thomas J. Jackson.
"Moses" was the epithet given to Harriet Tubman, a "conductor" on the "Underground Railroad."

> An *epithet* is often used as an adjective, as in "Catherine the Great."
> *Appellation* is another word for a name, but it is not necessarily descriptive: "Resurrection man" was an appellation that grave robbers once used.

6. fiend (fēnd)   *a demon or monster*

According to local legend, a spiteful fiend inhabited the dangerous rapids.
Mischief-makers often work with fiendish energy.

> *Fiend* has lighter uses. A chemistry "fiend" is very fond of chemistry.

7. harbinger (här'bĭn jər)   *a forerunner, herald*

Dark clouds are not always harbingers of rain.
Sorrow is often a harbinger of joy; floods can be harbingers of spring.

> *Precursor,* derived from Latin, is another word of similar meaning but less poetic flavor. See -curs- (p. 304).

Harbinger is of *Germanic* origin, coming from *heri* (army) + *berga* (shelter) in Old High German, referring to the couriers who rode ahead to seek lodging for their leaders.

8. lament　(lə mĕnt′)　　　　　　*an expression of sorrow or grief*

"Annabel Lee" is a haunting lament over the loss of a lover.
Prisoners lament their loss of freedom.
A Roman family depended on the noisy lamentations (lăm′ən tā shəns) of hired mourners to make a funeral impressive.
Is death always a lamentable event?

> Accent *lamentable* on the first syllable.
> To *rue* a mistake or a failure is to regret it: Does an *F* on a test make you feel *rueful*? Do you shake your head *ruefully* when you lament a misfortune?
> Review *plaintive* (p. 21).

9. omen　(ō′mən)　　　　　　*a portent, prophetic sign*

The Greeks prayed for a favorable omen from the gods before battle.
The hooting of an owl was an ominous (ŏm′ə nəs) (threatening) sound.

Related words:

> A *fateful* day is one which will decide someone's destiny.
> A *foreboding* or *presentiment* is a feeling beforehand that something disastrous is going to happen.
> A *foreshadowing* is an advance indication or suggestion of something to come.

10. pestilence　(pĕs′tə ləns)　　　　　　*a widespread disease*

The Black Death was a pestilence that destroyed one third of the people of Europe about the year 1350.
False ideas can be as pestilent (harmful, poisonous) as a smallpox epidemic.

> A *pestilence* may be either a disease or the epidemic it causes.

Word forays

1. Add a letter to one of the entry words and get something very pleasant to have.
2. Rearrange the letters of one entry word, change the first letter, and get a word cited in the previous entry.
3. What does the stem -vade- mean? Other -vade- words include *invade* and *evade*. Look them up. List their variant forms.
4. Study the *anger* words under *resent* and write a paragraph telling how they differ in usage and meaning.

First practice set

Which entry word best replaces the *italicized* word or words?

1. The danger that the knight's horse might slip into the *deep chasm* began to *decrease*.
2. *Beguiled* by a favorable *portent*, the captain of the doomed ship set sail.
3. *Brief stories* of those who failed to qualify for flight training *thwart* the plans of young people who hear them.
4. Did the *monster* at any time *reveal* fear?
5. The *widespread disease* made many *feel sorrow* for their sins.
6. Can you *mention* examples of how unwise it is to *take offense at* a kindly criticism?
7. The smells of baking which *spread through* the house proved unpleasant to those who had already managed to *satisfy (to excess)* themselves.
8. The ancient mariner was an *outcast* who, by telling and retelling his story, sought to *clear away* his sense of guilt.
9. The *descriptive title* "Pandora" was intended to *upbraid* Debbie for being too curious.
10. The sleet which we watched through the *opening* in the tent was a *forerunner* of a freezing mountain weekend in June.

Second practice set

Which of the supplementary words in the list at the left best replaces each *italicized* word or group of words?

presentiment
rueful
beguile
diminish
dotage
reprimand
glut
chide
wane
circumvent
lure
upbraid
incite
precursor
cajole
waxes
foil
appellation
sate
fissure
permeate

1. School spirit *increases* and *fades* like the tides.
2. Did the coach *rebuke (in a formal manner)* the player who goes by the *title* "Bulldog"?
3. Though her low grade made Yvonne *regretful*, its effect was to *arouse* her to greater effort.
4. It is useless to *scold* elderly people who are in their *second childhood due to old age*.
5. The hiker who stepped into a *cleft* in the rocks had had a *feeling beforehand* that something was going to happen.
6. The girls tried to *tempt* the squirrels with peanuts, but could not *bewitch* one of them into coming close.
7. How much knowledge does it take to *satisfy* you to the *full*? Do your teachers *flood* you with it week after week?
8. His father knows how to *coax* him into doing his work or to *scold him strongly* if necessary.
9. Thanksgiving is a *forerunner* of Christmas, and one's enthusiasm for it does not *grow less* from year to year.
10. If you do not find a way to *get around* the falls, the water will *spread through* my sneakers.

Third practice set

Write the numbers of the *italicized* words. Beside each, place the number of the matching word or group of words from the second column.

A

1. *Ominous* rumblings
2. *Fiendish* glee
3. *Anecdotal* writing
4. *Cloying* music
5. *Manifest* readiness
6. *Purgative* remedies
7. *Pestilent* thoughts
8. *Abysmal* despair
9. *Irreproachable* conduct
10. *Reproachful* words

1. distasteful
2. resentful, chiding
3. harmful
4. sorrowful
5. immeasurably deep
6. demonic
7. threatening
8. filled with brief stories
9. excessive in effect or duration
10. apparent, evident
11. cathartic
12. faultless

B

1. *Lamentation* of refugees
2. Temporary *satiety*
3. *Abatement* of the illness
4. Lingering *resentment*
5. Literary *manifesto*
6. A police *citation*
7. A guide's *dereliction*
8. Microscopic *aperture*
9. A treacherous *fissure*
10. A beginner's *frustration*

1. lessening
2. defeat
3. abandonment of duty
4. sensitiveness
5. formal declaration
6. fullness to excess
7. regretful wailing
8. narrow opening or cleft
9. distress
10. mention in form of a summons
11. opening
12. slow-burning indignation

unit five

PLUS

In each case, which of the choices is most appropriate?

1. Shoe plus gum on the sole will   (a) adhere   (b) alter   (c) emulate   (d) diverge
2. Mischievous prank plus discovery means that parents will   (a) disperse   (b) chastise   (c) assail   (d) forage
3. Shopper plus revolving door that sticks will result in someone's trying to   (a) augment   (b) assail   (c) extricate   (d) emulate himself
4. One clue plus no facts about a crime will lead to   (a) apathy   (b) clarity   (c) conjecture   (d) enhancement
5. A football game plus victory adds up to feelings of   (a) aggravation   (b) torpor   (c) elation   (d) exertion
6. One surgeon plus accident victim creates need for   (a) defiance   (b) avarice   (c) antagonist   (d) dexterity
7. One girl plus another she admires means that the first will try to   (a) enhance   (b) emulate   (c) reform   (d) assail the second
8. One miser plus nothing means   (a) avarice   (b) castigation   (c) defiance   (d) increment
9. One boy plus unwanted invitation displays   (a) defiance   (b) discretion   (c) apathy   (d) emulation
10. Road branching south plus another going east means that they will   (a) alter   (b) inflect   (c) augment   (d) diverge

VERBS

1. adhere   (əd hêr′)   *to stick fast, cling*

The paint will not adhere to a polished metal surface.
Adhesive tape adheres to the skin.
Adhesion (əd hē′zhən) of internal organs causes much pain. See -here- (p. 280).
No matter how costly adherence to the agreement may be, the company will honor its commitment.
The Christian religion now has nearly a billion adherents in the world.

2. alter   (ȯl′tər)   *to change or modify*

So called ready-to-wear clothes often require alterations.
Our plans will be alterable to suit weather conditions.
The laws of the Medes and Persians were unalterable.

> An *alter ego* is a close associate, literally an "other self" who thinks and acts much as you do. *Alter ego* is an unaltered Latin phrase meaning "Another I."

Alter words:

> To *veer* or *deviate* is to swing or turn from an intended plan or course of action. See -via- (p. 341).
> To *diversify* a line of goods is to alter it so as to serve a variety of needs. You diversify a business by offering more kinds of products or services. See -vers- (p. 299).
> To *mutate* is to change, especially in biology. A plant or animal will undergo some sudden mutation that may be inheritable.
> To *transfigure* is to alter the shape, nature, or appearance: Spring transfigures the landscape (p. 141).
> To *transmute* is to change the very nature of something: Scientists can now transmute one element into another by fission or fusion.

3. assail   (ə sāl′)   *to attack*

This editorial assails the chief of police for failing to catch a burglar.
Feelings of guilt often assail a person.
The man who was knocked down cannot identify his assailant.
The lawyer's defense proved unassailable.

> An *assault* is an attack, usually violent, often bodily: The assault on the city failed. See your dictionary for legal definition.

4. augment   (ȯg mĕnt′)   *to increase, make or become larger*

During the summer Ulrica took a job to augment the family income.
Governor Lopez recommends augmentation of flood-control measures.
Prefixes like "per" in "peroxide" are augmentative, implying more than the normal amount.

Modes of augmentation:

> An *increment* is an increase, especially of salary.
> *Intensification* is an increase of the amount, quality, or determination of an effort: You intensify your effort to win a writing prize.
> *Enhancement* is a heightening of attractiveness or value.
> *Accretion* is growth, especially by addition or accumulation: Knowledge is an accretion of facts and insights.
> *Dilation* is an increase in the size of an aperture like the pupil in the iris of the eye.
> *Aggravation* is a worsening or increase in the seriousness of an illness or problem (p. 36).
> *Amplification* is a form of enlargement used chiefly of verbal statements and radio-television signals.

5. chastise   (chăs'tīz')   *to punish*

It is unjust to chastise a person who intended no offense.
Junior deserved the chastisement he got for tormenting his brother.

Related punishment words:

> *Castigation* (usually severe and often public verbal criticism); *retribution* (well-deserved punishment or recompense).

6. disperse   (dĭ spûrs)   *to scatter, separate*

As soon as the sun comes up, it will disperse the mists in the valley.
The prism caused a dispersion of the light into a rainbow of colors.
Dispersal of the crowd after the game took over an hour.

> See -sperse- (p. 332).

7. diverge   (dĭ vûrj')   *to branch off, go in different directions*

The two routes to Nashville diverge near Memphis.
Otto and Bela expressed divergent views during the debate.
At times, considerable divergence exists between Democrats and Republicans on key issues.

8. emulate   (ĕm'yə lāt')   *to strive to equal or excel*

President Truman was in many ways a man to emulate.
Stories of heroes encourage emulation.
The emulative urge is usually strong in young people.

> *Vie* implies rivalry between persons of similar status: Bankers, plumbers, scouts vie with each other.

9. extricate   (ĕk'strə kāt')   *to disentangle*

It is difficult to extricate oneself from an embarrassing situation.
Extrication of the racers from their wrecked autos was shown on TV.

The cat was extricable (ĕk′strĭk ə bəl) from the skein of wool only by our using a pair of shears.

The tax suit became inextricably involved in government red tape.

10. forage (fôr′ĭj)   *to search for, ravage, plunder*

Hungry teenagers often forage for food in the refrigerator.

During the long drought, forage for the herds had to be dropped by plane on the plateau.

> To *ravage* is to destroy, plunder, or devastate: Floods ravage the countryside.
> To *pillage* is to take food, money, or property by force; to plunder or loot, especially by an invading army.

NOUNS

1. antagonist (ăn tăg′ə nĭst)   *a rival, opponent, adversary*

Brutus is the antagonist in Shakespeare's *Julius Caesar*.

A boastful person antagonizes many potential friends.

In his funeral oration for Caesar, Cassius stirred up the peoples' antagonism against Brutus.

2. apathy (ap′ə thē)   *lack of feeling, indifference*

Apathy in a society can lead to political tyranny.

No longer apathetic (ăp′ə thĕt′ĭk), the townspeople began to concern themselves with local problems.

> *Apathy* comes from Greek elements meaning "no feeling" *(a + pathos)*. See -path- words (p. 342).

Related words:

> *Lethargy* is drowsiness or sluggishness from some physical cause, such as drugs or overeating.
> *Torpor* is sluggishness from temporary loss of physical powers due to a cause such as very cold weather.
> A *stupor* is a deadened state of mind, as from drugs or shock.

3. avarice   (ăv′ə rəs)   *greed for money, cupidity*

The miser's avarice gained him a fortune but cost him his friends.
An avaricious (ăv′ə rĭsh′əs) art dealer would not verify the genuineness of the painting.

> To be *covetous* is to desire something too strongly, especially something forbidden: Do you covet your cousin's transistor radio?

4. clarity   (klăr ə tē)   *clearness*

Cultivate clarity in writing and speaking.
Clarify your ideas before you share them.
Ask for clarification of the proposal before you buy.

Related words:

> A *clarion* call is clear, sharp, shrill.
> *Elucidation* of a plan is the process of making it clear. See -luc- (p. 357).

5. conjecture   (kən jĕk′chər)   *a guess, inference*

One conjecture is that a spark of static electricity touched off the explosion.
The conjectural nature of racing predictions makes them unreliable.

Related words.

> A *supposition* pretends (supposes) for the moment that it is true.
> A *speculation* is an imaginative guess, whereas a *surmise* is a guess based more definitely on facts.
> An *assumption* accepts a guess or belief as if true: Law operates on the assumption that you are innocent until proven guilty.
> A *presumption* is much the same thing: You pretend (presume) that there are other worlds like ours because it seems probable.
> A *postulation* accepts as fact what must be true because of something else one knows to be true: You postulate the existence of God because it is difficult to explain certain facts in any other way.
> A *proposition* or *thesis* is a statement that you will undertake to demonstrate. You propose to prove, for example, that small nations dominate the United Nations.
> A *hypothesis* is a plausible theory or explanation: The nubular hypothesis is a theory of the origin of the planets of our solar system from a hot gaseous nebula.

6. defiance   (dĭ fī′əns)   *bold opposition, open challenge*

Ahab cried defiance at the angry sea and at the white whale, Moby Dick.
Randy became less defiant when he had more time to think about the consequences of his actions.
Many secrets of life deep in the ocean still defy scientists.

7. dexterity   (dĕk stĕr′ə te)   *skill, adroitness*

Surgeons must possess special digital dexterity.
Are you dexterous (dĕk′stər əs) enough to perfect a few tricks of magic?

The gambler handled the dice dexterously while his partner shuffled the cards.

Related words:

> *Adroitness* denotes skill, chiefly mental: The president commended the mayor's adroitness in handling the water shortage.
> *Proficiency* is knowledge and skill: A teaching post in Zaire requires proficiency in French.
> *Facility* is ease in doing or demonstrating something: Facility in grammar is not enough for a writer.

8. discretion   (dĭs krĕsh′ən)   *prudence, wise restraint*

Irma could invite her friends to the house at her own discretion.
Carl was discreet (dis krēt′) enough to remain silent while his two friends argued.
All U.N. council members spoke discreetly during the debate.

Related words:

> *Judiciousness* is wise judgment in action: Kevin's judiciousness in selecting his courses is typical.
> *Prudence* is caution mixed with wisdom, especially in managing one's affairs: It takes prudence to succeed in business.
> *Circumspection* is caution characterized by looking at a problem from all sides and considering its possible results. See -spect- (p. 342).

9. exertion   (ĕg zûr′shən)   *vigorous effort*

Climbing three flights of stairs daily was too much of an exertion for the ailing building superintendent.
Exerting themselves to the utmost, the movers lifted the piano into the truck.
Players do not hesitate to exert their utmost power and skill.

> *Endeavor* is sustained but less vigorous and less muscular effort than exertion: The sale of Christmas Seals is a nationwide endeavor.

10. exuberance   (ĕg zoo′bər əns)   *overflowing spirits, zestfulness*

Sparkling with youthful exuberance, the volunteer group set out to clean up the riverbank.
May is an exuberant month in the north temperate zones.
The choral group sings exuberantly.

Related words:

> *Ebullience* is a bubbling or overflow of enthusiasm, like exuberance, but it is used chiefly with reference to persons.
> *Elation* is a quieter kind of high spirits over some success or good news: Sylvia was elated at being chosen for the school play.
> *Transport* (p. 7) is like rapture or ecstasy and means literally being carried away with delight.

First practice set

Which entry word from this unit best replaces each *italicized* word or group of words?

1. On the treasure hunt, did you *cling* strictly to the rules when you went out to *search for* listed items?
2. Both leaders saw with perfect *clearness* that their views would sooner or later *go in different directions*.
3. "A mere *guess* on your part does not *modify* my attitude," she said.
4. Her *opponent* began to *attack* her for praising the party in power.

5. She watched the game with *overflowing spirits*, he with complete *lack of feeling*.
6. To *punish* Gunnar, his parents assigned him a month of *vigorous effort* in the garden.
7. In practice, the football players learned to *disentangle* themselves from the heap and to *scatter* as quickly as possible.
8. You will swim faster if you *strive to equal* a champion's *skill*.
9. The captain had the *prudence* to accept the penalty rather than to challenge it.
10. *Greed* made the merchant try to *increase* his income in *bold opposition* to current prices.

Second practice set

Which of the words in the list at the left best replaces each *italicized* word or group of words?

transmute
torpor
elation
diversify
stupor
prudence
proficiency
covetous

1. Knowing how our classmates feel about the victory will *heighten* our *high spirits (quieter kind)*.
2. You are lacking in *caution (mixed with wisdom)* if you let yourself be *too strongly desirous* of your boss's job.
3. If you had approached the holiday feast with *caution*, you would not now be suffering from *sluggishness*.

accretion
intensification
alter ego
assault
elucidate
endeavor
enhance
increment
transfigure
ebullience
lethargy
circumspection
aggravation
mutation
transport
ravaged

4. Being *carried away* by the music can *transform* a person—at least while the spell lasts.
5. *Augmentation of the feeling* of pain indicates *increase in the seriousness* of the disease.
6. If you *alter* your interests *(to serve a variety of needs)*, you will experience a wholesome *growth (by accumulation)* of useful knowledge.
7. The critics' *attack* began to reduce the artist's natural *overflow of enthusiasm*.
8. After the *sluggishness (from temporary loss of power)* of winter, the bear regained its *skill* at scooping fish from the stream.
9. The astronaut's *associate (other self)* was on the ground supporting the mission with less risk but more *effort*.
10. The role of the Red Cross is to *transform* contributions into food, medicine, and shelter for those *devastated* by natural or human disasters.

Third practice set

On a separate sheet of paper, write the numbers of the *italicized* words. Beside each, write the number of the matching word or group of words from the second column.

A

1. *Extrication* from difficulty
2. *Amplification* of the report
3. An *assault* on one's honesty
4. *Torpor* because of the heat
5. Gentle *chastisement*
6. *Prudent* purchases
7. *Adherence* to a building code
8. *Dispersion* of clouds
9. *Augmentation* of one's resources
10. *Emulation* of heroes

1. increase in quantity
2. striving to equal
3. increasing dislike
4. scattering
5. disentanglement
6. punishment
7. slow wasting away
8. attack
9. act of sticking to
10. enlargement
11. sluggishness (temporary)
12. cautiously wise

B

1. *Apathetic* attitude
2. *Unalterable* reluctance
3. Her *discreet* praise
4. *Antagonistic* remarks
5. The *exuberant* enemy
6. *Lethargic* behavior
7. *Dexterous* movements
8. *Defiant* gestures
9. *Elated* grandparents
10. *Retributive* action

1. unfriendly
2. drowsy
3. skillful
4. prudent, judicious
5. boldly challenging
6. exultant
7. indirect
8. punitive
9. unchangeable
10. distressed
11. indifferent
12. highly pleased

unit six

QUIBBLES

What is the best response to each question?

1. Which is luminous?   (a) a mine shaft?   (b) a firefly?   (c) an electric blanket? (d) an eyeshade?
2. Would a vindictive person be   (a) spiteful?   (b) lenient?   (c) resentful?   (d) fretful?
3. Which makes one languid?   (a) coffee?   (b) a good movie?   (c) sharp criticism   (d) a hot afternoon?
4. Would a regal wedding be   (a) lavish?   (b) ominous?   (c) quiet?   (d) frugal?
5. Are noxious beverages   (a) sour?   (b) sweet?   (c) alcoholic?   (d) harmful?
6. Where would a nomadic person live?   (a) in the slums?   (b) in a trailer?   (c) in a castle?   (d) in a lighthouse?
7. Would nocturnal habits be   (a) musical?   (b) evil?   (c) adventurous?   (d) practiced at night?
8. Would copious supplies be   (a) plentiful?   (b) adequate?   (c) high in quality?   (d) well arranged?
9. Would an eminent banker be   (a) haughty?   (b) extravagant?   (c) outstanding?   (d) defiant?
10. Would a lenient coach be   (a) merciful?   (b) generous?   (c) stingy?   (d) hard to please?

ADJECTIVES

1. copious   (kō′pē əs)   *abundant, plentiful*

Copious supplies for the colony arrived on the next ship.
The copiousness of the harvest made the island self-sufficient.
Roddy wept copiously when his pet raccoon died.

Plenty words:

> *Ample* appreciation is more than enough.
> *Bountiful* appreciation is generous and abundant.
> *Profuse* appreciation is lavish to the point of excess.
> Look up *cornucopia*.

2. eminent   (ĕm′ə nənt)   *outstanding, prominent*

An eminent Austrian surgeon is now lecturing in this country.
Her eminence grows out of her research on lung diseases.
From an eminence (elevation or hill), Napoleon watched the battle.

> What is the right of *eminent domain*? Has it been invoked recently in your community?

Fame words:

> *Renowned* (widely known); *celebrated* (widely praised, recognized); *distinguished* (outstanding, readily "seen"); *illustrious* (outstanding in the sense of brilliant, shining forth); *notorious* (widely noted or noticed). Which word ordinarily has an unfavorable connotation?

3. frugal   (froo′gəl)   *sparing, thrifty, economical*

Young Benjamin Franklin was frugal in his habits.
The townspeople of Hamlin were renowned (if not notorious) for their frugality (froo găl′ə tē).
Is frugality still an important virtue?

> **Synonyms:** A *thrifty* person avoids waste and manages well. An *economical* person buys wisely and does not spend too much.

> **Antonyms:** *prodigal* (wasteful, extravagant) Who can tell us the story of the *Prodigal* Son?

4. languid   (lăng′gwĭd)   *drooping, listless*

Warm days make people feel languid.
At high altitudes one experiences a soothing languor (lang′gər).
June is likely to be a languorous month in Hong Kong.

> To *languish* is to droop or pine away in grief, in prison, or in illness.
> *Lassitude* is a feeling of weakness or weariness, whereas *languor* is limpness or relaxation from indolence, weather, or mood.
> Compare *apathy* (p. 37).

5. hostile   (hŏs'təl)   ***unfriendly, warlike***

It is normal at times to feel hostile toward a friend.
The hostility (hŏs tĭl'ə tē), however, usually does not last very long.

Related words:

> *Adverse* (turned against; opposing): an adverse judgment; *averse* (turned away from; unfavorable to): You are averse to long speeches or you have an aversion to snakes; *inimical* (unfriendly, unfavorable): Bad air is inimical to health; *antagonistic* (struggling against, often dramatically): Cats and dogs are often antagonistic (p. 37).

6. laudable   (lòd'ə bəl)   ***praiseworthy, commendable***

The hikers made a laudable effort to climb Mt. Whitney.
A laudatory article about the Pilgrims appeared in a historical journal.
Our track team performed laudably, but it did not win the meet.

7. lenient   (lē'nē ənt)   ***mild, merciful***

The prison warden is lenient with convicts who prove trustworthy.
The judge was accused of excessive leniency.
Should teachers grade their students more leniently?

8. luminous   (loo'mə nəs)   ***glowing, giving off light***

Lighted signs vary from softly luminous to harsh and glaring.
The moon owes its luminosity to light reflected from the sun.
Tall buildings shine luminously at night against the New York skyline.

Related words:

> *Luminary* (a heavenly body or, figuratively, an illustrious celebrity on earth); *luminiferous* (light-bearing); *luminescence* (capacity for glowing or for giving off "cold" light): Lettering or figures that glow in the dark are *luminescent.*

9. nocturnal   (nŏk tûr'nəl)   ***occurring at night***

Thomas Wolfe wrote of his nocturnal wanderings in New York City.
Nocturnal flowers bloom at night.

> A *nocturne* is a dreamy musical composition, often dealing with or referring to night. It may also be a painting of a night scene.

10. oblique   (ō blēk')   ***slanting, indirect***

The oblique lines in the blueprint indicate the concrete foundation.
The prosecutor's oblique questioning led the suspect to admit his guilt.

> An *oblique* line is neither parallel to nor at a right angle with a given line. An *oblique* angle is any angle except a right angle.
> *Oblique* questions are calculated to trap a witness. *Oblique* actions are tricky or *devious* (roundabout) in order to mislead someone.

11. obnoxious (əb nŏk′shəs)   *offensive, hateful*

Weeds, bugs, and filth are obnoxious.
Our class will discuss the obnoxiousness of some television advertising.

> A *noxious* substance is poisonous or harmful: Carbon monoxide is a noxious gas.
> *Odious* (p. 194) is a stronger word: Rats and traitors are odious in any language.

12. obtrusive (əb trōō′sĭv)   *pushing, demanding attention, showy*

Are salesclerks in that bookshop obtrusive or is one free to browse?
The canoeists resented the obtrusiveness of motorboats on the usually quiet lake.
Barking obtrusively, the huge dog advanced.
Mother unobtrusively confiscated Andy's squirt gun.

> If you *obtrude* yourself upon a group, you may be accepted.
> An *officious* person is forward, meddlesome, inclined to interfere where not wanted. The word is milder than *obtrusive* and used chiefly of persons.

13. perpetual (pər pĕch′ōō əl)   *unending, lasting forever*

The peak of Mt. Everest is covered by perpetual snows.
The Jefferson Memorial perpetuates the memory of the third President of the United States.
We hold in perpetuity (pûr pə tōō′ə tē) the land on which our home is built.

Degrees of endlessness:

> A *continual* feast is intermittent, i.e., a series of feasts.
> An *incessant* noise is ceaseless, i.e., it keeps occurring for hours, days, months, or years.
> An *interminable* (seemingly endless) speech is quite long but seldom lasts more than a few hours, even in Congress.
> A *marathon* (an endurance) speech is also very long, and implies a contest or struggle. It may last for days.
> *Eternal* is used carelessly, but it really means forever; *eternity* is unchanging reality beyond time and space.

14. regal (rē′gəl)   *royal, notably excellent*

The retiring council members walked from the hall with regal dignity.
Crowns and scepters are ancient symbols of regality (rĭ găl′ə tē).

> The word *regalia* (rĭ găl′yə) once denoted the privileges, emblems, and decorations of royalty. Today it is a sometimes disrespectful term for the costumes, trappings, or robes of office, as in a fraternal order.

15. vagrant   (vā′grənt)   *roaming, wandering, or wayward*

The trapper led a vagrant life.
Three vagrants were arrested for loitering near the railroad station.
Tourism is a form of regal vagrancy abroad, though tourists are rarely caught
penniless.

Related words:

A *vagrant* lives a *nomadic* life, having no fixed home.
Itinerant workers go wherever they can find employment.
A *nomad* moves from place to place, rarely staying anywhere for very long.
A *vagabond* is more likely to be a true vagrant than a nomad.
What is a *vagrancy* charge? See dictionary.

16. vehement   (vē′ə mənt)   *violent, passionate*

The Senator made a vehement speech against the banking bill.
Though he sounded violent, his vehemence was mixed with humor.
A Marxist vehemently denounced all capitalists.

17. vindictive   (vĭn dĭk′tĭv)   *vengeful, seeking revenge*

A vindictive former employee planted the bomb.
The Count of Monte Cristo searched out and vindictively punished his enemies.

Related words:

Vindictiveness often creates wars.
Resentment is passive, slow-burning anger (p. 54).
Rancor is bitter hatred or ill will.

18. vociferous   (vō sĭf′ər əs)   *vocally noisy, clamorous, loudly insistent*

The children next door are a vociferous quintet.
The vociferousness of the angry crowd finally abated.
At the convention, rival groups shouted vociferously for their candidates.

Related words:

> *Clamorous* (urgently noisy); *obstreperous* (noisy, unruly); *boisterous* (noisy and unrestrained, but confused rather than unruly); *strident* music (noisy, but harsh and grating).

19. vulnerable   (vŭl′nər ə bəl)   *susceptible to injury or attack*

People who live in glass houses are vulnerable to vindictive assailants.
Poor nutrition increases the body's vulnerability to disease.
In Greek myth, the warrior Achilles was invulnerable, except for his heel.

20. zealous   (zĕl′əs)   *very active, eager, devoted*

Drug firms should be zealous in testing new medicines before putting them on the market.
Is zealousness more important than brilliance in getting good grades?
Not all who pray zealously can be called religious zealots.

Related words:

> A *zealot* is deeply and even vehemently devoted to a cause.
> A *fanatic* is an overzealous person. Fanaticism is redoubling your zeal when you have lost your aim.
> A *bigot* is zealous in a blind, intolerant, or self-glorifying way, particularly in behalf of a cherished belief.

First practice set

Which entry word best replaces the *italicized* word or words?

1. *Clamorous* bells, ringing out early in the morning, make Uncle Herbert *violent*.
2. *Undesirably showy* billboards along the road are *offensive* to many travelers.
3. Thora's *unending* devotion to worthy causes showed in her *glowing* face.

4. A *wandering* rabbit made frequent forays, largely *restricted to night,* into our vegetable patch.
5. Pug was a *vengeful* dog who nevertheless liked *abundant* displays of affection.
6. Are you *susceptible* to the temptations of a *listless* existence?
7. Housecleaning demands that we be *warlike* toward dirt and *very active* in the use of soap.
8. Is a *merciful* judge always *praiseworthy?*
9. The *prominent* author was very *economical* in her living habits.
10. At the *royal* ceremony, a councilor made an *indirect* reference to the state of the economy.

Second practice set

Which of the depth words in the list at the left best replaces each *italicized* word or group of words?

marathon
celebrated
luminescent
nocturne
obstreperous
fanatic
profuse
itinerants
bigot
odious
noxious
renowned
prodigal
lassitude
adverse
vagabond
interminable
averse
inimical
incessant
languish
strident
devious
apathetic
illustrious
boisterous
notorious

1. One *overzealous person* in the group wore on her back a sign that was *glowing in the dark.*
2. Some people are *wasteful;* others *pine away* for lack of food.
3. The *musical work dealing with night* is *widely known* for its quaint but soothing melody.
4. In court, the *vagrant* told his story in a very *roundabout* way.
5. At the meeting, praise for the plan was *poured forth to excess,* making its opponents *unruly and noisy.*
6. Once the town's smokestacks belched forth a *seemingly endless* stream of *harmful* fumes.
7. The swimming *endurance contest* was a *widely noted* way to attract tourists to the resort.
8. Laborers who are *movers from place to place in search of work* dread hearing *unfavorable* reports about the season's harvest.
9. *Ceaseless* complainers are often *hateful* to those around them.
10. People of good will are soon *turned away from* the opinions of *blindly zealous persons.*
11. Even persons usually *noisy and unrestrained* can be made *indifferent* by the extremes of both tropical and Arctic weather.
12. *Drooping weariness* does not make one *outstanding (brilliant)* in one's studies.

Third practice set

Write the number of the *italicized* words. Beside each, place the number of the matching word or group of words from the second column.

A

1. *Luminousness* of the firelight
2. *Frugality* in praising
3. *Zealot* for peace
4. The invalid's *lassitude*
5. *Vehemence* of the attack
6. The candidate's *obtrusiveness*
7. The writer's *eminence*
8. A criminal's *vindictiveness*
9. Ownership in *perpetuity*
10. *Obliqueness* of the rain

1. great violence
2. weariness
3. endlessness
4. deeply devoted worker
5. slanting quality
6. glowing quality
7. fiery glow
8. vengefulness
9. longing for home
10. sparing tendency
11. pushing quality
12. prominence

B

1. Arabian *nomads*
2. The guard's *officiousness*
3. Sign showing a *cornucopia*
4. The player's *vulnerability*
5. *Zealousness* in politics
6. Condition of *vagrancy*
7. Academic *regalia*
8. A parent's *leniency*
9. A bully's *obnoxiousness*
10. Hidden *hostility*

1. horn of plenty
2. hatefulness
3. unfriendliness
4. robes, decorations
5. mildness
6. meddlesomeness
7. formality
8. idle wandering
9. susceptibility to injury
10. commendation
11. persons without fixed homes
12. devoted activity

Rather personal

Think of a classmate, acquaintance, or celebrity to whom one or more of the adjectives in this unit may be applied. Write a description of this person. Contrast the person with someone having other, different characteristics mentioned in this unit.

unit
seven

WHICH WORD?

Which is the best answer to each question?

1. Which does one find in a grave? (a) a retinue (b) sanction (c) repose (d) succor
2. What, most of all, made George III obnoxious to Americans? (a) his tyranny (b) strategy (c) insolence (d) retinue
3. What does the Red Cross chiefly furnish? (a) obeisance (b) repose (c) sanction (d) succor
4. Which word describes an angry person? (a) exorbitant (b) erratic (c) indignant (d) tyrannical
5. Which word expresses approval? (a) strategy (b) sanction (c) succor (d) exultation
6. Which word best describes senseless chatter? (a) exultant (b) infernal (c) inane (d) errant
7. Which word is the most important in football? (a) acuteness (b) strategy (c) agility (d) retinue
8. Which word best describes a dog's faith in its master? (a) implicit (b) inane (c) inferior (d) agile
9. Which word indicates a happy frame of mind? (a) implicit (b) exultant (c) erratic (d) inert
10. Which word best fits a lazy person? (a) inert (b) inferior (c) errant (d) implicit

ADJECTIVES

1. acute (ə kyo͞ot′)   *sharp, severe, perceptive*

The pain of a heart attack is often acute.
The acute shortage of nurses made wage increases necessary.
College studies require mental acuteness as well as good study habits.

Clothing ads make one acutely aware of changing fashions.
Your visual acuity (ə kyo͞o′ət ē) is excellent if it is found to be 20/20.

Related words:

> *Discernment* (clear seeing) may be mental insight or physical vision.
> *Astuteness* is shrewdness or mental sharpness, with a hint of *wiliness* or cunning.

2. agile   (ăj′əl)   *nimble, quick and skillful*

You may be intellectually acute, but a monkey is more agile.
English author G. K. Chesterton was renowned for his mental agility (ə jĭl′ə tē).

> Anything *nimble* is quick, alert, and deft of mind or body; e.g., a nimble brain or nimble fingers.
> Anything *supple* is flexible, yielding in mind or body, quick to respond and adapt.

3. erratic   (ĭ răt′ĭk)   *irregular, wandering, having no fixed course;*
                                      large rock deposited by a glacier

An erratic player may perform well one day and poorly the next.
Its rudder broken, the ship drifted erratically in the North Atlantic, waiting for assistance.
The huge boulder was an erratic transported to the valley by an ancient glacier.

Err- words:

> *Erratic* comes from the Latin verb *errare,* to wander.
> To *err* is to wander from the path of virtue, duty, or truth.
> A knight-*errant* in medieval times was a wandering knight, and knight-*errantry* was his profession.
> An *erroneous* belief is a wrong, deviant, or mistaken belief.
> *Aberration* is a word for a mental derangement, or for a deviation or error in scientific observation.

4. exorbitant   (ĕg zȯr′bə tənt)   *excessive, unreasonable*
                                               (in what one asks)

Bridget feared that the price of the clock would be exorbitant.
The exorbitance of the kidnapper's demands staggered the police.
As a manufacturer of luxury goods, he charges exorbitantly for his products.

> *Exorbitant* applies mainly to prices, values, and qualities.

Related words:

> *Extravagant* (lavish); *inordinate* (beyond reason, without restraint); *immoderate* (not sufficiently restrained).

5. exultant   (ĕg zŭl′tənt)   *joyful, jubilant*

Winning the trophy made the team exultant.

Ted, unfortunately, likes to exult over a rival's downfall.
Olympic heroes enjoy the exultation of the cheering crowd.

Related words:

> *Jubilation* is wholehearted rejoicing and is thus more vociferous than exultation.
> A *jubilee* is a celebration, a time or occasion of rejoicing: The ancient Hebrews
> observed every fiftieth year as a jubilee.
> A *jocund* manner is cheerful and gay but not quite exultant.

6. implicit   (ĭm plĭs'ĭt)   *unquestioning, implied*

Most people have implicit confidence in banks.
Small children trust their parents implicitly.
Good art must transcend the implicit danger of triteness.

> *Implicit* permission is implied permission; *explicit* permission is clearly stated.
> Certain powers of the President are *explicit* in the Constitution; others are *implied*.

7. inane   (ĭn ān')   *senseless, empty*

The talk-show guest made several inane remarks about his slow rise to fame.
Both political speeches were full of inanities (ĭ năn'ə tēz).
Many a conversation has died of inanition.

> Pronounce the *a* in *inanity* and *inanition* as in *tan*.

8. inert   (ĭ nûrt')   *inactive or lifeless*

An inert gas, neon will not combine chemically with anything.
The lifeguard laid the child's inert body on the beach.
The campaign for a new park died of inertia (ĭ nûr'shə) (lack of action).
The city council deliberated inertly.

Related words:

> A *passive* person is unwilling to act or lead and therefore always wants someone
> else to take the initiative.
> An *indolent* or *slothful* person is lazy and thus inactive.
> A *dormant* condition is literally a temporary condition of inactivity like sleep.
> A *listless* manner is indifferent, uninterested, or languid (p. 44).
> Review *lethargy, torpor, stupor* (p. 37).

9. inferior   (ĭn fêr'ē ər)   *low(er) in place or quality*

Cars twenty years ago were inferior to present models in many ways.
The inferiority (ĭn'fêr'ē ôr'ə tē) of the new synthetic fabric soon drove it off
the market.

> *Ersatz* material is a substitute, usually inferior.

10. infernal   (ĭn fûr′nəl)   ***hellish, fiendish***

An infernal howling and shrieking filled the air.
Bunko artists are often infernally clever.
The wind and fire soon made the house a blazing inferno.

Hell words:

> A *diabolic*(al) scheme is devilish, fit only for, or devised by, a devil.
> An *execrable* temper is bad, ugly, hellish—literally, worthy of curses.
> *Execrations* are curses.

NOUNS

1. fugitive   (fyo͞o′jə tĭv)   ***one who flees, a runaway***

The fugitive was wanted in three states for various crimes.
For a fugitive moment, she saw a face at the train window.

Related words:

> A *refugee* is one who flees from home or homeland to escape some human or
> natural danger.
> *Elusiveness* is the quality that makes a fugitive hard to catch.
> *Evasiveness* is skill in dodging something, usually by the use of cunning. Used
> chiefly in the abstract sense, the word generally means avoiding either the issue
> or a definite verbal commitment.

2. indignation   (ĭn dĭg nā′shən)   ***justifiable anger***

The murder stirred a tidal wave of popular indignation in the town.
Indignant taxpayers stormed the mayor's office.

Anger words:

> *Pique* is the mildest form. You are merely ruffled.
> *Vexation* is strong annoyance, milder than anger. A broken dish or a flat tire causes
> vexation.
> *Resentment* is restrained, slow-burning anger (pp. 29, 47).
> *Exasperation* is intense irritation, often violent.
> *Wrath* is rage, fury, or intense anger, with a desire to punish or to avenge a mis-
> deed or offense.
> *Animosity* is strong hostility, usually personal: A person who humiliates you could
> become the target of your strong animosity.

3. insolence   (ĭn′sə ləns)   ***insulting behavior, impudence***

The scoutmaster would tolerate no insolence from the boys.
Insolent taunts greeted the appearance of the once-popular singer.

> Review *impudence* under *brusque* (p. 18).

4. obeisance   (ō bā′səns)   *a bow or curtsy, respect*

The travelers made a low obeisance as they entered the royal presence.
Tipping one's hat is an old-fashioned form of obeisance seldom if ever seen
today.
The speaker in her introduction did obeisance to the founders of our country.

Some forms of obeisance:

> *Curtsy* (a once-popular woman's salutation, a dipping of the body); *genuflection*
> (knee-bending in worship); *salaam* (a Middle-Eastern greeting in which one bows
> very low); *kow-tow* (Chinese kind of obeisance).

5. repose   (rĭ pōz′)   *rest, quiet*

Voltaire had a few years of repose in his home in Switzerland.
A mountain cabin has a reposeful atmosphere.
You repose (place) great confidence in your friend's integrity.

> A *repository* is a place of storage for objects, ideas, or materials, especially of
> cultural value. A person may be a repository of wit, wisdom, or ideas.
> *Repose* (to place) and *repository* come from the Latin *ponere* (to place), whereas
> *repose* (rest) derives from *pausare*, to pause or rest.

6. retinue   (rĕt′ə n̄oo′)   *a group of attendants*

The President travels with a retinue of secretaries and advisers.
A bride's retinue may often include a flower girl.

Related words:

> A *cortège* is a procession of followers or attendants.
> A *convoy* is a protecting escort at sea or a group of ships being escorted.

7. sanction   (săngk′shən)   *approval, authorization*

To marry before the legal age, one must have a parent's sanction to obtain a
license.
Is it your opinion that churches should never sanction a war?
Sanctions are punitive measures imposed by the U.N. on offending nations.

Modes of sanction:

> A *warrant* is an official approval or order by a government agency for an expen-
> diture.

A *dispensation* is approval by the church of some exception or variation from its rules or laws.

Indulgence is enjoyment, satisfaction, or leniency (p. 45), either yours, or permitted by you for others.

Condonation is approval of something questionable by seeming to overlook it.

8. strategy (străt′ə jē)   *skill in maneuvering* or planning*

The boxer's strategy was to feint and dodge until the chance came to land a well-placed left hook.

The offshore island had great strategic (strə tē jĭk) value as a defensive outpost.

The foreign firm's business practices were strategically sound.

Flattery is a stratagem often used on teachers.

A graduate of West Point should be a skillful strategist.

> In military affairs, *strategy* includes methods and plans in the largest sense, whereas *tactics* are specific devices and operations.

9. succor (sŭk′ər)   *aid, help*

Naomi's role as a volunteer was to give counsel and succor to those in need.

The boy made a brave though ineffectual attempt to succor his drowning brother.

10. tyranny (tĭr′ə nē)   *oppressive or unjust government*

Who said: "Taxation without representation is tyranny"?

Free people will always resist any kind of tyrannical (tĭ răn′ĭ kəl) rule.

The football coach was a tyrant, but the players admired him.

Forms of tyrants:

> An *autocrat* is a tyrannical person who may dominate a schoolroom, a home, a business, or a nation.
>
> A *dictator* is a tyrant or absolute ruler who ordinarily seizes power and does not transmit it to a successor in a family line.
>
> A *despot* is a tyrant belonging more likely to a regular line of succession, like Louis XIV of France or Ivan IV of Russia.

Form and substance

1. Write the adverbial or -<u>ly</u> form of fourteen of the entry words in this unit.
2. Make a list of -<u>pose</u>- words and their variant forms.

First practice set

Which entry word best replaces the *italicized* word or words?

1. The *runaway,* who was *without a fixed course,* was discovered traveling in circles.

*See pp. 96, 154.

2. With her *sharp* hearing, Sibyl easily detected which recording was *low in quality*.
3. The captain's *justifiable anger* was great when *aid* did not come.
4. The *jubilant* jester's *insulting behavior* enraged the Court.
5. After the *hellish* confusion came an era of well-earned *rest*.
6. The *quick-moving* performers made their *bow of respect* to the audience.
7. The paper reported some of the *senseless* comments made by the committee members and their *train of attendants*.
8. *Oppressive government* brought *excessive* prices.
9. Will the captain's *skillful planning* be enough to stir up the *inactive* imaginations of the players?
10. Sarah had *unquestioning* faith that her friends would *approve* her decision.

Second practice set

Which of the depth words in the list at the left best replaces each *italicized* word or group of words?

vexation
resentment
indulgence
dispensation
diabolical
inordinate
execrable
cortège
animosity
salaam
immoderate
jubilee
passive
repository
wrath
indolent
listless
jubilation
autocrat
despot
malevolent
nimble
aberration

1. *Whole-hearted rejoicing* took the place of *strong annoyance* when our team finally won.
2. The leader of the *procession* showed no *quiet, slow-burning anger* when delayed by the police.
3. The tyrant may be *slothful* but he is not *unwilling to act*.
4. The *alert* waiter did a graceful *low bow*.
5. Some *derangement* of political vision afflicted the *tyrant (in the line of normal succession)*.
6. An *unrestrained* love of praise is normal for a *tyrannical person*.
7. The captain's *strong hostility* toward the fugitive left no room for *leniency*.
8. The Pope granted an *exemption* from the usual fasting during the *time of rejoicing*.
9. The food was *worthy of curses,* but the starving refugees ate it in *unrestrained* quantities.
10. Far from *devilish* in appearance, the visitor from Mars seemed harmless and *indifferent*.

Third practice set

On a separate sheet, write the numbers of the *italicized* words. Beside each, place
the number of the matching word or group of words from the second column.

A

1. The *agility* of a panther
2. *Inferiority* of the soil
3. *Exorbitance* of the demands
4. *Inertness* of a turtle
5. *Implicitness* of a child's faith
6. Songs of *exultation*
7. *Inanity* of purpose
8. *Inanition* from weariness
9. Mental *acuteness*
10. Modern *knight-errantry*

1. inactivity
2. jubilation
3. emptiness
4. sharpness
5. nagging fear
6. excessiveness
7. nimbleness
8. adventuresomeness
9. animal energy
10. lower quality
11. trustfulness
12. senselessness

B

1. *Tyrannical* habits
2. His *passivity*
3. *Fugitive* thoughts
4. *Indignant* parents
5. Unexpected *sanction*
6. Faulty *strategy*
7. A *supple* body
8. *Erratic* thoughts
9. An *insolent* remark
10. "Jack, be *nimble!*"

1. maneuvering
2. quick-moving, deft
3. oppressive
4. impudent
5. careful, cautious
6. fleeing, runaway
7. justifiably angry
8. unwillingness to act
9. bending readily, lithe
10. irregular, uneven
11. catching, tending to adhere
12. approval

unit eight

ARMY NOTES

Which is the best answer in each case?

1. What word describes warlike music?   (a) redundant   (b) martial   (c) servile (d) intricate
2. What must every soldier be?   (a) valiant   (b) obstinate   (c) unvaunted (d) requisite
3. What does an army try to do to the enemy?   (a) impute it   (b) reprimand it (c) traverse it   (d) subjugate it
4. When an attack comes, it is necessary to   (a) segregate it   (b) surmount it (c) vilify it   (d) traverse it
5. If orders have not been posted, someone has been   (a) martial   (b) precarious (c) negligent   (d) servile when on duty
6. To get to the other side of the field, the soldiers must   (a) surmount it   (b) renounce it   (c) traverse it   (d) segregate it
7. Some recruits regard the job of cleaning up the mess hall as   (a) negligible (b) tenacious   (c) sundry   (d) servile
8. Persons unjustly accused of neglecting their duty should   (a) surmount the charge   (b) renounce it   (c) remonstrate against it   (d) vilify it
9. Which word applies to the situation of a soldier caught between two enemy patrols?   (a) precarious   (b) obstinate   (c) negligible   (d) redundant
10. Which word describes the phrase "martial war"?   (a) redundant   (b) precarious   (c) vituperative   (d) dogged

VERBS

1. impute   (ĭm pyo͞ot′)   ***attribute or ascribe (to another)***

"You impute to me more courage than I possess," he said.
The errors in the expense account imply carelessness, but carry no imputation of dishonesty.

2. renounce   (rĭ nouns′)   *give up, cast off, deny a claim (formally)*

If you were a king or queen, would you, like Edward VIII of Great Britain, renounce the throne to marry a commoner?
A nun must take vows of renunciation (rĭ nŭn′sē ā′shən) when she enters a convent.
The rescuer, in a renunciatory mood, refused to claim her reward.

Give-up words:

Relinquish (give up, abandon, let something go): You relinquish a claim or title. *Relinquishment* is a rather passive act of giving up something, while *renunciation* is active, forthright rejection.
Forgo (deny oneself a privilege or right): You forgo your chance to win a prize if you do not enter the contest.
Cede: A nation may cede (give up) part of its territory to another nation. See *concede* (p. 132): You concede defeat.
Waive (put aside, forgo a claim or right, withhold): You waive your right to claim an inheritance. *Waive* has a legal flavor, *forgo* a personal and social application.
Abdicate (give up a post or responsibility): A ruler may abdicate a throne; parents may abdicate their parental role.

3. reprimand   (rĕp′rə mănd′)   *to rebuke formally or severely*

The company will reprimand any employee who misrepresents its products.
One of the city officials received a well-deserved reprimand.

Degrees of rebuke:

Reproof is mild rebuke: You reprove someone for a mistake or fault.
Remonstrance is a pleading or protesting rebuke: You remonstrate with the children for slamming the door as they go in and out.
Expostulation is stronger: You expostulate (reason earnestly) with a person who causes you injury or persists in a wrong attitude. You take him or her to task.
Censure is strong and rather formal criticism, not kindly or friendly: The Congress voted to censure an irresponsible member of the House.
To *upbraid* or *berate* is to rebuke someone bitterly, violently, vigorously: You upbraid a person for cowardice or failure.

4. requite   (rĭ kwīt′)   *to repay, reward*

"May God requite you for your kindness!" the old man exclaimed.
The years have brought full requital for the sufferings and sacrifices of the pioneers.
In the Arthurian legends, Elaine's affection for Lancelot was unrequited.

Related words:

Requital may be either retaliation or reward.
To make *reparation* is to repair or pay for damage done.
To make *restitution* (p. 202) is to restore, compensate, or make amends for injury or damage one has done.
To *rectify* (p. 340) a mistake or wrong condition is to correct it.
To *redress* a wrong or injustice is to make amends.

5. segregate (sĕg'rə gāt')   *to separate, set apart*

The Supreme Court decided in 1954 that schools could no longer segregate children of one race from those of another.
Segregation of contagious diseases is necessary in a hospital.

6. subjugate (sŭb'jə gāt')   *to bring under control, subdue*

The Romans were able to subjugate many nations.
A monk's life requires subjugation of worldly desires.

Related words:

> *Quell* is used of small affairs: You quell a riot or your fears, but you subjugate powerful passions or other such forces.
> *Vanquish* is a more resounding way to conquer: You vanquish the most formidable foes, fears, and follies.

7. surmount (sər mount')   *to rise above, overcome*

A spire surmounts the tower of the new church.
No matter how scared, you must surmount your fears.
The obstacles of space travel have proved to be surmountable.
Few dare to face the almost insurmountable hazards of climbing Mount Everest.

8. tabulate (tăb'yə lāt')   *to organize (data) in tables and columns*

After an election, TV news commentators tabulate the results for the viewers.
The newspaper tabulation will show how each precinct voted.
Census statistics may be presented in either tabular or graphic form.

> Adding machines and bookkeeping machines are mechanical *tabulators.*
> A *computer* not only tabulates information, but also "remembers" it, "analyzes" it, and "reaches conclusions."

9. traverse (trə vûrs')   *to move across or pass over*

Experienced sailors can traverse the ocean without a compass.
To reach the bottom of the mountain, the skier had to traverse the slope many times.
The draperies are held up by traverse rods across the window.

10. vilify (vĭl′ə fī′)   *to speak evil of, defame*

The dealer was too honest to vilify a competitor.
Vilification of opponents is the curse of many political campaigns.

> To *revile* is to abuse or defame. It formerly meant to regard as vile.
> To *vituperate* is to condemn or abuse with violence and anger: The argument deteriorated into angry *vituperation*.
> *Defamation* consists of distributing information damaging to a person's reputation.

ADJECTIVES

1. intricate (ĭn′trĭ kət)   *complicated, complex*

A space vehicle is an exceedingly intricate mechanism.
Only an accountant can understand the intricacies of corporate finance.

2. martial (mär′shəl)   *warlike, military*

Followed by their school band, the students paraded with truly martial briskness and rhythm.
One onlooker, in jest, said that he would not know a field marshal from a court-martial.

> *Martial* law is military rule. Disasters sometimes weaken or overload civil authority to the point where sterner control is exercised.
> *Marital* (p. 204) affairs and problems are those related to marriage.

3. negligible (nĕg′lə jə bəl)   *trifling, unimportant*

If you had only one line in the play, your part was negligible.
Our garden received only negligible care that spring.
A dollar a week adds but negligibly to one's bank account.

> A *negligent* person is careless or neglectful of duty. The machine broke down because of the operator's negligence. *Negligent*, like *negligible*, comes from the Latin verb *negligere*, not to heed. What element of meaning do the two words have in common?

4. obstinate   (ŏb′stə nət)   *stubborn, dogged, not easily subdued*

The coach proved obstinate in not letting Jill play in the game.
Ron obstinately refuses to eat vegetables.
The obstinacy of the fever puzzled the doctors.

Forms of tenacity:

> *Doggedness* is stubborn adherence to a plan or goal: The pickets doggedly refused to go home.
> *Tenacity*, the will to hang on, to hold fast, is more a matter of will power and brain than doggedness: It takes tenacity to win a football game.
> *Pertinacity* is stubborn, tough-minded determination, more than tenacity indicates: A crusader needs to have unusual pertinacity.
> *Perseverance* is stick-to-it-iveness, endurance, but it is less intense than doggedness or tenacity: The tortoise won by perseverance.
> *Resoluteness* is strong determination: A resolute determination drove Edison on for weeks at a time.
> *Inflexibility* is an unbending determination that does not yield, either temporarily or slightly, to adverse circumstances.
> *Obduracy* is hardness, toughness, hard-heartedness, especially against moral influence.

5. precarious   (prĭ kâr′ē əs)   *insecure, uncertain*

A seat on top of a telephone pole is a precarious perch.
The precariousness of the negotiations made a strike possible.
Artists often live precariously, with poor lodgings and little food.

6. redundant   (rĭ dûn′dənt)   *repetitious, unnecessary to the meaning*

"Hot" in "hot water heater" and "stubborn" in "stubborn mule" are redundant terms.
Conversations are often loaded with redundancies.
The book deals redundantly with the problems of urban renewal.

7. requisite   (rĕk′wə zĭt)   *necessary, indispensable*

Nearness to raw materials is a requisite in selecting a site for a plant.
An A.B. degree is a prerequisite for admission to most law schools.
Hal's first assignment at the plant was to requisition a hundred pairs of overalls.

8. servile   (sûr′vĭl′)   *yielding, submissive, befitting*
                                                                      low position

Executives need to be teachable, but they should not be servile.
The cowed dog approaches its master with an air of servility.

Our early settlers often paid their passage across the Atlantic by several years of voluntary servitude (sûr'və tōōd') in the new land.

Related words:

A *subservient* person adapts readily to your wishes and authority, but in a less cringing way than one who is servile.
Menial work is humble, lowly, and usually disagreeable.
An *obsequious* person is servile, with a fawning attitude.

9. sundry   (sŭn'drē)   ***various, assorted, diverse***

The children help around the house in sundry ways.
Drugstores are well stocked with sundries.

To *sunder* old ties is to break them *asunder* or apart.

10. valiant   (văl'yənt)   ***brave, courageous***

"The valiant never taste of death but once."
Many groups work valiantly to preserve American freedoms.
Valor is highly esteemed in any field of endeavor.
The *Iliad* is full of ignoble as well as valorous deeds.

A *gallant* fighter is plucky, staunch, brave.
An *intrepid* fighter is fearless, daring, skillful.

First practice set

Which entry word best replaces the *italicized* word or words?

1. They asked *repetitious* questions about my *slavelike* duties.
2. We made *complicated* plans to *rise above* our financial problems.
3. The guard, appearing very *courageous,* marched back and forth with a *military* air.
4. Dad *severely rebuked* the boys because they had *attributed* such selfish motives to him.
5. All efforts to *set apart* those who had the disease met with *stubborn* resistance.
6. Our enemies failed to *subdue* us because they considered rigid discipline a *trifling* matter.
7. If you *speak evil of* a chum, your friendship will become very *insecure*.
8. It is *necessary* to find a way to *reward* the heroism that cost the nurse his eyesight.
9. The spy had to *give up* the citizenship which permitted her to *go across* enemy territory.
10. I had to *organize in tables* dozens of *assorted* expense items.

Second practice set

Which of the depth words in the list at the left best replaces each *italicized* word or group of words?

intrepid
tenacity
berate
vituperative
rectify
subservient
vanquish
waive
reprove
cede
menial
inflexible
restitution
negligent
obsequious
quell
pertinacity
gallant
censure
abdicate
forgo
remonstrance
obduracy
revile

1. The cousins were *unbending* in their refusal to *put aside (legally)* their claim to the estate.
2. The youth promised to *correct* his mistakes and to make *compensation* for work poorly done.
3. The leaders' *pleading rebuke* was met with *violently abusive* language from the offender.
4. The envoy's *hard-hearted determination* made our leaders less *adaptable to* (their) *wishes* than they otherwise would have been.
5. It takes *tough-minded endurance* to withstand *strong criticism.*
6. You may *deny yourself* your responsibility as an officer, but you must *give up* the privileges too.
7. *"Bitterly rebuke* me if you must,'' the Senator said, ''but I was not *neglectful* in doing my duty.''
8. Our *fearless and daring* guide showed a great *will to hold fast* until we scaled the cliff.
9. Many will *abuse and defame* you for being too *fawningly servile* in your reply.
10. Is it harder to *conquer* an army than to *overcome* one's fears?

Third practice set

On a separate sheet, write the numbers of the *italicized* words. Beside each, place the number of the matching word or group of words from the second column.

A

1. Tardy *relinquishment*
2. Several *sundry* items
3. *Renunciation* of pay raises
4. A reporter's *valor*
5. *Subjugation* of neighboring peoples
6. A pig's *obstinacy*
7. Life's *precariousness*
8. *Requital* of services
9. Scandalous *imputation*
10. Newspaper *vilification*

1. bravery
2. act of delaying
3. accusation
4. uncertainty
5. abandonment
6. repayment
7. an active giving up
8. defamation
9. miscellaneous
10. the subduing
11. obtuseness
12. stubbornness

B

1. *Resolute* hope
2. *Dogged* insistence
3. *Requisite* courtesy
4. *Intricate* strategy
5. *Negligible* cost
6. *Obdurate* attitude
7. *Gallant* bird
8. *Menial* duties
9. *Vituperative* letter
10. *Marital* laws

1. military, warlike
2. hard-hearted, tough
3. lowly, disagreeable
4. strong, determined
5. very complicated
6. staunch, plucky, brave
7. violently abusive
8. pertaining to marriage
9. stubborn, unyielding
10. mildly critical
11. trifling, insignificant
12. necessary, indispensable

Changes and charges

1. Change one letter of each of the following and get a more familiar word: *impute, requite, martial.*
2. List other words ending in -<u>nounce</u>, -<u>mand</u>, -<u>verse</u>, -<u>ile</u>.
3. Write a paragraph describing a fictitious incident in which you deserved a severe reprimand either from your parents, the school, or any higher authority. Include as many words from this unit as you can. Use your imagination to make the paragraph interesting for your classmates.

unit nine

EXAMPLES

Which of the words or situations at the left is best exemplified by each of the following statements?

nadir
enervation
apocalypse
anomaly
consolation
initiative
complement
exaltation
hypothesis
apogee
perquisite
litany
maxim
mosaic
arson

1. A teenager starts a fund to help a friend seriously injured in an accident.
2. You find a cow tied to the davenport in your living room.
3. The police think the burglar crawled in through a ventilating duct.
4. You get a typewriter as a prize if you sell enough tickets.
5. You are too exhausted from hard work and late hours to sell any tickets at all.
6. Your ship has the normal number of persons on its crew.
7. Your fortunes are at the very lowest point possible.
8. You feel very exhilarated because, in addition to good grades, you have received several honors in activities.
9. You are thirty years older and have reached the pinnacle of your career.
10. You comfort a child in deep grief for a beloved pet that has died.
11. You give the police information about a person you saw lurking about just before the fire broke out.
12. Your forte is comedy; you are not equipped to write about any remarkable revelation or prophecy.
13. You enroll for a course to learn to create inlaid artwork composed of bits of stone or glass.
14. You join with the congregation in intoning a fixed response to the clergy's series of prayers.
15. Your grandmother has a wise saying or pithy statement of a general truth for every occasion.

NOUNS

1. anomaly   (ə nŏm'ə lē)   ***an abnormal, irregular fact***
or occurrence

Snow in August is an anomaly almost anywhere in the U.S.A.
Laughter at a funeral is anomalous behavior—embarrassing, too.
Palm trees above the Arctic Circle would be anomalistic.

Compare with *incongruity* (p. 251).

2. apogee   (ăp'ə jē')   ***highest or farthest point (in an orbit);***
climax

The apogee of the new communications satellite is 160 meters from the earth.
Its perigee (nearest point) is 115 miles. (Gr. *perigeios*)
The perigean and the apogean figures imply an elliptical orbit.
British actress Vivien Leigh attained the apogee of her career in the film *Gone
with the Wind,* based on the novel by Margaret Mitchell.

Related words:

> *Zenith* (zē'nĭth) is an earthbound word for the highest point a planet or star attains
> in the sky above a given point on the earth. *Nadir* (nā'dĭr, -dər) is the lowest
> point: When Venus is directly overhead, it is at its zenith; when it is directly be-
> low, it is at its nadir. Figuratively, then, a career, a campaign, or any kind of
> undertaking has its zenith and its nadir.

3. apocalypse   (ə pŏk'ə lĭps')   ***vision of future (well-being);***
revelation

Images of war, revolution, and apocalypse fill the book.
The Book of Daniel in the Bible contains apocalyptic visions.
The play had an apocalyptic final scene, hinting that good would triumph.

> The *Apocalypse,* or Book of Revelation in the Bible, was written for Christians
> who were suffering severe persecution in Rome.

4. arson   (är'sən)   ***act of setting fire(s) purposely***

When a mysterious fire occurs, the police suspect arson.

The arson squad investigates. If evidence of arson is found, police look for the arsonist.

Mudslinging against an opponent in a campaign is political arson.

Related words:

> *Sabotage,* willful destruction of property, especially in strikes or war, involves more than *arson* and has more forms: Putting defective parts in the plane was an act of sabotage. A *saboteur* is a person who destroys property willfully.
>
> An *incendiary* is a person who starts fires or one who deliberately stirs up strife, hostility, or rebellion. The word functions as an adjective too: Cyd has an incendiary temper.

5. client   (klī′ənt)   *person for whom a lawyer, accountant,*
                                                              or agency is acting; customer

A young lawyer is happy to find a new client.

If an agency acts on your behalf, a cliental relationship exists.

Tiffany's has a wealthy or exclusive clientele (habitual customers as a group).

6. hypothesis   (hī pŏth′ə sĭs)   *theory; unproved explanation*

One hypothesis about the earth's origin states that the earth condensed from a cloud of gas hurled from the sun.

The lawyer constructed a hypothetical (hī′pə thĕt′ĭkəl) case of arson to prove his point.

Scientists were able to hypothesize the existence of Uranus before it was actually seen by telescope.

Earth life is hypothetically impossible on Venus.

> A *hypothesis* is a scientific guess or assumption made on the basis of incomplete information until it can be confirmed or proved erroneous.

7. incidence   (ĭn′sə dəns)   *process of a happening, an occurrence*

The U.N. reported on the incidence of illiteracy in the world.

Is the incidence of the disease decreasing now?

> *Incidence* also means the striking of a surface by a ray of light, bullet, line, or other body: Our physics teacher figured out the angle of incidence of the sun's rays. An *incident* is a distinct event, sometimes minor. An *incidental* remark is one you just happened to make.

8. initiative   (ĭ nĭsh′ə tĭv)   *unprompted action, the first*
                                                              step, enterprise

One can always depend on Phyllis to take the initiative in any crisis.

The initiative is in the hands of a committee that promises action.

A vice-president was the initiator of the new sales plan.

One of our school societies is about to initiate new members.

9. litany   (lĭt′ə nē)   *a responsive prayer or religious service*

The peoples' responses during the litany resounded throughout the church.
School cheers echoed like litanies during the game.

> The *liturgy,* or religious ceremony, of a Catholic mass is much more elaborate
> than the prescribed form for public worship of Baptist or other non-liturgical
> churches. Rites associated with religious service are called *liturgical* forms. The
> liturgy of a Jewish synagogue is based on the Old Testament.

10. maxim   (măk′sĭm)   *a wise saying, aphorism, proverb*

"Haste not, rest not" is a familiar maxim from Goethe.
Horace Greeley did not follow his maxim, "Go west, young man."

Related words:

> *Maxim* is akin to "maximum." Both come from the superlative of the Latin
> *magnus* (great). A *maxim* is thus by implication a saying of the maximum, or
> utmost, wisdom.
>
> A *proverb* states a familiar, obvious, widely accepted truth: "A stitch in time
> saves nine."
>
> An *adage* hints of its age. It has been in popular use for a long time: "He who
> goes a-borrowing goes a-sorrowing." Compare *saw.*
>
> A *dictum* is formal, authoritative, and likely to come from an expert: "Stars do
> not twinkle."
>
> A *canon* is a law, a body of laws (especially of the church), or a principle that
> cannot be disregarded: "Thou shalt love thy neighbor as thyself" is a major
> canon of Christianity and Judaism.
>
> A *truism* is obvious—too obvious in form or fact to be very impressive: "All men
> are mortal." Compare *axiom, postulate, theorem.*
>
> An *aphorism* or *apothegm* is a typically terse and pithy saying, somewhere be-
> tween the folksy and the authoritative, like a proverb: "Art is long, and time is
> fleeting."
>
> An *epigram* is likely to be witty but more involved, more comprehensive, or more
> poetic. Often it uses antithesis, and often is about a person: "My ancestors did
> not come over on the *Mayflower;* they went out to meet it," said Will Rogers.

11. mosaic   (mō zā′ĭk)   *inlaid art work, design made from bits*
of glass or stone set in cement

The top of the coffee table is a mosaic depicting a scene in a Persian garden.

When observed from the air, the prairie states form a mosaic of fields, woods, and towns in a rather regular pattern.

Life is a mosaic of joys and sorrows.

12. perquisite   (pûr′kwə zət)   *an extra benefit or remuneration*

One of the perquisites in the United States Air Force is free vacation transportation in military planes if space is available.

Wage dividends, profit sharing, and free health insurance are other kinds of perquisite, as is the discount on goods purchased from an employer's firm.

Related words:

A *bonus* is something special given over and above one's regular wages—extra pay, a dividend, or a gift; it is not a privilege or something customary like a perquisite.

A *bounty* is usually a reward for doing something that the government wants done, like exterminating a pest or producing extra crops.

A *premium* is something extra, given usually for purchasing an item.

A *dividend* is a share of the earnings from an investment of either money or effort.

VERBS

1. complement   (kŏm′plə mənt)   *to round out, make complete*

The two women complement each other admirably as business partners because one is a shrewd buyer and the other a genius in sales strategy.

A ship's complement is the number needed to operate the vessel.

Marriage is a highly complementary relationship.

2. console   (kŏn′sōl)   *to comfort (a person), make less sad*

Friends came to console the family in its loss.

Amy tried to find consolation for her grief in community service.

At first the refugees seemed inconsolable at having to leave their homes.

The storm forced the travelers to spend a few disconsolate days in a gloomy old hotel.

3. consummate   (kŏn′sə māt′)   *bring to fulfillment*
                                          or completion

It takes months to consummate a complex business deal in aircraft.

When very discouraged, Hamlet said of death, " 'Tis a consummation devoutly to be wished."

Chris plays tennis with consummate (kən sŭm′ət) skills.

4. enervate   (ĕn ər vāt′)   *weaken, take strength from,*
                                                  debilitate

Long hours with little exercise will enervate a person.
Loss of self-confidence has an enervating effect too.
Bad habits eventually lead to enervation.

Related words:

Barbarian invaders found Roman society in a state of *debilitation*.
Muscular dystrophy produces gradual physical *debility*.
Atrophy is a wasting away of bodily tissue or a failure to develop. The word may
also be used in referring to an institution or an enterprise: The fraternal orders
suffer from atrophy. The economy seemed atrophied that year.

5. exalt   (ĕg zȯlt′)   *to lift up, elevate*

Wealth alone did not exalt them to the top levels of society.
Stimulants produce a short-lived sense of exaltation.
Myrna found the exalted atmosphere of the university's school of music
exhilarating.

6. perforate   (pûr′fə rāt′)   *punch hole(s), pierce*

Darts began to perforate the outer rings of the target, but none scored a
bull's-eye.
Perforations in the chute allow the small peas to fall through.
A perforated lung is a serious condition.

7. propagate (prŏp'ə gāt')　　　　　　　　　*to reproduce, spread abroad*

Germs, flies, sparrows, and rabbits propagate rapidly.
Missionaries go out to propagate their faith.
Communists are dedicated to the propagation of Marxism.
Thomas Jefferson was a propagator of agrarian democracy.

> *Propaganda* is the spreading or promoting of ideas, doctrines, or information by people dedicated, paid, or otherwise obligated to do so. The word may also refer to the ideas, facts, or rumors themselves.

8. stipulate (stĭp'yə lāt')　　　　　　　　*to specify, include explicitly*
　　　　　　　　　　　　　　　　　　　　　　(in an agreement)

Be sure to stipulate in the printing order the kind of paper you want.
The contract contains the stipulation that it must be signed within three days.
In a buyer's market the buyer is usually the stipulator of price and quality.

First practice set

Which entry word or variant form best replaces each *italicized* word or group of words?

1. The law *states explicitly* that *setting fires to property purposely* is a felony demanding imprisonment.
2. An *inlaid art work* made of Jell-o would be quite an *abnormal occurrence*.
3. By not taking the *first step* in seeking business, the accountant kept the number of *persons for whom he could act* to a minimum.
4. It was hard to *comfort* the scientist when space probes disproved her *theory* about Mars.
5. The *responsive leader-and-group prayer* reaches its *highest point* at the end.
6. The *occurrence* of the disease on the island was high enough to *weaken* a large proportion of the work force.
7. The *vision of future well-being* contains a *saying of the highest wisdom:* be ready.
8. The *extra benefits* of this particular job have a tendency to *elevate* the employee in the eyes of her friends.
9. The party's leaders could not *bring to fulfillment* their plan to *spread abroad* their political beliefs.
10. Be sure to *punch holes in* these sheets which *round out* your biography before you insert them in the notebook.

Second practice set

Which word from the list at the left best replaces each *italicized* word or group of words?

proverb
bounty
zenith
clientele
maxim
enervate
saw
mosaic
postulate
adage
consummate
theorem
truism
propagate
dictum
aphorism
bonus
perigee
epigram
stipulate
exaltation
canon
atrophy
axiom
initiator

1. The lawyer's *habitual customers* will all work to help him *bring to fruition* his political ambitions.
2. A *formal, authoritative statement* sounds less formidable than a *principle that cannot be disregarded*.
3. "A rolling stone gathers no moss" may be properly called *a widely accepted truth* but hardly a *too-obvious saying*.
4. "Easy come, easy go," an *old traditional saying readily accepted*, doesn't *specify* what it is that comes and goes so easily.
5. "He never said a foolish thing nor did a wise one" was a *witty saying using antithesis* about Charles II of England.
6. "Many are called but few are chosen" is a *saying of the utmost wisdom* or a *saying between the authoritative and the folksy*.
7. "You must start at the bottom" is not a *principle to be proved* but an *accepted but unprovable principle* offering little comfort to beginners.
8. The *nearest point* (here, the lowest or least significant) of the writer's life was in her youth, before education, travel, and critical acclaim carried her toward the *highest point* of her career and the *state of elevation* that fame brings.
9. Once a *government reward* was given for killing mountain lions; now one is given for preserving them.
10. The *launcher or beginner* of the new project deserves (a) *something special over and above her regular pay* for her originality.

"What's the good word?"

Third practice set

On a separate sheet of paper, write the numbers of the *italicized* words. Beside each, place the number of the matching word or group of words from the second column.

A

1. Prudent *stipulation*
2. Long awaited *consummation*
3. Well-concealed *arson*
4. Melodious *litany*
5. Team's *nadir*
6. State of *exaltation*
7. Imperfect *perforation*
8. Expected *enervation*
9. A promised *perquisite*
10. One's own *initiative*

1. religious ritual
2. unprompted action
3. undeserved praise
4. fulfillment, fruition
5. hole punched in something
6. specific requirement
7. intense irritation
8. extra remuneration
9. lowest point
10. intentional setting of fire
11. weakening, debilitation
12. uplifted feeling

B

1. A *hypothetical* explanation
2. *Apocalyptic* writings
3. *Anomalous* behavior
4. *Propagative* capacity
5. A *disconsolate* victim
6. The *perigeal* point
7. An *atrophied* condition
8. *Incidental* meeting
9. *Complementary* relationship
10. A *mosaic* floor

1. sad, sorrowful
2. alarming, fear-arousing
3. theoretical
4. wasted or withered
5. nearest-to-the-earth
6. rounding out, completing
7. chance or casual
8. abnormal, irregular
9. composed of pieces forming a pattern
10. visionary or revelatory
11. simple, uncomplicated
12. reproductive

unit
ten

THEY CREATED WORDS

Which definition below belongs to each mythologic figure and the *italicized* English word that is derived from this figure?

1. Pluto gave us the word *plutocrat*.
2. The *Dionysian* way of living derives from the Greek god Dionysius.
3. Its counterpart, the *Apollonian* lifestyle, goes back to Apollo, the Greek Helios (Sun), god of poetry, music, medicine, and prophecy.
4. An *odyssey* is so named for the ''godlike'' Odysseus (Ulysses in Latin), Greek hero of the Trojan wars.
5. The Titans were a breed of giant deities from whom the word *titanic* comes. They were overthrown by the Olympian deities.
6. The word *hermetic* is traceable to Hermes Trismegistus who, it was believed, invented a magic seal for vessels or bottles sometime early in the Christian era.
7. A *Pyrrhic* victory reminds the reader of Pyrrhus, who ''won'' such a victory.
8. *Palladium* commemorates Pallas Athene, whose husband was Zeus.
9. A *promethean* gesture reminds one of Prometheus, who stole fire from the gods and gave it to earth.
10. A *terpsichorean* genius practices an art that calls to mind Terpsichore, who became the Muse of this art.
11. Procrustes was a mythical Greek giant whose *procrustean* hospitality still flourishes in some areas of thought.

intellectual–aesthetic	dancing (as an art)
too costly	living chiefly for sensual pleasure
daring on behalf of humanity	extended journey
wealthy power figure	powerful, gigantic
airtight or magical	a haven or heavenly place
something that insures safety	taking ruthless action to attain conformity

NOUNS

(This unit is an adventure in mythology as its symbolic meanings survive and flourish in the twentieth century.)

1. aegis   (ē′jes)   *protection, sponsorship*

The pony league baseball series operates under the aegis of the Kiwanis Club.
The Winter Concert series was organized under the aegis of the Office of Public
Events.

> *Aegis* comes from the Greek word for the shield borne by Zeus and later by his
> daughter, Athene.

Other *ae* words from Greek mythology include:

> *Aeolus,* god of the winds, from whose name we derive *Aeolian* harp, a musical
> instrument operated by air; *(a)eonian,* lasting forever; *Aeneas,* the legendary
> Trojan who founded Rome; *aesthetic* (or *esthetic*), sensitive to beauty.

2. amazon   (ăm′ə zŏn′)   *a large strong or athletic*
                                                                   woman, a female warrior

The women of the new army unit call themselves the Amazons.
The sculptured figure was of a woman of amazonian (ăm′ə zō′nē ən) pro-
portions.

> In Greek mythology, the *Amazons* were a race of female warriors believed to live
> near the Black Sea.

3. aurora   (ȯ rôr′ə)   *the dawn or similar luminosity*

Aurora was the Roman goddess of dawn.
The aurora borealis or northern lights look like the glimmers of a misplaced
dawn when they appear in the northern skies.
The aurora australis, an occurrence similar to the northern lights, takes place
in southern skies.

> *Aurora* (dawn) suggests the golden colors of dawn and also the words pertaining
> to gold formed from the Latin *aurum,* gold; *aureate,* golden or brilliant; *aureole,*
> a halo of golden radiance encircling a body; *auric* or *aureous,* containing gold.

4. odyssey   (ŏd′ə sē)   *extended journey or wandering*

In 1890, newspaper reporter Nellie Bly completed an odyssey around the world in seventy-two days, an astonishing feat at that time.

Three college students wrote a book about their odyssean (ō dis′ē ən) adventures in ten African countries.

Odysseus, starting for his home in Ithaca (Greece) after the Trojan War, wandered around the Mediterranean world for ten years.

5. paean   (pē′ən)   *song of thanksgiving, joy, praise, triumph*

Francis Scott Key wrote "The Star Spangled Banner" in 1814 as a paean of thanksgiving and triumph after the British failed to take Fort McHenry from the Americans.

Paeans of spiritual joy ring out on Easter Sunday.

> *Paean* comes from the Latin name *paian,* an epithet of Apollo.

6. palladium   (pə lā′dē əm)   *safeguard, something to insure safety*

The safety of ancient Troy was believed to depend on its Palladium, a cherished statue of Pallas Athene.

The Palladium in a city today is thought of as insuring its self-respect if not its safety.

One could say that the legislative process comprises the palladium of democracy.

> *Pallas Athene,* the Greek goddess of war and protectress of Athens, possessed as one of her many attributes that of wisdom.

7. plutocrat   (ploo tə krăt′)   *a wealthy person, especially one*
                                                   whose wealth means power

The town was named for a well-known plutocrat whose grandparents had once
owned the land for miles around.
Some people insist that the United States is a plutocracy (ploo tŏk′rə sē), a
country controlled by a very few wealthy families.
Plutocratic groups have never been able to prevent the passage or operation of
antitrust laws.

8. siren   (sī′rən)   *a bewitching or irresistible woman;*
                                                   fascinating, captivating

The sirens in the *Iliad* were nymphs who lured sailors to their death on the
rocks by their singing.
A siren voice today is one which, be it male or female, lures persons to harm
or destruction—physical, economic, moral, or political.
Sirens on ambulances or fire trucks, on the other hand, protect us from destruction.

> *Siren* comes from a Greek word for a rope or cord, perhaps because Odysseus
> saved himself from the sirens of classical fame by having his sailors lash him to
> the mast of his ship so that he could not yield to their allurement.

9. Valhalla   (văl hăl′ə)   *hall of feasting heroes*

Valhalla, the hall of Odin where slain heroes were received, is the ''heaven''
of Norse mythology.
Arlington National Cemetery is a kind of Valhalla in that it contains the remains
and memorials of our nation's heroes.

Heaven words:

> The Paradise of Adam and Eve in Genesis offered a complete array of earthly
> delights.
> The Moslem Paradise was a place primarily for warriors, with physical pleasures
> in abundance.
> The *Paradiso* of Dante was a place of purer delights.
> The Christian Heaven promises delights so unearthly that eye hath not seen nor
> ear heard what they are like.
> The ''heaven'' of the ancient Greeks was the Elysian fields (Elysium) or Isles
> of the Blest, the most delightful part of the underworld. Only virtuous people and
> heros were permitted to live there.

ADJECTIVES

1. ambrosial   (ăm′brō zhē əl)   *fragrant, delicious, superior*

In Greek mythology, ambrosia and nectar were the foods of the gods.

For Rita, a creamy fruit salad was ambrosial fare.

> The word *ambrosia* comes from a, not + *brotos*, mortal. Thus the name Ambrose has implications of wishful immortality in it. See *St. Ambrose of Milan* (340?– 397 A.D.).

2. Apollonian   (ap ə lō′nē ən)   *godlike, living by enlightened, aesthetic, intellectual values; harmonious, spiritual*

The new swimming champion is a young Apollo (ə pŏl′ō) in appearance.
A Rhodes scholar should be a true Apollonian.
Admirers talk about the new teacher's Apollonian lifestyle.

> *Apollo* was the Greek god of the arts, prophecy, and medicine, the model of youth-ful manhood and beauty. As the sun god, he was to Greeks the light of the world in an earthly sense. It is hard to find any other word that connotes so many aspects of handsomeness, athletic prowess, and intellectual enlightenment.

3. Dionysian   (dĭ ə niz(h) ē ən [or nis(h)])   *living for sensual and material delights*

The Dionysian lifestyle, which is the antithesis of the Apollonian style, con-sists primarily of the sensuous pleasures and revelry.
Life at its best is to some degree a well-controlled alternation between the Dionysian and Apollonian modes.

> *Dionysus* was the Greek god of wine and revelry.
> Compare *Bacchanalian*. Bacchus was the Roman counterpart of Dionysus, but a bacchanal is likely to be merely a drunken carouser.

4. hermetic   (hər mĕt′ĭk)   *completely sealed, airtight, hard to understand, relating to the occult or the magical*

One of Houdini's hermetical tricks was to be trapped inside a hermetic box and yet escape within a few minutes.
The submarine hatch closes hermetically.

> *Hermes* was the swift messenger of the gods, but *hermetic* comes from Hermes Trismegistus, a legendary author, and his magical and obscure doctrines.

5. procrustean   (prə krəs′tē ən)   *taking fanatical or ruthless action*
to attain conformity

Requiring all pupils to buy expensive gym uniforms is procrustean.
Making every worker pick the same amount of fruit in a day is also procrustean.

> *Procrustes* was a mythical giant in Greece who took in travelers at night and then
> stretched them, or cut off enough of their legs, to make them fit his bed exactly.

6. Promethean   (prə mē′thē ən)   *daring, creative, or heroic on*
behalf of humanity

Moses would be a Promethean figure if he had himself taken the initiative in
liberating his Hebrew people and had suffered divine punishment for his action.
Einstein qualifies as a truly Promethean figure, except that he suffered no
punishment.
The pretensions of a dictator are almost always Promethean, but not valid, and
punishment usually comes from outraged humanity rather than from the deity.

> In Greek mythology, *Prometheus* was a Titan who stole fire from the gods to bene-
> fit humanity. For punishment, the gods chained him to a rock, with a vulture
> eating his liver, which was replenished each night by the gods. A Prometheus
> today is thus a person who (1) performs an act of liberation or appropriation,
> (2) offends the deity by this act, and (3) suffers prolonged and painful punishment.

7. Pyrrhic victory   (pĭr′ĭk)   *a too-costly victory*

Gene and Jeanette won a Pyrrhic victory when they got ahead of the others in
a drag race but lost control of their car and suffered near-fatal injuries.
A person who sacrifices fortune and health for either a civil law suit or a national
election is said to have won a Pyrrhic victory.

> *Pyrrhus* was an ancient Greek king famous for military successes gained at too
> great a cost in lives and treasure on both sides. Is this true of all wars or only cer-
> tain wars?

8. stygian   (stĭj′ē ən)   *dark, gloomy, hellish*

The stygian darkness of the cave was terrifying when the light gave out.
Bones littered the shore of the River Styx (stĭks) in the Stygian setting fabricated by Rhoda for the Halloween party in our school gym, while a ferry (a
disguised dolly) waited to take the guests across.

> The *River Styx* in Greek mythology encircled Hades, and Charon, the ferry oper-
> ator, carried the souls of the dead over the water for a small fee.

9. tantalizing   (tăn′tə līz ing)   *teasing, tormenting*

The picture of a pizza is tantalizing to a hungry person.
While Sara carried the jug of milk, her brother tantalized her for being clumsy.

> In Greek myth, *King Tantalus,* a son of Zeus, was tormented in Hades by having
> to stand in water and under the branches of a fruit tree, only to have the water and
> fruit elude his grasp when he wished to drink or eat.

10. terpsichorean   (tûrp′sə kôr′ē ən)   *pertaining to dancing*

A ballerina displays marvelous terpsichorean skills.
After many years of practice, Janet is considered a talented terpsichorean.

> *Terpsichore* (delighting in the dance) was the Greek Muse of dancing.
> Used as a noun, *terpsichorean* has a humorous flavor.

11. titanic   (tī tăn′ĭk)   *extremely large, strong, or powerful*

In Greek mythology, the Titans (tī′tənz) were a race of giant deities overthrown
by Zeus and the other Olympian gods.
Titanism is revolutionary defiance of the established order.
A hydrogen fusion bomb produces a titanic explosion.

> What was the *Titanic*? Why was it so named? What happened to it in 1912?
> *Titanium* is the metallic element now almost indispensable in the manufacture of
> aircraft. Find out and explain how it is used if you can.

First practice set

Which entry word or variant form best replaces each *italicized* word or group of
words?

1. The Renaissance, a rebirth of arts and letters, was like the *dawn,* greeted by
   poets with happy *songs of joy*.
2. How does the mode of life that is *based on reason and enlightenment* conflict
   with the mode of life that is *devoted to the sensual and material*?
3. Heroic *female warriors* would qualify for *the hall of feasting heroes*.
4. The group's *lengthy journey* will operate under the *sponsorship* of a university.
5. A *wealthy person* quite naturally thinks of property as (a) *something to insure
   safety*—a guarantee that all material advantages, including a supply of *delicious,
   superior* food, will never cease.
6. In the New Testament, Salome, a *seductive woman,* could be said to have had
   a *too-costly* victory when she claimed the head of John the Baptist as a reward
   for her dancing.

7. Sometimes society inflicts *fanatically conforming* limitations on a modern-day *figure who is heroic, creative, and daring on behalf of humanity.*
8. The antique *dancing* doll is kept in a *completely sealed* container.
9. Steel technology was a *tormenting* process before use of titanium became practicable. It took a *wealthy power figure* to finance the improvement.
10. Carlsbad Caverns, vast and *hellish*, contain *extremely large* rock formations which at times suggest an enormous pipe organ.

Second practice set

Which word from the list at the left best replaces each *italicized* word or group of words?

<table>
<tr><td>tantalizing</td><td>1. *Fragrantly delicious* refreshments will be served under the *sponsorship* of the *Female Warriors,* Inc.</td></tr>
<tr><td>ambrosial</td><td></td></tr>
<tr><td>procrustean</td><td>2. For the inmates of the *Isles of the Blest,* there is no thrilling experience of *dawn.*</td></tr>
<tr><td>hermetic</td><td></td></tr>
<tr><td>amazons</td><td>3. Dante's *place of delight* is reserved for those who are *living by intellectual and spiritual values.*</td></tr>
<tr><td>stygian</td><td></td></tr>
<tr><td>aureate</td><td>4. Treatment that is *ruthlessly imposed to achieve conformity* would be a *too-costly achievement* for the victim as well as for the *extremely powerful creature* who inflicted it.</td></tr>
<tr><td>aurora</td><td></td></tr>
<tr><td>plutocrat</td><td></td></tr>
<tr><td>odyssey</td><td></td></tr>
<tr><td>Paradiso</td><td>5. The *dance* performance takes place in the *dark, gloomy* atmosphere of a cellar restaurant in town.</td></tr>
<tr><td>Promethean</td><td></td></tr>
<tr><td>aegis</td><td>6. The solution of the mystery is very *teasing* to the brain, for it is as *hard to understand* as the riddle itself.</td></tr>
<tr><td>palladium</td><td></td></tr>
<tr><td>Titan</td><td></td></tr>
<tr><td>terpsichorean</td><td>7. Satan pretended to be truly *daring on behalf of humanity* when he intruded on the *happy world* of Adam and Eve.</td></tr>
<tr><td>paean</td><td></td></tr>
<tr><td>aureole</td><td></td></tr>
<tr><td>Apollonian</td><td>8. The travel agent's description of the *extended tour* of the European wine country painted it as *living for sensual and material pleasure.*</td></tr>
<tr><td>Paradise</td><td></td></tr>
<tr><td>aeonian</td><td></td></tr>
<tr><td>Pyrrhic victory</td><td>9. For the *wealthy power figure,* any *safeguard* of one's possessions would deserve a *joyful song.*</td></tr>
<tr><td>Dionysian</td><td></td></tr>
<tr><td>Elysian fields</td><td></td></tr>
</table>

Third practice set

On a separate sheet, write the numbers of the *italicized* words. Beside each, place the number of the matching word or group of words from the second column.

A

1. *Procrustean* law	1. deliciously superior
2. *Promethean* ambitions	2. brilliant, glorious
3. An *ambrosial* diet	3. fanatically ruthless, unbending
4. An *auroral* splendor	4. sorrowful, sad
5. An *Apollonian* appetite	5. money-conscious
6. *Plutocratic* persuasiveness	6. hard to understand
7. An *aureate* era	7. dark and gloomy
8. *Dionysian* extravagance	8. heroic on behalf of humanity
9. *Hermetic* writings	9. bewitching
10. *Stygian* surroundings	10. intellectual, rational, spiritual
	11. dawn-like
	12. sense-appealing

B

1. A modern *Titan*	1. protection, sponsorship
2. A fanatic *terpsichorean*	2. irresistible singers
3. The *aegis* of Zeus	3. object of ridicule
4. A year-long *odyssey*	4. safeguard, an assurance of safety
5. *Paean* of peasants	5. drunken reveler
6. Legendary *sirens*	6. godlike giant
7. Writers' *Valhalla*	7. powerful female performer
8. Wealthy *amazon*	8. song of joy
9. A colorful *bacchanal*	9. a tormentor
10. A *palladium* of democracy	10. hall of heroes
	11. dancer
	12. wandering

Contrasts

1. Discuss the Apollonian and the Dionysian lifestyles and their interrelationship. Consider the role of sentiment and the sensuous aspects of life in these two outlooks. The novel *Death in Venice,* by Thomas Mann, presents the contrast especially well as it affects a writer. The two ways of living are stated in a number of other pairs of terms, each pair subtly different. The oldest and most universal is reason and passion (or strong desire). Intellect and emotion is another way of stating the strange duality of human existence, while classicism and romanticism refer to these diverse viewpoints as expressed in art and literature. At one time the terms body and soul were used to comprehend the tensions and fullness of life wholly lived. Spiritual and carnal (bodily) are two other, older, antithetic terms. Today a strong tendency exists to put all the emphasis on the body and its animal life, while discounting or denying the spiritual aspect altogether.

2. Discuss the concept of the Promethean hero. Is it valid? Would Karl Marx qualify? Is it true that "increase of knowledge brings increase of sorrow"? Can such sorrow be a blessing?

part two

unit one

CAVEAT EMPTOR*

Which word from the list at the left gives the best answer to each question?

contrive
acquiesce
indulgent
corroborate
discriminate
livid
internal
arid
dubious
dilate
abridge
depreciate

1. Before you buy a manufacturing plant, what must you do about its reported profits?
2. If the seller seems too eager to sell, how should you feel about buying?
3. What should you do if invited to visit the plant?
4. What will the value of the mechanical equipment do as time goes on?
5. What word describes problems between workers and management?
6. What might the pupils of your eyes do if the owner cuts the price in half?
7. What would you like to do with the long and involved sales contract?
8. What must you do when comparing the product with that of other firms?
9. What kind of attitude toward your employees is risky?
10. How are you likely to look if infuriated by the manager's carelessness?

VERBS

1. abridge   (ə brĭj′)   ***to shorten or condense***

If your report is too long, you must abridge it.
The papers printed an abridgement of the governor's speech.
An unabridged dictionary contains many words not in a college edition.

Related words:

An *abstract* (formal summary) gives the main facts of an article, a book, a legal document, or any compilation too long or too technical to be read in its entirety.

*"Let the buyer beware."

A *digest* is another kind of summary, which may employ the style, form, and manner of the original article or book.

A *synopsis* is a summary of a story, speech, or series of events.

A *compendium* is a comprehensive summary or a concise treatise in some field of learning. It may thus be quite a lengthy condensation.

2. acquiesce   (ăk'wē ĕs')   *to consent, agree passively*

The general acquiesced to the proposal for an exchange of prisoners.
Urged to buy a new wardrobe, Aaron gave a nod of acquiescence.
Ask for the favor when your parents are in an acquiescent mood.

> If one asks, "Will you meet me at 12:35?" you do more than acquiesce: You *assent* (say yes) in a more positive way.
> If one says firmly, "Meet me at 12:35," you do more than assent: You *accede* (yield) to a demand.
> If one says, "We ought to meet at 12:35 to talk this over," you may *concur* (agree) and say so. *Concurrence* will dispose of argument.

3. allude   (ə lōōd')   *to refer to or mention casually*

Do not allude to Andrew's defeat in the ring; he's still sensitive about it.
Rosa enjoyed searching out literary allusions in her reading.
Allusive phrases about death or disease are usually avoided at social gatherings.
Mia's constant allusiveness to home revealed how nostalgic she was for family and friends.

> This is a good place to cite *cite* (p. 27) and to allude to *casual* (offhand, incidental) (p. 231).

4. constitute   (kŏn'stə tōōt')   *to form, or make up*

One half of the members will constitute a quorum, the number needed to transact business.
A senator receives many letters from his constituents (kən stĭch'ōō ənts). If he wants to stay in office, he must please his constituency.

> A *constituent* is a part or component of something: Thus, the citizens of a district are the constituents of that district. Similarly, formic acid is one of the constituents of honey.

5. contrive   (kən trīv')   *to plot, scheme, devise a way*

When you give someone a surprise party, you must contrive to have the person present.

Cassie contrived to keep her car going until she could find a mechanic.
A can opener is a contrivance for getting at the contents.

6. corroborate   (kə rŏb′ə rāt′)   *to verify, confirm, substantiate*

Do photographs corroborate the existence of flying saucers?
The bloodstains provide corroborative evidence of the crime.
Corroboration of the ghost story would be difficult.

7. culminate   (kŭl′mə nāt′)   *to reach the highest point*

Four years of hard work at the Academy culminate when Air Force cadets get
their wings.
Passing the bar examination is the culmination of a lawyer's training.

> In the case of a mountain, a career, an ambition, or a campaign, the highest point
> is the *summit*.
> The highest point for a star or a career is its *zenith*. The word has a more romantic
> flavor than *summit* because it connotes the sky and the stars.
> A person, quality, or product may be the *acme* of perfection, or the highest point
> of excellence.

8. depreciate   (dĭ prē′shē āt′)   *to decrease in value, belittle*

A new car may depreciate 30 percent in value the first year.
Depreciation of the artist's efforts may discourage her.
Diamonds are a nondepreciable (nŏn dĭ prē′shə bəl) asset.

> See *decry, disparage* (p. 182).

> **Antonyms:** *Appreciate* means to add to the price or value: A home may appreciate
> in value if times are good.

9. dilate   (dī lāt′)   *to expand or enlarge*

He liked to watch the animal's nostrils dilate.
The drops an optometrist puts into one's eyes cause dilation of the pupils.
Athlete's heart involves dilation of its chambers.

10. discriminate (dĭs krĭm′ə nāt′)   ***to observe differences, make unfair distinctions***

A color-blind person cannot discriminate between colors.
Discrimination in music is a mark of good taste and good training.
It is unjust to discriminate against a person because of race.
A poll tax is deliberately discriminatory (dĭs krĭm′ə nə tôr′ē) in its effect.

ADJECTIVES

1. arid (ăr′ĭd)   ***dry, barren, parched, lifeless***

Arizona is an arid state with little rainfall.
This aridity of the land makes irrigation necessary.
Its aridness or "dryness" makes that textbook unpopular.

Related words:

Sear or *sere* (withered, dried up, or mildly scorched by heat): A cornfield in autumn, a desert, a life, or a city may be sear. A charcoal fire will sear the steaks.
Sterile (unfruitful, incapable of producing life, lacking vitality, free from micro-organisms): A life, a piece of land, a speech, or a surgical instrument may be sterile.
Desiccated (dried up): Deserts are desiccated areas. A marriage, like a garden, may end in desiccation if not well tended.
Jejeune (dull and flat, barren or dried up): A society, political system, book, or a set of ideas may be jejeune.
Effete (spent, worn, exhausted—and thus sterile): A life, a political system, a nation, or an enterprise may become effete.

Antonym: *humid.* Most tropical countries have humid air and soil, with plenty of rain.

2. chronic (krŏn′ĭk)   ***constant, habitual, recurring***

A chronic illness kept Quentin in bed for varying periods all his life.
No one likes a chronic complainer.
Do you know someone who is chronically afraid?

3. dubious (do͞o′bē əs)   ***doubtful, uncertain, causing doubt***

A dubious look on a doctor's face is very disturbing.
Her dubiousness may mean that she sees clearly what is wrong.
The nursing-home patient lives in a state of chronic dubiety (do͞o bī′ə tē).

A *dubitable* proposal is questionable, that is, it causes doubt.
An *indubitable* purpose is one not to be questioned or doubted.

4. indulgent (ĭn dŭl′jənt)   ***yielding, lenient, easy-going***

Indulgent parents let children eat, wear, and do whatever they like.
Uncle Joe smiles indulgently when you ask for advice.
Wealthy families often live lives of luxury and indulgence.

Forms of indulgence:

    Gratification (p. 315), *license, sanction, toleration, dispensation* (p. 56), *franchise.*

Forms of permissiveness:

    License, patent, authorization, sufferance, sanction (p. 55), *condonation* (p. 181).

5. internal (ĭn tûr′nəl)   ***inside, within (body, country, etc.), inner***

Internal injuries such as ruptured arteries may prove fatal.
Internal revenue is collected inside a country, not at ports of entry.
Persons who continually internalize strong feelings may get ulcers.
An intern is a doctor in training inside a hospital.

6. lethal (lē′thəl)   ***deadly, fatal***

A lethal dose of poison kills many troublesome rodents.
In the hands of a drunk or careless driver, a car is a lethal object.

    A *mortal* enemy, idea, or agent, is death-causing and may be a person, but *lethal* is applied only to objects and means, not to persons.

7. livid (lĭv′ĭd)   ***pale, lead-colored, grayish blue***

Illness, imprisonment, violent anger, or fear may make one's face livid.
The lividness of the heavily overcast sky was quite depressing.

    Livid may mean black and blue or discolored when describing a bruise or scar.

8. overt (ō vûrt′)   ***open, unconcealed***

The verbal attack on the committee members was an act of overt hostility.
After months of secret preparation, the enemy struck overtly.
The overtness of the drive for new members assured the town that no discrimination existed in the club's policies.

Related words:

A *conspicuous* object is one that is unconcealed and thus attracts attention. See -spic- (p. 342).

An *ostensible* motive for disagreeing is the apparent, seeming motive, not the real one.

Manifest (p. 28) plans and ideas are open, plain, unconcealed, yet not so obtrusive as overt actions.

Flagrant actions are not only overt. They are also startling because they are scandalous. See flagr- (p. 359).

Palpable deeds or wrongs are those you can feel or see readily. They make a strong or clear impression because they stir the senses.

9. senile (sē'nīl') *characteristic of old age*

Loss of memory in old age is an example of senile infirmity.
Living mostly in the past is also a mark of senility (sĭ nĭl'ə tē).
What are the evidences of senility in a nation or society?

Senile dementia is the mental derangement that often occurs in old age, including disorientation (not knowing where you are or live).

Related words:

Dotage is senility with weak-mindedness or abnormal fondness for certain persons or possessions (doting).

Superannuation is the condition of being retired or disqualified for active duty.

Longevity is merely long life.

10. virtual (vûr'chōō əl) *almost, for all practical purposes,*
being something in effect but not actually

Mr. Phillips is meek at work but a virtual tyrant at home.
The athletes won virtually every important event for their school.

The *virtual* image in a mirror or lens is not where it appears to be. Ask a science teacher.

First practice set

Which entry word best replaces each *italicized* word or phrase?

1. The complaint will *refer casually* to a trap *devised* for trespassers.
2. The red letters on the label help one *see a difference* between *deadly* chemicals and harmless ones.
3. The ailment is *constantly recurring* in the *extremely dry* climate.
4. The lawyer will *assent* to the plan to nominate him only if his reelection is a *seeming* certainty.
5. The fact that Lincoln decided to *shorten* his remarks at Gettysburg did not cause them to *decrease in value*.
6. Because Sandra's parents were not usually *lenient,* her eyes *enlarged* with surprise when her allowance was increased.

7. Neighbors *confirm* the *old-age* behavior of Mr. Cordozo.
8. Deep hatreds often *reach the highest point* in *open* violence.
9. *Inside* bleeding makes the bruise *lead-colored*.
10. Angry words *make up* a *doubtful* ground for legal action.

Second practice set

Which word from the list at the left best replaces each *italicized* word or group of words?

livid
accede to
concur
chronic
constituent
dilation
sear
dotage
superannuation
assent
synopsis
senile dementia
digest
ostensible
senility
conspicuous
humid
longevity
compendium
palpable
allusion
manifest
abstract
sterile

1. The editor will *comply with* the request that she print a *summary* of the novel about Russia.
2. If Father will *say yes* to the plan, I am sure Mother will *agree*.
3. Does a *lead-colored* complexion indicate that a person will attain *long life*?
4. *Senility with abnormal fondness for certain achievements* is an evidence of *being beyond the age of usefulness.*
5. You go from the *moist* air of the coastal plain to the dry winds and the *mildly scorched* vegetation of the arid plateau.
6. Moby Dick contains a *large compilation* of information about whaling by an author whose knowledge of the sea is *evident* on every page.
7. Senator Simpson sent to each *voter in his district* the *formal summary* of his speech on poverty.
8. Each issue contains a *summary (in the same style)* of a novel with *attention-attracting* captions.
9. A person's life seems quite *unfruitful* when *mental derangement of old-age* sets in.
10. The *seeming* reason for refusing the gift contradicts the *plain, readily felt* evidence.

Third practice set

Which of the lettered items is most nearly *opposite* in meaning to the word printed in capital letters?

1. ACQUIESCE: (a) consent (b) dissent (c) resent (d) incense (e) present
2. LETHAL: (a) gas-dispelling (b) memory-restoring (c) life-giving (d) slow-acting (e) having an antidote
3. DILATE: (a) grow narrow (b) amplify (c) intensify (d) move fast (e) explain

4. ABRIDGE: (a) lengthen (b) corroborate (c) restrict (d) intensify (e) amplify
5. VIRTUAL: (a) seeming (b) intentional (c) wicked (d) benevolent (e) actual
6. INDULGENT: (a) lovable (b) lenient (c) low in social rank (d) unyielding (e) ambitious
7. ARID: (a) humid (b) flat (c) mountainous (d) livid (e) well populated
8. DEPRECIATE: (a) deteriorate (b) increase in value (c) display (d) admire (e) sell wisely
9. OVERT: (a) unwarlike (b) hostile (c) tricky (d) hidden (e) slavish
10. SENILE: (a) intelligent (b) doubtful (c) youthful (d) rich (e) emotional

The correct choice

Write the number of the *italicized* word. Beside each, write the number of the matching word or words from the second column.

A

1. Spring at its *zenith*
2. *Concurrence* of experts
3. Inevitable *superannuation*
4. *Summit* of a mountain
5. *Digest* of an article
6. The *acme* of artistry
7. *Compendium* on birds
8. *Synopsis* of the speech
9. Unexpected *longevity*
10. Manifest *disorientation*

1. compilation of much knowledge
2. summary (in same style)
3. highest point (in poetic-romantic sense)
4. length of life
5. loss of usefulness through age
6. essential facts or statements
7. loss of the sense of where one is
8. highest point
9. agreement
10. greatest breadth
11. highest point (in definite, practical sense)
12. height of excellence

B

1. *Seared* sausage
2. *Casual* compliment
3. *Indubitable* insult
4. A *doting* mother
5. *Palpable* lies
6. *Sterile* leadership
7. *Ostensible* ignorance
8. *Internal* disorder
9. Forests *sere* and stunted
10. *Flagrant* disregard

1. not to be doubted
2. unproductive, lacking vitality
3. dark, treacherous
4. mildly scorched
5. startling, shocking
6. readily felt or recognized
7. unwise, foolish
8. offhand, incidental
9. overfond, excessively fond
10. apparent, seeming
11. withered, dried up
12. inner, within (a country)

unit two

PARTY

Which word from the list at the left fits best in each blank?

promulgate
humiliate
simile
exaggerate
jeopardize
accelerate
metaphor
recuperate
moron
simulate
impale
improvise
resuscitate
nonentity
scroll
tenacity

1. We arrived at the party late because the car would not _____ properly.
2. In one of the contests, each person had to _____ an illness, such as whooping cough.
3. One game involved _____s. For example, Corinne's card had "as lovely as" on it, and the card she drew said "a scaffold."
4. Marilyn, who liked to _____, said the party was like a night at the circus.
5. "I'm so exhausted I'll never _____," she exclaimed once. "Won't somebody please _____ me?"
6. "Don't _____ our friendship!" Sophie warned when Ferdinand pushed her toward the swimming pool. "You are a _____."
7. Fay tried to _____ him by saying, "Why don't you grow up," but someone interrupted.
8. For refreshments, each one had to _____ a hot dog and roast it over a fire.
9. Rex, Fay's dog, snatched some hotdogs from the grill and hung on to them with fierce _____.
10. Later, José unrolled a _____ and began to _____ the rules for another word game.
11. Each guest, upon receiving a list of animals, was asked to _____ figures of speech, to create implied comparisons or _____s.
12. Ada, usually withdrawn, drew loud applause for the originality of her comparisons. "I'll never be a _____ again," she said, laughing.

VERBS

1. accelerate (ăk sĕl′ə rāt′) *to speed up, increase the speed*

Unfilled orders made it necessary to accelerate production.
Acceleration of atomic particles takes place in a cyclotron.

Speed words:

> *Velocity* is speed or rate of motion in a quantitative sense.
> *Celerity* is speed or swiftness in a qualitative or literary sense.
> To *expedite* a project is to speed it up. The word is used of a process or of an action but not of objects.
>
> **Antonym:** *decelerate.*

2. compensate (kŏm′pən sāt′) *to make up for, pay, remunerate*

Do high grades in English compensate for low grades in science?
A wage earner's compensation takes the form of a weekly paycheck.
Compensatory (kŏm pən′sə tôr′ē) damages in a lawsuit cover the actual loss; punitive damages make up the actual penalty or fine.

Ways to compensate:

> To *recompense* is to provide compensation in the form of good or evil. For other -pens- words, see p. 289.
> To *reimburse* is to pay back money someone has spent for you.
> To *indemnify* a person is to pay or agree to pay for losses he or she may suffer on your account. An *indemnity* is the sum paid or promised.
> To make *reparation* is to pay in some way for damage one has done or caused to someone else.

3. exaggerate (ĕg zăj′ə rāt′) *to overstate, magnify, inflate*

Early reports often exaggerate the death toll in a catastrophe.
Calling one inch of rain a flood is quite an exaggeration.
The book gives a clear, unexaggerated account of the Gold Rush.

Related words:

> *Adulation, blandishments, idolization, panegyric,* and even *eulogy* spring from an exaggerated view of a person's worth. (See p. 350.)

Grandioseness is an exaggerated sense of the bigness, importance, or magnitude of a plan, a dream, or an undertaking.

Hyperbole (p. 247) is poetic exaggeration.

Caricature is the exaggeration of certain typical details of a face, a policy, or a work of art, usually for amusing or satiric effect.

Antonyms: *underestimate, belittle, deflate, depreciate* (p. 88).

4. humiliate   (hyoo mĭl'ē āt')   ***to lower the self-respect of, mortify***

Failure to win the trophy does not humiliate Abdul, for he did his best.

The humiliation of having her work ignored made Maxine try harder.

You admire humility (lack of overbearing pride) in your friends because it makes you feel on a par with them.

> *Humiliate* and *humility* derive from the Latin *humus,* meaning *earth.* Thus to humiliate someone is to bring that person down to the ground, and humility is self-abasement or down-to-earth behavior.

> **Antonyms:** *exalt, honor, glorify, pride, vanity, conceit.*

5. impale   (ĭm pāl')   ***to pierce, thrust through***

Pins were used to impale the insects and mount them for the exhibit.

Criminals are often impaled by their own admissions and thus convicted.

The detective examined the hole made by the impalement of a stray bullet through the door.

> **Synonym:** *transfix.* The centurion stood transfixed (as if pierced) at the sight of Rome in flames.

6. jeopardize   (jĕp'ər dīz')   ***to endanger***

Careless driving jeopardizes many lives every day.

It is seldom desirable to put one's life in such jeopardy.

7. perpetrate   (pûr'pə trat')   ***to perform, carry out***

It took three people to perpetrate the bank robbery.

One perpetrator was soon caught, but the others escaped.

The perpetration of the crime showed careful planning.

Related words:

> To *transact* business means to carry it out in a simple, direct manner.
>
> To *evolve* a plan or solution is to "roll" it out very gradually, by slow and steady improvement. See -volve- words (p. 291).
>
> To *effect* a change or improvement is to bring it about.
>
> To *execute* is to act or take action on a matter so as to carry it to completion. An *executive* is a person, presumably possessing initiative and good judgment, appointed to administer laws, business, or other affairs.
>
> To *prosecute* is to follow up, or follow through, on something that needs to be done, especially with regard to bringing criminals to court for trial.
>
> To *maneuver* is to use indirect or even underhanded means to accomplish something.

8. promulgate   (prŏm′əl gāt′)   *to make known, spread widely*

Executives employ messengers to promulgate their decrees.
Promulgation of weather reports is now a government function.

Related words:

To *propagate* (p. 73) truth, ideas, and beliefs is to spread or promote them, especially by persons dedicated to the task.
To *disseminate* information or knowledge is to distribute it widely.
To *proclaim* a deed or a discovery implies oral announcement with authority and often with joy.
To *bruit* a report or rumor is to spread it quietly but insistently: The location of the hideout was soon bruited about.

Four forms of promulgation:

An *edict* is an order, once the privilege of rulers, now a means used by bureaucrats and entrepreneurs.
An *encyclical* is a message from the Pope, especially for Roman Catholics.
A *pronouncement*, or a dictum, is a statement from an authority, usually after careful consideration.
A *manifesto* is a rather formal and somewhat pretentious pronouncement for all to see. See *manifest* (p. 28).

9. resuscitate   (rĭ sŭs′ə tāt′)   *to revive, bring back to life*

Every Scout learns how to resuscitate a drowning person.
Mouth-to-mouth resuscitation has saved many lives.

To *recuperate* is to regain strength, to recover from exhaustion, illness, or some other debilitating experience: The stock market usually recuperates after a sharp decline.

10. simulate   (sĭm′yə lāt′)   *to feign, pretend, imitate*

A toy engine will simulate the noise and smoke of a real one.
Most war games feature a simulated enemy attack.
Proud persons may simulate humility quite successfully.
Drama is the simulation of life's conflicts and crises on the stage.

NOUNS

1. metaphor   (mĕt′ə fôr′)   *an implied comparison*

"All the world's a stage" is a familiar metaphor.
Calling life a bullfight is a metaphorical way of saying that it is a dangerous combat—but are you the matador, the bull, or a spectator?

A *mixed metaphor* is confused and ridiculous because it telescopes or merges two metaphors, thus: "I began life's voyage with a flat tire." If life is a voyage, you might begin it in a leaky boat or grounded on a reef, but not in a car.

2. moron   (môr′ŏn)   *person of low intelligence, fool*

It is easier for a moron to wreck a car than to build one.
Making faces at the teacher is moronic behavior.

> *Moron* comes from a Greek word meaning foolish. Technically, a moron is above
> an imbecile or idiot, has an IQ of perhaps 50–75, and can learn a trade or craft.

3. nonentity   (nŏn ĕn′tə tē)   *a person or thing of no importance*

Alex was a nonentity until the coach discovered how well he could play basketball.
After thirty years, the trade treaty has become a virtual nonentity.

4. parity   (păr′ə tē)   *equality, equivalence*

A new treaty between the two countries provides for parity in arms.

> *Disparity* is difference—the state of being unequal: A very great disparity exists
> between baboons and human beings.
> The *par* value of the stock, *i.e.,* the price at which it was originally sold or the
> legally established price, was 10, but Mr. Rogers bought it at 6, or below par.

5. satellite   (săt′ə līt′)   *a small body revolving around*
a larger one; a person, group, nation
dependent on a larger one

The planet Jupiter has at least twelve satellites.
Telstar is one of the communication satellites revolving around the earth.
Courtiers revolved like satellites around the person of the king.
Finland is not a satellite of the U.S.S.R.

6. scroll   (skrōl)   *an ancient rolled manuscript*

The Hebrew texts of the Old Testament were written on scrolls.
The first of the famous Dead Sea Scrolls was discovered in 1947.
Scroll-shaped carvings adorned the altar.

7. simile   (sĭm′ə lē)   *an expressed comparison*

"My love is like a red, red rose" is a tired simile from Robert Burns.
Poets and novelists, in their similes, often compare an abstraction with an object.
Pilgrim's Progress by John Bunyan is a story told in the similitude (sə mĭl′ə tōōd′) (likeness) of a dream.
Stories have verisimilitude if they present the appearance of reality.

> A simile differs from a metaphor only in that the comparison is stated, using *like* or *as:* Protest letters poured in like an avalanche (simile). We were buried under an avalanche of protest letters (metaphor).

8. sovereign   (sŏv′rən)   *the supreme ruler, monarch*

The British sovereign is the titular head of the Church of England.
In the United States, the sovereign power belongs to the people.
A world government can prevent war only if each nation surrenders part of its sovereignty to that government.

9. stratum   (strā′təm)   *a layer or level*

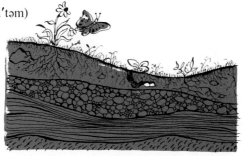

The earth's crust consists of one stratum or "plate" on top of another.
In a gorge one may study stratified (străt′ə fīd′) rocks from various geologic eras.
James Farrell wrote novels about the lower strata of American society.
In her lecture she discussed the stratification of society in three different cultures.

10. tenacity   (tə năs′ə tē)   *unyielding firmness*

Bulldogs are widely known for their tenacity.
Sales personnel are at times so tenacious (tə nā′shəs), it is hard to escape from them.
The physicist clung tenaciously to the belief that no life exists on Jupiter.

Firm words:

> *Perseverance* (patience plus tenacity); *persistence* (implies repetition or determined continuance); *obstinacy* or *pertinacity* (stubborn perseverance). Compare *doggedness* and other words (p. 63).

First practice set

Which word from this unit best replaces each *italicized* word or group of words? All but one are entry words.

1. Three boys irresponsibly *carried out* a fake drowning to see whether the lifeguard knew how to *revive* a person. (He did.)
2. The guard decided to retaliate, or at least *make up,* for this attempt to *mortify* him.
3. Determined to *pretend* anger, he threatened them with an oar until they stood helpless as if *pierced through.*
4. Constructing a *comparison (implied),* they called him a *dependent planet* of the City Park Department.
5. The guard declared that each of them was a *person of no importance* to act such a *dull, stupid fool.*
6. "You can claim *equality* with kings yet act like a demented donkey," laughed one of the boys, using a(n) *expressed comparison.*
7. "You *magnify* the extent to which your remarks can *endanger* my position," said the guard.
8. "The *unyielding firmness* with which you annoy me is amazing," he continued. "Please *speed up* your departure."
9. "As *supreme ruler* of this sandy shore, with my *rolled document* of punishments in hand, I banish you from this beach for one week."
10. "You come from the lowest *layer* of Hillville society, and I will *make known* your mischievousness throughout the town."

HE ALWAYS HANGS ON PEOPLE'S EVERY WORD

Second practice set

Which word from the list at the left, with perhaps a slight adjustment, best replaces each *italicized* word or group of words?

obstinacy
transact
pronouncement
disseminate
persistence
prosecute
bruit
recompense
simulate
perseverance
evolve
recuperate
encyclical
propagate
maneuver
velocity
celerity
manifesto
grandioseness
caricature
proclamation
exalt
hyperbole

1. The leader read a *formal, pretentious pronouncement* with the *exaggerated lordliness* of a strutting dictator.
2. The cartoon was a(n) *exaggeration of certain amusing details* of the sovereign's reading his *oral announcement*.
3. The news was *spread about in a quiet way* through the city that the assassin would be *brought to court* soon.
4. "*Feign* a virtue if you have it not," said Hamlet as he sought with *tenacious patience* to carry out his mission.
5. With *stubborn perseverance,* the sick man continued to *carry out* the business he had promised to complete.
6. It is the function of the U.S.I.A. to *spread abroad widely* both favorable information and appropriate *statements from authority*.
7. Whenever possible, the artist would *effect by indirect means* an invitation to dinner as a *compensation* fully deserved.
8. If she has enough *determined continuance,* she will *regain strength and recover* from the illness.
9. The Pope in his *message* to Roman Catholics everywhere urged new efforts to *spread abroad (by dedicated persons)* the faith.
10. Experts were called upon to *work out gradually* rockets that could attain the *speed* needed to go into orbit.

Third practice set

On a separate sheet, write the numbers of the *italicized* words. Beside each, place the number of the matching word or group of words from the second column.

1. Costly *reparation*	1. a thrusting through
2. Slow *recuperation*	2. imitation
3. Unexpected *jeopardy*	3. supreme control
4. Striking *similitude*	4. payment for damage done
5. *Impalement* with spears	5. resemblance
6. Skillful *simulation*	6. danger, hazard
7. Ample *indemnification*	7. payment for losses
8. Disputed *sovereignty*	8. recovery of strength

Antonyms

Which of the lettered items is most nearly *opposite* in meaning to the capitalized word?

1. EXAGGERATE: (a) tell the truth (b) explode (c) distort (d) minimize (make smaller) (e) reconsider
2. HUMILIATE: (a) make proud (b) abase (c) inflate (d) destroy (e) applaud
3. ACCELERATE: (a) impel (b) retard (slow down) (c) protect (d) examine (e) exhilarate
4. NONENTITY: (a) good-for-nothing person (b) saint (c) celebrity (d) coward (e) generous giver
5. PARITY: (a) inequality (b) farm losses (c) business gain (d) deflation (falling prices) (e) inflation (rising prices)
6. SOVEREIGN: (a) poverty (b) misrule (c) loss of throne (d) humility (e) slave
7. PROMULGATE: (a) discuss (b) suppress (c) file away (d) verify (e) censor
8. MORONIC: (a) imbecilic (b) very witty (c) talkative (d) intelligent (e) treacherous
9. METAPHORICAL: (a) comparable (b) fantastic (c) literal (d) imaginary (e) moronic
10. TENACITY: (a) laxity (b) irresponsibility (c) impatience (d) courage (e) willingness

Similarities and differences

1. List and verify the prefix opposite of five of the entry words or their variants in the verb clusters.

2. Which of the entry verbs has a noun suffix other than -tion?

3. Examine one of the following metaphors closely and list five or more of the similarities that you find:

> Life is a time game like football.
> Life is a dance.
> Life is a drama.

Ask such questions as these: What is your role? In what specific ways is the metaphorical situation like life? What aspects of life does the tone or nature of the metaphorical situation bring out? Do the same with the simile ''life is like a roller coaster.'' Do you think it is a valid simile? Why?

4. Devise ten fresh similes by thinking what familiar faces or objects really resemble.

Word square

Try to concoct one or more word squares of your own, using the following as a sample.

f	l	a	t
l	y	r	e
a	r	t	s
t	e	s	t

Share and share alike

What adjective do the two words in each set share?

A

1. cross, river
2. sentence, neck
3. faced, foot
4. Alaska, apple
5. coffee, winner
6. bug, rush
7. sense, law
8. horn, doors
9. wind, nature
10. boy, tide
11. shaven, break
12. elm, eel
13. door, scale
14. motion, poke
15. rounded, read

B

16. cowboy, hearts
17. brother, pressure
18. ice, bread
19. streak, fish
20. brow, jinks
21. end, weight
22. Christmas, maker
23. doors, trouble
24. cat, lamb
25. dollar, pasture
26. score, spirits
27. rot, run
28. kingdom, spirits
29. fiddle, hand
30. individualist, terrain

Another word game

Can you tell the difference?

1. Looking forward on a ship, which side is on the right: *starboard* or *port*?
2. Which instrument is smaller: *viola* or *violin*?
3. Which hat is military: *mortarboard* or *busby*?
4. Which indicates an omission: *caret* or *carat*?
5. Which singer has the higher range: *coloratura* or *alto*?

unit three

WOULD BE

Which is the best answer for each question?

1. Would an effigy be: (a) a ghost? (b) a monster? (c) a cartoon character? (d) a likeness?
2. Would a hybrid be: (a) a large bird? (b) a crossbred plant? (c) a pedigreed animal? (d) a kind of fish?
3. Would a despot be: (a) a servant (b) a dullard? (c) a tyrant? (d) a laborer?
4. Would an affinity for monkeys be: (a) an attraction? (b) a dislike? (c) a distrust? (d) a fund to help them?
5. Would opulence be: (a) poor eyesight? (b) abundance? (c) weariness? (d) fullness from overeating?
6. Would facile talking prove to be: (a) hard? (b) tiring? (c) easy? (d) useless?
7. Would a spontaneous outburst be: (a) fiery? (b) impulsive? (c) wild? (d) carefree?
8. Is punitive action intended to: (a) amuse? (b) chastise? (c) impair? (d) fix the blame?
9. Would amazing precision be: (a) sensitiveness? (b) sharpness? (c) exactness? (d) painstaking skill?
10. Would proximity to a source of supply be: (a) closeness? (b) danger? (c) distance? (d) suspicion?

NOUNS

1. affinity (ə fĭn′ə tē)   *attraction, kinship*

Rosa probably acquired her affinity for horses from her mother.
Sheila has quite an affinity for antiques.
Mercury has a well-known affinity for gold.

> *Affinity* also means "readiness to combine with" in chemistry: Oxygen has an affinity for hydrogen. It is mutual, as affinities often are.

2. despot   (děs′pət)   *a ruler with absolute power, a tyrant*

After President Hindenburg of Germany died, Adolf Hitler became a dangerous despot.
The treasurer's control of the company verges on despotism.
Julius Caesar became the despotic (dĭ spŏt′ic) ruler of ancient Rome.

Ruler words:

> A *chieftain* is the head man of a tribe or small nation.
> A *potentate* is a ruler very conscious of his power, but the word is often used in a humorous sense. See -pot- (p. 315).
> A *viceroy* is a deputy ruler who takes the place of the king in the area assigned to him.
> See *sovereign* (p. 99), *autocrat, dynast, dictator, monarch, tyrant, oligarch, patriarch,* and others under -arch- and patri- (p. 314).

3. effigy   (ĕf′ə jē)   *image, likeness*

A float in the Tournament of Roses portrayed Johnny Appleseed in effigy.
Mobs sometimes hang in effigy someone they despise.
Effigy Mounds National Monument in Marquette, Iowa, has thirty figures in the form of bears and birds.

Likenesses:

> Your *image* is what you appear to be to others. Your character is what you actually are.
> A *counterpart* is that which completes, balances, corresponds to, or closely resembles something.
> A *counterfeit* is a false or deceptive likeness, especially of coins, paper money, or a work of art.
> An *icon* is an image, figure, or painting, especially one having religious significance. *Iconography* is the study of these paintings and images.
> A *facsimile* is an exact likeness or copy, usually of a document, object, or artifact. A *photostatic* copy is one form of facsimile.
> A *replica* is a copy, especially of a work of art, made by the artist, or a model of a temple or other monument.
> A *mannequin* is a life-sized likeness of the human body used by a tailor, a dress shop, or a department store.

4. hybrid   (hī′brĭd)   **a cross between two varieties**

Most varieties of corn raised in Iowa are hybrids.
These hybrid varieties give a higher yield per acre than older kinds.
Efforts to hybridize citrus fruits have produced new kinds such as the tangelo
from the tangerine and the grapefruit.
A hybrid culture is one which combines two quite different sources.

5. illusion   (ĭ lōō′zhən)   **something not what it appears to be**

The pools of water which seem to lie across the pavement ahead are an illusion.
This illusion is one form of mirage.
The promises of a drunken person often prove illusive.

> *Disillusionment* is the loss of deceptive or unfounded beliefs about life or people.
> To disillusion a child about Santa Claus is to tell the truth and thus eliminate de-
> ceptive beliefs.
> A *delusion* is a false idea, like believing that 13 is an unlucky number or that
> laziness pays.
> A *mirage* is an optical illusion caused by atmospheric conditions.
> A *hallucination* is an illusion wholly within a person's mind. Something is per-
> ceived that does not exist and is not explainable as illusion.

6. opulence   (ŏp′yə lens)   **wealth, abundance**

Automobile manufacturer Henry Ford's opulence reputedly made him "the
first billionaire."
One of the most opulent persons of antiquity was Croesus, the last king of
Lydia, who ruled from 560–546 B. C.
Nature's opulence ranges from the scenery of the Rocky Mountains to the oil
fields of Arabia.

> An *affluent* person is a wealthy person, especially one who spends money as freely
> as it is acquired. See -flu- (p. 333): Poverty and affluence often exist side by side.

7. precision   (prĭ sĭzh′ən)   **exactness, accuracy**

Watchmaking requires extraordinary precision.
Brain surgery is a very precise (prĭ sīs′) operation.
An astronaut must fire the retro-rockets at precisely the right instant.

8. proximity   (prŏk sĭm′ə tē)   **nearness**

The proximity of our house to the river put us in danger of spring floods.
A proximity fuse depends on the nearness of the object which sets it off.

Nearness words:

> The *approximate* cost is a figure very near the actual cost.
> An *approximation* of the distance is a near or close estimate.
> *Propinquity* is nearness in space, time, or blood relationships. Thus, propinquity
> is a barrier to marriage.

9. reminiscence   (rĕm′ə nĭs′əns)   *a calling to mind, recollection*

At times one likes to indulge in reminiscences.
Parents like to reminisce about their youthful adventures.
Spinning wheels are reminiscent of Colonial days.

Related words:

In *retrospect* (looking backward); *memorabilia* of the Bicentennial celebration
(memorable incidents or moments); *memoirs* of the Boer War (personal record of
events); *memento* (souvenir or reminder) (p. 339) to *commemorate* (celebrate) an
important event.

10. reprisal   (rĭ prī′zəl)   *act of retaliation, especially in war*

The destruction of a whole town was an act of reprisal by the enemy for the
loss of a scouting party.
If you try to injure an enemy, you must expect reprisals.

Compare *vengeance* (p. 154).

ADJECTIVES

1. adroit   (ə droit′)   *skillful, clever*

Tess is very adroit in guiding our canoe through the rapids.
Adroitness in parrying blows will enable the prizefighter to hold out longer.
The governor managed his campaign for reelection very adroitly.

Antonyms: *clumsy, awkward, inept, maladroit.*

2. facile   (făs′əl)   *easily done, moving easily or quickly*

The facile fingers of the concertmaster never err.
Gary had a facile explanation for forgetting his appointment.
Bronislaw's sister Paula speaks French with remarkable facility (fə sĭl′ə tē′).
The university has adequate facilities for scientific research.

3. feline   (fē′līn′)   *catlike, sly, stealthy*

With feline patience and caution, the burglar approached the open window.
The larger felines, such as tigers and leopards, make dangerous pets.

Animal adjective zoo:

Canine behavior is doglike: Curb canine courtesy.
Bovine behavior is cowlike: Elephants have bovine traits.
Porcine is piglike: Gluttons exhibit porcine behavior.
Lupine (wolflike, rapacious): Lupine tactics are ferocious.
Vulpine (foxlike, crafty): Beware of vulpine maneuvers.
Equine (horselike): Some officials move with equine solemnity.
Simian (like a monkey, idiotic): Watch simian capers.
Asinine (like a jackass): Don't ask asinine questions.

4. mediocre   (mē′dē ō′kər)   *average, commonplace*

A mediocre player will win a game occasionally.
Do socialistic beliefs foster mediocrity (mē′dē ŏk′rə tē)?

5. prodigious   (prə dĭj′əs)   *enormous, marvelous, superhuman*

Paul Bunyan, the lumberjack hero of American folklore, performed prodigious muscular feats.
Foreigners admire the prodigiousness of American productive capacities.
Mozart, a child prodigy (prŏd′ə jē), was a skillful pianist at a very early age.

Compare *prodigal* (wasteful).

6. prosaic   (prō zā′ĭk)   *dull, monotonous, uninteresting*

Their prosaic letters did not reveal how exciting their safari in Africa actually was.
Fiction is vivid prose that sparkles and crackles with sharp detail.
Why are many poems so very prosy?

7. punitive   (pyōō′nə tĭv′)   *intended to punish,*
                                                        bringing punishment

The punitive raid on the camp was an act of retaliation.
The child's parents sued for punitive as well as compensatory damages.
No one should be able to kill or steal with impunity.

> *Impunity* is freedom from, or avoidance of, the loss or punishment one deserves.

8. spontaneous   (spŏn tā′nē əs)   *arising naturally from within,*
                                                        bubbling up

Performers desire spontaneous applause, not a polite spattering of noise.
The fire started spontaneously in a pile of old oily rags.
Tanya's refreshing spontaneity (spŏn′tən ē′ə tē) proved contagious.

> Spontaneous combustion in wet hay or oily rags arises from within the material.
> Spontaneous generation of life would arise from lifeless substances, not from any
> kind of life or "parents."

9. subtle   (sŭt′əl)   *delicate, artful, requiring acuteness*

The ice cream had a subtle cinnamon flavor.
Colors in a sunset change slowly and subtly.
Marie's subtle humor was lost in the loud spontaneous merriment of her friends.
Can you follow the subtlety of his argument?
A well-trained ear takes deep delight in the subtleties of a Shostakovich symphony or a Verdi aria.

10. transient   (trăn′shənt)   *fleeting, short-lived*

Transient beams of sunlight burst through the broken clouds.
The transience of sorrow makes it more endurable.
Transients in a hotel are travelers who stay only a day or two.

Related words:

An *ephemeral* delight lasts for a very short time: Most newspaper writing is highly ephemeral.
An *evanescent* joy vanishes soon. It fades quickly.
Sic transit gloria mundi means ''The glory of the world passes away.''
What is the root meaning of *transient*? See also prefix <u>trans-</u> (p. 278).

First practice set

Which entry word from this unit best replaces each *italicized* word or group of words below?

1. *Arising naturally,* the unexpected *cross between two varieties of plants* seemed more hardy than any artificial creation.

2. The *attraction* of plants for sunlight is no *deception.*
3. The *image* on the float was that of an All-American football player, though his skill in other sports was known to be *average.*

4. The *great wealth* of the Rockefellers did not prove to be as *short-lived* as the man who amassed it.
5. The *acts of retaliation* were carried out with great *exactness*.
6. The *nearness* of the mountain caused Mrs. Talkwell to *recall stories* about the many times she had climbed it in her youth.
7. The *tyrant* was a person of *artful* wit.
8. The mayor's election strategy was *skillful* as well as *smoothly done*.
9. The *punishing* measures taken by society provide a very *monotonous* life in prison for many offenders.
10. The strength of the largest *catlike* creatures is great but by no means *enormous* if compared with that of an elephant.

Second practice set

Which of the words at the left best replaces each *italicized* word or group of words?

impunity
replica
vengeance
affluent
memento
retrospect
memoirs
mirage
delusion
counterfeit
vulpine
mannequin
potentate
viceroy
ephemeral
counterpart
hallucination
equine
icon
facsimile
memorabilia
porcine
commemorate

1. The *deputy ruler* suffered from an *illusion wholly within his mind* that he was pursued by a fiery poodle.

2. This *life-sized likeness of the human body* has a *corresponding figure* in the store window across the street.

3. *Backward View* was the title of the racecar driver's *personal record of events*.

4. The *copy or model* of the sculpture showing the raising of the flag on Iwo Jima will *celebrate the memory of* the battle for that island.

5. The coin will make a good *souvenir* even though it is a *deceptive likeness*.

6. Elizabeth I of England was a *powerful ruler*, famous for her *foxlike* cunning.

7. It was a *false idea* to believe that the family was really *wealthy*.

8. If *infliction of injury as a recompense* is ever justified, can it be accomplished with *freedom from loss*?

9. To study the *image having religious significance*, the antique dealer had several *exact copies* made.

10. The *memorable incidents* of the Emperor Nero should include his *piglike* behavior at the banquet.

The right word

On a separate sheet of paper, write the numbers of the *italicized* words. Beside each, place the number of the matching word or group of words from the second column.

A

1. Disappointing *mediocrity*
2. A very large *effigy*
3. *Subtlety* of mind
4. Acts of *reprisal*
5. *Prodigy* of nature
6. *Hallucination* at night
7. *Delusion* of wealth
8. Delightful *spontaneity*
9. Exciting *reminiscence*
10. *Transience* of sunbeams

1. fleetingness
2. spirited naturalness
3. mystery
4. commonplaceness
5. persistent quality
6. illusion wholly within one's mind
7. acuteness
8. marvel
9. false idea
10. likeness
11. recollection
12. retaliation, especially in war

B

1. *Ephemeral* fame
2. *Feline* gentleness
3. *Illusory* gains
4. *Affluent* beggar
5. *Hybrid* rabbits
6. *Facile* charm
7. *Bovine* calmness
8. *Despotic* madness
9. *Approximate* perfection
10. *Punitive* action

1. providing punishment
2. easy, smooth
3. uninteresting, commonplace
4. tyrannical
5. near or approaching
6. cowlike
7. lasting but for a day
8. wealthy
9. imaginary
10. catlike
11. crossbred
12. irregular

Tangents

1. Look up the effigy-burning custom under *Effigy* in an encyclopedia.
2. Each animal adjective is in effect a simile. Take one and generate similes from the numerous strands of meaning it contains. For example, note how facets of appearance or behavior in the animal indicated suggest comparisons:

> As gentle as a kitten.
> As cruel as a cat catching a mouse.
> As soft as a rabbit's fur.

What is a *lycanthrope*? What is *lycanthropy*?

3. What is the root meaning of *hallucination*? What are hallucinogens?
4. What significance do the following have in common as applied to persons: *bovine, simian, asinine, senile,* and *puerile*?

MARKET REPORT: ALTERNATELY ORSINE & TAURINE

unit four

ADJECTIVITIS

Which word or phrase, by defining the *italicized* word, best completes the sentence?

1. A *querulous* housekeeper is   (a) queer   (b) quiet   (c) quick to complain   (d) quaintly curious.
2. A *plebeian* custom is   (a) luxurious   (b) commonplace   (c) Roman   (d) humiliating.
3. An *inscrutable* expression is one that is   (a) vain   (b) unchanging   (c) sad   (d) hard to interpret.
4. *Capricious* behavior is   (a) given to dancing   (b) fond of fun   (c) subject to whims   (d) light and airy.
5. *Morbid* details are   (a) sad   (b) horrible   (c) vivid   (d) related to death.
6. A *lugubrious* scene is   (a) dismal   (b) bloody   (c) terrifying   (d) humiliating.
7. An *inveterate* dislike is   (a) gained in wartime   (b) of animal origin   (c) firmly established   (d) unreasoning.
8. An *avid* interest is   (a) boring   (b) eager   (c) amazing   (d) dry.
9. An *austere* person is   (a) lean   (b) outstanding   (c) relaxed   (d) stern and sober.
10. A *meticulous* worker is   (a) tiresome   (b) painstaking   (c) stubborn   (d) polite.

ADJECTIVES

1. austere   (ȯ stêr′)   *rigorous, stern, severely simple*

The Pilgrims in New England led austere lives.
A call for national austerity (ȯ stĕr′ə tē) followed a failing economy.

Related words:

> *Austerity* implies harsh restraint and the absence of warmth, liveliness, or adornment: The austere grandeur of the Rocky Mountains was captured by the photographer.

Asceticism is self-denial. One avoids pleasure and finds virtue in painful acts of self-discipline.

Sobriety is serious, restrained, temperate living—solemn and grave, but not ascetic and hardly austere.

Rigor (p. 22) is stiffness, implying strong discipline, from within or without. The rigors of camp life are grim in winter.

Stringency means strictness or tight controls: The stringency of the tax laws leaves little leeway for deductions. See -stringe- (p. 308).

2. avid   (ăv'ĭd)   *eager, greedy*

Many high school students are avid readers.
Quite a few listen avidly to popular music.
Hundreds read the sports page with avidity (ə vid'ət ē).

Degrees of eagerness:

A *preference* is a mild eagerness, hypothetical or mildly emotional.
Partiality is a stronger preference, deliberate or unreasoning.
Keenness is desire with a sharp edge and is thus mildly thrilling.
Ardor is spirited or fiery eagerness (p. 184, 361).
Zeal or *zealousness* is warm, strong, energetic eagerness.
Rapacity is a ruthless or even immoral eagerness which leads to the wrongful or violent seizure of that which one wants.
Covetousness is rapacious eagerness for something that belongs to someone else.
A *mania* is eagerness verging on madness and obsession (p. 12).

3. capricious   (kə prĭsh'əs)   *subject to whims, changeable*

The weather on the island is so capricious, it is foolish to plan for a picnic outdoors.
Sometimes Raoul's capriciousness gets him into trouble.
One of his recent caprices (kə prēs'əs) was to avow a severe distaste for sailing while in the process of building a boat.

Other words for variable behavior:

Whimsical behavior is droll or sensible in a humorous, unexpected way.
Erratic behavior is uneven or irregular: The ball bounced erratically across the field. (See p. 52.)
Spasmodic behavior is sudden, irregular, and sometimes violent because of strong changes in mood or emotion: Penny's interest in music is spasmodic.

4. competent   (kŏm'pə tənt)   *capable, skillful, well qualified*

A competent secretary commands a good salary.
Brenda's competence in Spanish made her a valuable translator.
The upholsterer's incompetence destroyed the usefulness and beauty of the antique chair.

Related words:

Proficiency is a high degree of mastery in some specific skill or field: A competent chemist is proficient in chemical analysis.

Dexterity is primarily muscular skill and often speed.
Adroitness (p. 39) is the ability to handle a situation or problem skillfully.
Finesse is adroitness, gracefulness, smoothness in handling a situation.
Facility (p. 39) is competence with ease as well as skill.

5. diffident (dĭf′ə dənt) *shy, timid, unassertive*

Carolyn's diffident behavior keeps her from getting much attention.
Could diffidence be a subtle form of pride?

Related words:

Bashful, retiring, taciturn (p. 223), *demure* (quietly charming), *sedate* (dignified and serious), *modest* (unassuming).

6. diminutive (dĭ mĭn′yə tĭv′) *undersized, small*

A midget is a diminutive human being.
"Piglet" is a diminutive which denotes a small pig.
Tom Thumb became a celebrity because of his diminutiveness.

Compare *diminish* (p. 26), to decrease: The world's supply of petroleum will continue to *diminish*, this *diminution* adding fuel to the energy problem.

7. formidable (fôr′ mĭ də bəl) *hard to overcome, causing fear or dread*

This year Central High School has the most formidable team in the league.
Sixty years ago the formidability of the obstacles to space travel made them seem insuperable.
For many students trigonometry is a formidable subject.

8. inexorable (ĭn ĕk′sər ə bəl) *unyielding, unrelenting*

The union was inexorable in its demand for shorter hours.
The management was inexorably opposed to granting the demand.

Related words:

Inflexible (p. 279), *unalterable* (p. 347), *obstinate* (p. 63), *obdurate* (p. 63), *implacable* (p. 307), *irrevocable.* See -<u>voke</u>- (p. 299).

9. inscrutable   (ĭn skrōō′tə bəl)   *mysterious, unfathomable,*
beyond comprehension

The inscrutable stranger looked steadily at us, then turned and ran.
Einstein well exemplified the inscrutability of genius.

> Compare *scrutinize* (p. 141).

10. inveterate   (ĭn vĕt′ər ət)   *habitual, deeply established*

Most Americans are inveterate coffee drinkers.
The inveteracy of Kurt's smoking habit has convinced him that it is impossible
to reform.

> *Inveterate* is used of practices which have become habitual through long repetition
> and are not easily changed.
> A *chronic* condition like asthma is a long-established and recurring condition
> (p. 89). See also -chron- (p. 341).

11. lugubrious   (lə gōō′brē əs)   *mournful, doleful, dismal*

''The Song of the Shirt'' by Thomas Hood is a lugubrious poem.
When overdone, as in melodrama, lugubriousness has a comic effect.

Related words:

> *Funereal, lachrymose* (tear-producing or tearful), *lamentable, grievous, morbid*
> (gruesome, horrible), and *macabre* (p. 20), all grimmer words than lugubrious.

12. melancholy   (mĕl′ən kŏl′ē)   *gloomy, brooding,*
sadly thoughtful

The death of Ann Rutledge made Lincoln very melancholy.
Hamlet is called the ''melancholy Dane.''
The words of his monologues, the thoughts that he spoke aloud, were full of
melancholy.

Related words:

> *Melancholia* is a mental disorder characterized by exceedingly low spirits and
> severe depression.
> *Wistfulness* is slight, very gentle melancholy (p. 21).
> *Depression* is a state of low spirits, not so deep as dejection and due more to physi-
> cal or temporary conditions. See -press- (p. 332).
> *Dejection* is the state of being downcast, discouraged, lacking hope. See -ject-
> (p. 288).
> *Despondency* stresses lack or loss of hope that the situation will improve.
> *Disconsolateness* is the condition of being uncomforted, especially over a specific
> cause of grief.
> *Despair* is despondency at or beyond the breaking point, where one abandons
> hope and faith.

13. meticulous   (mə tĭk′yə ləs)   *scrupulous about details*

An accountant must be very meticulous in listing expenditures.
The engine in a racing car must be meticulously tuned.
Police officers inspected the abandoned car with great meticulousness, but found no clues.

> A *punctilious* person is scrupulously exact about details, practices, customs, and schedules.
> A *punctual* person makes a habit of being on time.

14. munificent   (myōō nĭf′ə sənt)   *very generous, lavish*

The trip to Europe was Deborah's munificent reward for writing a sonnet.
Nature's munificence makes May a beautiful month.
The townspeople contributed munificently to build a new hospital.

Related words:

> *Liberal* giving is free, ample, more than enough.
> *Generous* giving is spontaneous, unselfish, wholehearted.
> *Bounteous* giving is abundant, unrestrained, more than merely liberal.

15. opportune   (ŏp′ər tōōn′)   *timely, advantageous, seasonable*

January is an opportune time to go to Florida.
Being an opportunist, the dictator accepted aid from both the U.S.S.R. and the U.S.A.
The new vaccine arrived opportunely, for an epidemic seemed imminent.
As tensions between nations grew, opportunistic speculators bought stock in munitions.

> *Opportunism* is the act of seizing an unexpected chance and turning it to one's advantage. Being *opportunistic* implies a lack of moral scruples.

16. plebeian   (plĭ bē′ən)   *common, ordinary, low-class*

Camp fare consisted of plebeian foods like mashed potatoes and meat loaf.
Most movies are a plebeian form of entertainment.

> A *plebiscite* is a vote by the people (plebs-) on a specific issue, especially a choice of sovereignty. First-year students at Annapolis and West Point are called "plebes."

17. precipitous   (prĭ sĭp′ə təs)   *very steep*

The car plunged down a precipitous mountainside.
It was very precipitate to ask for a date before being introduced.
The knockout blow precipitated the challenger into the ropes.

> As adjectives, *precipitate* and *precipitant* mean sudden, rash, too hasty; as a verb, *precipitate* means to hurl, to throw violently.
> Compare *impetuous* (pp. 221, 332).

18. precocious (prĭ kō′shəs)   *ahead in development (especially mental); exhibiting exceptionally mature qualities*

Loren is a precocious sixth grader who could do ninth-grade work.
It would be unfair, however, to expect adult behavior from her because of her precociousness (precocity) (prĭ kŏs′ə tē).

19. pugnacious (pŭg nā′shəs)   *quarrelsome, inclined to fight*

A pugnacious attitude gets one into needless trouble.
Well-controlled pugnacity (pŭg năs′ə tē) is an asset to a fighter.
An ill-tempered person often behaves pugnaciously.

Related words:

A *combative* person has the wary, pugnacious attitude of a soldier in combat.
A *contentious* person keeps stirring up trouble.
A *pugilistic* person is not necessarily pugnacious but has a connection with boxing; a *pugilist* is a boxer or prizefighter.
A *belligerent* person is very quarrelsome (p. 159).
A *bellicose* person is warlike.

20. querulous (kwĕr′ə ləs)   *fretful, complaining*

Job's numerous misfortunes made him querulous.
Mrs. Beebo's inveterate querulousness annoys her neighbors.

Related words:

A *petulant* person is peevish and irritable, especially in the sense of being bad-tempered. See -pet- (p. 332).
A *peevish* person is fretful and ill-humored, especially in petty ways.

First practice set

Which word from this unit best replaces each *italicized* word or group of words? One is not an entry word.

1. *Unrelenting* hardships made existence in the prison camp very *dismal*.
2. The governor, who took office at a *timely* moment, proposed a *severely simple* solution for the state's fiscal problems.
3. Frances, an extremely *capable* nurse, can successfully handle even those patients who are *subject to whims*.
4. The attorney's *firmly established* cautiousness makes her defense of her client especially *hard to overcome*.
5. My cousin is *timid* and very *scrupulous about details*.
6. Eric's dog is much like some humans: very *complaining* if neglected, yet *inclined to fight* if approached.
7. To the rather *gloomy* Anglo-Saxon warriors, life was *unfathomable*.
8. *Advanced in mental development beyond her years*, Janet was able to appreciate how *lavish* her uncle always was to her.

9. *Eager* pursuit by an enemy made the animals rush down the *very steep* hillside and into the water.

10. Does using an *undersized* court instead of a king-sized one make table tennis a *common* pastime?

Second practice set

Which word from the list at the left best replaces each *italicized* word or group of words?

erratic
sobriety
proficiency
depression
asceticism
whimsical
ardor
disconsolate
rapacity
despair
finesse
punctiliousness
lachrymose
mania
pugilistic
petulant
adroitness
combative
partiality
despondency
spasmodic
dejection
precipitate
morbid

1. *Restrained, temperate, solemn behavior* is more moderate than *finding virtue in painful acts of self-discipline.*

2. *Irregular, uneven* habits make it difficult to attain *mastery in some specific area.*

3. A lack of *maneuvering ability* in handling his ship may have been what made Captain Queeg *irritable and bad-tempered.*

4. Some people's *scrupulousness in observing customs and practices* becomes a(n) *eagerness verging on madness.*

5. *Loss of hope that the situation will improve* often makes a person *pugnacious.*

6. The *fiery, spirited eagerness* of youth for service changed slowly into *ruthless eagerness* for gain.

7. She performs her *tearful* role on the stage with *adroit, graceful skill.*

8. *Unconsolable* over the loss of his eyesight, he approached *the breaking point where one gives up.*

9. *Discouragement* filled her mind with *unwholesomely horrible* thoughts.

10. While recovering from a broken leg, Ingrid was warned against *sudden irregular* actions from changes in mood or *rash and hasty* attempts at walking.

Third practice set

On a separate sheet, write the numbers of the *italicized* words. Beside each, place the number of the matching word or group of words from the second column.

A

1. *Whimsical* remarks
2. A *dejected* champion
3. A *pugnacious* bulldog
4. A *diffident* person
5. *Lugubrious* scenes
6. *Melancholy* truth
7. *Inflexible* habits
8. *Querulous* anxiety
9. *Wistful* eagerness
10. *Contentious* cousins

1. mildly sad
2. argumentative
3. doleful
4. rigid, unbending
5. petulant
6. full of fear
7. shy
8. bellicose
9. depressing
10. quaintly different
11. gloomy and sad
12. sad (in downcast sense)

B

1. A long-awaited *plebiscite*
2. *Rigor* of winter
3. Wholesome *sobriety*
4. A tailor's *meticulousness*
5. *Inscrutability* of fate
6. Unexpected *competence*
7. Military *punctiliousness*
8. *Inveteracy* of one's vanity
9. *Diminution* of gold reserves
10. Unnatural *precocity*

1. incomprehensibility
2. reduction, decrease
3. capability
4. deep-seatedness
5. evasion or escape
6. being ahead in development
7. stiffness, harshness
8. temperate living
9. scrupulousness about details
10. lack of ability
11. ballot or vote
12. exactness in observances

Antonyms

Which word in each group is most nearly *opposite* in meaning to the word in capital letters?

1. MELANCHOLY: (a) illusive (b) ugly (c) happy (d) ambitious (e) laughable
2. CAPRICIOUS: (a) severe (b) consistent (c) diffident (d) demure (e) plebeian
3. INEXORABLE: (a) loose (b) yielding (c) changeable (d) free from strain (e) indistinct
4. MUNIFICENT: (a) unfortified (b) half-crazy (c) cautious (d) stingy (e) morbid

5. DIMINUTIVE: (a) generous (b) oversized (c) expansive (d) abundant (e) musical
6. AUSTERE: (a) self-indulgent (b) healthy (c) undignified (d) capricious (e) incompetent
7. QUERULOUS: (a) uncomplaining (b) laudable (c) courageous (d) creative (e) hopeful
8. OPPORTUNE: (a) appropriate (b) unpleasant (c) upright (d) ill-timed (e) unresponsive
9. LUGUBRIOUS: (a) horrible (b) inspired (c) cheerful (d) easy to explain (e) witty
10. FORMIDABLE: (a) friendly (b) easy to overcome (c) diminutive (d) easygoing (e) cowardly

Explorations

1. This unit includes five roots, each of which appears in several other words:
   -belli- in *bellicose, belligerent(ly), belligerency, nonbelligerent, rebellion*
   -dur- in *endure, durable, duration*
   -melan- in *melancholy, Melanesia, melanoma*
   -pugn- in *impugn, repugnant, pugnacious*
   -punc(t)- in *punctual, punctuate, compunction, punctilious*
   What does each root mean? How does the meaning of the root affect the meaning of the word? What is the value of knowing what a root means?
2. In addition to *piglet*, list examples of -let words, like *ringlet*, where the diminutive indicates a decrease in size.
3. What is the root meaning of *patrician*? Of *precocious*? Of *morbid* in literary and medical use?
4. Write a paragraph about a family party or reunion, using ten or more of the words covered in this unit.

unit five

DO YOU

Which is the best answer for each question?

1. If you disburse a thousand dollars, do you (a) steal it? (b) eye it with disgust? (c) pay it out? (d) refuse it?
2. If you incriminate someone, do you (a) exonerate him? (b) implicate him? (c) condemn him? (d) suspect that person?
3. If you arraign a youth, do you (a) call him before a court? (b) adjust a claim for him in court? (c) give him authority? (d) set him up in business?
4. If you encroach, do you (a) decorate? (b) refuse? (c) spread out? (d) infringe?
5. Do actuarial statistics have to do chiefly with (a) bankers? (b) real estate? (c) insurance? (d) manufacturing?
6. Is bereavement (a) loss? (b) physical injury? (c) confusion? (d) a funeral?
7. Is an option (a) an exclamation? (b) a curtain? (c) a bill of sale? (d) a choice?
8. If you allege a loss do you (a) state it? (b) sustain it? (c) admit it? (d) conceal it?
9. If you libel someone do you (a) endanger that person? (b) sue that person? (c) attack that person? (d) defame that person?
10. Is a debenture (a) damage in an accident? (b) a claim against you? (c) a statement of indebtedness? (d) a list of your debts?

VERBS OF BUSINESS AND LAW

1. allege (ə lĕj′)   *to declare or assert*

The defense alleges that the prisoner is insane.
The prisoner allegedly denied being guilty.
The allegations (ăl′ə ga′shənz) of the prosecuting attorney are well supported.

2. arraign (ə rān′)   *to call before a court, summon to trial*

Those people arrested for trafficking in stolen goods will be arraigned tomorrow.
The law requires prompt arraignment of suspects.

The process of *prosecution* (from -sequ- p. 307):

1. Someone commits a *felony* (major crime).
2. The police arrest and *imprison* him.
3. *Arraignment* follows in the next day or two.
4. The *alleged* felon pleads not guilty.
5. He is taken back to prison for continued *detention* or released on *bail* (bond guaranteeing he will return for trial).
6. His case is put on the *docket* (calendar of cases to be tried).
7. The case is finally brought to trial. The *prosecutor* starts off by presenting the case to the jury, and the *defense attorney(s)* responds.
8. The *verdict* of the jury *acquits* the defendant or *convicts* him.
9. If he is convicted, the judge *sentences* him.

3. bequeath (bǐ kwēt̲h′) *to give or bestow in one's will*

Mrs. Nathan will bequeath all her property to her daughter Leah.
This bequest (bǐ kwĕst′) should be worth $350,000.

The process of *inheritance:*

Had Mrs. Nathan died *intestate* (without a will), the amount of her daughter's bequest would be less.
The will goes to *probate* (testing by the court) in a few days.

4. disburse (dǐs bûrs′) *to pay out, expend (money)*

It is the duty of the treasurer to disburse funds as directed.
The process of disbursement is subject to stringent regulations.
Disbursable funds are not always sufficient to meet needs.

Disburse is a more technical word than *expend* and a more formal word than *pay*.
To *reimburse* a friend who paid a bill for you is to pay him back.
The *bourse* in Paris is the stock exchange.
The *bursar* in a college is the treasurer.

5. encroach (ĕn krōch′) *to intrude, trespass*

Visitors who stay too long encroach upon your study time.
Your neighbor can sue you for encroachment if your house extends onto his or her land even by an inch or two.

Related words:

To *invade* is to move in like a hostile army, disregarding the rights and wishes of the victim: Your parents invade your room.

To *infringe* is to violate someone's rights or privileges, especially in a patent: Xeroxing large amounts of material from a book is an infringement of the copyright unless you have permission.

To *presume* is to take it upon oneself to say or do something not ordinarily permissible: You presume to correct your teacher.

To *arrogate* to oneself a privilege or right is to seize it boldly: Do you ever arrogate to yourself the use of your father's favorite chair?

6. exonerate   (ĕg zŏn′ə rāt′)   ***to clear from blame or guilt***

If accused of a crime, you hope that the court will exonerate you.
Occasionally exoneration comes only after several years in prison.

Related words:

To *absolve* a person of guilt is to release him from the consequences by requiring penance or granting forgiveness. See -solv-, -solut- (p. 290).

To *acquit* is to clear a person after his innocence is proved.

To *exculpate* a person is to free him from blame either because he was not guilty or because he was justified in what he did.

7. incriminate   (ĭn krĭm′ə nāt′)   ***to involve or implicate in a crime***

A pair of blood-stained gloves served to incriminate the caretaker.
To avoid self-incrimination, the caretaker refused to talk.

Related words:

Discrimination (skill or prejudice in observing differences), *recrimination* (counter-accusation).

NOUNS OF BUSINESS AND LAW

1. actuary   (ăk′chо̄о ĕr′ē)   ***an insurance analyst and statistician***

An actuary deals in insurance statistics, computing risks and rates.
When buying insurance, be sure that the company is actuarily sound.
Actuarial studies show that, on the average, people live longer now than they did fifty years ago.

Additional act words (from Latin *actus,* act):

To *actuate* a pump is to put it in operation.
To *actualize* a plan or dream is to carry it out.
To *activate* a squadron or a base is to begin using it officially.
To *counteract* a pest is to act against it. See counter- (p. 295).

2. alibi   (ăl′ə bī)   ***the claim of having been elsewhere
when an offense was committed***

The police will check the suspect's alibi meticulously.
The burglary suspect had an airtight alibi.

In common speech, an *alibi* is simply an excuse.

3. debenture   (dĭ bĕn′chər)   *interest-bearing bond,*
voucher of indebtedness

The corporation is offering 30-year debentures at 8 percent interest.
The county issued debentures to meet its welfare costs.

Related words:

A *debit* in bookkeeping or bills is a sum that you owe.
A *deficit* is the amount by which a sum of money falls short of what is expected,
needed, or owed: The city faces a deficit.

4. increment   (ĭng′krə mənt)   *an increase (usually at*
specific intervals)

A salary increment is always very welcome.
The incremental value of a house is the added value that it acquires, if prices
go up.

Compare *appreciation* in the financial sense of growth in value. (See p. 88.)

5. libel   (lī′bəl)   *written or printed defamation*

The scientist sued a newspaper for libel because of statements damaging to her
reputation.
The coach claimed $100,000 in damages from a sports magazine for its libel-
ous article exposing him to public ridicule.

Related words:

Defamation consists of *false and malicious* attacks on someone's character or
reputation: de + fame, take fame or credit from.
Slander is spoken defamation, false report, or damaging statements.
Calumny is defamation, the making of false or malicious misrepresentations, either
written, spoken, or otherwise expressed.
Compare *derogation, disparagement* (p. 182).

6. litigation   (lĭt ə gā′shən)   *a lawsuit, or legal disputation*

The litigation over the industrialist's will lasted for ten months.
One of the litigants (lĭt′ə gənts) kept trying to break the will.

Litigious persons like to start or prolong a lawsuit whenever a *litigable* problem
arises.

7. option   (ŏp′shən)   *a choice or a right of choice*

The buyer had the option of paying in cash or in six installments.
The latter option meant he must pay interest on his indebtedness.
Before one buys a building or piece of land, he may purchase an option which
prevents its sale to anyone else for a given period of time.
Radios are optional equipment in many cars.

Compare *prerogative*. See -rog- (p. 306).

8. solvency (sŏl′vən sē) *ability to meet all financial obligations*

No one questions the solvency of the General Motors Corporation.
Each of its subsidiaries is solvent, too.
When a firm is insolvent, it is, in effect, bankrupt.

Related words:

Liabilities are dangers one must face, especially sums of money that one must or
may have to pay.
The *fiscal* year is the financial year, which begins at some time other than January 1.

NOUNS—FUNERAL WORDS

1. bereavement (bĭ rēv′mənt) *loss or desolation,*
especially by death

The dead girl's parents never really got over their bereavement.
Bereaved of his gold, Silas Marner found solace in Eppie.
Bereft (bĭ rĕft′) of hope, the prisoner was near despair.

Bereave comes from an Old English word meaning to rob.

2. condolence (kən dō′ləns) *formal expression of sympathy*

When someone dies, friends send condolences to the bereaved family.
The three sisters condoled with each other over their sudden loss.

Related words:

Compassion is pity or sympathy, with an urge to help in some way: "Jesus was
moved with compassion."
Commiseration is strong sympathy expressed in a more personal, more intimate,
and less formal or distant manner than condolence: Job's friends commiserated
with him after his bereavement.

3. dirge (dûrj) *a funeral hymn, a song or poem of grief*

The choir sang a dirge at the diplomat's funeral.
Wind and waves sounded a dreary dirge at the height of the storm.

Related words:

A *requiem* is a musical composition or a dirge for the repose of the dead; a *Requiem
Mass* is a religious service for the dead.
An *obituary* is a death notice, usually in a newspaper, with a short biography.
A *necrology* is a list of persons who have died. See <u>necro-</u> death, corpse (p. 332).

4. epitaph   (ĕp′ə tăf′)   *a tombstone inscription*

Collecting epitaphs in old cemeteries was Elsa's weekend pastime.
Jonathan Swift wrote his own epitaph.

Tomb words:

A *mausoleum* is a large tomb built above ground.
A *sepulcher* is a tomb somewhat less imposing than a mausoleum.
A *cenotaph,* meaning empty tomb, is a monument honoring a person buried else-where.
A *sarcophagus* is a stone coffin, especially one with a carving or inscription on it.
See -carn-/-sarc- (p. 343).

5. interment   (ĭn tûr′mənt)   *burial*

Interment of the dead pilot took place the day after the crash.
The musician's wife decided to inter the body of her husband in his home town.

Related words:

Cremation, reducing a body to ashes, often takes the place of burial.
Many persons *bequeath* their bodies to medical schools for dissection and research,
or donate specific parts for transplantation, as circumstances permit.
To *disinter* or *exhume* a body is to remove it from the ground after burial. Both
words are used metaphorically of objects or memories that have been "buried"
for a long time.

First practice set

Which entry word from this unit fits best in each blank?

1. The *process of carrying on a lawsuit* over the alleged *written defamation* in a
   magazine article lasted nearly a year.
2. Payment of the *interest-bearing bonds* made possible only a small *increase* in
   salaries this year.

3. When *called before a court,* the suspect offered a convincing *claim of having been elsewhere when the crime was committed.*
4. The couple who wrote their own *tombstone inscription* made plans for *burial* in the place where they were born.
5. The jury refused to *clear* the broker of the charge that he *paid out* company funds illegally.
6. The company *declares* that the directive from the union *intrudes* upon the rights of management.
7. The *ability to meet all financial obligations* of an insurance company depends on the skill of *insurance statisticians.*
8. *Funeral hymns* are intended as *expressions of sympathy* for those bereaved.
9. The deceased mother cannot *give (in her will)* an exemption from the pangs of *loss by death.*
10. A prizefighter had the *choice* of *implicating* himself or losing the $50,000 purse.

Second practice set

Which of the words at the left best replaces each *italicized* word or group of words?

commiseration
fiscal
intrude
invasion of
libel
bursar
compassion
cremate
cenotaph
requiem
subsidiary
sarcophagus
deficit
infringement
acquit
necrology
calumny
recrimination
prosecutor
obituary
derogation
exhume
mausoleum
defamation

1. The *treasurer* of the college found that the *financial year* had ended with a *shortage of funds.*
2. When the jury did not *clear* the accused of the charge, he began to hurl angry *counteraccusations* upon the *initiator of legal proceedings.*
3. The historian's body was *reduced to ashes* and scattered, a choral group sang a *religious service,* and the family erected a *monument for one whose remains were elsewhere.*
4. *Strong sympathy* from those who can do nothing is often more comforting than *deep sympathy with an urge to help.*
5. To *push one's way* into a telephone conversation is held by some authorities to be a(n) *hostile moving in on* one's privacy and thus a(n) *violation* of one's rights.
6. Is it difficult to *remove from the ground* a body from a *large stone coffin*?
7. *A malicious attack on one's character* is not easy to distinguish from *the making of false and harmful statements.*
8. Can the heirs win an award for *written defamation* in the *death notice*?

Third practice set

On a separate sheet, write the numbers of the *italicized* words. Beside each, place the number of the matching word or group of words from the second column.

1. Tardy *arraignment*
2. Fruitless *exhumation*
3. Detailed *obituary*
4. Unusual *bequest*
5. Systematic *infringement*
6. Unexpected *acquittal*
7. Egyptian *sepulcher*
8. A libelous *allegation*
9. Unwanted *commiseration*
10. Lapsed *option*

1. business deal
2. claim or statement
3. misfortune
4. right of choice
5. strong sympathy
6. death notice
7. removal from the ground
8. item given in a will
9. moderately imposing tomb
10. summoning to trial
11. encroachment
12. release from charges

For more practice

1. What is the significance of *habeas corpus? mandamus? certiorari?*
2. Write the noun form of each verb under *encroach*. Compose a paragraph using several of the words.
3. List twenty depth words in this unit and write beside each a variant form of the word, using the dictionary if necessary. Write a paragraph using several of the depth words and their variants.
4. What is the root meaning of *prosecute? disburse? debenture? verdict? exonerate? solvent? epitaph? sarcophagus? condolence? interment? dissection?*
5. Write about a court procedure or trial, using words from this unit.

Mrs. Constance Baker Motley
Judge, United States District Court, Southern District of New York

unit six

STANCES

Which word or phrase best completes each statement?

1. To set a value on something is to: (a) elicit it (b) assimilate it (c) assess it (d) deprecate it.
2. A strange figure floating in mid-air is (a) an apparition (b) a clairvoyant (c) an alien (d) a facade.
3. Deceptive behavior is (a) reconnaissance (b) alienation (c) duplicity (d) dissipation.
4. A stranger in a country is (a) a confederate (b) an apparition (c) an abstainer (d) an alien.
5. A person credited with strange seeing power is (a) a deprecator (b) a dissipater (c) a confederate (d) a clairvoyant.
6. A half-joking way of getting cooperation is (a) exasperation (b) cajolery (c) condescension (d) evocation.
7. A somewhat violent way of getting information is to (a) elicit it (b) educe it (c) deprecate it (d) extort it.
8. Refraining from something is (a) abstinence (b) ascertainment (c) elicitation (d) anguish.
9. An excited dispute or quarrel is called (a) an assimilation (b) an altercation (c) a holocaust (d) a barrage.
10. An estimate of the value of something is (a) an assessment (b) an apparition (c) a concession (d) an assimilation.
11. The right granted to conduct a business is (a) a foreclosure (b) a forfeiture (c) a concession (d) a sell out.
12. A noisy ghost is (a) a polygon (b) a poltergeist (c) a polyglot (d) a go-between.
13. A widespread raging fire is (a) a concussion (b) a dissolution (c) a flamingo (d) a conflagration.
14. Sharpness and bitterness of speech is (a) acerbity (b) dissipation (c) extraction (d) assimilation.
15. A manner that shows a feeling of superiority is (a) superstitious (b) roundabout (c) patronizing (d) superabundant.

VERBS

1. abstain   (əb stān′)   *to refrain, keep oneself from*

Pickets must at all times abstain from violence.

A teetotaler is a total abstainer from alcoholic beverages.

The abstention (əb stĕn′shən) of seven senators from the voting kept the bill from passing.

For diabetics, abstinence (ăb′stĭ nəns) from rich foods is necessary.

Related words:

> An *abstemious* person eats and drinks sparingly or moderately.
>
> To *refrain* is to keep from acting or responding to a stimulus or a provocation: You refrain from criticizing a friend.
>
> To *forbear* implies self-restraint growing out of patience, consideration, or tolerance: "Love is forbearing and kind."
>
> To *desist* is to cease doing something.

2. alienate   (ā′lē ə nāt′)   *to make hostile or unfriendly, to estrange*

If you gossip about your friends, you will probably alienate them.

Alienation often results from a misunderstanding or long separation.

The Declaration of Independence states: "All men are endowed by their Creator with certain unalienable (ən′al′yə nə bəl) rights.

Each alien (foreign citizen) must register in January.

Generosity is alien (foreign, a stranger) to avarice and selfishness.

> *Alienation* is estrangement from persons to whom one was once attached, or from anything of which one was once a part.

3. assess (ə sĕs′) *to estimate; to impose a tax, fine, payment*

Ask a friend to assess the value of the car before you buy it.
Each county has an assessor who estimates the value of every piece of property.
Taxes are based on such assessments.
Societies assess their members to raise money for special projects.

Related words:

> To *appraise* something is to set a price or value upon it.
> To *evaluate* is to estimate the merits of a plan or performance.

4. assimilate (ə sĭm′ə lāt′) *to absorb, incorporate, make or become like or part of (that which incorporates it)*

Our bodies assimilate the ingredients they need from the food we eat.
Similarly, one assimilates ideas and insights from one's reading.
The assimilation of new members in a club is often difficult.
What are the chief assimilative forces for aliens or strangers who come to live in your community?

5. cajole (kə jōl′) *to coax or wheedle, persuade by flattery*

Joel's mother does not compel him to work; she cajoles him into doing it.
Cajolery works better than force in getting stubborn people to cooperate.

Related words:

> *Blandishments* (flattering remarks) are a kind of cajolery which stresses the element of flattery more than persuasion.
> *Persiflage* (banter, raillery) is a light, sometimes frivolous way of speaking to amuse, not to induce someone to do something.

6. concede (kən sēd′) *to admit, yield, grant*

Since Beverly won, you must concede that her skill is superior.
A chess player will concede the game when no hope of winning exists.
Each side must make concessions (kən sĕsh′əns) if the dispute is to be settled.

> The word *though* has *concessive* force. It admits something: Though I dislike you, I will help you.
> A *concession* at a fair, carnival, or stadium is a privilege *granted* to someone (the *concessionaire*) to sell something.

7. condescend (kŏn′də sĕnd′) *to come down to another's level, deign*

Francesca would not condescend to notice Sergio when he passed her house.
An air of condescension is irritating in anyone.
Perhaps the biochemist did not realize that he spoke condescendingly when addressing people outside his field.

> A *patronizing* manner is a condescending way to show favor or kindness.

8. deprecate   (dĕp′rə kāt′)   *to disapprove, protest against*

It is easy to deprecate modern art if you do not understand it.
Older persons often look with deprecation on new ways of doing things.
Thumbs down is a deprecatory (dĕp′rĭ kə tôr ē) gesture.

> *Deprecate* means literally "to pray down or away." Compare *imprecate,* to pray
> against or curse, and *imprecation.*

9. dissipate   (dĭs′ə pāt′)   *to dispel, waste, live dissolutely*

It takes the sun all morning to dissipate the mist along the coast.
A few of the players dissipated too much energy on sports and failed their exams.
The emperor was given to drinking and other forms of dissipation.

> *Dissolute* living is immoral, profligate (given to vice), and wanton.

10. elicit   (ĭ lĭs′ĭt)   *to draw forth (information)*

A spy tries to elicit military secrets from the general's aide.
By cajolery, Delilah elicited from Samson the secret of his strength.
Torture is a very grim method of eliciting information.

Related words:

> To *educe* information is to draw or lead it forth. See ex- + -duc- (p. 296).
> To *extract* information is to drag or pull it out, overcoming reluctance by insistence.
> See -tract- (p. 290).
> To *extort* a reply is to use threats, force, or unusual pressure. See -tort- (p. 290).

11. emaciate   (ĭ mā′shē āt′)   *to make very lean*

A hunger strike will emaciate a person rapidly.
Underfed victims of war suffer from emaciation and disease.
We tried in vain to build up the emaciated animal we had rescued from a trap.

12. exasperate   (ĕg zăs′pə rāt′)   *to irritate thoroughly, infuriate*

Cy's carelessness was enough to exasperate any employer.
Nancy in *Silas Marner* was "exasperatingly quiet and firm."
Godfrey's exasperation over the loss of his horse exceeded that of Dunstan,
who had caused the animal's death.

Related words:

> *Asperity,* from the same root as *exasperate,* is harshness or roughness of manner,
> weather, sound, or materials.
> *Acerbity* is sharper, more bitter than asperity, but also harsh, especially in temper
> and words. To *exacerbate* a problem or difference is to make it sharp, sour, irritat-
> ing, and thus to *aggravate* it (make it worse) (p. 288).

NOUNS

---

1. altercation   (ŏl′tər kā′shən)   ***an angry dispute or quarrel***

The altercation between the drivers of the damaged cars was noisy and protracted.

Kinds of discord:

> *Dissension* is strong feeling against a regime, situation, or belief.
> A *feud* is a little war which may go on for years and may range from recurring exchanges of insults between two persons to the kind of warfare that existed between the Hatfields and the McCoys in Kentucky annals.
> A *fracas* is a noisy fight, quarrel, or brawl.
> *Litigation* (p. 125) is the sometimes dramatic process of legal dispute.
> A *dispute* or *disputation* is a verbal argument or quarrel.
> An *imbroglio* is a confused entanglement or disagreement.

2. anguish   (ăng′gwĭsh′)   ***intense suffering***

Screams of anguish came from the girl pinned under the wrecked car.
Arnie spent an anguishing hour of suspense waiting for the doctor's report.
The anguished testimony of the victim's wife brought tears to our eyes.

Modes of suffering:

> *Agony* is extreme torment, with undertones of struggle.
> *Mortification* and *chagrin* indicate suffering from embarrassment, shame, or humiliation.
> An *ordeal* is a severe trial of one's courage, fortitude, endurance, or skill: Exams are always an ordeal.
> *Tribulation* is prolonged misery, distress, affliction, or sorrow: The Jews in Germany suffered agonized tribulations.
> *Purgatory* in Catholic doctrine is a place of prolonged expiation and purification by which one qualifies for Paradise.
> *Crucifixion* was an especially prolonged and harrowing ordeal. From the same root, *crux, crucis* (cross), come *excruciating,* and *crucial.*

3. apparition   (ăp'ə rĭsh'ən)

*specter or phantom,
a sudden appearing*

The new tenants of the old manor house thought they saw an apparition.
Ghost stories are still popular, though belief in apparitions is less prevalent than
it was in the 1800s.
The apparition in the living room turned out to be Father in pajamas.

> *Apparition* is only partly a ghost word: The Apparition to the Shepherds was the
> act of appearing.

Related words:

> A *phantom* or *phantasm (fantasm)* exists only in the mind and is thus an illusion:
> Her hopes were phantoms, *i.e.,* they had no basis in reality.
> A *specter* is something seen, a visible ghost or apparition, or any object of fear
> and dread: Valjean's past rose like a specter to haunt him.
> An *aura* is a kind of vapor or mysterious atmosphere surrounding a person. A *halo*
> is an aura, real or symbolic.
> A *poltergeist* is a noisy, usually mischievous, ghost supposed to specialize in table
> rappings, furniture topplings, and other such happenings.
> *Ectoplasm* is the luminous aura allegedly emanating from the body of a spiritist
> medium during a trance.
> A *zombi(e)* is a corpse animated by a diabolic power, or just a person either chilling
> and terrible or dull and unattractive.
> A *banshee* is a female spirit wailing a warning of an imminent death in the family.

4. barrage   (bə räzh')

*a shower (of artillery fire),
a heavy onslaught*

The enemy laid down a heavy barrage to keep our men from advancing.
A barrage of rotten apples convinced the cow that boys can be cruel.
A barrage of highway noises made it difficult to get to sleep.

Related words:

> A *salvo* is a burst of fire from small arms or artillery, or a burst of cheers or applause.
> A *fusillade* is the discharge of many firearms all at once or in rapid succession—
> or a figurative equivalent like an outburst of boos at a prize fight.

5. clairvoyant   (klâr voi'ənt)

*one who has unusual or
preternatural insight*

For the new President, the clairvoyant predicted a successful term in office.
When it came to planning a tour, the actor was no clairvoyant.
Many experiments in extrasensory perception and clairvoyance have been per-
formed.

> *Preternatural* powers are beyond what is natural or normal.

6. duplicity   (dōō plĭs′ə tē)   *double-dealing, deception*

You will be accused of duplicity if you tell one friend you are sick and then go
to the movies with another.
A double agent must be skilled in duplicity.

> See du- (two) words (p. 321).

7. facade   (fə säd′)   *the front, or face*

The facade of the Supreme Court in Washington is massive and august.
Behind a facade of wealth, the man lived a lonely, impoverished life.

8. holocaust   (hŏl′ə kȯst′)   *widespread destruction, especially by fire*

Nagasaki was the victim of a holocaust that brought a quick end to the war in the
Pacific.
Thousands lost their possessions in the holocaust.

Related words:

> A *holograph* is something written wholly in the handwriting of the author: A holo-
> graph will is hard to break.
> A *conflagration* is a very large fire. See -flagr- (p. 359).

First practice set

Which entry word or variant form best replaces each *italicized* word or phrase?

1. The lawyer *admitted* that he had a prejudice against *persons with preternatural insight.*
2. Insurance investigators spent a week trying to *estimate* the damages from the *massive fire.*
3. Attempts to *refrain* from the habit of smoking often bring *intense suffering.*
4. The speaker made *disapproving* remarks about a belief in *specters.*
5. The news reporter hoped to *draw forth* the secret information, but to *coax* the officer would only make him wary.
6. A *heavy onslaught* of paper wads *infuriated* the teacher.
7. They were *made very lean* by the severe diet, which they would not abandon even though it almost *estranged* their family.
8. It takes hours to *absorb* all the subtleties of such spectacles as the *front* of the Taj Mahal.
9. How could anyone *stoop* to such *double-dealing*?
10. The *angry dispute* is a result of an uncle's *dissolute behavior.*

Second practice set

Which word from the list at the left best replaces each *italicized* word or group of words?

refrain	1. The principal tried with considerable *harshness* to *drag out* a promise from the failing student.
desist	
appraise	2. The *flatteries* of a third party did not prevent the *noisy quarrel.*
blandishment	
dissolute	3. It would be hard to *set a price on* a Shakespearean (play) *written wholly in his own handwriting.*
chagrin	
extract	4. Rumors about a *noisy, table-rapping ghost* got the two youths into a(n) *confused entanglement.*
asperity	
acerbity	5. The great religions urge one to *keep* from *immoral living.*
dissension	
fracas	6. The Florida hurricane was a(n) *severe trial of courage,* bringing *suffering from shame* to those who did not prepare for it.
feud	
litigation	7. The *extreme physical torment* of the disease did not produce *harsh bitterness* in the sufferer.
imbroglio	
agony	8. A *wailing, female spirit* warned of the *prolonged distress* which the drought would bring to her family.
ordeal	
tribulation	9. The *strong feeling against* (the regime) led to a prolonged *process of legal dispute.*
holograph	
zombi	10. At one point the story of the *corpse animated by a demon* brought forth a *burst* of loud shrieks from the listeners.
poltergeist	
specter	
banshee	
preternatural	
salvo	

The right word

On a separate sheet, write the numbers of the *italicized* words. Beside each, place the number of the matching word or group of words from the second column.

1. A *concession* to labor	1. rapid discharge
2. Incredible *forbearance*	2. indulgence in harmful pleasure
3. *Emaciation* from disease	3. displeasure
4. *Fusillade* of curses	4. coming down to another's level
5. Frantic *dissipation*	5. extreme irritation
6. Resorting to *cajolery*	6. claim granted
7. Unrelieved *acerbity*	7. drawing forth
8. Scoutmaster's *exasperation*	8. self-restraint
9. *Elicitation* of grievances	9. disclosure
10. Lordly *condescension*	10. leanness
	11. coaxing and flattery
	12. harsh bitterness

Extra action

1. Each of the entry verbs has a root meaning that contributes to its connotative effect. What is the root meaning of *assimilate*? *cajole*? *clairvoyant*? *condescend*? *duplicity*? *incorporate*? *patronize*? *specter*?
2. Write in dialogue form a page of cajolery which you have heard, used, or could use to get a parent, brother, or sister to do something for you.

3. *There Is a River* by Sugrue is a biography of Edgar Cayce, a remarkable clairvoyant of the twentieth century. A student interested in clairvoyance should read it and report.

unit seven

SITUATIONS

Which lettered item best completes the statement?

1. The national flag is an object most Americans   (a) vitiate   (b) ostracize   (c) scrutinize   (d) venerate.
2. An hourly news summary is   (a) iterative   (b) prevaricating   (c) vicious   (d) venerable.
3. A clergyman biblical or traditional in matters of belief is   (a) pious   (b) godly   (c) devout   (d) orthodox.
4. A radiant bride in her wedding dress looks   (a) reinstated   (b) scrutinized   (c) pallid   (d) transfigured.
5. A dangerous criminal is   (a) skeptical   (b) vicious   (c) turbulent   (d) intolerant.
6. Persons excluded from a social group to which they once belonged have been   (a) perverted   (b) exiled   (c) ostracized   (d) depraved.
7. Shoppers unable to make up their minds are   (a) juvenile   (b) vacillating   (c) vitiated   (d) tolerant.
8. Television advertising is generally   (a) mercenary   (b) vicious   (c) provident   (d) galvanic.
9. A speech teacher is expected to be   (a) pallid   (b) mercenary   (c) articulate   (d) turbulent.
10. A nun is probably   (a) pious   (b) lucrative   (c) juvenile   (d) turbulent.
11. A copy that is made to defraud or deceive is   (a) an imbalance   (b) a model   (c) a resemblance   (d) a counterfeit.
12. Childish behavior in an adult is   (a) puerile   (b) engaging   (c) whimsical   (d) plaintive.
13. A strong desire or craving for another's possessions is   (a) craftsmanship   (b) detention   (c) covetousness   (d) debilitation.
14. Skin that is "black and blue" from a bruise is   (a) listless   (b) livid   (c) blatant   (d) erratic.
15. A person who is stingy is   (a) dextrous   (b) penurious   (c) openhanded   (d) opulent.
16. Needless repetition of an idea is called   (a) tautology   (b) extravagance   (c) luminosity   (d) delinquency.

VERBS

1. galvanize (găl′və nīz)   *to stimulate, excite*

Criticisms galvanize the manager into acting promptly.
A galvanic (găl văn′ĭk) (electrifying) thrill goes through the stands when our team makes a touchdown.

The word *galvanize* comes from the name of Luigi Galvani, who discovered that electricity can be produced by chemical action. Galvanized sheeting is iron coated with zinc to prevent rust.

2. iterate (ĭt′ər āt)   *to utter again, repeat*

Parents insist on iterating and reiterating their warnings.
Iteration of the accusations by the lawyer made the jury more conscious of them.
Octogenarians often become iterative in their old age.

Related words:

To *reiterate* is to repeat or keep repeating something.
To *recapitulate* is to summarize the main points you have made.
Tautology is needless reiteration of an idea in other words or phrases: "Golden flaming bonfire" is a tautological and therefore *redundant* (wordy, excessive) phrase.

3. nurture (nûr′chər)   *to nourish, foster, rear*

You nurture an idea or a plan until you can carry it out.
Churches provide religious nurture for their members.
George Eliot wrote of pale-faced weavers as having "unnurtured souls."

Related words:

To *cherish* something is to cling to it with affection.
To *espouse* an idea or a cause is to adopt and support it as one does a husband or wife (spouse).

4. ostracize   (ŏs′trə sīz′)   *to banish, exclude*

If respectable people ostracize an ex-convict, how can he reestablish himself
in society?
Social discrimination is a form of ostracism (ŏs′trə siz′əm).

> *Banishment, exile, deportation,* and *expatriation* all denote separation from the
> country one is in. All are forms of ostracism, but *expatriation* reverses the process
> in that you banish your country by leaving it.

5. prevaricate   (prĭ văr′ə kāt′)   *to evade the truth, lie or quibble*

It is foolish to prevaricate to oneself about the reason for low grades.
The suspect tried to defend himself by prevarication and deceit.

Deceitful doings:

> *Mendacity* is simple, deliberate lying not always intended to mislead.
> *Fabrication* is creative or imaginative lying. (It is also the literal process of creating
> something out of its component parts.)
> *Duplicity* (p. 136) is double-dealing with its deceitful effects.
> *Perjury* is deceit or lies, especially in court under oath. "At lovers' perjuries, they
> say, Jove laughs." *(Romeo and Juliet)*
> A *counterfeit* is a deceptive imitation of what it represents: A counterfeit smile
> or counterfeit courage is often overdone.
> *Simulation* (p. 97) is acting or pretending, sometimes to deceive, often to entertain.
> *Dissimulation* and *dissembling* are forms of deliberate, unqualified pretense,
> which appear more often under other names today.
> *Hypocrisy* is the feigning of qualities opposite to the ones actually possessed.
> *Forgery* is found in a signature, article, book, or artwork which purports to be
> someone else's but is actually your own fabrication. Compare *plagiarism* (p. 211).

6. scrutinize   (skrōō′tə nīz′)   *to examine closely*

Petra scrutinizes her actions with self-questioning concern.
By leaving early for school, Fred escaped his parents' scrutiny.

> Compare *inscrutable* (p. 116), which comes from the same Latin root *scrutari,*
> to search carefully.

7. transfigure   (trăns′fĭg′yər)   *to transform, glorify*

Reforestation will transfigure the barren hills around the town. Such trans-
figuration is a gradual process. It will take all of twenty years.
" 'Twas a land transfigured," wrote Vachel Lindsay of the African country
now known as Zaire.

> *Transfigure* applies chiefly to the outward appearance.

Related words:

> *Transmute* implies a complete change in the nature or form of a quality or sub-
> stance: Alchemists tried to transmute lead into gold.

Metamorphose is used of a complete change of form in a living organism: A caterpillar metamorphoses into a butterfly. See meta- (p. 330).

8. vacillate　(văs′ə lāt′)　　　　　　　*to waver or be changeable*

The translator was advised not to vacillate too long between two job offers—one at home, the other abroad.
Falling prey to vacillation, the embezzler alternated between a claim of innocence and an admission of guilt.

9. venerate　(věn′ə rāt′)　　　　*to regard with deep respect, revere*

Americans venerate the courageous signers of the Declaration of Independence.
Veneration for George Washington verges, at times, on idolatry.
For many years, Mother Cabrini has been a venerable (věn′ər ə bəl) figure in American religious life.

Related words:

Deference (p. 11) is respectfulness, but not so reverent as veneration.
Adoration is deep affection with awe and reverence. It can refer to the respect and worship one accords to the deity, or the kind of feeling a bride and groom have for each other.
Venerable, beatified, and *canonized* are three degrees of sanctity in the Roman Catholic Church. *Venerable* implies advanced age as well as reverence. The word comes indirectly from *Venus,* the Roman goddess of love.

10. vitiate　(vĭsh′ē āt′)　　　*to contaminate, debase, or render worthless*

Selfishness and jealousy vitiate a person's character.
Does the reading of inferior fiction lead to the vitiation of literary taste?

In legal use, *vitiate* means to make ineffective or invalid: Because one of the parties to the contract was insane at the time, the agreement was vitiated.

Related words:

To *debauch* a person is to lead him morally astray in the grosser ways of sensual indulgence: Excessive drinking led to worse forms of debauchery.
To *deprave* a person is to corrupt him, especially in the sense of debasing his character: Depravity breeds a hundred kinds of guilty fears.
To *pervert* (p. 162) a person is to turn him away from right thinking or actions: Bribery perverts justice.

ADJECTIVES

1. articulate (är tĭk′yə lət′)   *spoken distinctly,*
able to express (oneself)

A teacher needs to be very articulate.
You can understand Olaf's English, but he does not articulate (är tĭk′yə lāt′) very well.
An articulate person expresses ideas and feelings clearly.
Because of his inarticulateness, Herman Melville's Billy Budd struck out and killed his accuser.

2. juvenile (jōō′və nĭl′)   *youthful, for children, immature*

Dueling with squirt guns is a juvenile pastime.
A juvenile court is usually not open to the public.

Related words:

> An author's youthful writings are called *juvenilia*.
> *Puerile* means childish in an uncomplimentary sense. It is often applied to adults who behave in a childish way: Jumping up and down in anger is very puerile.

3. lucrative (lōō′krə tĭv)   *profitable, remunerative*

Buying apples for ten cents apiece and selling them for twenty-five would be very lucrative if you had several hundred to sell.
The alleged lucrativeness of gold mines has often proved illusory, but fortunes have been made selling pins or matches.

4. mercenary (mûr′sə nĕr′ē)   *acting from desire for money*

A mercenary doctor charges exorbitantly for his services.
Mercenaries are soldiers hired by a government other than their own.

Related words:

> *Cupidity* is greed or excessive desire for wealth.
> *Avarice* is an active, grasping appetite for money or gain.
> *Niggardliness* is stinginess that pays the smallest amount possible for articles purchased.
> *Parsimoniousness* is excessive frugality and economy to the point of niggardliness.
> *Penuriousness* carries stinginess to the point where one appears poverty-stricken.
> *Miserliness* carries avarice to the point of penuriousness, or beyond.

5. pallid (păl′ĭd)   *pale, wan*

Illness often makes a person pallid, though normal color will return as one recovers.
Chronic pallidness or pallor may indicate poor health.

Related words:

An *anemic* paleness is often a result of disease and implies weakness.
A *sallow* face is yellowish and looks unhealthy.
Ghastly is very pale, like a ghost. The word is a variant of *ghostly*.
A *cadaverous* face is pale like a corpse.
A *hoary* person or object is white or gray with age.
Ashen paleness suggests fright or terror.
A *livid* face is gray or blue gray, typically from cold or anger (p. 90).

6. pious (pī′əs)   *outwardly religious, godly*

A pious expression lights up the face in the painting, though the model who sat for the artist was not religious.
The radiant piety of St. Francis was simple and sincere.
The clergyman spoke piously about living a good life.

Related words:

A *devout* person is fervent and deeply religious.
An *orthodox* person holds closely to traditional or standard beliefs or practices.

7. provident (prŏv′ə dənt)   *exercising foresight, thrifty*

Mary has a provident father who plans carefully, buys wisely, and saves something every week.
A seemingly providential cloud cover enabled more than 300,000 trapped British soldiers to escape from Dunkirk in 1940.
Horace said Providence gave us the country, but the art of man built the cities.

Providence is often used as a synonym for Deity. How did Providence, R.I., get its name? *Providential* may also mean fortunate or lucky.

8. tolerant (tŏl′ər ənt)   *forbearing, respectful*

Tolerant parents do not always have well-trained children.
What kinds of behavior do teachers refuse to tolerate (tŏl′ə rāt)?
The Canadian tourists found the hot, humid weather of New Orleans intolerable.
Tolerance toward other people's beliefs is an admirable trait.

9. turbulent (tûr′byə lənt)   *disorderly, tumultuous*

When the crowd began to grow turbulent, the police intervened.
A plane is often shaken by turbulence in the upper atmosphere.

-Turb- words come from the Latin *turba*, tumult or crowd. *Turbid* words are muddy or muddled. Do not confuse this with *turgid* words, which are swollen, distended, or bombastic to the point of seeming muddled.
Perturb and *disturb* both imply agitation or disorder. A *turbine* creates an orderly but powerful "disturbance."

10. vicious (vĭsh′əs)   *evil, destructive, savage*

The mortality rate among vicious dogs is likely to be very high.
No one could account for the viciousness of the attack on the governing body.
Rats will fight viciously when cornered.

Related words:

Villainous acts, like arson, are the acts of a villain.
Diabolical acts, like inciting riots, are devilish.
Nefarious deeds, like robbing blind people, are very evil indeed.

First practice set

Which word from the unit best replaces each *italicized* word or group of words?

1. The woman *uttered again* her very *distinctly spoken* protest.
2. *Electrified* by the *evil* rumor, the police investigated promptly.
3. The *youthful* culprits tried to *evade the truth* about their part in the theft.
4. Many Republicans were *forbearing* enough to *regard with deep respect* President Franklin D. Roosevelt for successfully steering the country out of the Great Depression.
5. *Tumultuous* seas soon *rendered worthless* the swimmer's efforts to reach the shore.
6. When the visitors entered the hospital room, the child's *wan* face was *transformed* by happiness.
7. Many wished that the Empress would *inspect closely* Rasputin's *outwardly religious* behavior.
8. The youth is *acting from a desire for money* in choosing what he thinks is the most *remunerative* vocation.
9. The Agnellos are *thrifty* parents who *rear* their children with affection and understanding.
10. Because Fritz was apt to *waver* too much in a crisis or emergency, he should have been *excluded* by the mountaineering party.

Second practice set

Which word from the list at the left best replaces each *italicized* word or group of words?

depraved
mendacity
perverted
perjury
devout
nefarious
ghastly
transmute
debauchery
perturb
diabolical
tautology
puerile
cadaverous
miserliness
metamorphose
dissimulation
forgery
covetousness
hypocrisy
counterfeit
adoration
cupidity
dissemble

1. The youth's *deliberate lying* must *agitate* his parents very much.
2. *Childish* behavior will often *transform* good will into ill will.
3. *Led astray* from pious ways, some of the people were allured into *unrestrained indulgence*.
4. *Excessive desire for anything someone else possesses* is a more inclusive vice than *excessive desire for wealth*.
5. An unscrupulous agent tried to win acceptance by *deliberate pretension* (older term) and by *feigning good qualities*.
6. A *corpse-like* pallor made the boy look *pale as a specter*.
7. Expressions of sympathy that are *falsely imitative* are not likely to *change form* into the genuine quality.
8. It is *very evil* to try to sell a holographic literary *fabrication (or deception)* as a genuine manuscript.
9. *Unnecessary repetition of an idea* is one evidence of a *corrupted* literary style.
10. *Lying in court under oath* is a *devilish* act.

Third practice set

Which of the lettered items is most nearly *opposite* in meaning to the capitalized word?

1. GALVANIZED: (a) vacillated (b) bored (c) fabricated (d) venerated (e) counterfeited
2. VITIATE: (a) enliven (b) make joyful (c) deaden (d) enhance (e) nurture
3. LUCRATIVE: (a) unremunerative (b) deferential (c) penurious (d) avaricious (e) unmercenary
4. VICIOUS: (a) virtuous (b) healthy (c) thrifty (d) gratifying (e) vigorous
5. MENDACITY: (a) cowardice (b) blandness (c) wholeness (d) piety (e) truthfulness
6. PROVIDENT: (a) irreligious (b) happy-go-lucky (c) vacillating (d) tolerant (e) intermittent

7. DEFERENCE: (a) veneration (b) candor (c) disrespect (d) hypocrisy (e) tolerance
8. TURBULENT: (a) calm (b) articulate (c) mendacious (d) provident (e) inactive
9. TOLERATE: (a) dislike (b) disturb (c) ostracize (d) actively oppose (e) harmonize
10. SCRUTINIZE: (a) disregard (b) iterate (c) nurture (d) transfigure (e) disapprove

The right word

On a separate sheet, write the numbers of the *italicized* words. Beside each, write the number of the matching word or group of words from the second column.

1. *Reiteration* of slogans	1. childishness
2. *Transfiguration* of society	2. evasion of the truth
3. Precise *articulation*	3. tumultuousness
4. Shameless *prevarication*	4. lack of color
5. Astonishing *puerility*	5. mild dislike
6. *Turbulence* of Niagara	6. exercise of foresight
7. An editor's *providence*	7. deep reverence
8. Words of *veneration*	8. exclusion from fellowship
9. *Pallor* of a monument	9. unexpected release
10. Professional *ostracism*	10. oral formation of words
	11. constant repetition
	12. glorifying transformation

Replacements

Which word from the list at the left best replaces each *italicized* word or group of words?

turbid	1. The author was a(n) *voluntary exile* in Switzerland.
deport	2. Joan of Arc was a *fervent, devoted* Catholic.
duplicity	3. *Muddy-looking* clouds boiled up in the east.
expatriate	4. The pistol shots had a(n) *electric* effect on the horse.
galvanic	5. The government will *ship* him *out of the country* as
turgid	an undesirable alien.
sallow	6. Cinderella's coach *changed into quite a different*
banish	*form*.
devout	7. A doctor is disturbed by a *yellowish* complexion.
metamorphosed	8. Treason is a form of *double-dealing*.
intolerance	9. *Refusal to forbear* causes arguments.
transmute	10. Good thoughts will *compel* bad ones *to leave*.

A tall tale

1. Prepare a paragraph or two about an adventure, such as an imaginary trip around the world, using several words from this unit.
2. Look up the Greek custom from which the word *ostracize* derives.
3. Since *vita* means life, how does *vitiate* come to have an evil meaning?

unit eight

FIND

Which word from the list at the left fits best in each blank?

ardent	1. A quality for which George Washington is famous: _____
celestial	
indolence	2. A word for a trick or artifice: _____
subterfuge	3. A word that implies burning: _____
futile	4. A word that tells what a wrongdoer receives when he gets what he deserves: _____
fluctuation	
veracity	5. A common cause for failure: _____
morale	6. A word especially applicable to the weather: _____
civil	7. One reason why good teams play well: _____
credible	8. A word applicable to one's regrets over lost opportunities: _____
retribution	
utility	9. A word that means polite, in a rather formal way: _____
	10. A word for the realms of sky and stars: _____

ADJECTIVES

1. ardent (är′dənt)   *fervent or zealous, burning*

An ardent supporter of a cause is expected to make fiery speeches.
The pilgrims prayed at the shrine with a rare religious ardor.
Mountain climbing is an arduous (strenuous) hobby.

> **Synonyms:** *fervent, passionate, vehement, zealous* (p. 48).

2. benign (bĭ nīn′)   *kindly, gentle and mild*

A good book review should be incisive, not benign.
The tumor proved to be benign rather than malignant.

"The rude mind with difficulty associates the ideas of power and benignity (bĭ nĭg′nə tē)," said George Eliot.

Related words:

Benevolence stresses well-wishing, but may imply charitable deeds.
Altruism stresses the charitable deeds, but it may indicate only a desire to help others.
Philanthropy denotes deeds, gifts, *benefactions,* often on a large scale.

3. celestial   (sə lĕs′chəl)   ***heavenly, of the sky***

Angels are celestial beings. The stars are celestial bodies.
Celestial navigation is based on positions of the sun, moon, and stars.

Anything *ethereal* is light, airy, delicate, angelic, or celestial.
The *empyrean* is an older, literary word for the sky, firmament, or heaven, literally the place of pure light or fire. See -pyr(o)- (p. 359).

4. civil   (sĭv′əl)   ***of a citizen or state, polite***

Civil defense, an emergency system in the event of military attack or natural disaster, provides a part-time activity for many Americans.
Civilian (sə vĭl′yən) life is considered less strenuous than military duty.
Shakespeare was a person of civil bearing.
When, in 1871, British explorer Stanley located Scottish missionary Livingstone in Africa, the two men merely exchanged civilities (sə vĭl′ə tēz).

Civil service is nonmilitary service in the local, state, or federal government. *Civil* war is internal war or war within a country.
Civic duties are the normal obligations of a citizen. See -civi- (citizen) (p. 317).

5. complacent   (kəm plā′sənt)   ***self-satisfied, contented, smug***

"If you weren't so complacent about your studies, you'd get better grades," Arne's father said.
Is complacency a good quality or a fault verging on egotism?
The coach smiled complacently when the team was praised for its victories.

6. credible   (krĕd′ə bəl)   *believable*

The sailor's account of his escape from the sunken ship through a porthole is
hardly credible.
Ignatius Donnelly wrote a book demonstrating the credibility of the tales of a
lost continent called Atlantis.

> A *credulous* person is too willing to believe and is thus easily deceived.
> *Credulity* is often a result of ignorance. See *plausible* (p. 21).

7. culpable   (kŭl′pə bəl)   *blameworthy, deserving blame*

The boy most culpable in the lunchroom accident was the one who started the
trouble. Realizing his culpability, he stayed at home the next day.
''Many and deep are the sorrows that spring from false ideas for which no one
is culpable.'' (George Eliot)

> A *culprit* is an offender, someone to blame for a crime or fault.
> Compare *exculpate, acquit,* and related words under *exonerate* (p. 124).

8. eccentric   (ĕk sen′trĭk)   *odd, peculiar*

Jane's chums thought her eccentric because of her fondness for snakes, insects,
and mice.
Uncle Pete's interest in old lamps verges on eccentricity (ĕk′sən trĭs′ə tē).

> *Eccentric* literally means off center. How is an eccentric wheel or cog used in
> machinery?

Related words:

> An *anomalous* occurrence like a flying saucer is irregular, abnormal, unexpected.
> See *anomaly* (p. 68).
> An *aberration* is a defect in character or vision which causes deviation from what
> is normal, right, or logical.
> *Capriciousness* is unpredictable behavior, subject to whim. See *capricious* (p.
> 114).
> *Idiosyncrasies* are minor peculiarities of personal behavior, like fitting the tips of
> one's fingers together.

9. futile   (fyoo′təl)   *useless, ineffectual*

All efforts to locate the missing plane proved futile.
The futility (fyoo til′ə tē) of the undertaking did not discourage the searchers.

> An *effectual* plan produces the desired results; an *ineffectual* plan does not. Compare *abortive*.

10. incipient   (ĭn sĭp′ē ənt)   *in the early or beginning stages, commencing*

A medical examination showed the man had incipient tuberculosis.
Cancer discovered in its incipiency is often cured.

> A *percipient* person sees clearly, keenly, or readily. See *discern* (p. 10).

NOUNS

1. fallacy   (făl′ə sē)   *false reasoning, mistaken idea*

It is a fallacy to suppose that wealth always brings happiness.
The idea that cleverness makes honesty unnecessary is fallacious (fə lā′shəs).
Advertising copy often encourages readers to think fallaciously.

> *Fallible* judgments are subject to error, or likely to be mistaken.
> Electronic computers are as infallible as their programmers.
> Compare *erratic, errant* (p. 52).

2. fluctuation   (flŭk′choo ā′shən)   *rise and fall, continual variation*

Opinion polls record each fluctuation of the candidates' popularity.
Prices of farm products fluctuate considerably each season.
Do fluctuating costs and capricious weather make farming more of a gamble than is manufacturing?

Kinds of variability:

> To *undulate* is to rise and fall evenly, like waves.
> To *vacillate* (p. 142) is to waver in one's mind, to be irresolute.
> To *falter* is to weaken momentarily or to waver in one's determination; also, to speak in hesitating words.
> To *alter* one's plans is to change them. *Alternation* (taking turns) is similar to fluctuation, only more regular. See alter- (p. 347).

3. indolence   (ĭn′də lĕns)   *love of ease, laziness*

Indolence keeps capable high school students out of college.
An indolent breeze barely moved the curtain.
The vacationers relaxed indolently on the beach.

Related words:

Sloth (p. 53) an older and more sinister word for laziness, is one of the seven deadly sins of medieval fame.

Lethargy is sluggishness, drowsiness, lack of energy.

Supineness (literally, lying down) is inactivity, sluggishness, passivity, with a hint of laxness but not of evil.

Somnolence is drowsiness or sleepiness.

Inertness is inactivity in a person or a substance.

4. inference (ĭn′fər əns)   *conclusion, deduction*

If you see police around a house with drawn guns, your inference is that there must be a dangerous person inside.

One would infer (ĭn fûr′) from the sailor's story that he had been in Africa.

> An *inference* is a conclusion *you* draw; an *implication* is an idea implicit or built into what someone says. Thus, the sailor's words *imply* a knowledge of Africa. From a page of statistics you *deduce* the conclusion that crime is increasing faster than the population. Deductions are more precise and perhaps more formal than inferences.

5. morale (mə răl′)   *spirit, state of courage or confidence*

School morale reached a new high when we won the crucial game.

Visits to the hospital by friends and family soon raised the patient's morale.

> *Esprit de corps* is a French phrase for *the spirit of the group*. The term implies pride, enthusiasm, and courage.

6. retribution (rĕ′trə byōō′shən)   *merited punishment, requital*

Swift retribution overtook the thief, for, trying to escape, he fell into a pool and was drowned.

Making children pay for the intentional damage they have done is retributive (rĭ trĭb′yə tĭv′) justice.

Related words:

> *Retribution* is compensatory justice. It tends to be impersonal or automatic and may be either a reward for good or a requital for evil.

Vengeance, retaliation, and *reprisal,* like *revenge,* are usually personal, extralegal forms of requital.

Requital is impersonal repayment for good or evil.

Review *chastise* and its synonyms (p. 36).

See *vituperate* (p. 62), *expostulate* (p. 60), *recriminate* (p. 124).

7. subterfuge   (sŭb′tər fyo͞oj′)   *a trick, scheme, or artifice (to escape something unpleasant)*

Pretending to be asleep when Father came to investigate the noise was not a very effective subterfuge.

The cook once feigned illness as a subterfuge to avoid preparing a hot meal.

Related words:

A *maneuver* or *stratagem* is a trick to outwit or deceive someone: A fugitive outwits his pursuer by the stratagem of doubling back on his path.

A *ruse* is a trick intended more to mislead than to outwit: A bird acts injured as a ruse to lead the enemy away from its nest.

A *feint* (p. 11) is a pretended action to mislead an opponent.

8. temerity   (tə mĕr′ə tē)   *rashness, reckless boldness*

Hitler in 1941 had the temerity to attack Russia while he was fighting the Western Powers.

A forward pass from behind one's own goal posts is a temerarious way to gain ground.

Don Quixote temerariously attacked a windmill.

Related words:

Audacity is bold courage, daring, or impudence, but is not rash like *temerity.*

Effrontery is shameless boldness, especially in a personal confrontation: Joe had the effrontery to blame the coach for the team's poor track record.

Impudence is shameless and often wanton boldness with a little hint of bravery to sweeten its ugliness: Gail addressed some impudent remarks to the principal when told that she could not graduate.

Presumption is assertiveness that goes beyond one's apparent rights or abilities: Though inexperienced, Boggs had the presumption to assume the leadership of a rescue party.

Imposture goes beyond presumption. An *impostor* is one who poses as a doctor, for example, but has no medical training.

Quixotism is visionary temerity, based on ill-considered idealism: Don Quixote imagined himself a knight-errant and went out righting what he thought were injustices.

9. utility   (yo͞o tĭl′ə tē)   *usefulness, something useful*

Flowers have little apparent utility, but they help one's morale.

Clothespins are a minor household utility.

In planning a home, one should utilize (yo͞o′tə līz′) every square foot of space. The utilitarian (practical) values of an education are numerous.

> *Utilitarianism* is a philosophy which takes as its practical goal the maximum happiness for the most people.

10. veracity   (və răs′ə tē)   *truthfulness*

The chronic liar had mixed fact with fancy for so long that veracity was now almost impossible for him.
Did Herodotus give a highly veracious (və rā′shəs) account of his travels?

> *Verity* is truth in the abstract sense: Philosophy seeks verity.
> *Verisimilitude* is artistic truth, or a similarity between artistic representation and reality. See -ver- (p. 341).

Setting-up exercises

1. List adverbs formed from the entry words. Use the dictionary when in doubt.
2. Write a paragraph about a bold person in a setting with which you are familiar.
3. What is the root meaning of *retribution*? Of *ardent*? Of *culpable*? Of *indolence*? What is the value of knowing each?

First practice set

Which entry word from the unit best replaces each *italicized* word or group of words?

1. That country's strategists cling with *rash boldness* to the *false reasoning* that air power alone can win a war.
2. With *burning, flamelike* eyes Napoleon watched the *continual variations* of the battle, drawing swift *conclusions* from each development.
3. *Love of ease* readily makes a person *self-satisfied*.
4. The threat of a(n) *commencing* invasion was cut short by *impersonal punishment* in the form of an earthquake.
5. With *kindly* satisfaction the doctor reassured the *peculiar* old lady that her health was good.
6. Adrift in the Atlantic, the survivor sought *heavenly* help to strengthen his failing *spirit*.
7. It seemed *useless*, if not a *trick* to obtain financial backing, to discuss the *usefulness* of the invention as if it existed.
8. In spite of a seeming *truthfulness*, the messenger proved *blameworthy*.
9. Remain *polite* even if the traveler's adventures are not *believable*.

Second practice set

Which word from the list at the left best replaces each *italicized* word or group of words?

alternation
altruism
philanthropy
benevolence
ethereal
exculpate
anomalous
lethargy
idiosyncrasy
credulity
vacillation
capricious
impudent
somnolence
presumption
sloth
inertness
esprit de corps
reprisal
ruse
imposture
stratagem
requital
effrontery
supineness
quixotism

1. *Sinful laziness* is less tolerable than sluggish *lack of energy* but not less productive.
2. *Sluggish passivity (lying down)* is as disastrous in a worker as *drowsiness.*
3. Feeling *subject to whims,* the eccentric millionaire chose an *abnormal* way to travel a mile to the city —he chartered a balloon.
4. It takes *shameless boldness (at confrontation)* to ask the principal to *free from blame* the boy who stole his car.
5. *Visionary temerity* is a form of *rash boldness beyond presumption;* it pretends to have police authority.
6. Hiding the loot is a familiar *trick to mislead,* not clever enough to be called a *trick to outwit.*
7. Sending three orphans to camp may be described as *charitable actions* but hardly *benefactions of impressive magnitude.*
8. Commander Queeg's *wavering* about the strawberries helped to lessen the *group enthusiasm* of his crew.
9. A(n) *wantonly bold* negative reply to a presumptuous invitation to dinner could be called *impersonal repayment of good or evil.*
10. Wearing two pairs of shoes in *turn (first one, then the other)* may be an amusing *peculiarity,* but both pairs will last longer.

Third practice set

Which of the lettered items is most nearly *opposite* in meaning to the words printed in capital letters?

1. ARDENT: (a) slow (b) even-tempered (c) indifferent (d) darkened (e) ungenerous
2. COMPLACENT: (a) uncivil (b) discontented (c) unselfish (d) clever (e) ardent
3. FUTILE: (a) effectual (b) encouraging (c) resourceful (d) dominant (e) impressive
4. ECCENTRIC: (a) round (b) benign (c) civil (d) complacent (e) normal
5. INCIPIENT: (a) healthy (b) prominent (c) terminal (d) unnoticed (e) futile

6. BENIGN: (a) undeserving (b) beneficial (c) irreligious (d) vengeful (e) malevolent
7. INDOLENT: (a) virtuous (b) energetic (c) humble (d) ethereal (e) generous
8. VERACIOUS: (a) untruthful (b) incredible (c) credulous (d) exciting (e) anomalous
9. CULPABLE: (a) laudable (b) civil (c) useful (d) credible (e) inert
10. FALLACIOUS: (a) misleading (b) altruistic (c) discreet (d) logical (e) incredible

The right word

Write the numbers of the *italicized* words. Beside each, write the number of the matching word or words from the second column.

A

1. Quick *retribution*
2. Obvious *utility*
3. A clever *subterfuge*
4. Great *benignity*
5. High *morale*
6. Claims of *infallibility*
7. Irritating *complacency*
8. Questionable *veracity*
9. A justifiable *inference*
10. Undue *civility*

1. truthfulness
2. politeness
3. self-satisfaction
4. deduction
5. belief in justice
6. trick to escape something unpleasant
7. trick of logic
8. kindliness
9. requital
10. state of courage
11. usefulness
12. inability to err

B

1. Fearless *altruism*
2. Unexpected *credulity*
3. Feline *culprit*
4. A writer's *eccentricity*
5. Harmless *aberration*
6. Pious *benevolence*
7. Musical *undulation*
8. Prolonged *vacillation*
9. Glacial *inertness*
10. The story's *verisimilitude*

1. offender
2. rise and fall
3. error of perception
4. charitable feelings and deeds
5. kindly error
6. odd idea or habit
7. adherence to reality
8. well-wishing
9. unusual honesty
10. willingness to believe
11. inactivity
12. wavering, irresolution

Bonus

Which word from the list at the left best replaces each *italicized* word or group of words?

morale
fluctuate
verity
ineffectual
imply
maneuver
civil
fervent
impudence
passionate
benefactions
temerity

1. The plan to end the *internal* warfare in that bitterly divided country proved *incapable of producing the desired results.*
2. The new senator, a person of many *good deeds and gifts,* has proved to be a very *ardent* supporter of our cause.
3. Student *spirit* seems to *rise and fall.*
4. Do the speaker's *overpowering emotional* criticisms of the proposal *hint* that he is a member of the opposing political party?
5. The sophomores thought of a *trick intended to mislead* which they used to expose the *rash boldness* of the freshman president.

Word wizardry

1. With an eye on the word lists and to prove the utility of a developing vocabulary, write ardently about eccentric persons you know or can envision.
2. Enumerate a few popular fallacies, or discuss human fallibility as you see it in school.

unit nine

FRENCH REVOLUTION

Which word from the list at the left fits best in each blank?

perversity
rancor
hypocrisy
vigilant
belligerent
insidious
venial
sanguine
oblivion
gluttony
morose
depravity

1. The peasants felt deep _____ (hatred) because of the oppressive rule of the aristocrats.
2. The attitude of the secret leaders was very _____ (gloomy) as they watched the poverty and suffering around them.
3. In order to escape detection, it was necessary for the Jacqueries to be very _____ (watchful) in guarding their maneuvers.
4. Meanwhile, the French dignitaries were much too _____ (hopeful) about their future.
5. The peasants were growing more _____ (warlike) all the time.
6. The aristocrats clung stubbornly to their ancient privileges, and this _____ (willful nonconformity) helped bring on the revolution.
7. There was much _____ (pretense) on both sides.
8. A fault of some aristocrats was _____ (eating to excess) while the ordinary person was near starvation.
9. The _____ (treacherous) spirit of rebellion gained headway rapidly.
10. La Guillotine brought _____ (state of being forgotten) to many aristocrats before the revolution had run its haphazard course.

SEVEN SINISTER ADJECTIVES

1. belligerent (bə līj′ər ənt)

quarrelsome or warlike,
engaged in warfare

Belligerent behavior often disrupts a friendship.
Sweden and Switzerland were not among the belligerents of World War II.

A state of belligerence exists when two persons or nations are fighting each other.

Warlike words:

A *bellicose* attitude is hostile or warlike. It applies to attitude not to behavior, whereas *belligerent* indicates either.
A *pugnacious* person (p. 118) likes to fight or quarrel.
A *martial* atmosphere (p. 62) is military or warlike.
Polemic(al) writing is word warfare, *i.e.,* argumentative or controversial speeches or writings.

2. incorrigible (ĭn kŏr′ĭj ə bəl) *incapable of reform, unmanageable*

An incorrigible liar soon shows his lack of credibility.
Incorrigibility makes a convict ineligible for parole.

Related words:

Inveterate (p. 116), *chronic* (pp. 116, 341), *intransigent* (irreconcilable, uncompromising).

3. morose (mə rōs′) *gloomy, sour*

Ill health makes some people quite morose.
Moroseness usually decreases, however, as health improves.
"What good does it do to study?" Ben asked morosely, after failing the exam because of unintelligent preparation.

Related words:

Sullen is silently gloomy, resentful or dismal.
Surly is brusque, bitter, ill-humored—often with a snarl.
Churlish is surly in a boorish, uncouth country manner.
Splenetic is spiteful and peevish.
Acrimonious is caustic, bitter, sharp, with a strong hint of jealousy.
Acrid is sharp, acid, stinging in taste, odor, or speech.

4. nefarious (nə fãr′ē əs) *very wicked or evil*

When uncovered, the nefarious plots of underworld hoodlums make startling news.
Deliberate cruelty heightened the nefariousness of the crime.

Related words:

Atrocious deeds are grimly evil or horribly wicked.
Reprehensible acts are illegal, unethical, or otherwise blameworthy but not shockingly evil: Carelessness is a reprehensible trait.
Review *vicious* and its group; also *vitiate* (p. 142).

Antonyms: *righteous, virtuous, saintly, upright, ingenuous* (p. 221).

5. pernicious   (pər nĭsh′əs)   ***highly injurious, deadly***

Heroin is a pernicious drug because, among other things, its use may lead to criminal acts.
Discussions with her peers made Celeste realize the perniciousness of prejudice.

Related words:

An *insidious* trait is treacherously or stealthily injurious: Jealousy is an insidious trait. Gossip works insidiously.
Baneful habits or attitudes are harmful like a poison: Fear of failure is baneful if it makes a person too tense or too cautious.
Pestilent ideas are harmful like a plague or disease: Gambling is a pestilent habit because it is hard to curb.
A *noxious* substance or idea is harmful because it is poisonous or offensive: Carbon monoxide is insidious because it is so noxious.
A *deleterious* substance or habit is harmful with a deteriorating effect: Certain pesticides have deleterious effects on human beings.

6. venial   (vē′nē əl)   ***pardonable, excusable***

While occasional tardiness is a venial fault, persistent tardiness is a pernicious habit.
The venialness (vē′nē əl nes)—or veniality (vē′nē al′ə tē)—of social errors decreases for those who repeat them.

Do not confuse *venial* (from the Latin word *venia*, grace or a favor) with *venal* (from the Latin word *venum*, meaning sale): A corrupt legislature or government is full of venality (readiness to accept bribes). In theology, a venial sin is opposed to a *mortal* or deadly sin.

7. venomous   (vĕn′əm əs)   ***poisonous, spiteful***

The cobra is a venomous snake found in Asia and Africa.
If it bites you, the venom will cause death in a few hours.
The venomousness of the speaker's attack on the police led to the discovery of his criminal record.

SIX KINDS OF EVIL

1. depravity   (dĭ prăv′ə tē)   ***moral corruptness, debasement***

Swift's Yahoos were vile creatures symbolizing human depravity.
The depraved inhabitants of the ancient city offered human sacrifices.
Bad habits slowly deprave the character of those who let them form.

Immorality is depravity, especially sexual, but, generally, it is any breaking of the society's moral code.
Turpitude is shameful baseness or vileness comparable to depravity.

2. gluttony   (glŭt′ən ē)   *indulgence to excess, especially in eating*

The four-hundred-pound person was a victim of gluttony.
With his huge appetite, Henry VIII of England developed into a glutton.
His gluttonous habits made him "goodly of girth."

Gluttony may express itself in forms of indulgence other than eating, such as reading. It is one of the Seven Deadly Sins of medieval fame. They are: (1) pride or
arrogance (p. 219), (2) covetousness (pp. 38, 114, 249), including avarice
(pp. 38, 143), (3) lust or lechery, (4) anger, (5) gluttony, (6) envy, and (7) sloth
(p. 53 under *indolence*).

3. heresy   (hĕr′ə sē)   *belief(s) differing from accepted view*

The idea that germs cause diseases was once a scientific heresy.
The heretic's teachings were condemned as false by his church.
A teacher holding heretical (hə rĕt′ĭ kəl) views about education may be ostra-
cized.

4. hypocrisy   (hĭ pŏk′rə sē)   *pretense of being what one is not, sham*

Judge Pyncheon's hypocrisy and greed made him the villain in Nathaniel Hawthorne's *The House of Seven Gables*.
A person who owns very little property is hypocritical (hĭp′ə krĭt′ĭ kəl) in pretending to be materially wealthy.
Tartuffe was a hypocrite who professed to be pious while scheming to get his
benefactor's wealth.

Insincerity is milder and much more venial than hypocrisy.

5. perversity   (pər vûr′sə tē)   *willfulness in nonconformity*
or wrongdoing, obstinacy

Is it perversity or hypocrisy that makes one refuse to wear a coat in cold weather?
The inveterate gambler proved perverse and unrepentant.
Judges who accept bribes pervert justice (turn it from the right course).
Bad art is a perversion of good taste.

Related words:

See -vert-, -vers- words (p. 299).
A *fractious* person or horse is unruly, rebellious, or irritable.

A *refractory* person is hard to manage, more resistant and stubborn than one who is merely perverse.

A *froward* person is perverse, but more headstrong and aggressive in wrongdoing.

A *wayward* person is perverse and disobedient in a whimsical, erratic manner.

6. rancor   (răng′kər)   ***bitter hatred, ill will***

Captain Ahab's rancor grew ever stronger against the white whale which had bitten off his leg.

Herod had a rancorous nature.

Related words:

Rancid butter or other fat is spoiled or partly decomposed and thus bitter. *Rancid* and *rancor* come from the same Latin word *rancere,* to have a sharp, bitter taste. *Rankle* comes from the Latin word *draco,* for dragon: Captain Ahab's loss rankled so deeply that it undermined his sanity.

Malignity is intense ill will, a strong desire to inflict harm.

Malice is ill will of a less intense kind than malignity.

Malevolence is merely evil-wishing. See -<u>mal</u>- words (p. 350).

SEVEN REMARKABLE ADJECTIVES

1. intrepid   (ĭn trĕp′ĭd)   ***fearless, dauntless***

The test pilot was an intrepid aviator, one of the first to fly more than two thousand miles per hour.

Walter Reed's intrepidity (ĭn′trə pĭd′ə tē) in exposing himself to yellow fever enabled him to discover the cause of the disease.

See *temerity* and related words (p. 154).

2. laconic   (lə kŏn′ĭk)   ***concise, terse, pithy***

The sayings of Confucius are laudably laconic.

Gretchen accepted the invitation with a laconic "yes."

Aunt Estelle thought Carl rude to answer her questions so laconically.

The word *laconic* commemorates the ancient Spartans or Laconians, who were trained from childhood to speak only when necessary and then in the briefest and most pointed manner.

For synonyms, see *succinct* and its group (p. 205).

3. militant   (mĭl′ə tənt)   *resolute, combative, eager to fight*

The Senator who addressed the group was a militant crusader for the rights of the unborn.
By organizing a march on Washington, the advocates of a constitutional amendment showed their militancy.
Poor eyesight militates against success in school.

> *Militant* applies chiefly to a resolute spirit and positive and forceful methods in peaceful pursuits: *The Church Militant.*
> *Martial* (p. 62) is a stronger word for truly warlike actions and activities.

4. oblivious   (ə blĭv′ē əs)   *unconscious, unmindful*

The runner was oblivious to the cheering in the stands.
Sleep provides temporary oblivion from weariness and worries.
A guard's obliviousness enabled the prisoner to escape.

> Compare *Lethe,* in Greek mythology the river of forgetfulness.

5. sanguine   (săng′gwən)   *hopeful or confident, bloody*

A sanguine person like Madeline is not overcome by despair.
The Reign of Terror was a very sanguinary affair (much bloodshed).
Consanguinity (kŏn′săng′gwĭn′ə tē) (blood relationship) does not exist between an adopted child and the foster parents' own child.

> *Sanguine* comes from the Latin word *sanguinis,* blood. It came to mean ruddy, as applied to faces, and thus in time it took on the meaning of having a warm-hearted, cheery nature.

Related words:

> *Effervescent* (p. 361) (spirited, lively, frothy), *buoyant* (lighthearted, good-natured), *exultant* (joyful, jubilant) (p. 52).

6. ubiquitous   (yo͞o bĭk′wĭ təs)   *everywhere present*

Fear was a ubiquitous and insidious foe which demoralized the town more than enemy gunfire could have done.
The ubiquitousness of the press made it impossible to conceal the discovery.

> Compare *onmipresent,* with the same meaning, but used often of Deity and perhaps for this reason less likely to imply mild annoyance as *ubiquitous* does: Mud may be ubiquitous after a heavy rain, but not omnipresent.

7. vigilant   (vĭj′ə lənt)   *alert to danger, watchful*

The nurse kept a vigilant watch over the sick child.
During a dry spell, vigilance to prevent forest fires is doubly urgent.
The knight's vigil (period of watching) at the altar lasted all night.
Soldiers guarded the palace vigilantly.

> Vigilantes were members of self-appointed vigilance committees which guarded a frontier community from desperadoes and outlaws.

First practice set

A

Which entry word (or form of the entry word) best replaces each *italicized* word or group of words?

1. His *moral corruptness* went unnoticed for a long time because he promoted his *very evil* schemes so blandly.
2. When the judge declared the mugger *incapable of reform* and imposed the maximum sentence, several people in the courtroom became *gloomy and sour*.
3. One face grew hard with *bitter hatred* while another spectator turned on the judge with a *warlike* gesture.
4. "You *poisonous* viper!" the convicted felon declared. "My misdeed is no worse than your *eating too much*."
5. "I'm not *unconscious* of the fact that I am grossly overweight," said the judge, "but I think my fault is a *pardonable* one. At least it is far less *injurious* than the *fearless* robberies that you have perpetrated."
6. "It would be *an unaccepted belief* in legal circles to think of reducing your sentence, and no honest judge would encourage you to be *hopeful* that a reduction would be approved."
7. "I admire you for not showing *pretended* remorse, but your *obstinacy* in doing wrong is well established," he added.
8. "You are too *combative*," was the culprit's *pithy* reply.
9. "The authorities were too *watchful*, and the police seemed *everywhere present*," he concluded angrily.

B

Which of the two words in parentheses fits best in each sentence?

1. The band played *(belligerent, martial)* music as the parade began.
2. *(Splenetic, laconic)* as ever, the guard greeted us with an unending series of complaints.
3. Because their fault was only *(venal, venial)*, the children were punished with a mild reprimand.
4. That *(ubiquitous, omnipresent)* phrase, "you know," indicates that speakers take a great deal for granted about their listeners.
5. Before the game the team was *(exultant, sanguine);* after the victory it was *(exultant, sanguine)*.
6. It was *(obvious, oblivious)* to his friends that Bart was *(obvious, oblivious)* to sound advice.
7. Lindbergh's *(effrontery, intrepidity)* in flying the Atlantic solo inspired many young aviators of his day.
8. *(Arrogance, gluttony)* is the regrettable fault that often brings on overweight.
9. A(n) *(chronic, incorrigible)* ailment kept the woman indoors.
10. If the stable attendants had been more *(militant, vigilant)*, they would have noticed that the horse chosen by the unskilled rider was *(fractured, fractious)*.

Second practice set

Which of the words in the list at the left best replaces each *italicized* word or group of words?

pestilential
polemical
surly
buoyant
churlish
splenetic
acrimonious
venomous
reprehensible
atrocious
insidious
immorality
noxious
turpitude
martial
omnipresent
fractious
refractory
wayward
rancid
venality
sullen
exultant

1. The child is *whimsically perverse* rather than *obstinate and unmanageable*.
2. The prison guard's *readiness to accept bribes* was a very *treacherous* defect in the administration of justice.
3. *Spiteful and peevish* remarks occur often in that columnist's *argumentative* writings.
4. When her identity became known, the recluse's manner was *silently bitter and resentful* rather than *brusquely ill-humored*.
5. *Jealously bitter* writings are at times *as harmful as a plague*.
6. *Spoiled* salad dressing will have a *poisonous* taste.
7. Treachery is *grimly wicked* and indicates *shameful baseness*.
8. Is a *military-warlike* manner *blameworthy* in a teacher?
9. Careless spending is a *harmful and poisonous* habit; indeed wastefulness may be considered *a violation of society's moral code*.
10. Annabel had a *light-hearted, floating* nature and her promotion made her *jubilant*.

Third practice set

Which of the lettered items is most nearly *opposite* in meaning to the word printed in capital letters?

1. INCORRIGIBLE: (a) healthy (b) capable of reform (c) resolute (d) sanguine (e) ambitious
2. MOROSE: (a) sharp (b) healthy (c) weak (d) good-natured (e) humble acting
3. MALIGNITY: (a) fullness (b) pleasure (c) benevolence (d) directness (e) fairness
4. OBLIVIOUS: (a) forgetful (b) careful (c) aware (d) vigilant (e) cheerful
5. LACONIC: (a) concise (b) implicit (c) frank (d) wordy (e) quite emotional
6. PERNICIOUS: (a) harmless (b) noxious (c) noisy (d) not a drug (e) unsuspecting

7. INTREPID: (a) slow-moving (b) watchful (c) brusque (d) painstaking (e) timid
8. VENIAL: (a) incorruptible (b) inexcusable (c) deliberate (d) saintly (e) morose
9. SANGUINE: (a) dishonest (b) easygoing (c) despairing (d) lifeless (e) unpromising
10. VIGILANT: (a) cautious (b) unwary (c) cowardly (d) sleepy (e) tiresome

The last enemy

Danger—in the air, on the desert, in a war, in an earthquake—is a logical topic for a militant paragraph. Many of the words in this unit are suitable for such a topic. Choose your dangerous locale and write a meaty paragraph on it.

unit ten

AMUSING

Which word from the list at the left fits best in each blank?

derision
jocularity
facetiousness
burlesque
satire
repartee
cajolery
bathos
irony
hilarity
levity
ludicrousness

1. A humorous skit of the President signing a bill: _____
2. The simple absurdity of a bearded goat's appearance: _____
3. The noisy gaiety of a basketball team that won a championship: _____
4. A parent's coaxing and flattery to get a child to go to the dentist: _____
5. The light-mindedness of a group of joking teenagers: _____
6. Clever or witty ways of describing an embarrassing situation: _____
7. Ridicule as a literary mode or form for exploiting human faults or follies: _____
8. Joking, good-natured conversation: _____
9. Rapid, witty interplay in a brisk conversation: _____
10. Anticlimax or abrupt descent from the lofty to the commonplace: _____

WORDS FOR RIDICULE

1. derision   (də rĭzh′ən)   *ridicule, mockery*

Robert Fulton's steamboat was called, in derision, "Fulton's Folly."
Beards were once a target for derisive (də rī′sĭve) (scornful) remarks.
It is fun to deride (dĭ rīd′) inventors for the absurd devices they often create.
Wits like to deride ridiculous titles of rank and royalty.

> *Risible* (laughter-producing) comes, like *derision* and *ridicule,* from the Latin verb *(de)ridere*. The past participle is *derisus*.

2. bathos   (băʹthōs′)   *anticlimax, false or excessive pathos*

The tourist's letter was full of bathos. "A splendid Greek pillar," he wrote, "stood out against the sky like a big cigar."
Sudden sentimentality and bathos in the third act bogged down an otherwise interesting play.
Life provides many bathetic (bə thetʹik) moments, like hearing a catfight outside just at the height of a stirring story on television.

> *Bathos* comes from the Greek word *bathos,* depth. It thus denotes a sudden descent from the sublime to the depths of commonplaceness or absurdity. From the same Greek word come *bathometer* (instrument for measuring water depths) and *bathysphere* (a chamber lowered to great depths in the ocean).

Related words:

> A *spoonerism* is a slip of the tongue in which sounds are transposed, with bathetic effect: "The boy rode down the street on a well-boiled icicle." The word *spoonerism* comes from the name of a notorious Oxford don, Dr. W. A. Spooner, 1844–1930, who often made such slips.
> A *pun* is a witty play on words: He's a boar.
> *Pathos* is from -path-, feeling or suffering (p. 342).

3. burlesque   (bûrʹlĕsk′)   *a comic imitation or takeoff*

The skit the students are preparing is a burlesque of two serious actors trying out for a comic role in television.
Bobby likes to burlesque his father's way of strutting down the street.

> A *burlesque* is a humorous distortion of an impressive situation or event. The term is also applied to a variety show consisting of outlandish songs, skits, comic bits, and dancing. A musical comedy usually contains burlesque scenes or elements.

Related words:

> A *parody* is a comic imitation of a well-known literary or musical composition. Thus . . . "Geoffrey's Tales from Chauffeur" is a parody or takeoff on Chaucer's *Canterbury Tales*.
> A *travesty* is a crude or grotesque imitation of something impressive, or it is a situation or incident which appears to be a distorted imitation: The trial was a travesty of justice.
> A *caricature* is a picture or account which exaggerates certain features of a person or situation in order to poke fun. A political cartoon usually caricatures a person or an event.

4. irony   (īʹrə nē)   *mild sarcasm, a grimly humorous effect of words,*
or a situation opposite to what one expects

The irony of the accident was that, in swerving to miss hitting a cat, the driver caused the death of a human being.
Ironically (ī rŏnʹī k(ə)lē), the accident victim had canceled her life insurance a week before the fatal occurrence.
An ironic detail of *Oedipus Rex* is that the blind priest "sees" the truth about Oedipus far better than Oedipus himself does.

Sarcasm is harsh, cutting derision in which irony is often used: "You are indeed a genius!" the golf pro exclaimed, as Tom's swing cut a deep wedge out of the green.

5. satire   (să′tīər′)   *ridicule, especially in literary form*

Gulliver's Travels is a famous satire ridiculing human follies.
The author, Jonathan Swift, was a skillful satirist (săt′ər ĭst), fond of ironic poses.
The satirical undertone of her speech was intended to effect a change in the attitude of her audience.

> A *lampoon* is a strongly satiric piece of writing, generally brief and usually directed at a person.

> **Note:** *Derision,* the key word for this group, quite properly appears first. *Levity* is the key word for the next group.

WORDS FOR LIGHT-HEARTED USES

1. levity   (lĕv′ə tē)   *light-mindedness, frivolity*

Levity is out of place in a cathedral, even for tourists.
New Year's Eve is a good time for unrestrained levity.

> *Levity* (from Latin *levis,* light or smooth) frequently implies an unseemly lack of seriousness. Other -levi- words: *levigate* (to make smooth or into a smooth paste), *levitate* (to rise into the air), *levitation.*

2. facetiousness   (fə sē′shəs nəs)   *witty levity*

In moments of facetiousness, Bob Witt's friends call him Half-Witt.
Mrs. Cook facetiously calls the kitchen range her altar of burnt offerings.
Coach Marinello often makes facetious remarks, addressing the football players as his ballet team.

3. flippancy   (flĭp′ən sē)   ***pertness, lightly disrespectful***
talk or action, sauciness

Her constant flippancy hid the intensely serious streak in her nature.
Robin spoke flippantly of school traditions.
Jon's flippant remarks at graduation irked the principal.

> *Flippant* probably comes from *flip,* to make a quick, light upward toss of a coin,
> a pancake, an egg, or some other object. A flip comment is thus quick, easy, glib,
> conceited, or frivolous, and often disrespectful.

4. hilarity   (hə lăr′ə tē)   ***boisterous levity***

The hilarity of the April Fool's Frolic lasted long past midnight.
The Senior Assembly with its burlesque classroom scene was a hilarious affair.

> *Merriment* is joyous but less comic and boisterous than *hilarity.*
> *Mirth* is prolonged amusement or merriment.

5. jocularity   (jŏk′yə lăr′ə tē)   ***good-natured, playful joyousness***

Franklin's jocularity reminded the children of Santa Claus.
They liked the jocular folk songs he sang to them.
The hospital attendants found that most patients responded well if treated
jocularly.

Joy words:

> A *jovial* mood is hearty and good-humored. The word comes from the Roman god
> Jove, who was sometimes jovial.
> *Jocose* remarks are light-hearted or intended to cause laughter.
> *Jocund* talk is cheerful, good-natured, and spirited. This word is older and more
> likely to appear in poetry:
>
> > *Night's candles are burnt out, and jocund day*
> > *Stands tiptoe on the misty mountain tops. (Romeo and Juliet)*

6. ludicrousness   (lōo′də krəs nəs)   ***laughableness, ridiculousness***

The ludicrousness of the cow costume brought howls of laughter.
What is it that makes a donkey ludicrous to look at?

> *Ludicrous* is used mostly of objects and situations.
> Compare *incongruous* (p. 251).

7. repartee   (rĕp′är tē′)   ***rapid, witty conversation or reply***

The French writer claimed a talent for repartee, but his American guests were
well able to match his wit. "Tea and Repartee" would make a good title for the
conversation.

ADJECTIVES

---

1. bohemian (bō hē′mē ən) *loose, arty, unconventional*

A number of American artists and writers of the 1920s lived a bohemian existence in Paris.

The "beats" and the "Beat Generation," the "hippies" and the "flower children," of later decades made up sects of bohemians.

Bohemia is a province of Czechoslovakia through which gypsies once passed in large numbers to reach Western Europe. Thus, the word *bohemian* came to mean a gypsy kind of carefree, nomadic existence.

2. catatonic (kăt′ə tŏn′ĭk) *marked by stupor or muscular rigidity, often alternating with excitement*

The youth was found in a catatonic state.

Some claim that a mystical nature, with its sluggish periods of apathy and occasional moments of ecstatic excitement, verges on mild catatonia.

> Cata-, a prefix meaning down(ward), against, away, or backward, appears in such words as the following:
> *Catalepsy* is a kind of seizure marked by muscular rigidity and temporary loss of consciousness. It may occur in epilepsy and schizophrenia.
> A *cataclysm* (a washing down or away) is a great flood or sudden upheaval.
> *Catacombs* are tombs or vaults underground, as in Rome.
> A *catalyst,* in chemistry or society, encourages a desired reaction by its presence.
> A *catapult* is a machine or other device for hurling rocks (down).
> Compare *catalogue, catastrophe, catarrh* (inflammation of mucous membrane), *cataract* (waterfall), but not *catamount.*

3. ecumenical   (ĕk'yə mĕn'ĭ kəl)   *worldwide, universal,*
church-uniting

The ecumenical conference brought together representatives of varied religious sects.
Ecumenicalism (ecumenism) (e kyü'mə niz'əm) has gained momentum in many churches that want to cooperate with each other more extensively than in the past.
The National Council of Churches is an ecumenical organization.

> Compare *sectarian*, devoted to one specific sect or denomination.

4. empirical   (ĕm pĭr'ĭ kəl)   *based on experience or experiment*

A rat in a maze gets food by the empirical method of trial and error.
Much has been learned empirically about the hazards of space travel.
The knowledge of electricity began long ago in Greek empiricism (ĕm pĭr'ə sĭz'əm).

> *Empirical* comes from the Greek *em* (into) plus *peira* (trial).
> *Empire*, however, comes from the Latin root imperium, from which comes also the word *imperial*.

5. nether   (nĕth'ər)   *down, below*

The nether regions of the earth are underground.
The Netherlands is a fitting term for the Low Countries of Europe; much of the land is below sea level.

6. palatable   (păl'ət ə bəl)   *tasty, savory, agreeable*

Marie does not find ripe California figs as palatable as oranges.
Opinions differ sharply on the palatability of avocados, mandrakes, and mushrooms.

> *Palatable* comes from *palate,* the roof of the mouth; but it also applies to the arts and to intellectual preferences: Musical comedy is more palatable to many Americans than opera.

7. paranoid   (păr'ə noid)   *characterized by suspiciousness and*
a feeling of being persecuted

The eccentric artist was particularly subject to the paranoid delusion that his friends hated him.
As his career progressed, he became increasingly paranoiac in his behavior.
Paranoia made the patient increasingly suspicious and irritable.

> *Paranoia* implies abnormality or mental imbalance.

8. psychedelic   (sī′kə dĕl′ĭk)   *producing an unnatural mental state*

Some of the Indians used peyote, a psychedelic drug, to produce weird visions and sensations.

A psychiatrist warned of the danger of using psychedelic drugs.

> The *hallucinogens* are known as psychedelic drugs because they produce a state of "heightened consciousness" which involves hallucinations.

First practice set

Which entry word from the unit best replaces each *italicized* word or group of words?

1. The ancient cuckoo clock produced a moment of *anticlimax* and *boisterous amusement* by sounding just as Father began telling how well he did in school.
2. Dillie enacted a *humorous takeoff* of school life that was full of *laughable antics*.
3. Mario's mother was as famous for her *rapid, witty conversation* as for her very *tasty* blueberry pies.
4. Sean's good-natured *joking, playful* joyousness made him popular with everyone, while his *witty levity* was widely admired.
5. We read a *work of ridicule* which treats animals with great *mockery*.
6. Some persons find *lightly disrespectful talk* and *loose, unconventional living* quite attractive.
7. The teacher did not encourage *light-mindedness* about the *lower* world of Dante's *Inferno*.
8. The standard treatment for behavior that is *marked by stupor alternating with excitement* is *based on experience*.
9. After taking the *hallucinatory* drug, he experienced delusions that were *characterized by suspiciousness and a feeling of persecution.*
10. That *universal, church-uniting* activities are so difficult to carry out is *characteristic of a situation opposite to what one would expect*.
11. While the play's situations were *ridiculous*, its *rapid, witty verbal exchange* was refreshing.
12. Who would be so *lightly disrespectful in talk or manner* as to approach a serious family crisis with *frivolity*?
13. The noisy, glaringly-lighted musical show at the fair was *jokingly* billed as a *mindblowing* experience.
14. Many famous comedians got their start in *theatrical entertainment employing comic imitations* that relied heavily on *mockery*.
15. The *mildly sarcastic* tone of the host's remarks seemed lost on the *unconventional* individual who had joined the party.
16. Research that is *reliant on experience or experiment* suits her temperament.
17. With *witty levity* our Australian friend frequently calls her country the *Down-Under* regions.
18. The protagonist was *filled with suspiciousness and a feeling of being persecuted*, a part that one actor did not find *agreeable*.

Second practice set

Which word from the list at the left best replaces each *italicized* word or group of words?

cataract
mirth
catarrh
catapult
catalyst
catatonia
catacombs
cataclysm
catalepsy
jocund
jocular
jocose
jovial
levitation
realistically
levigation
sarcasm
caricature
travesty
parody
spoonerism
pun

1. *Loss of consciousness with muscular rigidity* is a disease that does not warrant *laugh-arousing* remarks.
2. The chorus sang a *heartily good-natured* song that was a *comic imitation* of "Anchors Aweigh."
3. "I will sew you to a sheet" said the usher, thus creating not a *witty play on words* but a(n) *accidental transposition of sounds*.
4. A *hearty, good-humored* person is a good *encourager (by his or her mere presence)* of fun at any social gathering.
5. In *Don Quixote* we have a *picture exaggerating certain features* of a knight who did not see things *as they really were*.
6. Axel's *cheerful and spirited* behavior caused *prolonged merriment* and hilarity at the picnic.
7. *Rising and floating* of a table is a trick of clairvoyants, while *beating into a smooth paste* makes a pudding more palatable.
8. There was a grim relationship between the *alternate stupor and excitement* from which the victim was suffering and the *devastating flood*.
9. The entrance to the *underground tombs* began near a *swift waterfall*.
10. The *grotesque imitation of something impressive* on life in Antarctica is full of *harsh derision* about the loveliness and durability of ice.

Third practice set

Which of the lettered items is most nearly *opposite* in meaning to the word printed in capital letters?

1. SERIOUS-MINDEDNESS: (a) derision (b) irony (c) levity (d) caricature (e) ludicrousness
2. GLOOM: (a) hilarity (b) repartee (c) bathos (d) irony (e) flippancy
3. MOROSE: (a) satirical (b) jocular (c) ironic (d) ludicrous (e) bathetic
4. LEVITATION: (a) gloom (b) empiricism (c) cataclysm (d) gravitation (e) solemnity
5. PALATABLE: (a) ugly (b) distasteful (c) spiritual (d) inedible (e) disrespectful

6. VENIAL: (a) incorrigible (b) incorruptible (c) belligerent (d) pernicious (e) inexcusable
7. BATHOS: (a) sensibility (b) impressiveness (c) acceptability (d) grandeur (e) probability
8. ECUMENICALISM: (a) irreligiousness (b) narrowness (c) empiricism (d) sectarianism (e) obliviousness
9. LUDICROUSNESS: (a) luminousness (b) lugubriousness (c) paranoia (d) lamentation (e) catatonia
10. RESPECTFULNESS: (a) sarcasm (b) youthfulness (c) levity (d) flippancy (e) satire.

Matching verbs

On a separate sheet write the numbers of the items at the left. Beside each number place the number of the item in the right column which best defines the *italicized* word.

1. *Levitate* literally	1. act out a comic imitation of
2. *Satirize* the mayor	2. exaggerate pictorially, for comic effect, certain features of
3. *Deride* a hero	
4. *Parody* a prologue	3. gambol happily
5. *Travesty* a ceremony	4. hurl like a stone
6. *Caricature* a celebrity	5. cause to rise
7. *Catapult* a player	6. give a humorous imitation of
8. *Palatalize* a sound	7. ridicule in literary manner
9. *Burlesque* a singer	8. give a grotesque imitation of
10. *Empiricize* a problem	9. treat in terms of practical experience
	10. mock
	11. change the form of

Matching adjectives

1. *Ludicrous* gestures	1. imitative in a mocking, verbal way
2. *Hilarious* escapades	2. mocking, ridiculing
3. *Ironic* event	3. joking, playful
4. *Flippant* answers	4. bent on literary ridicule
5. *Derisive* shouts	5. wittily amusing
6. *Facetious* followers	6. anticlimactic, overdone
7. *Jocular* jests	7. pertly disrespectful
8. *Satiric* writers	8. perverse or bitter
9. *Parodistic* skill	9. opposite in effect from what is expected
10. *Bathetic* results	10. odd or erratic
	11. laughable, laughter-causing
	12. boisterously gay or merry

Extra

1. Write a parody, a burlesque sketch, a brief satiric allegory, a page of repartee, or an account of a ludicrous incident as your teacher suggests.
2. Read one part of *Gulliver's Travels* and make a list of the human follies Swift is satirizing.

3. Read *Animal Farm* by George Orwell, *The Screwtape Letters* by C. S. Lewis, or some other twentieth-century satire. Write a brief report discussing what the author is satirizing and whether or not you think the satire is effective.
4. List adverbs that may be formed from the entry words and write sentences using several.
5. How is *palatalize* related in meaning to *palatable*?

Ten defiant adjectives*

1. adiaphorous   (ad′ē af ər əs)   ***morally neutral or indifferent; doing neither good nor harm, as a medicine***

Should a teacher adopt an adiaphorous attitude when a moral issue comes up for discussion?

   Adiaphorous comes from *a-*, not + *diaphoros*, different or differing.

2. arcuate   (är′kyə wāt)   ***curved like a bow***

Arcuate eyebrows are attractive.

   Arcuate is simply *arc*, with an adjective ending. Both words come from the Latin verb *arcuare*, to form an arch, which in turn is derived from *arcus*, a bow.

3. ariose   (ŏ rē′ōs)   ***melodious, songlike***

The shower responds better than the family to Arnold's ariose moods.

*All but one of these words may be found in a college-size dictionary.

Ariose comes from the very familiar musical term *aria,* the air or melody in a musical work for voices, such as a cantata, opera, oratorio, etc.

4. mephitic   (mə fid′ik)   *bad smelling, noxious, offensive, or*
                                                 poisonous from any source

Marsh gas is a mephitic memory of those who camped along the pond.

> *Mephitic* takes its origin from a similar Latin adjective, *mephiticus.*
> *Mephitis* is a bad-smelling poisonous gas from the decomposition of organic matter in the ground.

5. nacreous   (nā′krē əs)   *lustrous, iridescent; yielding nacre*
                                                 or mother-of-pearl

Nacreous dewdrops glisten in the morning sunlight.

> The ancestor of *nacreous* is an Arabic word for a small kettledrum.

6. nugatory   (n(y)ü′gə tōr ē)   *of small value, worthless; not operative*

''The clock was slow'' is a nugatory excuse.

> The root of *nugatory* is the Latin verb *nugari,* to trifle, from *nugae,* trifles.

7. palpebral   (pal pē′brəl)   *of or having to do with the eyelids*

Eyeshadow is a form of palpebral decoration.

> *Palpebral* arises from the Latin word for eyebrows, *palpebra.*
> Compare *palpable,* readily felt (pp. 91, 206).

8. pejorative   (pi jȯr′ət iv)   *making or becoming worse; disparaging*

Carpetbaggers was a pejorative term for Northern adventurers who went to the South to seek their fortunes after the War between the States.

> *Pejorative* derives from the Latin verb *pejorare,* to make worse, which in turn arose from *pejor,* worse.

9. scissile   (sis′əl)   *capable of being readily cut or split*

Soft pine is a scissile kind of wood; mica is a scissile mineral.

> *Scissile* derives from *scissus,* past participle of *scindere,* to cut.
> Compare *scissors.* What then does *scission* mean?

10. stirious   (stē′rē əs)   *like an icicle*

A stalactite is a stirious rock formation.

> *Stirious,* listed in the dictionary as obsolete, comes from the Latin word *stiria,* icicle. Because it is very specific and could be quite useful, do you think this word should be revived?

part three

unit one

SOMETIMES

Which word from the list at the left fits best in each blank?

cavil
chagrin
emanate
calumny
alacrity
deter
collaborate
contemplate
immolation
coincide
dilemma
consternation
construe
condone

1. Scientists and businessmen _____ (work together) to develop a new product.
2. The political candidate refuses to _____ (approve indirectly) an opponent's tactics.
3. The prospect of punishment did not _____ (hinder) the murderer.
4. Investigators find themselves in a _____ (predicament) for which there is no obvious solution.
5. A respected public servant becomes a victim of _____ (slander).
6. A destructive flood or tornado causes the property owners _____ (dismay).
7. Students do their assignments with _____ (eagerness).
8. A person's goals and his achievements _____ (match exactly).
9. A good listener will _____ (interpret) a statement as you meant it.
10. Workable ideas often _____ (flow forth) from dreamy minds.

VERBS OF ATTITUDE AND SOCIAL RELATIONSHIP

1. cavil (kăv′əl) *to quibble, find fault frivolously*

Derek likes to cavil about local politics.
The lawyer's cavils relating to the evidence irritated the judge.
One council member spent an hour caviling about the cost of flood control.

> Compare *carp, captious* (p. 219).
> *Nitpicking* is an informal word for finding fault over minute or trivial details.

2. coincide   (kō ĭn sīd′)   *to match exactly, occupy the*
                                      same time or place

Hazel's air trip to London will coincide with her sister's trip to Paris.
By coincidence (kō ĭn′sə dəns) I met a college classmate on the streets of
Bombay.
The similarity of the two ballads supposedly by different songwriters is too
marked to be coincidental.

> *Identity* is the sameness of the essential character of two objects, situations, or
> points of view. For persons, it is who each one is.

3. collaborate   (kə lăb′ər āt′)   *to work together, cooperate*

Rodgers and Hammerstein collaborated on creating musical comedies.
Collaborators in the village helped the prisoners to escape.
Scientific experimenters have become more collaborative in recent years.

> *Collusion* is secret agreement or collaboration for a fraudulent purpose: That the
> car was near the scene of the robbery with the engine running suggests collusion.

4. condone   (kən dōn′)   *to excuse by seeming to overlook,*
                                  treat as if trivial

Employers who condone carelessness will suffer the consequences.
Eileen does not condone bad manners; she will admonish you.
Does publication of a convict's book imply condonation (kŏn′də nā′shən) of
his crime?

Modes of excusing:

> A *reprieve* literally or figuratively excuses a person temporarily from a penalty he
> must still pay.
> *Remission* is pardon or cancellation of sins, debts, or taxes; it also denotes the
> lessening or abating of a disease or of pain for a time.
> *Absolution* is release from sins or errors; complete forgiveness, especially by the
> Church or religious authorities. See -solu(t)- (p. 290).
> *Exculpation* and *exoneration* free one from blame for a crime or other offense one
> was accused of committing. Review *exonerate* (p. 124).
> *Amnesty* (p. 266) is pardon for political crimes against a regime.

5. construe   (kən strōō′)   *to interpret, explain*

Joyce construes her friend's bad manners as an affront.
Is a poor appetite construable as a sign of poor health?
Do not misconstrue the teacher's criticism; she simply wanted to help.

6. contemplate   (kŏn'təm plāt')   *meditate upon, gaze at,*
                                                    to intend or plan

Did you contemplate moving to the country in the spring?
From the brow of the hill, Jose contemplated the scene below.
A cathedral is a place especially conducive to contemplation.
Does Dvorak's *New World Symphony* make you contemplative (kən tĕm'plə
tĭv')?

   Review *meditate* and the "think" words (pp. 11–12).

7. deter   (dĭ tûr')   *to restrain through fear or doubt,*
                                               hinder or discourage

Failures did not deter climbers from the ascent of Mount Everest.
Do pictures of gruesome accidents have a deterrent effect on careless drivers?
Is a country's maintenance of vast military power a deterrent against war?

Other ways to restrain or discourage:

   To *dissuade* a person from climbing Mt. McKinley is to convince him he should
   not try.
   To *inhibit* him is to restrain him by making him deeply aware of the dangers and
   problems.
   To *enjoin* him is to urge him strongly to the point of forbidding, prohibiting, or
   taking legal action to prevent him.
   To *dishearten* a person is to reduce his eagerness so he no longer feels like climbing.
   To *daunt* him is to shake or weaken his courage to the point where he gives up.
   To *abash* or *overawe* him is to make him feel ashamed, uneasy, or unwise in con-
   templating the ascent.
   To *intimidate* him is to make him afraid, either of the mountain or of what you will
   do to him if he tries to climb it.

8. disparage   (dĭ spăr'ĭj)   *to belittle, speak slightingly of*

The coach is too wise to disparage a beginner's clumsy attempts.
Disparagement does not discourage a good debater.

Ways to belittle something:

   To *depreciate* it is to underrate or lower its value.
   To *detract* from it is to talk down its merits. See -tract- (p. 290).
   To *deride* it is to ridicule or make fun of it.
   To *minimize* it is to give the lowest estimate of its value or importance.
   To treat it with *irreverence* is to show lack of respect.
   To cast *aspersions* on it is to make derogatory or *disparaging* remarks.
   To *misprize* it is to scorn, despise, or undervalue its merits.

9. emanate   (ĕm'ə nāt)   *to flow or issue forth*

Reports which emanate from Peking often prove credible.
Bobbie knows that sincere courtesy emanates from sincere good will.
Emanations of energy from the sun include cosmic rays as well as light.

Related words:

> A river *emerges* (flows forth) from the hills, where it is said to "rise."
> A volcano or a riot *erupts* with much heat and considerable noise.
> Words *issue* (come forth) from one's lips. Each *issue* of *Mad* is eagerly read. The
> Army *issues* clothing and equipment.
> Coffee *percolates* (p. 277) when water flows through the coffee grounds.
> The pores of the skin *exude* (give forth) perspiration slowly. See <u>ex-</u> (p. 286).
> Many American words *derive* from Latin or Greek.

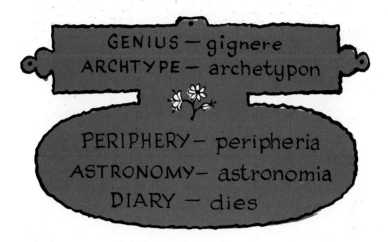

> GENIUS — gignere
> ARCHTYPE — archetypon
>
> PERIPHERY — peripheria
> ASTRONOMY — astronomia
> DIARY — dies

10. exemplify   (ĕg zĕm'plə fī')   *to serve as an example of*

A rainbow exemplifies the refractive action of sunlight on mist.
The life of Jesus offered a striking exemplification of His teachings.
The Chinese philosopher was a man of exemplary humility.

SITUATIONS AND RESPONSES

1. alacrity   (ə lăk'rə tē)   *lively willingness, briskness*

Ping Pong is a game requiring the alacrity of a grasshopper.
Firefighters must respond with alacrity to every alarm.

Modes of vitality:

> *Vivacity* is liveliness or aliveness (-<u>viv</u>-). A vivacious person is sprightly and full
> of life.
> *Verve* is liveliness plus enthusiasm and spirit. It may mark the dynamic imagination
> of a talented musician or writer.

Ardor (pp. 114, 361) is a burning eagerness, enthusiasm, or zeal.
Animation is aliveness, zest, or vivacious activity. See -<u>anim-</u> (p. 360).

2. calumny   (kăl′əm nē)   *slander, false and malicious statements*

The senator's record refutes the calumnies of his unscrupulous opponent, who accused him of dishonest practices.
Colleagues might calumniate (kə lŭm′nē āt′) a scientist holding unorthodox views.

> **Synonyms:** *defamation, vilification, traducement.* See *vilify* (p. 62).

Related words:

> *Scurrility* (obscene, coarsely jocular defamation); *lampoon* (comic or satiric abuse): *libel* (published vilification).

3. chagrin   (shə grĭn′)   *shame, vexation, humiliation*

The maestro who tripped on the podium tried to hide his chagrin.
Emily, stopping near the station to speak to a friend, was chagrined to see the train leave without her.
It was chagrining to Marty not to have a date for the class party.

> *Chagrin* comes from a French word meaning grief or sorrow. Compare *discomposure, mortification, embarrassment.*

4. consternation   (kŏn′stər nā′shən)   *amazement and terror, dismay*

The arrival of the Roman army spread consternation in Carthage.
The picnickers on the island stared at each other in consternation as their boat floated away.

> Compare *perturbation, palpitation, trepidation.*

> **Antonym:** *equanimity.*

5. dilemma   (dĭ lĕm′ə)   *a predicament, agonizing choice*

Manuela faced a dilemma: Should she remain silent about her friend's involvement in the incident?
The town's dilemma was how to maintain its air of quiet charm in the face of growing industrialization.

Related words:

> A *quandry* is a state of great anxiety or *perplexity* which is not, like a dilemma, a matter of clear-cut alternatives.
>
> An *impasse* is a deadlock or dilemma with no acceptable solution or escape: The strike had reached an impasse; neither side would compromise.

6. enigma (ĭ nĭg′mə)   *a puzzle, mystery, perplexing situation*

Sibyl's disappearance is an enigma the police cannot solve.

No one understood the student's enigmatic (ĕn′ĭg măt′ĭk) remark about having nothing to do.

The labor mediator, sensing the dilemma, smiled enigmatically (ĕn′ĭg măt′ĭ kəl lē).

Other puzzle words:

> *Anagram, charade, conundrum, cryptogram* (message in cipher), *labyrinth* (p. 6), *paradox* (p. 211).

7. erudition (ĕr′ə dĭsh′ən)   *learning, scholarly knowledge*

The publisher commissioned persons of great erudition to begin work on the encyclopedia.

One professor gave an erudite (ĕr′ə dīt *or* ĕr′yə dīt) answer to each of the questions on the subject of African history.

> *Sophistication* is "worldly" knowledge of what to eat, wear, and do; *erudition* is chiefly book knowledge or deep learning.
>
> Compare *savant, pundit*.

8. fecundity (fə kŭn′də tē)   *fruitfulness, productiveness*

Nature's fecundity depends on good soil and adequate rainfall.

Guinea pigs are noted for their fecundity.

Lope de Vega, a fecund genius, wrote more than a thousand plays.

> *Fruition* is fulfillment: The dreams of many pioneers found fruition in America.
>
> *Prolific* means productive or fruitful: Flies proliferate around open garbage cans.

9. immolation (ĭm′ō lā′shən)   *(act of) sacrificing or being sacrificed*

In a dramatic act of immolation, King Agamemnon sacrificed his daughter, Iphigenia, to obtain a favorable wind.
The hunger strike was an act of self-immolation.
Century by century, war mercilessly immolates its devotees.

10. innovation (ĭn′ə vā′shən)   *new method or custom, major change*

Standard-time zones in the U.S.A. were an innovation of the 1880s.
James Joyce was an innovator in stream-of-consciousness literature.

Acts of beginning:

> *Embarkation,* a going on board or a launching, is romantic. It calls up the picture of a ship setting sail for distant ports.
> *Inception* is an unromantic, businesslike word. It indicates the beginning of a method, system, plan, or affair.
> *Genesis* (p. 313) is a poetic word, often with hints of initial beauty and perfection: The genesis of painting may be found on the walls of ancient caves.
> *Initiative* (p. 69) is the act of beginning, or leading off: A person who wants friends should take the initiative.
> *Commencement* applies chiefly to graduations but has many other uses: The commencement of the business relationship at just that time had fatal consequences.
> *Inauguration* is a formal word. Typically, it puts a plan into operation or a person in office.

First practice set

What entry word in each unit best replaces each *italicized* word or group of words?

1. A *difficult choice* involving security made it impossible for the two scientists to *work together*.
2. It was a dangerous *new method* for the court to *excuse by apparently overlooking* a person's dishonesty.
3. An honorable person would not use *false and malicious statements* to *belittle* anyone.

4. *Shame* over her failure will not *restrain* Octavia *through fear* from taking the exam again.
5. One would hardly *interpret* the offhand remarks of the jockey as a piece of *scholarly knowledge*.
6. June's *terror* at the thought of performing in an assembly was surprising to *meditate upon*.
7. Dr. Browne refused to *find fault frivolously* about the reasons why a person would consider performing an act of self-*sacrifice* for society.
8. Set Enid any mathematical problem and with *lively willingness* she will devote herself to solving the *puzzle*.
9. Orders that *issue forth* from headquarters each day *serve as an example of* the unexpected way military units operate.
10. A graph showing the *productiveness* of the rabbit population almost *agrees* with the graph of the rainfall last year.

Second practice set

Which word from the list at the left best replaces each *italicized* word or group of words?

genesis
deride
depreciate
lampoon
libel
scurrility
absolution
emerge
inception
vivacity
incertitude
dissuade
verve
issue
scandal
flout
quandary
intimidate
animation
minimize
cryptogram
impasse
embarkation
exoneration

1. The *situation from which there is no escape* is far grimmer than a *state of great perplexity* would be.
2. It is easy to *underrate* the value of an education and to *give the lowest possible estimate of* its value.
3. *Eager liveliness* is a little more dynamic than mere *liveliness*.
4. After the rain you will see people *come out* from their homes and chat with *aliveness verging on vivacity*.
5. Speaking about the *beginning* of television and radio in the twentieth century, he traced their *poetic beginning* in the work of De Forest and Edison.
6. The church granted the man *complete release* from sin for the theft he had committed, and he gained *release from blame* for the crime he had not committed.
7. That *satiric abuse* is but one example of many to *come forth* from the pen of the student editor.
8. *Obscene defamation* is degrading to an author's reputation. *Printed defamation* may also lead to a lawsuit.
9. The *message in cipher* announcing the *departure* of a troop ship was handed to the general.
10. It is hard to *influence* Hal *away* from bad habits or to *make* him *afraid*.

Third practice set

On a separate sheet, write the numbers of the sentences. Beside each write the letter for the pair of words which best completes the sentence.

1. _____ and _____ are two qualities that make a personality lively and attractive.
   (a) Contemplation —
       emanation
   (b) Alacrity —
       initiative
   (c) Abashment —
       consternation
   (d) Innovation —
       calumniation

2. A writer and a composer may _____ on a musical comedy if their interests _____ to a sufficient degree.
   (a) disparage —
       exemplify
   (b) cavil —
       emanate
   (c) condone —
       disparage
   (d) collaborate —
       coincide

3. Without surgery, the patient would die, but she was too weak to survive an operation. Such was the _____ that _____ the doctor.
   (a) consternation —
       inhibited
   (b) dilemma —
       deterred
   (c) cavil —
       condoned
   (d) chagrin —
       emanated from

4. Stories that _____ the candidate's ability _____ from the opposition headquarters.
   (a) condone —
       issue
   (b) cavil about —
       collaborate
   (c) disparage —
       emanate
   (d) construe —
       derive

5. Political _____ _____ the treacherousness of those who invent them.
   (a) calumnies —
       exemplify
   (b) cavils —
       contemplate
   (c) dilemmas —
       condone
   (d) enigmas —
       disparage

6. "The Gold Bug" by Edgar Allan Poe describes an imaginary _____ which leads to _____ in finding Captain Kidd's treasure.
   (a) chagrin —
       indulgence
   (b) cryptogram —
       collaboration
   (c) alacrity —
       disparagement
   (d) consternation —
       contemplation

7. She may _____ , but do not _____ as indifference her reluctance to accept the gift.
   (a) erupt —
       condone
   (b) deter —
       disparage
   (c) coincide —
       contemplate
   (d) cavil —
       construe

8. A teacher cannot _____ laziness, however much he may sympathize with the _____ a reprimand causes.
   (a) condone —
       chagrin
   (b) contemplate —
       alacrity
   (c) collaborate —
       calumny
   (d) exemplify —
       absolution

9. The cause of the explosion was _____ , and the noise and smoke caused widespread _____ .
   (a) a dilemma —
       chagrin
   (b) a deterrent —
       impasse
   (c) cavil —
       coincidence
   (d) an enigma —
       consternation

10. Solitary _____ helps one achieve the _____ that grows into wisdom.
   (a) collaboration —
       construability
   (b) emanation —
       disenchantment
   (c) contemplation —
       erudition
   (d) fruition —
       condonation

The right word

Which word from this unit best replaces each *italicized* word or group of words?

1. The author advertised for a *cooperating person* to help with a book on Africa, someone who could write with *dynamic aliveness*.

2. The problem of dating the *beginning* of the crime wave created a *state of puzzled bewilderment* in the district attorney's office.

3. The director's *belittling comment* will not discourage the leading player or *make* her *uneasy* once she is on the stage.

4. The Eagle Scout is a person whose behavior is *worthy-of-serving-as-an-example,* an individual not susceptible to *slander.*

5. The study of rays which *flow forth* from radium helped scientists understand atoms long before the *beginning* of the Atomic Age.

WORD BY WORD THE BOOK IS MADE....

Word on word

1. Compile a list of words beginning with <u>viv-</u> (live or alive). Add words formed with one of the prefixes in IV, 1 and IV, 2, plus -<u>viv-</u> and endings.
2. See <u>hypo-</u> in p. 331 and then, using a dictionary, make a list of ten additional <u>hypo-</u> words worth knowing.
3. Assume that you are a judge, legislator, or editorial writer. Compose a paragraph on a recent murder, a political scandal, or a current issue. You will be able to use many of the words from this unit, such as *disparagement, calumny, chagrin, coincidence,* and *cavil.*

unit two

COUPLES

Which verb from the list at the left tells what one would probably do about:

subsidize
vindicate
repudiate
mediate
reconcile
temporize
reciprocate
emancipate
placate
usurp
relegate
felicitate

1. Slaves? _____ them.

2. Two friends who have quarreled violently? _____ them.

3. Deadlocked strike negotiations? _____ the differences.

4. Dinners and social affairs you have enjoyed with friends? _____ them.

5. A demented assailant armed with knife or gun? _____ him.

6. A friend misjudged or misunderstood? _____ him.

7. A broken chair? _____ it to the cellar or to oblivion.

8. A friend very angry with you? _____ her.

9. A mistaken or misquoted statement attributed to you? _____ it.

10. Two friends who have just become engaged? _____ them.

ADJECTIVES

1. altruistic   (ăl′trōō ĭs′tik)   *unselfishly concerned for others*

Altruistic youth groups will distribute food to needy families.
Altruism (ăl′trōō ĭz əm) is a favorite activity of wealthy Americans.
Volunteer work of various kinds attracts altruists of all ages.

Related words:

> A *charitable* act, like giving to the Salvation Army, is altruistic in a specific and limited way.
> A *philanthropic* project, like a youth center or a new hospital, serves the community in a larger way than individual charitable acts, and calls for large donations.
> A *humanitarian* undertaking, like a day nursery for working mothers or an anti-poverty program, aims at creating a better life for others.
> A *charismatic* figure like Lincoln is one beloved, romantic, and appealing in a broad humanitarian sense.
> Compare *beneficent, benevolent* (p. 150).

2. astute   (ə stoot′)   *shrewd, crafty, keen of mind*

Our team was astute enough to exploit our rival's weaknesses.
A detective's astuteness in tracking down clues led to the killer's capture.
Astutely appraising the situation, Eunice was able to offer the family some good advice.

> *Acumen* is mental sharpness or acuteness, especially in a business or activity where know-how and experience, but not craftiness, are involved.
> Compare *adroit* (p. 107), *wily* (p. 23), *discerning* (p. 10), *sagacious* (p. 202), *perspicacious* (pp. 200, 202).

3. authentic   (ȯ thĕn′tĭk)   *genuine, entitled to acceptance*

Verification of the signature proved the will to be authentic.
Precise geographical references show the authenticity (ȯ′thĕn tĭs′ə tē) of biblical stories about Hebrew migrations in the Arabian desert.
Affidavits authenticate the letter from Hawthorne to his wife.

> The *historicity* of Homer is his genuineness as a historical figure. Was there such a person, and did he write the *Iliad*? Did a woman write the *Odyssey*?

4. cumulative   (kyōōm'yə lə tĭv)   *tending to increase*
                                                        or accumulate

Stan's tireless exertions kept his cumulative average from declining.
A cumulativeness of fatigue and worry was the cause of Mona's exhaustion.

Related words:

> A library is an *accumulation* of books.
> A collection of facts about a subject is a *compilation*.
> An assortment of people or things is an *aggregation*.
> A mass of people gathered for worship is a *congregation*. See -greg- (p. 316).

5. despondent   (dĭ spŏn'dənt)   *dejected, despairing*

The sufferings of his young wife made Poe despondent.
David relieved Saul's despondency by playing on his harp.

> Compare *melancholy* (p. 116).

6. didactic   (dĭ dăk'tĭk)   *morally instructive*

Greek drama was intended to be didactic as well as entertaining.
Some parents tend to be too didactic and not exemplary enough.

7. ecclesiastical   (ĭ klē'zē ăs'tĭ kəl)   *pertaining to church or clergy,*
                                               especially as an established institution

A stray dog, intruding on the cathedral service, badly upset the bishop's ecclesiastical dignity.
Catholic ecclesiastical authority culminates in the Pope.
The Archbishop of Canterbury is an influential ecclesiastic.

> *Ecclesiasticism* attaches great importance to rituals, liturgy, and church traditions: Baptist churches forgo ecclesiasticism.
> *Ecclesiastes* (meaning the Preacher) is the title of an Old Testament book.

8. felicitous   (fə lĭs'ə təs)   *fortunate, aptly chosen,*
                                                        happily conceived

At eighty, Great-grandmother considered her birthday a felicitous occasion.
Shakespeare expressed himself with unusual felicitousness.
Always felicitate (congratulate) the groom, not the bride.
Wish the bride unqualified felicity (good fortune, bliss) instead.

9. imperial   (ĭm pêr'ē əl)   *majestic, befitting an emperor*

The bridal procession moved down the aisle with imperial solemnity.
Communists accuse the United States of imperialism, *i.e.*, of trying by force
or by intrigue to dominate other nations.
The owner had a right to order me off his property, but he did not need to be
so imperious (overbearing) about it.

Words of power:

Imperial and *empire* both come from the Latin word *imperium* (sovereignty).
A *regal* attitude is a royal one—that of a king or queen.
Monarchial privileges are those of a monarch.
Dynastic dreams are imperial: You want to rule and to establish a *dynasty* (succession of rulers).
Feudal power was that of a medieval lord over his serfs and retainers.
Patriarchal power is that of a father, especially an elderly father, whether as a respected family head, a tribal chief, or a dignitary of the Greek Catholic church.
Matriarchal, analogous to patriarchal, power is that of the mother or grandmother, as in some cultures.
Aristocratic power is that of wealth, prestige, upper-class birth, or great knowledge (*aristo,* in Greek, means the best).

10. odious   (ō′de əs)   *hateful, offensive*

The odors of decay are odious.
Laziness is an odious quality, but it may spur inventiveness.
The odiousness of treachery led Dante to relegate traitors to the lowest, or Ninth Circle, of his Inferno.

Hate words:

Detestable, abhorrent (p. 286), *obnoxious* (p. 46), *repugnant, despicable, contemptible, abominable, heinous.* See *antipathy* (p. 342).

VERBS

1. emancipate   (ĭ măn′sə pāt′)   *liberate, set free*

With her first real job, Irena felt completely emancipated from parental control.
Martin Luther King was a modern emancipator.
Knowledge brings intellectual emancipation: "Ye shall know the truth, and the truth shall make you free."

Ways to emancipate:

To *disenthrall* a person is to free him from literal or figurative slavery (*thrall* means slave). It is more specific, more individualized than *emancipate*.

To *redeem* a slave is to buy him back and thus liberate him; *redeeming* a debt or obligation is making good on it (pp. 12, 278).

To *ransom* a person or object is to redeem it by paying the sum demanded, especially in a kidnapping case.

To *disencumber* is to set one free from burdens or obligations less onerous than slavery, debt, or captivity.

2. mediate   (mē′dē āt′)   *to act as go-between, serve as harmonizing agent*

The strikers and the owners chose a lawyer specializing in labor problems to mediate their dispute.

She set up a mediation board to work out a settlement.

The lawyer had served as mediator in previous disputes.

Related words:

An *arbiter* (arbitrator) has more authority than a mediator.

To *arbitrate* a dispute is to settle it by giving a decision or judgment.

Sometimes *arbitration* is compulsory.

An *intercessor* pleads (*intercedes*) on behalf of one side or the other.

An *intermediary* is merely a go-between or messenger between two hostile parties.

Compare *interfere, intervene, interpose, interpolate.*

3. reciprocate   (rĭ sĭp′rə kāt′)   *repay an obligation, social or otherwise, exchange favors or courtesies*

If a new friend sends a Christmas gift, naturally you will reciprocate.

Reciprocation in cultural affairs was the backbone of the agreement between the two colleges.

Marriage demands much reciprocity (rĕs′ə prŏs′ə tē) (mutual sharing, give and take).

> **Query:** What are *reciprocal* trade agreements? What are the *reciprocating* parts of a bicycle? A locomotive?

4. reconcile   (rĕk′ən sīl′)   *to bring to agreement, harmonize*

All attempts to reconcile the overbearing father and his proud daughter failed.

Friends did all they could to effect a reconciliation (rĕk′ən sīl′ē ā′shən).

The offending country sent a conciliatory note to its outraged neighbor.

Heavy government spending and a lowered tax rate are considered by many to be irreconcilable.

Related words:

To *conciliate* is to pacify or satisfy: How do you conciliate a malicious enemy? *Conciliation* is typically a mutual process between equals.

To *placate* is to make agreeable or calm: You try to placate an angry or ferocious watchdog.

5. relegate   (rĕl′ə gāt′)   *to banish or to reduce to lower status*

We will relegate Woofer to the basement if he barks all night.
Why not give away some of the furniture we relegated to the attic?
Relegation of run-down cars to junk yards makes the highways safer.

6. repudiate   (rĭ pyōō′dē āt′)   *to disavow, disown, reject*

The company was quick to repudiate the agent's promise that its machines
would last a lifetime.
After the coup, the new rulers announced their repudiation of the debts of the
former government.

> One may repudiate a claim, a child, a belief, an accusation, a debt.
> The Latin verb *pudere* (to feel shame) appears also in *impudent* (shameless) and
> *pudency* (bashfulness).

7. subsidize   (sŭb′sə dīz′)   *to provide financial aid*

The federal government subsidizes farmers by buying their surplus crops at
prices above the market value.
Subsidies (sŭb′sə dēz) to developing countries or industries help them buy
what the United States must sell to keep production at normal levels.
The cost of transportation is a subsidiary (səb sĭd′ē ĕr′ē) (supplementary, but
not dominant) factor in selecting a site for the new factory.

Ways to give aid:

> *Donate, subscribe, patronize, sustain, succor.* What is the special use of each?

8. temporize   (tĕm′pə rīz′)   *to act evasively to gain time,*
                                                            yield temporarily to circumstances

The researcher found it safe to temporize by cautious or ambiguous statements
on ticklish topics he had not yet investigated.
Many young people will temporize by going out with a number of friends until
they can decide which ones they like best.

> See -temp- (time) words (p. 341).
> *Temporary*—lasting for a (short) *time* only: A temporary license.
> *Extemporaneous*—unpremeditated, done with little or no preparation.
> *Temporal*—limited in duration, not eternal; pertaining to this world only: Tem-
> poral blessings may obscure spiritual values.

9. usurp (yoō sûrp′)   ***to seize (power or control) unlawfully***

A small military group managed to usurp the power of the rightful government. Like most usurpers, the leaders found a way to make their usurpation sound legal.

> One may usurp an office, a place, powers, or rights.
> To *arrogate* to oneself a privilege or honor is to seize it in a high-handed or haughty manner: He arrogated to himself the right to order the guests around in his daughter's house.

10. vindicate (vĭn′də kāt′)   ***to justify, clear of a charge or criticism***

Police investigation vindicated the driver, who had been charged with criminal negligence.
Columbus was able to vindicate his belief that the earth is round.
It took two decades to effect the vindication of the judge.

First practice set

Which entry word in this unit best replaces each *italicized* word or phrase?

1. The letters of the *church* leaders were full of *aptly chosen* phrases.
2. It was *shrewd* of the labor leaders to stress their desire to *liberate* laborers from long hours and low pay.
3. The discovery that the letters showing the governor's guilt were not *genuine* should *justify* him.
4. The coach had to *banish* the two players to the second team because they could not *bring* their differences *to agreement*.
5. The lawyer, who is very *unselfishly concerned for others,* was glad to *serve as go-between* in the airline dispute.

6. The prince did not *yield temporarily to circumstances;* rather, he set about immediately to *seize wrongfully* his mother's throne.

7. The state's refusal to *grant financial aid to* the scientist for her experiment made her *dejected*.

8. His idea of the presidency became *one befitting an emperor*, which made him very *hateful* to the country that had elected him.

9. The effect of the politican's critical remarks was *increasing in quantity*, but he would not *disavow* them.

10. The parable is a *morally instructive* tale; for example, it may teach that you should *pay back* favors, or lend a helping hand to those in need.

Second practice set

Which word from the list at the left best replaces each *italicized* word or group of words?

temporal
impudent
patriarchal
charitable
historicity
dissent
disenthrall
placate
ransom
intermediary
extemporaneous
humanitarian
temporary
redeem
arrogate
heinous
charismatic
feudal
disencumber
intercessor
repugnant
philanthropist
acumen
regal
obnoxious
compilation
arbitrate

1. The rector plays the role of *one who begs or pleads,* and his curate or assistant is the *go-between*.

2. It was necessary for Doreen to *calm (down)* the belligerents before she could *settle* the dispute.

3. Henry II, not content with *worldly* power, wanted to *seize* for himself certain rights of the Church.

4. The *genuineness (as a historical personage)* of Paul Bunyan is immaterial; he has become a *beloved and romantic* figure.

5. Andrew Carnegie was a famous *altruist (donating large sums),* while President Franklin Roosevelt is remembered as an outstanding *leader in reducing human suffering*.

6. Mother expressed her strong *feelings of disagreement* when Roger refused to *make good on* his debt to the family.

7. Knowledge *frees* one from bondage to superstition and *sets* one *free* from the burdens of needless precautions.

8. The administrator's *unpremeditated* speech showed her *mental sharpness*.

9. A *medieval* landowner's power should not be confused with the *royal* powers of the monarch.

10. The *fatherly* authority of the archbishop made no impression on the *shameless* young lord.

Third practice set*

Which lettered pair of items comes nearest to having the same relationship as the pair printed in capital letters?

1. MEDIATE:ARBITRATE:: (a) usurp:elect (b) incinerate:scorch (c) pacify:reconcile (d) repudiate:reciprocate

2. EMANCIPATE:ENSLAVE:: (a) vindicate:incriminate (b) felicitate:authenticate (c) vindicate:reciprocate (d) relegate:reconcile

3. ODIOUS:HEINOUS:: (a) intentional:impudent (b) unselfish:altruistic (c) amorous:felicitous (d) amicable:inimical

4. EGOTIST:ALTRUIST:: (a) amity:amicability (b) illumination:incineration (c) accusation:vindication (d) usurper:inheritor

5. TEMPORAL:ECCLESIASTICAL:: (a) monarchial:imperious (b) didactic:felicitous (c) extemporaneous:premeditated (d) charitable:abominable

6. RELEGATE:FURNITURE:: (a) party:reciprocate (b) cremate:corpse (c) temporize:politicians (d) repudiate:agreement

7. SIGNATURE:AUTHENTICATE:: (a) party:reciprocate (b) cremate:corpse (c) reputation:vindicate (d) lawyer:mediate

8. VINDICATE:REPUDIATE:: (a) mediate:temporize (b) officiate:felicitate (c) emancipate:enthrall (d) relegate:placate

9. IMPERIAL:EMPIRE:: (a) despondent:mediation (b) authentic:letters (c) amicable:didacticism (d) humanitarian:altruism

10. UNHAPPINESS:FELICITY:: (a) slavery:emancipation (b) selfishness:egotism (c) usurpation:tyranny (d) public debt:taxes

---

*This is the first of several exercises to provide practice in finding a relationship or analogy between words paired together. Sometimes the pairs are related because they are synonyms *(cold:chilly)* or antonyms *(cold:hot)*. Sometimes one word in the pair may describe the other *(elephant:large)*, may indicate a product *(carpenter:porch)*, or may motivate the other *(fear:flight)*.

unit three

OPPOSITES

From the list at the left choose the word which is most nearly the *opposite* of each numbered item.

propriety
recumbency
propensity
surfeit
tentativeness
prerogative
perspicacity
predilection
succinctness
prostration
sagacity
vicissitude

1. Stupidity, obtuseness
2. Long-windedness
3. Finality
4. Recuperation
5. Invariability
6. Unsound judgment
7. Scarcity
8. Nonconformity
9. Upright position
10. Lack of fondness or of inclination toward

NOUNS

1. perspicacity   (pur′spə kăs′ə te)   ***mental penetration,***
discernment

Early Americans had the perspicacity to realize that some day the United States would be a great nation.
A perspicacious (pûr′spə kā′shəs) young person, Regina likes to play chess.
The speaker explained space travel with great perspicuity (pûr′spə kyōō′ə tē).

> *Perspicacity* and *perspicuity* come from <u>per</u>- (through) plus -<u>spic</u>- (p. 342). The first implies acuteness of discernment; the second includes clarity and lucidity of expression as well.
> See *acute* (p. 51) and *astute* group (p. 192).

2. predilection (prĕd'ə lĕk'shən)   *preconceived preference or partiality*

Beth has a predilection for the color blue.
Is the American predilection for large automobiles on the wane?

> **Antonym:** *prejudice,* a preconceived or irrational dislike.

Related words:

> A *bias* is an unreasoned preference or slant, favorable or unfavorable: The referee showed a bias for our team.
> A *predisposition* is a susceptibility, a bent, or a natural (but not preconceived) preference. Gladys, the daughter of an actor, has a strong predisposition toward a theatrical career. Because Jerome was raised in Atlanta, he was *predisposed* to root for the Braves.

3. prerogative (prĭ rŏg'ə tĭv')   *privilege, right*

It is your prerogative to choose your own career.
To select the pianist to accompany her at the concert was the singer's prerogative.

> See *option* and related words (p. 125).

4. propensity (prə pĕn'sə tē)   *natural tendency, bent*

From childhood Al had a propensity for getting into trouble.
A propensity for mathematics suggests a career in engineering.

Related words:

> A *penchant* is a strong liking or taste for some odd habit or objects: Lucy has a penchant for walking in the rain.
> *Propensity* and *penchant* both come from the Latin *pendere* (hang or weigh). See -pend- (p. 289).
> A *proclivity* is a propensity for something objectionable, like swearing.
> *Proneness* is a human weakness or leaning toward a quality or an attitude: Proneness to error is proverbial.

5. propriety (prə prī'ə tē)   *conformity to accepted standards of behavior, rightness or suitability*

An etiquette book crisply catalogs the rules of propriety.
War and riots disrupt many of the proprieties of human existence.

> Compare *decorum, amenity* (p. 246).

6. prostration   (prŏs trā′shən)   *a falling down in worship,*
                                                             exhaustion

In ancient Japan, one of the proprieties was the act of prostration before the
emperor.
Islam also requires a worshiper to prostrate himself in prayer.
The weary runner lay prostrate on the ground.
Nervous prostration and heat prostration are forms of exhaustion.

Related words:

A physical *collapse* frequently prostrates a person.
Invalidism is a state of chronic prostration if the person must stay in bed most of
the time.
Despair and *despondency* are figurative forms of prostration.

7. restitution   (rĕs′tə tōō′shən)   *restoration, reparation*

If you wreck a friend's car, you must make restitution.
Experts say restitution is vital in rehabilitating criminals.

Types of restoration:

To make *reparation* is to pay for the material damage one has done.
Compensation (p. 202) is payment to cover injuries or damage for which a person
is responsible: Workmen's compensation laws protect employees.
Indemnification is repayment by an insurance company for what one has lost, or
by a government agency for what one has spent: A person asks indemnification
for a car destroyed in a riot.
Reinstatement is restoration to a post or position from which one has been unjustly
removed: A dismissed employee may demand reinstatement.
Rehabilitation is the restoration of a person to health or usefulness: The rehabilitation of disabled war veterans is often a costly process.
Recuperation is usually recovery from illness or exhaustion.

8. sagacity   (sə găs′ə tē)   *shrewdness, sound judgment*

The pilot's sagacity kept the ship from foundering in the storm.
Queen Victoria was a sagacious ruler of an empire.
Emerson was called ''the sage (sāj) [profoundly wise man] of Concord.''
Franklin's *Poor Richard's Almanac* is full of sage advice.

Perspicacity stresses insight and the understanding of dark and difficult matters.
Sagacity, on the other hand, is practical wisdom with far-sightedness and the
ability to make intelligent decisions.

Other types of brain skill:

Penetration, judiciousness, discretion (p. 39), *acumen* (p. 192), *acuteness, astuteness* (p. 52).

9. surfeit   (sûr′fət)   ***excess, disgust from excess***

Members of the road company felt a sense of surfeit of travel and a longing for
a permanent home.
Surfeit of success often makes a person complacent and vain.
Thanksgiving dinner will surfeit (fill to excess) the heartiest eater.

Degrees of satiety:

   Suffice, satisfy, satiate (p. 29), *sate, surfeit, glut* (fill disgustingly full).

10. vicissitude   (vǐ sǐs′ə tōōd)   ***irregular change, ups and downs***

A political figure often finds the vicissitudes of public life and the uncertainty
of reelection hard to endure.
Most psychologists agree that adolescence is a time of emotional stress and
disturbing vicissitudes.

ADJECTIVES

1. lambent   (lăm′bənt)   ***softly radiant, playing lightly over a surface***
or subject

The lambent firelight filled the room with dancing shadows.
The principal was a kindly person whose lambent wit delighted us all.

2. latent   (lā′tənt)   ***hidden or unrevealed, potential***

The woman had latent executive ability no one knew about until she had to
take over the family business.
Coal contains latent heat. Do bulbs contain latent flowers?

   Potential skill is undeveloped or unrealized capability.
   Dormant ability is unawakened or not operative at the moment.

3. marital   (măr′ə təl)   *of, or relating to, marriage*

Marital responsibilities usually have a steadying effect on people.
A court of marital relations solves many problems of wedlock.

Related words:

> *Conjugal* harmony is harmony between persons joined together in marriage. See
> con- (with) and -juga- (join) (p. 307).
> *Nuptial* events are those pertaining to a wedding or to marriage.
> *Domestic* interests are those of the household or of one's country.

4. partisan   (pär′tə zən)   *one-sided; partial to a party or cause;*
                                             supporter of an idea or person

Often the election of judges becomes a partisan issue.
A partisan (supporter) of the public housing program will speak on Friday.
Baseball is a sport which stirs strong partisanship (taking of sides).
The amendment to the state constitution has much nonpartisan support among
the voters.

Related words:

> A *disciple* is a follower, literally a learner, attached to some great leader or teacher:
> Plato was a disciple of Socrates.
> An *advocate* is a supporter or champion of a principle, a cause, or an idea: Gandhi
> was an advocate of civil disobedience.
> A *patron* is a customer who buys from a given dealer, or a contributor to a phil-
> anthropic project.
> An *abettor* assists or supports a questionable undertaking of some kind: They
> were found to be abettors of a swindling ring.
> A *votary* is an ardent, devoted supporter of a cause or ideal, often with religious
> zeal: Yoga has its votaries.
> A *devotee* is a person deeply attached to a pastime, art, or religious goal: Devotees
> of drag racing die young.

5. recumbent   (rĭ kŭm′bənt)   *reclining or leaning, inactive*

The recumbent figure on the bed is my aunt taking her Sunday nap.
A hobo in a position of recumbency on the park bench was oblivious to the
passers-by.
The workers relaxed in recumbent positions against a stone wall while they
ate lunch.

> An *incumbent* duty is one which is obligatory, *i.e.,* it lies heavily upon a person:
> It is incumbent upon a worker to find a job.
> The holder of an office is called the *incumbent:* Mr. Mead, a candidate for county
> treasurer, denounced the incumbent bitterly.

6. salient   (sā'lē ənt)   *prominent, conspicuous, outward*
                                                         projecting angle

Major Rich outlined the salient points of the company's new recruiting plan.
One salient argument for a world government is the convenience it would provide for travel and commerce.
The left salient of the battle line was vulnerable because it was nearer to the
enemy's gun emplacements.

7. seditious   (sə dĭsh'əs)   *inciting discontent or rebellion*

A wave of seditious whispering stirred the crew.
Sedition was afoot, and the authorities searched for its leaders.

Related words:

> *Treason* is overt action like giving secrets to the enemy in wartime, or trying to
> overthrow the government by illegal means.
> *Subversion* is the seditious process of making a loyal citizen rebellious.
> *Mutiny, anarchy,* and *insurrection* (p. 211) are also results of discontent.

8. succinct   (sək sĭngkt')   *terse, concise*

The Indian's advice was eloquently succinct: "Go home."
How do telegrams encourage succinctness?

Other terse words:

> *Laconic* (p. 163), *concise, compact* (p. 210), *sententious* (terse, pithy), *aphoristic.*
> See *brevity* (p. 13).
> *Ellipsis* is a form of brevity attained by omitting words normally employed to com-
> plete or round out a sentence: Liked Jamaica. Decided to stay. *Ellipsis* is also
> used of words omitted and represented by three dots or, if a period is included in
> the omitted words, by four dots.

Antonyms: *prolix, verbose, garrulous* (p. 221).

9. tangible   (tăn'jə bəl)   *real, substantial, palpable*

There is no tangible evidence that ghosts exist.

The case against the hitchhiker lacks tangibility—no fingerprints, no witnesses, no weapon, no confession.

Faith and hope are intangible qualities one cannot touch or see.

Good will is an intangible asset in a business.

Tangible words:

> A *tangible* object is one you can touch or feel; a tangible idea is one you can grasp readily.
>
> A *palpable* fact is obvious, evident, one that makes itself felt (p. 91).
>
> A *perceptible* condition is just barely seen or sensed.
>
> A *discernible* detail can be seen or sensed more readily (p. 10).
>
> An *appreciable* difference is big enough to be recognized.
>
> A *manifest* shortcoming is immediately clear or evident (pp. 4, 28, 91, 343).

10. tentative   (tĕn′tə tĭv)   *provisional, experimental*

The tentative draft of the annexation plan can be changed before it is typed in final form.

The tentativeness of the diagnosis makes the doctor reluctant to tell the patient what apparently is wrong.

First practice set

Which entry word from this unit best replaces each *italicized* word or group of words?

1. Sylvia, the daughter of a professor, had a *preconceived preference* for friends with some *mental penetration*.
2. The depressed retiree had a *natural tendency* for thinking he was near the point of *exhaustion*.
3. The firm will make *reparation* to anyone it has wronged, especially those suffering from the *ups and downs* of an uncertain market.
4. The *provisional* topic for the discussion was *conformity to accepted standards* in dress for business and sport.
5. It is an employer's *privilege* to seek *potential* selling ability wherever it can be found among employees.
6. The store's buyers showed *sound judgment* in avoiding an *excess* of strictly seasonal stock.
7. The *softly radiant* twilight fell and breezes fanned the *reclining* figure of the family's patriarch.
8. Telex provides *substantial* examples of *concise* messages.
9. A *conspicuous* argument of those engaged in *activities inciting to rebellion* was that the head of state had in effect *usurped* the premiership.
10. Men and women often take opposite and thus *one-sided* views on *marriage* issues.

Second practice set

Which word from the list at the left best replaces each *italicized* word or group of words?

subversion
reinstatement
patron
rehabilitation
proclivity
advocate
compensation
devotee
discernible
potential
indemnification
palpable
manifest
conjugal
domestic
incumbent
predisposition
penchant
dormant
bias
reparation
disciple
recuperation

1. The referee had a clear *susceptibility beforehand* for our type of team but showed no *unreasoned preference* in calling fouls.
2. Ada has a *strong taste* for science fiction and also, unfortunately, a *propensity* for staying up too late reading.
3. A demand was made for *restoration (to his former position)* of the teacher ousted for alleged irregularity in *marital* affairs.
4. Brother Juniper was looking for *learner-followers* who would become *dedicated persons* of his faith.
5. Maple trees are *temporarily inactive* during the winter, but their buds are very *readily seen* in the spring.
6. Alexander Hamilton, a strong *supporter or champion* of federal power, had a strong *unrealized capability* as a future President.
7. The *present* (judge) says the *remuneration* is not enough.
8. Dynamiting the bridge was a(n) *evident* act of *sedition*.
9. After weeks of *recovery,* Julie was able to resume her *household* duties.
10. For its *obvious (strongly felt)* error of forgetting to put the oil back into the crankcase, the garage management offered to rebuild the engine by way of *paying for the damage*.

Third practice set

Which lettered pair of items comes nearest to having the same relationship as the pair printed in capital letters?

1. VERBOSITY:SUCCINCTNESS::   (a) redemption:treason   (b) reinstatement:prostration   (c) variability:vicissitude   (d) obtuseness:perspicacity

2. PROPENSITY:PENCHANT::   (a) perspicacity:sagacity   (b) prerogative:proclivity   (c) stability:vicissitude   (d) propriety:restitution

3. SAGACITY:FOOLISHNESS::   (a) salience:inconspicuousness   (b) restitution:reparation   (c) bias:propriety   (d) satiety:surfeit

4. INTANGIBLE:PALPABLE:: (a) sagacious:recumbent (b) treasonable:seditious (c) imperceptible:discernible (d) potential:latent

5. LACONIC:SUCCINCT:: (a) domestic:sagacious (b) incumbent:recumbent (c) palpable:tangible (d) salient:potential

6. PREDILECTION:PREJUDICE:: (a) tangibility:latency (b) predisposition:proclivity (c) sagacity:perspicuity (d) partisanship:sedition

7. RECUMBENT:PROSTRATION:: (a) nuptial:marriage (b) palpability:tangible (c) incumbent:reinstatement (d) seditious:treason

8. TENTATIVE DRAFT:FINAL DRAFT:: (a) candidate:incumbent (b) succinct speech:concise speech (c) lambent gazes:angry looks (d) reparation:redemption

9. SHORTAGE:SURFEIT:: (a) incumbent:recumbent (b) partisanship:discipleship (c) invariability:vicissitude (d) bias:predisposition

10. LOYALTY:SEDITION:: (a) lack of propriety:breach of etiquette (b) perspicacity:stupidity (c) palpability:tangibility (d) irreverence:prostration

A WORD SPOKEN IS AN ARROW LET FLY...

THOMAS FULLER

unit four

WEIRD OR SINISTER

Choose the word which completes each statement best.

1. A sorcerer delves in: (a) occultism (b) forensics (c) plagiarism (d) coalitions
2. Three countries, united for a time to face a common enemy, form: (a) a covenant (b) a coalition (c) an insurrection (d) an incentive
3. A crime that may be described as a kind of theft is: (a) aestheticism (b) exoticism (c) plagiarism (d) paradox
4. Ghostly monsters hiding in alleys are: (a) ineffable (b) occult (c) chimerical (d) aesthetic
5. Arabian food is likely to look and taste: (a) diabolic (b) fetishistic (c) exotic (d) chimerical
6. A person educated in the fine arts is considered: (a) occult (b) paradoxical (c) aesthetic (d) exotic
7. A question bearing on the subject under discussion is: (a) relevant (b) forensic (c) paradoxical (d) portentous
8. An object worshipped for its magical power is: (a) a paradox (b) a solstice (c) a fetish (c) a paragon
9. A conjunction of planets is considered: (a) exotic (b) paradoxical (c) occult (d) portentous
10. Spring sunshine could well be described as: (a) exotic (b) ineffable (c) chimerical (d) occult

NOUNS

1. coalition (kō ə lĭsh′ən)   ***combination or alliance (especially of opposing parties and usually temporary)***

An unexpected coalition of conservatives and liberals defeated the tax measure in the Senate.

After consultations, the Premier of France set up a coalition cabinet.

If you heat the crystals, they will coalesce (kō′ə lĕs′) (fuse, unite).

Labor wants a coalescence of the two unions.

Compare *league, confederation, federation, union.*

2. covenant   (kûv′ə nənt)   *solemn agreement or compact*

Marriage is a covenant between two people in love.
The Covenant of the League of Nations was also its constitution.
The church covenant condemns discrimination on the basis of race.

> A *covenant* generally includes an oath to uphold a principle or belief.
> What was the Solemn League and Covenant in English history? What was a Covenanter?
> A *compact* or a *pact* is a solemn agreement but with less of an intensely personal and religious flavor than a covenant.
> A *contract* is a legal agreement, usually written, by which one party agrees to perform some service for the other for some kind of compensation.

3. fetish   (fĕt′ĭsh)   *something worshiped for its magical power*

The chieftain kept the tribal fetish in his possession.
The student made a fetish of being the most popular person in the school.
Vitamin pills can become a fetish.
Among some peoples, fetishism may include the worship of animals.
Avoiding the number 13 is a fetishistic practice.

Related words:

> A *talisman* is a ring, stone, or other object carved with symbols which are supposed to have magic powers. It may also be any good-luck token.
> An *amulet* is a charm worn to ward off evil.

Devil words:

> *Diabolism* is devil worship, sorcery, or witchcraft: Faust had an adventure in diabolism. See *diabolical* (p. 145) under *vicious.*
> *Necromancy* is divination, *i.e.,* foretelling the future by communicating with the dead (p. 332).
> *Exorcism,* the process of driving away evil spirits, has been revived in certain churches.

Worship words:

> *Idolatry* (worship of idols); *heliolatry* (sun worship); *zoolatry* (animal worship); *bibliolatry* (worship of books).

4. incentive   (ĭn sĕn′tĭv)   *stimulus, that which stirs one to do or be*

The annual poetry prize at the college provides an incentive for all who write verse.
Overtime pay was an incentive for the laborers to work on weekends.

> *Incentives* ordinarily come from a source outside the person.
> *Motives* arise within a person, often as a result of outside influences.

5. incubus   (ĭng′kyə bəs)   *nightmare, depressing burden*

An incubus of fear haunted the killer day and night.
France at that time was staggering under an incubus of debt.

> An *incubus* was originally a demon supposed to cause nightmares by lying upon a sleeping person.

6. insurrection   (ĭn′sə rek′shən)   *armed uprising or rebellion*

Troops quickly quelled the insurrection in the Central American country that we were visiting.
Three leading insurrectionists were captured and convicted.

> *Insurrection* and *insurgent* come from the same Latin verb, *surgere,* to rise. An *insurgent* may be a rebel who opposes his own political party.

Modes of revolt:

> A *boycott* is a peaceful revolt in which one refuses the goods or services of the object of the revolt.
> A *riot* is a small, violent, ostensibly unorganized revolt against civil authorities.
> An *uprising* is an outbreak against the government, usually more deliberate and less spontaneous than a riot.
> A *mutiny* is a revolt, especially by a ship's crew or a military unit, in which the individuals refuse to perform their duties.
> A *revolution*, which may be violent or peaceful, is bigger and lasts longer than a riot or uprising. The term is often applied to a successful revolt.

7. paradox   (păr′ə dŏks′)   *self-contradictory statement*
                                                                  or condition

One can love and hate a person at the same time; this is the paradox of ambivalence.
Marcus Aurelius, a Roman ruler, was a paradoxical person who forgave his enemies, practiced brotherhood of man, and yet hated the Christians.
"Death, thou shalt die!" is a paradoxical line from Donne's poetry.

8. paragon   (păr′ə gŏn′)   *perfect model or pattern*

The captain of the basketball team is a paragon of modesty.
Shakespeare is a paragon of British dramatic poets.

9. plagiarism   (plā′jə rĭz′əm)   *the stealing of ideas,*
                                                                  the stolen ideas

Copying part or all of a term paper from a book or from another person's work is plagiarism.
A student or anyone else who thus steals material is a plagiarist.

Composers may plagiarize old music and modernize it as their own. Such plagiarism is venial because the music is no longer under copyright and the composer has contributed something substantial.

> *Plagiarism* comes from the Latin word for kidnapper.

> **Note:** Ideas cannot be copyrighted, only the words by which they are communicated. Paraphrasing thus prevents plagiarism, but anyone using material in this way must nevertheless acknowledge the source.

10. solstice   (sōl′stəs)   ***time when the sun is farthest from the equator***

In the northern hemisphere, the winter solstice comes just before Christmas, the summer solstice in June. What are the dates?

> *Solstice* may mean the farthest limit, culmination, or turning point. See -sol- (sun) (p. 357).

ADJECTIVES

1. aesthetic   (ĕs thĕt′ĭk)   ***responsive to beauty, artistic***

Trips to art galleries and museums cultivate one's aesthetic tastes.
Aesthetics is the study of the principles that govern the fine arts.
Aestheticism is the cultivation of artistic sensitivity.

> An *aesthete* is a person who knows and cultivates one or more of the fine arts: Henry James was an aesthete as well as a novelist.
> A *dilettante* is a mere dabbler in the fine arts, often pretending what he does not know or feel.

2. chimerical   (kə mĕr′ĭ kəl)   ***of the nature of fantasy, imaginary***

Are ghosts as chimerical as the hallucinations of a drug addict?
A Martian invasion was once a chimera (kī mêr′ə *or* kə mêr′ə) that haunted imaginative people.

Related words:

> In Greek mythology, a *chimera* was a fire-breathing monster with a lion's head, goat's body, and serpent's tail. The name was later applied to any frightful or foolish creature of the imagination.
> A *quixotic* (p. 154) person is a visionary or deluded individual, extravagantly chivalrous. The word comes from *Don Quixote* by Cervantes.

Imaginary creatures from mythology:

> *Hydra* was a nine-headed snake whose name became a symbol for persistent and growing evil because when one head was cut off, another grew in its place.
> The *centaur* was a monster having an upper torso like a man and the lower part like a horse.

3. exotic   (ĕg zŏt'ĭk)   ***strange, foreign***

The exotic aroma of oriental incense filled the room.
To an American, most Chinese foods look and taste exotic.
The exoticism (ĕg zŏt'ə siz əm) of the *Arabian Nights* makes the stories sound weird.

> *Exotic* comes from a Greek word meaning outside.

4. forensic   (fə rĕn'sĭk)   ***pertaining to public debate, oratorical***

Daniel Webster is remembered for his forensic skill.
Though the discussion on space law was forensically interesting, it was not very instructive.
The art of forensics looms large in courts of justice or in public debate.

> *Forensic* derives from the Latin *forum,* marketplace.

5. ineffable   (ĭn ĕf'ə bəl)   ***unutterable, inexpressible***

The ineffable stillness of evening slowly enveloped the lake.
In the silence of the shrine, an ineffable calm came over the troubled spirit of the pilgrim.
Finland in June is a good place to watch the ineffableness of cloud pageantry at sunset.

6. maudlin   (mȯd'lən)   ***weakly emotional, foolishly sentimental***

The class reunion was a medley of maudlin speeches about the good old days and the clever things students once said or did.
Leroy expressed the opinion that most of the agitation in behalf of the killer was maudlin.

> Compare *fatuous* (p. 220).

7. occult   (ə kult′ or ŏk′ŭlt′)   *of a magical nature, mysterious*

The palmist appeared to possess occult powers.
Occultism (ŏk′ŭl tĭz′əm), especially the extrasensory capacities of Edgar Cayce, engaged the attention of the study group.

> *Occult* originally meant covered up, hidden.
> Compare *recondite* (profound, abstruse), *esoteric* (known only to the initiated), *abstruse, mystical* (p. 232).

8. portentous   (pôr tĕn′təs)   *foreshadowing evil, awe-inspiring*

The portentous black funnel of an approaching tornado sent most of the townspeople to their cellars.
Some people still think that a black cat portends disaster.
The comet was regarded as a portent (omen) of evil.

> See *sinister* (p. 313) under -dexter-.

9. relevant   (rĕl′ə vənt)   *pertinent, bearing on the topic*

Though in an ancient-history class the life of Cleopatra is relevant, a discussion of baseball would be irrelevant.
No one could question the relevance of the witness's testimony about her fainting spells if they began after the accident.

Words for relevance:

> Anything *apropos* is to the point as well as relevant: She said that she had discovered some new information apropos of yesterday's argument.
> An *apposite* remark is one especially apt or suitable: "Siren Voice" is an apposite epithet for a shrill-toned alarmist.
> *Pertinent* facts are directly related to the topic: The size of the apartment door is pertinent if one is buying a piano.
> *Germane* information is closely related and highly appropriate: Tire sizes are germane to a discussion of auto racing.

10. sadistic   (sə dĭs′tĭk)   *cruel, fond of cruelty*

The troubled youth took a sadistic delight in mistreating animals.
The sadistic horrors of the concentration camp are difficult to believe.

> *Sadism* (love of cruelty) comes from the name of the Marquis de Sade (1740–1814), who wrote about his cruel pleasures.

First practice set

Which word best replaces each *italicized* word or phrase?

1. Jacob and Laban made a *solemn agreement* that was quite *pertinent* to the peace and happiness of both.
2. A *temporary alliance* of Latin American countries was formed to combat the *nightmare* of a Communist takeover.

3. The speaker used *debating* skill to prevent an *armed uprising* in her country.
4. Drug-taking is very dangerous even though the *fantastic, imaginary* world one enters seems *inexpressible* while the drug is having its effect.
5. *Strange* incantations and *magical* utterances followed the ritual of the seance.
6. Is it a *self-contradictory condition* for people to view an eclipse as both *awe-inspiring* and meaningless?
7. Despite his *cruel* treatment of wife and children, the bully regarded himself as a *perfect model* of family virtue.
8. At the summer *point when the sun is farthest north,* lazy rhymesters may be tempted to *steal (poetic) material verbatim.*
9. The memory of his *foolishly sentimental* remarks at the party gave him the *stimulus* to send his hostess a note of apology.
10. The carving of great *artistic* appeal has been made a(n) *object worshiped for its magical powers* by its admirers.

Second practice set

What word from the list at the left best replaces each *italicized* word or group of words?

quixotic
germane
heliolatry
uprising
zoolatry
pertinent
diabolism
amulet
necromancy
apposite
hydra
riot
anthropolatry
exorcism
compact
mutiny
talisman
apropos
bibliolatry
boycott
idolatry
revolution
chimera
insurgent

1. The odd nickname was an *especially apt* one for the man, for he annoyed many people and seemed *visionary or deluded* to them.
2. The traveler carried with her a *ring of magic power,* wearing this *charm to ward off evil* on a golden chain around her neck.
3. The *rebel* tried to stir up a *small, violent revolt against civil authorities* but failed.
4. The Boston Tea Party was the *deliberate outbreak* which came as a climax to a *peaceful revolt by refusing the goods.*
5. Drug addiction is a *nine-headed monster* that was of small importance in the days of the Mayflower *solemn agreement.*
6. Captain Ahab's *devil worship* made him as terrifying as a *fire-breathing monster.*
7. *The worship of books* is one form of *idol worship.*
8. Both *sun worship* and *animal worship* are common among primitive peoples.
9. The student's comment was *to the point,* but it came too late. The driver's news was *direct and important;* we were about to advance.
10. The article on *driving away evil spirits* seemed very *closely related* to the subject of the rector's recent lecture.

TAKE MY WORD FOR IT. WE'RE DEFINITELY PASSE!

Third practice set

Which lettered pair of items comes nearest to having the same relationship as the pair printed in capital letters?

1. SADISM:MERCIFULNESS:: (a) insurrection:boycott (b) incubus:covenant (c) fetish:amulet (d) plagiarism:originality

2. INCENTIVE:MOTIVE:: (a) meditation:forensics (b) lookout:visionary (c) reverie:forensics (d) covenant:contract

3. OMINOUS:PORTENTOUS:: (a) clear:chimerical (b) occult:rational (c) relevant:recondite (d) visionary:quixotic

4. APROPOS:IRRELEVANT:: (a) aesthetic:moral (b) earthly:ineffable (c) inapropos:germane (d) diabolic:fetishistic

5. FETISH:TALISMAN:: (a) hydra:chimera (b) aesthetics:exoticism (c) uprising:coalition (d) paragon:paradox

6. INSURGENT:INSURRECTION:: (a) aesthete:visionary (b) aesthetics:aesthete (c) orator:forensics (d) daydreamer:incubus

7. AMULET:FETISH:: (a) sadism:paradox (b) incentive:result (c) plagiarism:occultism (d) insurrection:revolution

8. SENTIMENTAL:MAUDLIN:: (a) fanciful:chimerical (b) native:exotic (c) relevant:evident (d) sadistic:sadism

9. ASTROLOGY:OCCULTISM:: (a) necromancy:diabolism (b) zoolatry:bull worship (c) riot:mutiny (d) chimera:quixotism

10. BULL WORSHIP:ZOOLATRY:: (a) antique hunting:idolatry (b) hydra:necrolatry (c) library:bibliolatry (d) sun bathing:heliolatry

The right word

Which word from this unit best replaces each *italicized* word or group of words?

1. Does a red sky *foreshadow* evil?
2. The idea that money is a blessing and a curse is an example of a *self-contradictory statement*.
3. A Democratic *rebel* in the Senate broke the tie by voting against his party.
4. The author was accused of *stealing another's ideas*.
5. Robert was full of *romantic, visionary, but impractical* schemes for eliminating pollution.
6. Visiting her Turkish cousins for the first time, Mara was fascinated by the *strange foreign* atmosphere of their home.
7. The new teacher is an *individual who cultivates a fondness for art, music, and poetry*.
8. The next step is to draw up a *solemn agreement* uniting the three religious bodies in beliefs.
9. Someone interrupted the speaker to ask a question which was completely *without bearing on the case in hand*.
10. The idea of living in a cave instead of a tent during our camping trip struck me as *fantastic (in the nature of a fantasy)*.

Queries

1. What would each of the following worship words mean: *hagiolatry, iconolatry, necrolatry, anthropolatry, matriolatry*? What others can you discover or devise?
2. Write the adjective form of each entry word that has one.

unit five

FAMILY GATHERING

Which word best completes each sentence?

1. A taciturn nephew is   (a) agile   (b) quiet   (c) tricky   (d) suave.
2. An arrogant uncle is   (a) fond of teasing   (b) fond of asking questions   (c) haughty   (d) roguish.
3. A fastidious aunt is   (a) facetious   (b) very discriminating   (c) rather giddy   (d) too economical.
4. An ingenuous sister-in-law is   (a) inventive   (b) unimaginative   (c) well-born   (d) frank and open.
5. A volatile niece is   (a) even-tempered   (b) spirited   (c) condescending   (d) talkative.
6. A silly, self-satisfied cousin is   (a) astute   (b) presumptuous   (c) dogmatic   (d) fatuous.
7. A brother-in-law fond of showing off is   (a) ostentatious   (b) sinuous   (c) truculent   (d) captious.
8. A mother-in-law who likes to go to social affairs is   (a) garrulous   (b) dogmatic   (c) unctuous   (d) gregarious.
9. A fault-finding father-in-law is   (a) captious   (b) jocular   (c) fastidious   (d) cynical.
10. A grandmother with strong opinions is   (a) tentative   (b) aggressive   (c) dogmatic   (d) amicable.

BEHAVIORISTICS

1. aggressive   (ə grĕs´ĭv)   *assertive, vigorously active, quick to attack*

The new sales representative, aggressive and self-confident, gets results.
The uninvited guest's aggressiveness made her doubly unwelcome.
The United Nations acted to prevent aggression in the Middle East.

Related words:

>A *forward* person is quick to take the initiative, but with less hint of contest or struggle than an aggressive person conveys.
>
>An *officious* person is forward in a meddlesome or objectionable manner (p. 46) under *obtrusive*), assuming too much authority.
>
>An *assertive* person is forward or insistent, but not quite officious.
>
>See -<u>gress</u>- (p. 279) with -<u>cede</u>-. Forms of aggressiveness include *invasion, incursion, foray, assault* (p. 35), and varieties of *revolt* (p. 211).

2. arrogant   (ăr′ə gənt)   ***haughty, overbearingly proud***

Three members of the committee seemed arrogant and aggressive.

The captain of the team showed his arrogance by continually trying to usurp the coach's prerogative.

Did the President arrogate (ăr′ə gāt′) (seize) to himself more power than the Constitution intended when he settled the strike?

>A *presumptuous* person assumes too much about, or for, himself, and thus becomes too bold or forward. See -<u>sumpt</u>- (p. 309).
>
>A *disdainful* person is haughty or contemptuous, but not overbearing.
>
>An *insolent* person is arrogantly rude and discourteous.
>
>A *supercilious* air is disdainful or scornfully aloof: The Pomeranian pup has a supercilious air. The root meaning is *with raised eyebrows.*

3. captious   (kăp′shəs)   ***fault-finding, hard to please***

Ernest often tries to show his sophistication by being captious.

The new drama critic's captiousness makes her reviews readable, but one tires of the obvious ill-nature behind them.

Related words:

>A *peevish* or *petulant* person is sulky and fretful about small matters.
>
>A *contentious* person likes to argue for the sake of arguing.
>
>A *querulous* person (p. 118) is likely to be ill-natured and merely a complainer.
>
>A *quibbler* or *caviler* (p. 180) grasps at trifles and is less serious or sincere than a captious person.
>
>A *hypercritical* person is hard to please, but likely to be more consistent and more serious than a captious critic.

4. cynical   (sĭn′ĭ kəl)   *scornfully distrustful*

A cynical person is skeptical of all motives and values, and to such a one all human actions are selfish.
The speech contained echoes of political cynicism (sĭn′ə sĭz′əm).

Similar to cynical:

A *satirical* (p. 170) person sees and ridicules the vices and follies of the world. The purpose of satire is to amuse and reform.
A *sarcastic* person has little love and much distrust for people and thus makes cruel and cutting remarks.
A *sardonic* nature is bitterly scornful and more biting than a sarcastic temperament with its ill-humor or a satiric nature with its often witty creativeness.
A *pessimistic* (p. 249) nature takes a dark, distrustful, and thus cynical view of people and of nature.
A *misanthropic* view of humankind is one of detestation rather than of merely pessimistic hopelessness.

5. dogmatic   (dȯg măt′ĭk)   *unduly positive, dictatorial*

Because Uncle Bill has lived in London for five years, he is dogmatic about what the British ought to do.
In discussing politics, the teacher avoids dogmatism (dȯg′mə tĭz′əm).

The *dogmas* of a church are its official doctrines or beliefs.
Compare *dictatorial* (p. 305), *doctrinaire, arbitrary.*

6. fastidious   (făs tĭd′ē əs)   *daintily refined, very discriminating*

The furnishings of the home testified to the owner's fastidious taste.
Fastidiousness in following recipes should make food more appetizing.

Related words:

A *particular* person is fussy about details.
A *squeamish* person is unduly sensitive to what is unsavory: Jane was so squeamish that a dead fly made her uncomfortable.
A *scrupulous* person is very precise and discriminating, but more on ethical than on aesthetic or emotional grounds.
A *prudish* person has an excessive sense of delicacy or propriety in speech, dress, or behavior.

7. fatuous   (făch′o͞o əs)   *complacently stupid or silly*

Millicent dislikes fatuous praise of her musical ability.
The comedian's wit soon deteriorated into fatuousness.

Synonyms: *foolish, oafish, asinine.*

The Latin word *fatuus* means foolish.
Infatuation, often mistaken for love, is a foolish or unreasoning fondness which makes up in intensity what it lacks in durability.
Compare *maudlin* (p. 213).

8. garrulous   (găr′ə ləs)   *talkative*

Garrulous characters are often introduced into serious drama for comic relief.
The speaker had the garrulity (gə rōō′lə tē) of a House filibusterer.

Modes of talkativeness: Why are there so many?

> *Loquaciousness* is excessive but endurable.
> *Garrulousness* is noisy and hardly endurable.
> *Volubility* is windy talk, ample, empty, hinting of "hot air."
> *Effusiveness* is an outpouring of words, especially of a flattering nature.
> *Diffuseness* is tiresome, taking too many words to make a point.
> *Glibness* is smooth, slick talkativeness, irresponsible and unrewarding.
> *Fluency* is an easy and ample command of language if not of ideas, but it has in part the faults of glibness.
> *Verbosity* is above all else wordy, whether it makes sense or not.
> *Prolixity,* like diffuseness, is wordy and roundabout, with little to say.

9. gregarious   (grə gâr′ē əs)   *sociable, inclined to go in groups*

Hermits are among the least gregarious of human beings.
High school gregariousness expresses itself in clubs and cliques.

> See -greg- words (p. 316).

10. impetuous   (ĭm pĕch′ōō əs)   *rushing with great force;*
                                                  impulsive, rash, hasty

Impetuous winter winds howled across the prairies.
Shelley was an energetic youth who often acted impetuously.
Maturity modified the dancer's youthful impetuosity (ĭm pĕch′ōō ŏs′ə tē).
Elizabeth Barrett and Robert Browning displayed lovers' impetuousness when they eloped.

Related words:

> An *impulsive* person is quick to act on emotional incitement.
> A *precipitate* person's actions are rash and hasty, as well as sudden.
> See *precipitous* (p. 117).

11. ingenuous   (ĭn jĕn′yōō əs)   *frank, genuine, free from reserve*

"I do it myself," was Judy's ingenuous response to Gary's apology.
The candidate's youthful ingenuousness appeals to many voters.

> An *ingenue* (ăn′jə nōō′) is either an ingenuous girl or an actress representing such a person.
> Compare *naïve,* artless, unsophisticated: Nancy was naïve enough to accompany the talkative stranger, and her naïveté almost proved fatal.
> Do not confuse *ingenuous* with *ingenious.*
> Review *candid* (p. 19).

Antonym: *disingenuous.*

12. nostalgic   (nŏ stăl′jik)   ***homesick, longing for something past***

As the printer recalled his boyhood home, he fell into a nostalgic mood.
How Green Was My Valley is the nostalgic title of a nostalgic novel.
The nostalgia (nŏ stăl′jə) for simpler times that was sweeping the country was
reflected, perhaps, most strongly in the movies.

The root of *nostalgic* is the Greek word *nostos,* a return.

13. ostentatious   (ŏs′tən tā′shəs)   ***fond of display, pretentious***

The newly rich are often ostentatious in dress and behavior.
A peacock strutted ostentatiously across the green at Warwick Castle.
A Hollywood movie can scarcely recapture the ostentatiousness of the French
court in the eighteenth century.

Related words:

A *garish* outfit or party is gaudy, overdone, and too colorful. Garishness may be
costly but it lacks quality.
Pomp and ceremony are necessarily ostentatious, with a majesty and grandeur
rarely recaptured today.
Histrionics is showy, stagy, theatrical behavior in real life: Mac's histrionics did
not impress the officer who arrested him.
Melodrama is ostentatious, overdone drama or behavior, often stereotyped on
the stage.

14. sinuous   (sĭn′yo͞o əs)   ***curving or winding, devious***

The High Sierras are laced with a network of sinuous trails.
The once majestic sinuousness of diplomatic language has yielded somewhat
to modern simplicity.

Negotiations for a new contract often proceed sinuously.
"Hunting" with a movie camera, the photographer caught on film the sinuous movements of the big cats.

Curvy words:

> *Undulating* waves or roads go up and down in even rhythms.
> A *circuitous* route is roundabout and thus devious or winding.
> A *serpentine* route or course of action twists and turns in a curving manner like a snake looking for food.

15. taciturn   (tăs′ə tûrn′)   ***habitually silent, uncommunicative***

John Alden was a taciturn young man who dared not propose to Priscilla.
President Coolidge became famous for his taciturnity and terseness.

Related words:

> *Tacit* means implied but not stated: By not objecting, Mother gave her tacit consent to the plans for a slumber party.
> A *reticent* person is reserved, hesitant about speaking or acting.

16. truculent   (trŭk′yə lənt)   ***fierce, savage, cruel***

A truculent parent stormed into the principal's office.
The suspects glared truculently at the officer who arrested them.
The driver's truculence, when he was asked to stop, earned him a reprimand from the judge.

17. unctuous   (ŭng′choo̅ əs)   ***excessively suave or bland, oily***

The undertaker was unctuous in making the funeral arrangements.
A hypocritical neighbor informed Gordon with great unctuousness that he should always tell the truth.
The orator spoke with unction (a smooth manner) of our noble pioneers.

18. valid   (văl′ĭd)   ***sound, effective, well-founded***

A valid argument against divorce is its effect on the children.
Courts are testing the validity (və lĭd′ə tē) of the prospector's claim.
The county clerk must record and validate (văl′ə dāt′) the documents.

<u>Val-</u> **words:** (from the Latin *valere,* to be strong)
> *Valiant:* "The valiant never taste of death but once." (p. 64)
> *Valor* (courage): Exploring Antarctica requires valor.
> *Valence* in chemistry is strength in the sense that it is the number of other atoms an atom of a given element can hold in chemical union.

Antonyms: *invalid, invalidate.*

19. versatile   (vûr′sə təl)   *many sided in abilities*

Only a versatile athlete can earn letters in four sports.
The next general manager must be a person of great versatility—skillful in
finance, in planning, in personal relations, and in other matters.

> See -vert-, -vers- words (p. 299).

20. volatile   (vŏl′ə təl)   *changeable, spirited, explosive*

Lucy is volatile and carefree. Nothing troubles her for very long.
That summer, Rene's volatility (vŏl ə tĭl′ə tē) made her as graceful and active as
a wild mustang.
The police entered a highly volatile situation when they quelled the incipient riot.

> When used of a liquid, *volatile* means quick to evaporate.

> **Antonyms:** *phlegmatic* (sluggish, unexcitable), *stable, bovine.*

If time permits

1. Write the adverb form of each entry word.
2. Write the noun form of each italicized adjective presented in the supplementary
   material, if it has one.

First practice set

Which entry word from this unit best replaces each *italicized* word or group of words?

1. A *habitually silent* shopper might dislike a *talkative* clerk.
2. An *overbearingly proud* manner and a *homesick* desire to be a carefree child
   again kept Wanda from making friends.
3. Salespersons are trained to be *assertive* in a tactful way and to have *sound and
   effective* answers to customers' questions.
4. The *many-sided* portrait painter is *fault-finding* and disdainful toward those who
   sit for him.
5. Though the butler has an *excessively suave* voice, he also has an extremely
   fierce manner.
6. The inspector on the case was both *complacently stupid* and *hasty* in his
   judgments.
7. The maestro is *spirited and changeable* and quite *inclined to join groups* after
   his evening concerts.
8. The scout leader is *frank and genuine* but *hard to please* about the way food is
   prepared around the campfire.

9. *Devious* in business dealings, the supervisor is nevertheless *unduly positive* about political matters.
10. Some of the club members justify their *pretentious* behavior by being *scornfully distrustful* about modest people.

Second practice set

Which word from the list at the left best replaces each *italicized* word or group of words?

undulating
prudishness
supercilious
fluency
infatuation
sardonic
gregarious
misanthropy
scrupulous
serpentine
contentious
asinine
naïve
impulsive
querulous
garish
reticent
glibness
sarcastic
effusive
insolent
circuitous
valiant
satirical
hypercritical
aggressive

1. It is *unsophisticated* to confuse *foolish, impetuous fondness* with the real thing.
2. The artist is *hesitant about speaking or acting,* but *precise and discriminating* about her choice of colors and media.
3. Rocco's *scornful, cutting* reply to his critics was that they were merely *arguing for the sake of arguing.*
4. Friends called the manager's verbal dexterity *smooth and easy talk commanding respect;* enemies called it *easy, irresponsible verbosity.*
5. One listens more willingly to a person who is *unduly critical but consistent and serious,* than to one who is *merely complaining.*
6. The *roundabout* trip over *wavy* roads and hills took all day.
7. *Twisting and turning like a snake* in his movements, the acrobat performed outside a midway tent, while a barker, *impressively pouring out words* and smiling, urged the crowd to go in.
8. A person who is *quick to act on emotional incitement* might prove to be a *brave* fighter.
9. *Excessive delicacy in what is moral* provided the playwright with a theme for his *ridiculing* talent.
10. The courtier's *detestation of mankind* made him *bitterly scornful.*

Third practice set

Which lettered pair comes nearest to having the same relationship as the two words printed in capital letters?

1. CYNICAL:SARDONIC::   (a) aggressive:unctuous   (b) loquacious:garrulous   (c) ostentatious:truculent   (d) taciturn:naïve   (e) presumptuous:precipitate

2. SARDONIC:SARCASM:: (a) fastidious:captiousness (b) impetuous:ingenuousness (c) sinuous:unction (d) dogmatic:dogma (e) ostentatious:naïveté

3. FATUOUS:INFATUATION:: (a) captious:captivation (b) taciturn:tacitness (c) dogmatic:dogmatism (d) ingenuous:ingenuity (e) volatile:volubility

4. VOLATILE:PHLEGMATIC:: (a) ostentatious:naïve (b) dogmatic:nostalgic (c) gregarious:social (d) maudlin:fatuous (e) garrulous:taciturn

5. IMPETUOUS:IMPULSIVE:: (a) ingenuous:ingenious (b) irresponsible:insolent (c) cynical:sarcastic (d) timid:presumptuous (e) supercilious:meek

6. INGENUOUSNESS:DISINGENUOUS:: (a) arrogance:arrogant (b) nostalgia:nostalgic (c) ostentation:unostentatious (d) gregariousness:segregated (e) unaggressive:aggression

7. NAÏVETÉ:ARTLESS:: (a) truculence:saturnine (b) arrogance:cynical (c) fatuousness:tranquil (d) gentleness:haughty (e) taciturnity:reticent

8. SUPERCILIOUS:DISDAINFUL:: (a) volatile:changeless (b) versatile:gregarious (c) presumptuous:unctuous (d) ferocious:truculent (e) captious:fatuous

9. GREGARIOUS:UNSOCIABLE:: (a) garrulous:voluble (b) ingenuous:sinuous (c) impulsive:impetuous (d) naïve:sincere (e) fastidious:undiscriminating

10. DOGMATIC:DOGMATIZE:: (a) presume:presumptuous (b) captious:captivate (c) valid:validate (d) garrulous:garrulity (e) prude:prudishness

unit six

A THRILLER

Which word from the list at the left fits best in each blank?

annihilate
extenuate
procrastinate
propitiate
capitulate
auspicious
egregious
expedient
fortuitous
aggravate
adumbrate
instigate

1. The plot centers on a clever spy who had a _____ (occurring by chance) opportunity to _____ (utterly destroy) a guerrilla outpost.

2. Shot down near the post, he thought he could infiltrate it and _____ (stir up) a mutiny.

3. He made a very _____ (promising) start when he was mistaken for a newly assigned officer whom he had captured and locked in a shed, and whose uniform he had put on.

4. He affronted the commander, however, when he attempted to slink by and then tried to _____ (appease) him with excuses.

5. One _____ (remarkably bad) slip of the tongue helped to _____ (make worse) his predicament and make his imperfect use of the enemy language too obvious to overlook.

6. He realized it would be _____ (advantageous) to escape if he wanted to save his life, and he tried.

7. Rifle fire disabled him, however. He was brought back and he had to _____ (surrender).

8. Since there was nothing to _____ (make less serious) what he had intended to do, he languished in prison until exchanged for an important guerrilla who had fallen into the hands of his own people.

VERBS

1. adumbrate   (ăd′əm brāt)   *to outline in a vague way;*
to foreshadow

George Orwell's novel, *1984,* adumbrates the trend toward perennial warfare, thought control, and the existence of superstates.
Early American methods of fighting were adumbrations of the guerrilla tactics of modern resistance movements.

Umbra- (shadow) words:

> *Umbrage* (cover or shadow), *penumbra* (partly lighted area around the shadow of an eclipse), *umber* (a color), and *umbrella.*

2. aggravate   (ăg′rə vāt′)   *make worse or more severe*

Headaches aggravate a person's natural irritability.
Aggravation of the famine was one result of the shipping strike.
Because a table leg was used as the weapon, the charge was aggravated assault.

> To *augment* one's resources is to increase them. See word and synonyms (p. 35).
> To *exacerbate* a crisis is to sharpen or heighten it.
> Compare *acerbity:* The acerbity of the woman's grief almost caused insanity.

3. annihilate   (ə nī′ə lāt′)   *destroy utterly*

One hydrogen bomb could annihilate a city of several million.
With supersonic planes and satellite communication, the annihilation of time and distance in world affairs is almost complete.

Related words:

> *Nihilists* believe in nothing because they have no basis for certain knowledge: Some nihilists would destroy all social and moral law.
> To *obliterate* is to destroy by rendering unrecognizable: Rain obliterated every clue that would have helped police find the murderer.
> One may *obliterate* an inscription, but one is more likely to *raze* a building.
> To *exterminate* is to wipe out, in the sense of killing: Madame DeFarge, in *A Tale of Two Cities,* wanted to exterminate the Evremond family.
> To *extirpate* or *eradicate* an evil is to root it out: Extirpation of slavery was an achievement of the nineteenth century. Modern science eradicates many diseases.
> See *abolish* and synonyms (p. 2).

4. capitulate   (kə pĭch′ə lāt′)   *surrender on certain terms*

Do you think the company will capitulate to the strikers' demands?
The rebels' capitulation to superior forces brought peace at a price.
Premier Khrushchev of the Soviet Union was once a capitulationist because he yielded to President Kennedy's demand for the removal of missiles from Cuba.

5. extenuate   (ĕk stĕn'yo͞o āt')   *make less serious, diminish*

"Ignorance of the law does not extenuate a crime," the judge declared.
"My client's youth is an extenuating circumstance," the lawyer replied.
In extenuation of the crime, the lawyer also pleaded the client's limited knowl-
edge of English.

> *Extenuate, attenuate* (to lessen, weaken, make thin), and *tenuous* (thin, slight,
> weakened) come from the Latin word *tenuis,* thin.

6. fulminate   (fo͞ol'mə nāt')   *to explode, erupt, shout violently*

The candidate fulminated against her opponent's vituperative attacks.
Angry fulminations echoed from the crowd meeting in the stadium to protest
the new law.

> *Fulminate* comes from the Latin word *fulmen,* thunderbolt or lightning.

7. instigate   (ĭn'stə gāt')   *provoke, incite*

How did a false message instigate an attack on the city?
Satoru entered the contest at the instigation of his English teacher.
The instigator of the crime is as guilty as the actual criminal.

> Compare *impel, goad, spur, tempt.*

8. mitigate   (mĭt'ə gāt')   *lessen, make milder*

A large lake tends to mitigate the climate along its shores.
The governor would not consider mitigation of the arsonist's sentence.

Related words:

> To *assuage* a person's grief is to soften or reduce it. *Assuage* is used chiefly of
> feelings, whereas *mitigate* is more often used of the weather and outward events
> or conditions.
> To *pacify* angry persons is to quiet them and calm them down.
> To *alleviate* pain or hardship is to relieve it.
> To *allay* a hardship is to lessen, relieve or make it less onerous. It is used especially
> of fears.
> See *relent* and synonyms (p. 12).

9. procrastinate   (prə krăs'tə nāt')   *to delay, put off*

It is especially easy to procrastinate about seeing a dentist.
Uncle Ignatius had always planned to go to college after working a year or two,
but procrastination kept him from ever getting there.
Queen Elizabeth I was a skillful procrastinator who often temporized, and
thus postponed decisions on difficult problems.

> The Latin word *cras* (tomorrow) appears in *procrastinate* and helps explain its
> meaning.

10. propitiate   (prə pĭsh′ē āt′)   ***appease, conciliate***

One life was not enough to propitiate the tyrant's vengeance.
The box of candy was an act of propitiation.
The appearance of the dove was a propitious (prə pĭsh′əs) (favorable) sign.

Related words:

To *mollify* is to appease or pacify a power one has offended: Promises will not
mollify thousands of unemployed who want to live creatively. Enraged strikers
shouted down the mediator's efforts at mollification.
To *expiate* or *atone* for an offense is to make amends by suffering punishment or
making reparation: Sue tried to expiate the wrong she had done her sister.
A smile or gesture of resignation will often *placate* an angry parent.

Note: Each of these words denotes the act of appeasing a person or power which
one has offended. Three, *propitiate, expiate,* and *atone,* have special religious
or Christian meanings. All, unlike *assuage* and its synonyms above, involve acts
of reparation or compensation. You propitiate a person. You expiate a sin or error.
You atone for sin or error.
Compare *Yom Kippur,* the Jewish Day of Atonement.

ADJECTIVES

1. auspicious   (ȯ spĭsh′əs)   ***promising, favorable***

Government spending made the year auspicious for new business.
The hobby show is under the auspices (ȯ′spə səz) (sponsorship) of Kiwanis.

Compare *propitious,* above.

2. egregious   (ĭ grē′jəs)   ***remarkably bad, flagrant***

Don made an egregious fool of himself at the party when, with ostentatious
flourishes, he jumped into the pool to save a floating dummy.
The "super-colossal" movie was egregiously disappointing.

Egregious originally meant *out from the herd.* See the ex- words (p. 286) and
-greg- words (p. 316).

3. equivocal   (ĭ kwĭv′ə kəl)   ***vague, ambiguous, questionable***

The manager's equivocal reply to the reporter's question made it difficult to
guess what her opinions really were.
The suspect is a person of equivocal character who has a police record.

Still popular after twenty years, the singer prefers to equivocate about his age.

Related words:

An *obscure* message can be understood only with great difficulty.
A *vague* message is hazy, indefinite, and unclear by its very nature.
An *ambiguous* message can be read equally well with two or three meanings.
See -ambi- (p. 348).
An *enigmatic* message puzzles or perplexes its readers (p. 185).
A *cryptic* message is intentionally puzzling, usually by its ambiguity as well as
its brevity.

4. expedient (ĕk spē′dē ənt) *suitable, advantageous but*
not necessarily right

Is military might the most expedient way to avoid war?
The expediency of taking turns at the bedside of the patient was understandable,
but eventually a full-time nurse would be needed.
Temporizing is an expedient to frustrate hijackers.

5. fortuitous (fȯr tyōo′ə təs) *occurring by chance or accident*

A fortuitous encounter with a beggar provided a valuable clue.
The fortuitousness of the inspector's arrival almost guaranteed that the plant
would soon be operating in a normal way.

> *Fortuitous* implies good fortune as well as chance. Compare *casual* (unplanned,
> incidental), *adventitious* (accidental).

6. intrinsic (in trĭn′zik) *actual, essential, or inherent*

''Sandwich'' (clad or bonded) coins have intrinsic value much below their
face value.
A person's intrinsic qualities come out clearly when danger arises.

> The intrinsic, or *inherent,* value of something is the value belonging to it by its
> very nature: The intrinsic value of a check is only that of a piece of paper. The
> *extrinsic* value of the check depends upon factors outside itself, such as the money
> in the bank behind it.

7. mystical   (mĭs′tĭ kəl)   *participating in mysterious spiritual experience or knowledge*

The Oracle at Delphi in Greece was known for her mystical messages.
Whitman's mystical utterances often sound unbalanced at a first reading.
Rufus Jones, like most Friends, was something of a mystic.
The insights of mysticism have a spiritual meaning beyond the ordinary range of human experience.

   Antonym: *rational.*

8. sacrilegious   (săk′rə lĭj′əs)   *irreverent, blasphemous*

In Scotland it was once sacrilegious to whistle on Sunday.
Some churches in the 1700s considered the use of an organ sacrilegious.

9. salubrious   (sə lōō′brē əs)   *healthful, promoting health*

The salubrious mountain air brings color to one's cheeks.
Many people are drawn to California because of the salubriousness of the climate.
A warm atmosphere, good meals, and frequent exercise soon worked salubriously upon the young patient.

   Salutary means conducive to health or well-being: The sharp decrease of polio cases showed the salutary effects of Salk vaccine.

10. synthetic   (sĭn thĕt′ĭk)   *artificial, manufactured*

Synthetic rubber is superior to natural rubber for many purposes.
The sympathy that the stranger offered was synthetic, not genuine.
"Poetry is the synthesis (sĭn′thə səs) of hyacinths and biscuits," said Carl Sandburg.
The artist attempted to synthesize form and content.

First practice set

Which entry word from this unit best replaces each *italicized* word or group of words?

1. Nothing would *conciliate* the manager or *soften* his bitterness about losing the championship.

2. The speaker began to *thunder and curse* against all who claim to be *participating in mysterious spiritual knowledge.*
3. The British Government finds it *advantageous* to *yield conditionally* to the terms of the new trade treaty.
4. Mountain climbing is a *health-promoting* pastime capable of *lessening* even the fiercest restlessness.
5. *Artificial* gasoline has *inherent* qualities similar to those of the natural product.
6. The Roman general, a Christian, tried to satisfy the angry king by *ambiguous* praise without being *irreverent.*
7. The *(occurring-by-) chance* mistake proved *favorable* for the scientist because it led to the discovery of a new element.
8. The dictator was a *flagrant* example of a tyrant; he almost managed to *destroy utterly* all his enemies.
9. The behavior of radium *provoked* the study of atoms and *foreshadowed* the main achievements of nuclear physics.
10. The governor's desire to *delay action* indefinitely will *worsen* the public dissatisfaction.

Second practice set

What word from the list at the left best replaces each *italicized* word or group of words?

abolish
salutary
extirpate
alleviate
allay
extrinsic
impel
tenuous
synthesis
assuage
exterminate
mollify
nihilist
cryptic
placate
enigmatic
eradication
obliterate
augment
mysticism
propitious
equivocate
attenuate
rational
atone

1. The evidence is *slight* (thin) that the cook, to *increase* his income, took part in the crime.
2. Will current efforts to *root out* poverty *relieve* the situation?
3. What can now *make amends* for failing to place the invalid in a *health-fostering* environment?
4. The letter is *puzzling (by its brevity),* but its arrival was a *favorable* warning.
5. One *outward* advantage of going out for a sport lies in being able to *satisfy* (please) your family that you are getting sufficient exercise.
6. Long hours of labor may tend to *lessen* (make thin) one's resistance to colds, but the pay received does *relieve* (lighten) the burden of one's debts.
7. Peggy tried to *appease* her irate relative with *puzzling* references to family pride.
8. Nothing will really *soften* or *destroy (by rendering unrecognizable)* the deepest grief.
9. To prevent the plague from spreading, it was necessary to *wipe out* all rats, and a necessary step in this *rooting-out (process)* was the burning of the houses along the river.
10. A *person who has no basis for certain knowledge* rejects the *reasoning* as well as the mystical approach.

Third practice set

Which pair of words (a, b, c, or d) best completes the meaning of each sentence below?

1. The advent of the automobile served to _____ the traffic problem at Haymarket Square, but a way has been found to _____ it.
   - (a) mitigate—extenuate
   - (b) mollify—synthesize
   - (c) aggravate—alleviate
   - (d) capitulate—procrastinate

2. One's heredity is a rather _____ process rather than one of _____, such as one might desire.
   - (a) fortuitous—expediency
   - (b) egregious—expiation
   - (c) equivocal—procrastination
   - (d) auspicious—synthesis

3. Myrna's grief was _____ as she turned over in her mind the memories which nothing could ever _____ .
   - (a) synthesized—exterminate
   - (b) extenuated—mitigate
   - (c) enigmatic—mollify
   - (d) assuaged—obliterate

4. The _____ message was too intentionally puzzling to _____ the king's wrath; quite the contrary, his wrath grew.
   - (a) clear—propitiate
   - (b) cryptic—mitigate
   - (c) enigmatic—synthesize
   - (d) vague—aggravate

5. The inmates, who had taken over the prison, wanted to _____ certain conditions before talking of _____ .
   - (a) extenuate—mitigation
   - (b) procrastinate—propitiation
   - (c) equivocate—assuagement
   - (d) eradicate—capitulation

6. An agitator set out to _____ dramatic acts of violent _____ .
   - (a) instigate—sacrilege
   - (b) extenuate—expediency
   - (c) equivocate—egregiousness
   - (d) assuage—adumbration

7. It would be _____ folly to _____ any longer about having the brakes fixed.
   - (a) inexpedient—extenuate
   - (b) fortuitous—atone
   - (c) egregious—procrastinate
   - (d) ambiguous—propitiate

8. The _____ law to increase old-age pensions was passed to _____ the elderly voters in the state.
   - (a) expedient—alleviate
   - (b) egregious—assuage
   - (c) equivocal—aggravate
   - (d) auspicious—mollify

9. The girl had to _____ in order to _____ a rejected suitor's disappointment.
   (a) adumbrate—instigate
   (b) equivocate—assuage
   (c) extenuate—mitigate
   (d) procrastinate—synthesize

10. Nothing could _____ the crime he had committed, and he worked years to _____ it to some degree.
    (a) mollify—extirpate
    (b) extenuate—expiate
    (c) annihilate—pacify
    (d) aggravate—procrastinate

A word for it

Which word from this unit best replaces each *italicized* word or group of words?

1. The powder will *root out* ants if you do not *delay action* in using it.
2. The new law is a *combining of ideas* of several different bills to *make amends (through reparations)* to local farmers for the indifference of county officials.
3. It was *advantageous* for the skiers to find shelter before the blizzard grew worse. The *chance* discovery of a cave solved their problem.
4. The proposal has *inherent* merit; besides, this is a very *favorable* time for new legislation.
5. Nothing could *lessen* the seriousness of his *flagrant* error.

TIMBER !

unit seven

Which word from the list at the left goes best with each phrase?

coterie	1. A guardian of valuable treasures: _____
curator	2. A middle-class citizen: _____
bourgeois	3. A highly skilled performer: _____
critique	4. A competent judge of painting: _____
repertoire	5. A wise counselor: _____
mercury	6. A specialist in retribution: _____
debutante	7. A swift messenger or guide: _____
connoisseur	8. A social set or clique: _____
liaison	9. A society girl: _____
virtuoso	10. A connection in a spy ring: _____
mentor	
nemesis	

EIGHT WORDS OF FRENCH FAME

1. bourgeois   (boŏrzh′wä′)   ***(member of) the middle class***

The new police chief in Marseilles had a bourgeois origin.
Bourgeois virtues include thrift, industriousness, and honesty.
Karl Marx had a special dislike for the bourgeoisie (boŏrzh′wä′zē′) (middle class).

> Traditionally, society is divided into three classes: the *aristocracy,* or patrician, landowning class; the *bourgeois,* or shopkeeping, merchant class; and the *proletariat,* or laboring class. Does such a division exist in the United States today?

2. connoisseur   (kon′ə sûr′)   ***competent judge***

Our dinner guest, a connoisseur of classical music, directs a symphony orchestra.
Linda's training makes her a connoisseur of French cooking.
A connoisseur is an expert, especially in one of the fine arts.

> **Antonym:** *charlatan.*

Related words:

> A *dilettante* is a dabbler in the fine arts.
> An *arbiter* is a judge or umpire in a dispute, but an *arbiter elegantiarum* is an authority in matters of taste.
> *Pundit* is a Sanskrit word, often used with humorous effect, for a person of vast knowledge.
> An *epicure* is a person who especially enjoys delicately flavored foods and drinks.
> A *gourmet* is less given to mere enjoyment than an epicure, and is more of a connoisseur.

3. coterie   (kō′tə rē′)   *social set, clique*

Rebecca's little coterie of artists represents a galaxy of fine talent.
A coterie of bridge fans takes over a corner of the school lounge every noon.

Society words:

> A *clique* is a small, exclusive coterie, often snobbish: In the senior class several well-established cliques are evident.
> A *set* is a large group, often of society people, linked by common interests: Edith Wharton wrote fiction about the life of the smart set in New York in the early 1900s.
> A *plebeian* (p. 117) concept or *plebeian* tastes are those of the common people or working class.
> A *patrician* air or attitude belongs to the upper class—in terms of wealth or education.
> A *parvenu*, being a newcomer in society, perhaps a social climber, is looked upon with suspicion and a certain degree of condescension.
> *Sansculotte* (without breeches) was a term of scorn applied by French aristocrats to the poorly clad soldiers of the Revolutionary Army, who wore pantaloons instead of knee breeches.

4. critique   (krĭ tēk′)   *written analysis of a work of art*

Each pupil wrote a critique of a favorite poem.
The *Times* is famous for the literary critiques it publishes.

Related words:

> An *exegesis* is an intensive analysis or interpretation of a poem, short story, or biblical passage.
> A *disquisition* is a formal discussion, oral or written. The word is often used in a disparaging or humorous sense.
> A *treatise* is a formal essay or book on a subject.
> A *thesis* is a proposition to be proved or the essay defending it.

5. debutante   (dĕb′yo͞o tänt′)   *young woman making her formal appearance in society*

Six debutantes were chatting happily about the charity ball.
One had just made her debut (dā′byo͞o′) (first appearance in society).
The Finnish pianist made his debut in Stockholm.

Related words:

A *debut* is any first appearance before the public. *Debut* is a French word.
See *ingenue,* also French, under *ingenuous* (p. 221).

6. intrigue   (ĭn′ trēg)   *plotting, scheming; to arouse or stir the interest or curiosity of*

A state senator started a political intrigue against the governor.
Realistic novels intrigue Clara.

Related words:

Intrigue may also mean an illicit love affair.
A *cabal* is a group of people secretly united in some scheme or plot, especially one to overthrow the government.
A *junta* can be a legislative or administrative council, especially in South or Central America; a group of people in control of a government, especially after a revolution; or, like a cabal, a number of persons gathered together for some secret—usually political—purpose.
A *coup d'etat* is an illegal overthrow of a government by a small group, usually by force.

7. liaison   (lē′ə zŏn′)   *unofficial linkage*

The Department of the Army has a liaison with the State Department in order to coordinate their activities more effectively.
The President has a liaison officer in the Pentagon.

Originally, *liaison* meant an illicit love affair. How does this fact illuminate its present meaning? See *paramour* (p. 360).

8. repertoire   (rĕp′ər tuär′)   *(list of) works a person or a company can perform*

The singer has a repertoire ranging from operatic arias to folk songs.
The actor from the repertory (rĕp′ər tôr′ē) company has played many roles.

> A *repertory* company is a theatrical group which presents new plays and also maintains a repertoire of classic plays.

SIX WORDS FROM NAMES

1. malapropism   (măl′ə prŏp′ĭz′əm)   *blunder in choice of words*

Phil accidentally used a malapropism: Meaning to use the word "restitution," he said instead, "The police demanded immediate destitution of the stolen goods."

> In Sheridan's play *The Rivals,* Mrs. Malaprop, who was especially fond of long words, was always using a word which sounded like the one she thought she was using. For example, she declared that a girl should know something of "contagious countries," and should "reprehend the true meaning of what she is saying." The name *Malaprop* comes from *malapropos,* a French word meaning unseasonable, ill-timed, or inappropriate.
> Compare *apropos* under *relevant* (p. 214).

2. mentor   (mĕn′tör′)   *a wise, trusted adviser*

Because the coach of the drama club was often an adviser and counselor to the players, he was sometimes called its mentor.
Aunt Harriet was her niece's mentor and friend.

> Mentor was the friend to whom the Greek hero Odysseus entrusted his household and his son, Telemachus, before leaving for the Trojan War.
> Compare *sage* (wise person), *solon* (wise leader), *savant* (learned person), *tutor* (teacher, counselor). *Tutor* is closer to *mentor* in meaning than any of the others, but its use is chiefly academic, whereas a mentor is a guardian and monitor as well as a tutor.

3. mercury   (mûr′kyə rē)   *messenger, carrier of news*

The *American Mercury* is a western literary periodical.
A mercury thermometer measures temperature by the expansion and contraction of the heavy mercury liquid.
A mercurial (mər kyo͞or′ē əl) person is volatile, quick-witted, changeable.

Related words:

> An *emissary* is a messenger, often a secret agent, sent on a specific mission.
> A *nuncio* or *legate* is a papal ambassador or representative.
> A *missionary* or *apostle* is a person sent on a religious or good-will mission.

In Roman mythology, Mercury was the eloquent, clever, swift-footed messenger of the gods. The planet was named in his honor. Medieval alchemists gave the same name to the heavy, metallic liquid once known as *quicksilver*. Can you explain why?

4. nemesis (nĕm′ə səs)   ***agent of retribution, a just punishment***

In the French Revolution, Marat's nemesis was Charlotte Corday, who stabbed him to death while he bathed.
King Saul was his own nemesis; he committed suicide.

Nemesis was the Greek goddess of retribution or vengeance. See *retribution* (pp. 36, 153).

5. protean (prō′tē ən)   ***highly versatile,***
readily taking numerous forms

A business executive must be a truly protean kind of person.
Because he could delineate such a variety of characters so well, Shakespeare was probably the most protean of all English playwrights.

In Greek mythology, Proteus was a sea god who could assume many different forms, such as a lion, a snake, a tree, or fire.

6. stentorian (stĕn tôr′ē ən)   ***very loud or powerful***

The foghorn gave forth a stentorian blast at regular intervals.
Mr. Eppling addressed his classes in stentorian tones.

In the *Iliad*, Stentor was a herald with a very powerful voice.
There are many noise words, such as *pandemonium, hullabaloo, detonation, fulmination* (p. 229), and *clangorous*.

SIX WORDS FROM FINE ARTS

1. allegory   (ăl′ə gôr′ē)   ***story in which characters are symbolic***

Animal Farm, by George Orwell, is an allegory in which various animals symbolize social forces.
Idylls of the King has an allegorical meaning. In ''Gareth and Lynette,'' Death, the most terrible and most feared of the knights, turns out to be a young boy, easily overthrown.

> The characters of an allegory are usually personified virtues or vices and their actions are often symbolic, too. Church pageants often abound in allegorical figures.

2. ballet   (băl′ā)   ***style of dancing, (a kind of) dance performance***

A ballet is an elaborate dance, employing pantomime (often allegorical) and set to music.
Scheherazade is a well-known ballet, set to the music of Rimsky-Korsakov. Russians have excelled in ballet; Nijinsky and Pavlova were two of the world's greatest ballet dancers.

> A *ballerina* (female dancer) needs years of training before she is able to execute the ballet steps with ease and grace.
> The art of devising and arranging the dances of a ballet is called *choreography*. The composer of dances is the *choreographer*.

3. curator   (kyо̄о̄r′ā′tе*r*)   ***custodian of a museum or art collection***

The curator of the art gallery purchased a Renoir painting.
The curatorship of the new museum will go to Dr. Martha Maggione.

Related words:

> A *steward(ess)* takes care of another person's property or estate, or serves the passengers on a plane.
> A *croupier* takes care of the betting at a gambling table.
> A *custodian* is the caretaker of a building. See *custody* (p. 14).

4. denouement   (dā′nо̄о̄ män″′)   ***outcome, solution***
                                           (of a story or play)

The denouement of the O'Casey play is believable and fitting.
Discovery of the missing document hastened the denouement of the legal battle to settle the dead man's estate.

> *Denouement* comes from a French verb meaning to unravel or untie.

5. symmetry   (sĭm′ə trē)   ***balance, correspondence of parts***

The intricate symmetry of a snowflake shows up under magnification.
The Parthenon was a symmetrical (sĭ mĕ′trĭ kəl) structure—both vertically and
lengthwise—with subtle curves that escape notice.

> *Symmetry* denotes a rather exact balance in the size, shape, and position of the parts
> on either side of a dividing line.

6. virtuoso   (vûr′cho͞o ō′sō)   ***person especially skilled in***
                                                     one of the fine arts

The violinist is a world-famed virtuoso.
She maintains her virtuosity (vûr′cho͞o ŏs′ə tē) by practicing six hours a day.

> *Virtuoso* comes from the Latin *virtuosus* (virtuous). Because it was a "virtue" to
> become learned or skilled in the arts, the term *virtuoso* began to be applied to the
> artist.
> Compare *savant* (p. 239), *maestro*.

First practice set

Which entry word from this unit best replaces each *italicized* word or group
of words?

1. The *society girl* was not interested in *middle-class* culture.
2. A *social set* of young people who consider themselves *competent judges* of
   popular music gathers weekly to play records.

3. The governor's political *trusted adviser* maintained *unofficial linkage* with the judges of the state supreme court.
4. The *custodian* of the museum, who came to America from another country, slips into an occasional *blunder in the choice of words*.
5. The *outcome* of the *pantomimic dance performance* brought the audience to its feet.
6. One part in the alto's operatic *works she can perform* requires the fullest use of her *very powerful* voice.
7. Gareth becomes the *agent of retribution* for Death in Tennyson's *story (in which characters and incidents are symbolic)*.
8. The *Daily (Messenger)* contained a fine *analysis* of the play.
9. The *vastly variable* range of the *person (skilled in one of the arts)* impressed everyone.
10. *Murder in the Cathedral*, a drama of court *plotting*, displays in its structure a pleasing *correspondence of parts*, with the King pitted against Thomas à Becket.

Second practice set

Which word from the list at the left best replaces each *italicized* word or group of words?

patrician
ingenue
croupier
epicure
repertory
gourmet
sage
savant
sansculotte
junta
plebeian
parvenu
emissary
clique
disquisition
nuncio
treatise
arbiter
repertoire
demimonde
cabal
tutor
coup d'etat
inapropos

1. A *man of learning* became the center of a *Latin American legislative and administrative council* formed after a revolution in his country.
2. The papal *representative* served as *umpire and judge* in the dispute between the two countries.
3. The election of a political *newcomer* was especially *inappropriate* at this time.
4. The *upper-class* Roman matron and her husband presided at a feast attended by well-known *persons who enjoyed delicately flavored foods*.
5. The *group of plotters* that engineered the *illegal overthrow of the government* met in a beer hall.
6. Emerson, the *wise man* of Concord, was one of a *small exclusive group* of intellectually elite who lived in or near Boston.
7. A *teacher charged with the instruction of another* was enlisted to coach the person chosen for the role of a *naïve young girl* in the play.
8. A *special connoisseur of foods* would be the obvious person to write a *book* on elegant eating.
9. The vagrant soon exhausted his *stock* of *lower-class* curses.
10. The *secret messenger* left after hearing the prime minister's *oral discussion* on the penalties of failure.

Third practice set

Which lettered pair of items comes nearest to having the same relationship as the pair printed in capital letters?

1. CRITIC: VIRTUOSO:: (a) connoisseur: ballet (b) mercury: gods (c) ingenue: debutante (d) ballerina: mentor

2. NEMESIS: RETRIBUTION:: (a) intrigue: liaison (b) newspaper: Mercury (c) Stentor: herald (d) Proteus: variability

3. CABAL: COUP D'ETAT:: (a) ballerina: ballet (b) pundit: parvenu (c) mentor: virtuoso (d) bourgeois: denouement

4. AUTHOR: ALLEGORY:: (a) curator: museum (b) choreographer: ballet (c) arbiter: coterie (d) repertoire: actor

5. MALAPROPISM: SPOONERISM:: (a) critique: intrigue (b) liaison: demimonde (c) cabal: junta (d) drama: ballet

6. ACTOR: REPERTOIRE:: (a) music: connoisseur (b) choreographer: allegory (c) ballerina: ballet (d) curator: museum

7. PROTEUS: PROTEAN:: (a) gourmet: epicure (b) Stentor: stenographic (c) Odysseus: Odyssey (d) Mercury: mercurial

8. COTERIE: CLIQUE:: (a) cabal: coup d'etat (b) choreographer: virtuoso (c) debutante: dilettante (d) aristocrat: patrician

9. EPICURE: GOURMET:: (a) disquisition: thesis (b) custodian: croupier (c) plebeian: proletariat (d) sage: savant

10. PLEBEIAN: PROLETARIAT:: (a) junta: cabal (b) patrician: aristocracy (c) critique: treatise (d) ballet: repertory

THIS JOB'S NO CHALLENGE. THERE'S NOT AN EPICURE OR GOURMET AMONG THEM.

Bonus

Which word from this unit best replaces each *italicized* word or group of words?

1. *Laboring class* leaders were not skillful in maintaining *unofficial linkage* with their political mentors.
2. She laughingly admitted that what she had originally chosen to wear in making her *first appearance in society* was *inappropriate*.
3. The characters of the ballet are *symbolic*, and their actions portray the *retribution* of wasted talent.
4. The *correspondence (balance of parts)* of the blocks *arouses the interest of* my four-year-old brother.
5. The violinist is known for her *volatile* temperament and extraordinary *skill in execution*.

Word hunt

1. Look up *The Rivals* by Philip Sheridan. Scan Mrs. Malaprop's speeches and list several more of her blunders. Can you devise two or three she might have made if she were living today?
2. Browse through a dictionary of mythology and list several words not in this unit which have come from mythological names.
3. What is *reconnaissance? croquet?* a *debacle?* the *Ballet Russe?* a *billet-doux?* a *claque?* an *allegorist? asymmetry? savoir faire?* a *virtuoso* of the 1660s in England? What are *belles lettres?*

unit eight

CRUCIAL DISTINCTIONS

Make the correct choice in each case.

1. A compatible person is   (a) easy-going   (b) easy to get along with   (c) easy to dislike   (d) easy to get rid of.

2. A person who observes the amenities is   (a) superstitious   (b) forgetful   (c) polite   (d) lacking in courage.

3. Intuition is   (a) instinctive knowledge   (b) cost of education   (c) reasoning power   (d) native ability.

4. A specious excuse is   (a) prompt   (b) scornful   (c) deceptive   (d) vague.

5. A criterion is   (a) mythical creature   (b) a competent critic   (c) a model of moral perfection   (d) a standard of judgment.

6. Comity pertains to   (a) the theater   (b) diplomacy   (c) astronomy   (d) beauty culture.

7. A crucial event is primarily   (a) decisive   (b) regrettable   (c) injurious   (d) prolonged.

8. Hyperbole is   (a) a missile   (b) cold weather   (c) exaggeration   (d) abandon.

9. A nonchalant person is   (a) indifferent   (b) easy-going   (c) negative   (d) abstinent.

10. A deleterious substance is   (a) hateful   (b) laugh-producing   (c) light and flaky   (d) harmful to health.

DISTINCTIVE NOUNS

1. amenity   (ə mĕn′ə tē)   *a pleasing way or custom*

The amenities in India are quite different from those in Europe.
Father is not always amenable (ə mē′nə bəl *or* ə mĕn′ə bəl) (submissive) to suggestions.

MY FATHER THANKS
YOU.... MY MOTHER THANKS
YOU..... MY SISTER THANKS YOU.....

Saying *thank you* is an everyday amenity that makes life more pleasant.

Related words:

Amenable also means liable: Speeders are amenable to arrest.
Etiquette is merely codified propriety in social situations.
Civility is politeness in a routine and impersonal way. See *civil* (p. 150).
Comity is courtesy, consideration, and civility between nations in observing each other's laws and amenities.
Diplomacy is courteous, tactful strategy in gaining national or personal ends.

2. criterion   (krī têr′ē ən)   ***basis or standard for judgment***

Is a college degree a valid criterion of intelligence?
Leadership, scholarship, character, and service are the criteria for membership in the National Honor Society.

The plural of *criterion* is *criteria*. The plural of *phenomenon* is *phenomena*. From what language do these words come?

3. hyperbole   (hī pûr′bə lē′)   ***exaggeration for rhetorical effect***

"The waves were mountain high" and "I almost died laughing" are common examples of hyperbole.
To say of the body, " 'Tis but a tent for one day's rest" is a hyperbolic (hī′pər bol′ĭk) metaphor.

See <u>hyper-</u> words (above, beyond normal) (p. 331); *hypertension, hypertrophy, hypersensitive, hyperacidity.*
Litotes is understatement, of which the British are fond. An example: Napoleon caused a slight commotion in Europe.

4. integrity (ĭn tĕg′rə tē)   ***moral soundness, uprightness***

The cabinet appointee was a woman of the utmost integrity, honest in all her dealings and unimpeachable in character.
The gatekeeper showed his integrity by refusing to accept a bribe.

> *Integrity* literally means oneness or wholeness of character.
> An *integer* is a whole number.
> To *integrate* a school or other area is to make it open and available to all races.
> To *disintegrate* physically or morally is to *deteriorate, degenerate,* and thus lose one's wholeness or soundness.
> An *unintegrated* mass of data is one that has not been organized or analyzed.
> Compare *rectitude* (p. 340) which indicates a sound moral character and is more self-conscious than integrity.

5. intuition (ĭn′tōō ĭsh′ən)   ***instinctive knowledge***

Gladys knew by intuition that she could not trust the glib stranger.
Religious faith is primarily intuitive (ĭn tōō′ə tĭv) rather than rational.

> Compare *tuition,* the charge for instruction in a college or private school.

6. nonchalance (nŏn′shə ləns′)   ***indifference, unconcern***

Isabel's nonchalance under cross-examination reassured her friends that she was innocent.
The heiress nonchalantly faced her accusers.
Ingrid was nonchalant about the prizes she had won.

> Compare *inert* and synonyms (p. 53) and *apathy* (p. 37).

7. optimism (ŏp′tə mĭz′əm)   ***tendency to take the most hopeful view***

The doctor's optimism gave the sick man courage.
Past victories made us optimistic about winning the pennant.
Being an optimist, Frank had no doubts about passing the tests.

> See also *optimum,* most favorable: The optimum temperature for a home is 68°–70°.
> Review *sanguine* (p. 164). *Buoyancy* is cheerfulness of spirit.

8. pertinacity (pûr′tə năs′ə te)   ***stubborn perseverance***

In the business of selling, one must have the pertinacity to face strong resistance from potential customers.
Boswell was a pertinacious (pûr′tə nā′shəs) young man who attached himself to Dr. Johnson despite the latter's dislike.

> *Pertinacity* has somewhat unfavorable connotations, with a hint of excess that *tenacity* (p. 99) does not imply.
>
> **Synonyms:** *doggedness, persistence, resoluteness, steadfastness, stubbornness, obstinacy* (pp. 63, 99).
>
> Compare *unwavering, unfaltering, unswerving, unflinching, unflagging, unremitting.*

9. pessimism   (pĕs′ə mĭz′əm)   ***tendency to expect the worst***

Mr. Gobel's pessimism was a natural result of his incompetence.
Cloudy skies made the grownups pessimistic about our having the picnic.
''Nothing disappoints a pessimist like the refusal of things to go wrong'' is an obvious truism.

Pessimistic modes:

A *splenetic* (p. 160) person is bad-tempered, peevish, irritable.
A *cynical* person distrusts human motives.
A *saturnine* person is gloomy and grave.
A *lugubrious* person is heavily sad and doleful, as only a pessimist can be (p. 116).
A *despondent* person feels hopeless, gloomy, dejected, and near despair (p. 193).
A *disconsolate* (p. 116) person is without provision for cheer or hope.
A *melancholy* person is darkly sad and gloomy. See synonyms (p. 116).
A *misanthropic* person, hating humanity, can hardly have an optimistic view of the future.

10. rapacity   (rə păs′ə tē)   ***violence or greed,***
eagerness for plunder

Barbarians from the north began plundering the weakened Roman Empire with the rapacity of wild beasts.
Rapacity for patronage plagued the state administration.
A rapacious (rə pā′shəs) hoodlum demanded ''protection'' payments.

Degrees of greed:

Covetousness (p. 114) is excessive desire for that which one has no right to possess.
Cupidity is greed for money or power—on a large or small scale.
Avarice is greed a shade more intense, with determination to match (pp. 38, 143).
Predacity is primarily the animal urge to prey on other animals. Human beings are often *predatory* in business, love, and sports.

Query: Is the Hindu ideal of desirelessness the remedy or the antidote for greed?

PRECISE ADJECTIVES

1. clandestine (klăn dĕs′tən)   *secret, stealthy*

The rebel leaders held a clandestine meeting in a cave.
Gems worth many thousands of dollars were brought into the country clandestinely.

Varieties of secrecy:

> A *covert* glance is disguised, secret: The child threw covert glances at the forbidden box of candy.
> A *furtive* glance is sly and wary: The pickpocket in one furtive glance discovered the location of the man's wallet.
> A *surreptitious* visit is stealthy and concealed, although without the same sense of guilt that a clandestine visit might imply.
> See *incognito* under -cogn- (p. 339).

2. coherent (kō hêr′ənt)   *sticking together, connected*

The nurse tried to give a coherent account of what had happened.
Frank's tale was confused and lacking in coherence (logical order).
Though the victim was conscious, fever made her incoherent.
A magnet causes iron filings to cohere in a symmetrical pattern.

> *Coherence* is usually applied to figurative or abstract (immaterial) things, *cohesion* to material things. The wet clay formed a cohesive mass.

3. compatible (kəm păt′ə bəl)   *capable of being harmonized*

The woman's garb was hardly compatible with her cultured speech.
The class discussed the compatibility of various temperaments.
Often dogs and cats are incompatible pets.

> Compare *congruous, consonant, conformable, consistent* (p. 298), *reconcilable* (p. 195).

Kinds of incompatibility:

Incongruity is lack of harmony or correspondence of parts: Chickens would look incongruous in the living room. Surrealistic art, such as Dali's, features incongruities.
Intractability is the failure to yield to a teacher's, leader's, or employer's direction: The intractability of the local people made it difficult to employ them in the making of the film.
Recalcitrance is refusal to obey or conform to what is required in the circumstances: France's recalcitrance weakened NATO.

4. concomitant   (kən kŏm′ə tənt)

an attendant condition, varying at the same rate

The growth of crops is concomitant with the tipping of the earth's axis toward the sun.
Inverse concomitance exists between atmospheric pressure and altitude.
Blood pressure and pulse rate tend to vary concomitantly.

Related words:

Concurrent terms of imprisonment run simultaneously. See -cur(r)- (p. 304).
Corresponding points of similarity prove that the fingerprints at the scene are those of the suspect.
Coincidence (p. 251) is typically an incidental and accidental occurrence, like having a fiancé with the same birthday as yours; a *concomitance,* however, is usually a process related by cause and effect.
A *synchronous* motor keeps in time with the generator, *i.e.,* turns at the same speed.

5. crucial   (krōō′shəl)

supremely important or decisive, severe

The fourth quarter proved crucial because we were one point behind.
Misfortune offers a crucial test of character.

Crucial comes from the Latin word *crux* (cross). Thus it suggests severe, climactic suffering. Other cross words are *crucify, crucifix, cruciform, crucifer, excruciating, crucible.*

6. deleterious   (dĕl′ə têr′ē əs)

harmful to health, injurious

The new medicine sometimes has deleterious side effects.
The essay discusses the deleteriousness of bad habits.

Related words:

Baneful (p. 161), *narcotic, noxious* (pp. 46, 161), *detrimental, noisome, insidious* (p. 161), *pestilent* (p. 161), *septic, venomous* (p. 161), *pernicious* (p. 161), *mephitic* (bad smelling, poisonous) (p. 178).

Antonym: salubrious (healthful) (p. 232).

7. impervious   (ĭm′pûr′vē əs)   *impenetrable, unaffected by*

Plastic materials are impervious to water.
Jerry proved impervious to criticism, no matter how blunt or how subtle.
Imperviousness to praise keeps a person from becoming vain.

> The root meaning of *impervious* is no (im-) way (vi-) through (per-).

8. iridescent   (ĭr′ə dĕs′ənt)   *glistening with colors, glittering*

Diamonds and dewdrops are remarkably iridescent.
The iridescence of fine mist in bright light creates rainbows.

> In both Greek and Latin, the word *iris* means rainbow; thus *iridescent* literally means becoming a rainbow.

Color words:

> *Prismatic* lighting is brilliant, dazzling.
> A *polychromatic* (many-colored) display is like light reflected through a prism.
> *Kaleidoscopic* effects are constantly changing in pattern as well as color.

-Escent (becoming) words include:

> *Reminiscent* (becoming alive in memory); *phosphorescent* (becoming luminous without heat); *putrescent* (becoming rotten); *incandescent* (becoming white hot); *recrudescent* (becoming alive again, breaking out again).

9. peremptory   (pə rĕmp′tə rē)   *imperative, positive, dictatorial*

''No visitors at all!'' was the doctor's peremptory command.
The angry father peremptorily ordered his son out of the house.

> A *peremptory* command or demand is absolute. It permits no refusal, denial, or delay. For the legal meaning, consult the dictionary.
> Compare *imperious* under *imperial* (p. 193).

10. specious   (spē′shəs)   *fair-seeming, deceptive, plausible but not genuine*

Pat invented a specious excuse for not going to the party.
The article was full of misleading statements and specious logic.
Connie recognized the speciousness of the plan to pay for welfare by a lottery.

Related words:

> A *specious* plan sounds good, but it is unsound.
> A *meretricious* scheme (deceptively alluring) looks good: The colorful folders put out by the land-developing company obscured the meretriciousness of the offer.
> A *plausible* (p. 21) plan is reasonable and, unlike a specious one, may be sound.
> An *ostensible* reason is not the real reason but a pretended one.

First practice set

Which entry word from this unit best replaces each *italicized* word or group of words?

1. To call the loss of a *supremely important* football game Franklin High's Waterloo was a startling *exaggeration for effect*.

2. Greeting a guest with a mild compliment is one of the *pleasing customs* that give a hostess a glow that is *glittering with colors*.

3. Some employers regard punctuality as a *basis (for judging)* a person's *moral soundness*.

4. *Instinctive knowledge* told Dora that pills to keep one awake are *harmful to health* if taken too often.

5. Public opinion holds that diplomatic negotiations should not be *stealthy* or *dictatorial*.

6. *Stubborn perseverance* will not help a candidate who has a reputation for *violent greed*.

7. The arguments for *expecting the worst* where human nature is concerned are *logically connected* and convincing.

8. Chuck's apparent *unconcern* about school work is not quite *consistent with, that is, not capable of being harmonized with,* the good grades he gets.

9. In the case under discussion, the decision of the Supreme Court may seem *deceptive* and its judges virtually *unresponsive* to public opinion.

10. Millie's fluctuating *tendency to expect the best* seems to be *varying (at the same rate)* with the state of her health.

Second practice set

Which word from the list at the left best replaces each *italicized* word or group of words?

incongruous
mephitic
insidious
disconsolate
surreptitious
intractability
kaleidoscopic
ostensible
concurrent
rectitude
litotes
recalcitrance
civility
prismatic
optimum
integration
splenetic
consonant
recrudescence
unremitting
phosphorescent
diplomacy
comity

1. Brenda's *upright character* did not, however, make tolerable her *inability to yield to an employer's direction*.

2. The *peevish, bad-tempered* bus driver was more *cheerless* than usual today.

3. *Most favorable* conditions exist in October in that country before the *subtly treacherous* onset of malaria begins.

4. *Dazzling, iridescent* colors danced on the gray walls of the *bad-smelling* cell.

5. *Courtesy between nations* calls for *tenacious* patience on the part of their diplomats.

6. *Skill in difficult negotiations* made it necessary to give the *pretended, seeming* reason for wanting to delay action.

7. It was *inharmonious* to find winter weather in July but we accepted it with routine *politeness*.

8. "The world will little note, nor long remember" turned out to be an *understatement* quite *harmonious* with the speaker's character.

9. Fred's *refusal to obey* led to a *concealed* departure from the camp during the night.

10. A *colorful, everchanging* adventure in London brought a *breaking out again* of the author's old creativity.

Third practice set

Select the pair of words (a, b, c, or d) which best completes the meaning of each sentence below.

1. One _____ by which we may estimate the character of a person in public office is his _____ .
   (a) hyperbole—intuition
   (b) amenity—civility
   (c) criterion—integrity
   (d) intuition—nonchalance

2. While _____ often helps a person know what he ought to do, he must avoid excessive _____ , knowing that the most inspired plans sometimes fail.
   (a) intuition—optimism
   (b) nonchalance—pertinacity
   (c) pertinacity—pessimism
   (d) diplomacy—intuition

3. The little _____ of negotiation play an important part in the larger and more inclusive strategies of _____ .
   (a) criteria—optimism
   (b) amenities—diplomacy
   (c) civilities—rapacity
   (d) pertinacities—integrity

4. The driver's account of the accident was _____ , but it was not _____ with the victim's account.
   (a) incongruous—reconcilable
   (b) deleterious—plausible
   (c) specious—recalcitrant
   (d) coherent—compatible

5. _____ love affairs may pervert one of life's most _____ decisions.
   (a) Recalcitrant—iridescent
   (b) Clandestine—crucial
   (c) Deleterious—surreptitious
   (d) Recalcitrant—pessimistic

6. Most voters thought the losing candidate's promises were _____ and his influence highly _____ .
   (a) crucial—impervious
   (b) specious—deleterious
   (c) incongruous—amenable
   (d) synchronous—insidious

7. Because of his _____ honesty, employers tolerated his _____ outbursts and did not fire him.
   (a) rapacious—amenable
   (b) nonchalant—civil
   (c) unwavering—splenetic
   (d) specious—misanthropic

8. Is it _____ to say that American writers are barbarians who foster only _____ in their readers?
   (a) hyperbole—pessimism
   (b) amenity—intuition
   (c) pertinacity—optimism
   (d) nonchalance—integrity

9. Violet thought she was _____ to fear, but her _____ disappeared when she saw that a crash was inevitable.
   (a) incongruous—diplomacy
   (b) amenable—criterion
   (c) impervious—nonchalance
   (d) recalcitrant—optimism

10. Our _____ about the future is based on the fact that the campaign is so terribly _____ in its operation.
    (a) criterion—recalcitrant
    (b) optimism—incongruous
    (c) pessimism—unintegrated
    (d) nonchalance—rapacious

unit nine

APPLICATIONS

Which word from the list at the left gives the best answer to each question?

onerous
alleviate
connive
hibernate
indigenous
amortize
amalgamate
indigent
mundane
obsolete
clement
ribald

1. Which one applies to the Model T Ford (1909–1927)?
2. Which one describes a plant that is native to the region where it is found?
3. Which pertains to winter?
4. Which one is in need?
5. Which one is coarse? and mocking?
6. Which tells how you pay a huge debt?
7. Which applies to something burdensome?
8. Which one unites or combines?
9. Which applies to commonplace, everyday matters?
10. Which makes you approve or assist in wrongdoing?

EXECUTIVE OPTIONS

1. abrogate   (ăb′rə gāt′)   *to abolish, annul, do away with*

The new tax law abrogates several provisions of the old one.
Abrogation of the treaty was inevitable.

Compare *revoke* (p. 299), *repeal, nullify, rescind, negate, cancel, invalidate.*

2. adulterate   (ə dŭl′tə rāt′)   *to cheapen or debase with inferior or harmful ingredients*

Cornstarch is sometimes used to adulterate ice cream.
Pure food and drug laws control the adulteration of foods.
Penalties are prescribed for the use of adulterants.

> *Adulterate* goes back to the Latin <u>ad</u>- (to) and *alter* (other, different).

3. alleviate   (ə lē′vē āt′)   *to lessen, lighten, relieve*

A nurse tried to alleviate the patient's pain.
Many measures have been taken for the alleviation of poverty.

Relief words:

> *Allay, mitigate* (p. 229), *assuage.*
> Compare *ameliorate* (to make better).

4. amalgamate   (ə măl′gə māt′)   *to combine, unite, fuse*

The two insurance firms voted to amalgamate.
Details of the amalgamation will be worked out by the officers.

> An *amalgam* is an *alloy* or *fusion,* especially of mercury with some other metal. The amalgam fillings which a dentist uses are an alloy of mercury and silver.
> The word *alloy* was originally applied to a base metal used to cheapen or adulterate other metals. Thus the word *unalloyed* has come to mean *genuine, sincere:* Christmas brings unalloyed delight to children.

Related words:

> *Integration* is a merging or unification of separate plans, races, or processes.
> *Interfusion* is the process of mixing such ingredients as cultures, races, or ideas.
> *Consolidation* is the process of combining material assets or gains.
> *Coalescence* (p. 257) is combining by the gradual process of merging or growing together. It is a word used especially of ingredients.
> A *coalition* (p. 209) is a temporary union or combination, particularly of political forces when one of them cannot obtain a majority by itself.
> A *merger* is a combination, especially of two business firms.

5. amortize   (ăm′ər tīz′)   *to write off a debt by regular payments*

The Burkes will amortize the cost of a new house by paying 1 percent a month.
At 8 percent interest, how long will the amortization take?

> How do you account for the -<u>mort</u>- root in *amortize* and in *mortgage*? (See your dictionary.)

6. connive   (kə nīv′)   *to approve of or secretly aid the wrongdoing of another*

The police were foolish to connive with gamblers in illegal pay-offs.
Bruce expected his brother to connive at the sale of land which had no assured water supply.

The sale of narcotics went on with the connivance of the city officials.

Connive originally meant to wink or shut one's eyes. It is followed by *at* or *with*.

Related words:

To *condone* a practice is to approve it by seeming to overlook it (pp. 181, 307, 351).
To *collude* is to conspire for fraudulent purposes: Ananias and his wife were guilty of *collusion*.
To *conspire* is to devise a plot or plan against someone.

7. effect (ĭ fĕkt′) *to bring about, accomplish*

It took only one day to effect a compromise in the wage dispute.
The new method of checking orders proved effectual (ĭ fĕk′cho͞o əl).
Judge Rizzo found the lawyer's arguments for a suspended sentence interesting but ineffectual.

Related words:

Compare *fruition* (p. 185), *consummate* (p. 71).
An *eventuality* is an ultimate outcome.
The *execution* of a command or a commission is the performance of it.
The *effectuation* of a plan is its accomplishment, the putting it into operation. It is less direct and less personal than *execution*.

8. hibernate (hī′bər nāt′) *to spend the winter (in a resting state)*

Those who can afford it like to hibernate in California, Florida, or the French Riviera.
For bears, hibernation means a dormant condition.

Compare *aestivate,* to spend the summer.
A *Hibernian* is a native of Ireland. The word derives from the Latin *Hibernia* (Ireland).

9. pacify (păs′ə fī′) *to make calm, appease*

It took two hours to pacify the woman when her husband died.
Pacification of the enraged farm owners was not easy.
The invaders made it clear that their intentions were pacific (pə sĭf′ĭk).
Like most others of the sect, the young Quaker is a pacifist.
Many idealists today advocate pacifism.

10. stultify (stŭl′tə fī′) *to render absurd or useless*

Inattention in Congress serves to stultify speech-making, but the printed speeches look good to constituents in a representative's home state.
Stultification of the campaign for free bus service was a gradual process.

Related words:

Farce is a form of absurdity, to which a court trial may be reduced by frivolous evidence, a mistaken case, or an uninformed jury.
Ludicrousness is much more laughable than is stultification.
Preposterousness is startling or shocking absurdity.

QUALITIES AND CONDITIONS

1. clement   (klĕm'ənt)   *mild, merciful*

Clement December weather is unusual in Minnesota.
The jury recommended clemency because the culprit meant only to scare his
victim, not to injure her.

> **Review:** *lenient* (merciful, mild), *leniency* (p. 45).

> **Antonym:** *inclement.*

2. indigenous   (ĭn dĭj'ə nəs)   *native, characteristic of a*
specific region

The botanist pointed out plants indigenous to North America.
The indigenousness of the animal to a similar Australian climate indicates that it
will thrive in Illinois.

Related words:

> *Indigenous,* like *congenital,* belongs to the -gen-, or birth, words (p. 313).
> *Aboriginal* plants are the oldest, earliest known species in a region or area. The
> *aborigines* are the earliest, or native, inhabitants of a land.
> An *endemic* plant or disease is one prevalent in a specific region and therefore in-
> digenous to that region.

3. indigent   (ĭn'də jənt)   *needy, poor*

The church prepares Christmas baskets for indigent members.
Is indigence an insurmountable handicap?

Poverty words:

> An *impoverished* person is one who formerly had wealth.
> An *impecunious* person never has much money, partly because of bad management.
> A *destitute* person is extremely poor, lacking even enough for food.
> Compare *pecuniary, mercenary* (p. 143).

I'M PRACTICALLY INDIGENT. I'VE BEEN IMPECUNIOUS ALL WEEK AND NOW THE MATER IS WITHOLDING MY ALLOWANCE

4. mundane   (mŭn′dān′)   *earthly, commonplace*

The game of tic-tac-toe is a mundane activity.
Joyce voiced her annoyance at having to spend so much time on mundane matters.

> *Secular* means worldly in the sense of nonreligious. The church is concerned with religious, the state with secular, affairs.
> *Secularish* is a preoccupation with worldly concerns.
> *Sectarianism,* however, is excessive devotion to one sect or its beliefs.

Pairs of opposites:

> *Earthly—heavenly; secular—sacred; terrestrial—celestial* (p. 150); *temporal—eternal; sectarian—nonsectarian.*

5. obsolete   (ŏb′sə lēt′)   *outmoded, out of use*

Do guns and cannon make armor obsolete?
Machinery in a modern factory often becomes obsolescent (ŏb′sə lĕs′ənt) (passing out of use) before it wears out.
Although rapid obsolescence is costly, it is less costly than the operation of outmoded, inefficient equipment.

Related words:

> *Antique* furniture is usually less than three hundred years old, but *ancient* furniture may be over two thousand years old.
> *Archaic* words or objects are still in use but nearly obsolete.
> *Decadent* customs or practices are on the decline. Some consider our society to be in a state of *decadence,* as Rome was in A.D. 200.

6. onerous   (ō′nər əs)   *burdensome, oppressive*

The onerous task of translating a twenty-volume history kept the Cabral sisters busy for several years.
Widespread protest arose over the onerousness of the taxes the state imposed.

> The Latin word *onus* (a load) has become an English word meaning burden: The onus of arranging the reception fell upon the teacher.
> *Exonerate* (p. 124) comes from the same root as *onus.*
> Compare *opus* (a major work or masterpiece).

7. reputable   (rĕp′yə tə bəl)   *well thought of, respected*

A reputable firm will guarantee its product.
The reputability of the college is well attested.
The new make of car performs reputably.

The shabby old house is reputed (rǐ pyōō′təd) to be over a hundred years old.
Courtesy and consideration will always be in good repute (rǐ pyōōt′).

Antonyms: *disreputable, disrepute.*

See -<u>pute</u>- words (p. 340).

8. ribald   (rǐb′əld)   *coarsely mocking, scurrilous*

Ribald laughter greeted the remarks of the latest arrival at the bar.
The tavern reechoed with unrestrained ribaldry (rǐb′əl drē) for several hours.

Coarse words:

> *Indelicate, unrefined, vulgar, indecent, gross, obscene, scurrilous:* A *scurrilous* remark is mockingly abusive. An *obscene* remark is loathsome and ugly. A *vulgar* gesture is crude, coarse, unrefined. See variant forms of each word in your dictionary and note original root meaning.

9. traumatic   (trə măt′ĭk)   *painful, resulting from violent physical injury or emotional shock*

The traumatic effect of finding the maniac in her room nearly unbalanced the woman's own psyche.
The trauma (trou′mə) of being severely injured left mental as well as physical scars.
Was it the injury he received or the terror from being pinned under his car that traumatized the tailor?

10. voluptuous   (və lŭp′chōō əs)   *giving delight to the senses*

Riding on the roller coaster was a voluptuous experience.
Prince Henry lived a life of carefree voluptuousness.
The party-goers danced voluptuously to the orchestra's primitive beat.

Related words:

>A *hedonistic* existence assumes that pleasure is the highest good.
>*Epicurean* delights are sensuous, especially eating and drinking.
>A *Sybarite* is a person fond of luxury and pleasure, *i.e.*, a *voluptuary*.

First practice set

Which entry word from this unit best replaces each *italicized* word or group of words?

1. The two organizations, which provide housing for the *poor*, will *combine* next year.

2. Mr. Santucci will soon *accomplish* his plans to *write off (by regular payments)* the purchase of an automobile dealership.

3. Realtors must *appease* the city council or it will refuse to *annul* the old zoning law.

4. The realtors also fear that the banks may *secretly work* with the council to make the financing too *burdensome*.

5. The plan of the bank has a certain *native* logic, and it is not likely that its implementation will prove *deeply painful*.

6. Though most of the council members are rather *commonplace* in their thinking, they are not the *coarsely mocking* characters they are reputed to be.

7. Nothing can *debase* their honesty, and they do all they can to *lessen* the problems of the city.

8. The newspapers call the council's proposal to abolish *outmoded* housing a plan that is clearly *well thought of*.

9. Critics say that the mayor lives too *sensual* a life to win their confidence and that this kind of life will ultimately *render* his career *useless*.

10. As the weather was *mild* on the island, the archeologists preferred to *spend the winter* in a cave rather than to live in inadequate dwellings.

11. Environmental scientists *brought about* a change in the river flow that would *relieve* somewhat the dryness of the desert region.

12. Though Bob found the work rather *oppressive*, he knew it would be more difficult to *appease* his conscience if he failed.

Second practice set

Which word from the list at the left best replaces each *italicized* word or group of words?

impecunious
execution
effectuation
secular
hedonistic
disrepute
ludicrousness
antique
epicurean
nonsectarian
ameliorate
fruition
pacifists
aestivate
lenient
amalgam
coalesence
impoverished
disreputable
archaic
eventuality
conspire
destitute
integration
inclement

1. Is a life *not respectable* that is *marked primarily by love of pleasure*?
2. If *war haters* faced the slaughter of loved ones as an *ultimate outcome*, what would they do?
3. Some think that artists are *prone to have little money* and live a life that is quite *filled with sensuous delights (especially eating)*.
4. Wits often dwell on the *ridiculousness* of *almost obsolete* customs like housewarmings.
5. *Putting into operation* of a plan to help *extremely poor* people support themselves awaits the council's approval.
6. *The gradual process of growing together* takes place when a piece of bone is transplanted.
7. *Unmerciful* weather abetted the author's desire to *spend the summer* in Norway; thus his *carrying out* of the workshop plans was postponed.
8. When warm winds from the south *make* the climate *better*, parents are more *merciful* about letting small children play outdoors.
9. *Merging* (making into one) of the two recreational programs will take place today, if no one *devises a plot* to undermine it.
10. Because of poor billing, the performer fell unjustly into a state of *not being respectable* and was, as a result, *greatly without money*.

Third practice set

Which lettered pair of items comes nearest to having the same relationship as the pair printed in capital letters?

1. REFINED:RIBALD:: (a) decadent:obsolete (b) terrestrial:earthy (c) affluent:indigent (d) onerous:ludicrous

2. CLEMENT:ALLEVIATE:: (a) dead:amortize (b) stultify:absurd (c) integrated:coalesce (d) lenient:mitigate

3. SECULAR:RELIGIOUS:: (a) ribald:sacred (b) farcical:onerous (c) temporal:contingent (d) mundane:terrestrial

4. COALESCE:INTERFUSE::   (a) revoke:consolidate   (b) connive:pacify
  (c) integrate:amalgamate (d) ameliorate:alleviate

5. NEGATION:ABROGATION::   (a) hibernation:refrigeration   (b) allevia-
tion:assuagement   (c) condonation:connivance   (d) onerousness:dis-
reputability

6. PACIFIC:MILITANT::   (a) ribald:religious (b) voluptuous:destitute (c)
amalgamated:invalidated (d) eternal:temporal

7. CONSOLIDATE:DISINTEGRATE::   (a) consummate:stultify   (b) amal-
gamate:abrogate (c) pacify:secularize (d) amortize:collude

8. TERRESTRIAL:CELESTIAL::   (a) onerous:obscene   (b) sybaritic:volup-
tuous (c) sectarian:secular (d) reputable:ludicrous

9. RIBALD:OBSCENE::   (a) aboriginal:decadent   (b) mundane:sectarian
 (c) indigenous:traumatic (d) indigent:destitute

10. HIBERNATE:AESTIVATE::   (a) integrate:adulterate (b) condone:stultify
 (c) abrogate:consummate (d) secularize:conspire

A word for it

Which of the words in this unit best replaces each *italicized* word or group of words?

1. Writing is *burdensome,* but many writers are not so *lacking in money* as you
may imagine.
2. Watching the robbery and murder was a *painful and harmful* experience, especially for a *person who rejects war and violence.*
3. Evidence existed of (a) *secret agreement for fraudulent purposes* between the
security guard and the burglar, both of whom were fond of *coarse mockery.*
4. Children from *extremely poor* homes usually have a *commonplace* existence.
5. That college is *not devoted to one religious sect,* but it is by no means a *nonre-
ligious* institution.

unit ten

CREDO FOR HARD WORK

Which word from the list at the left fits best in each blank?

analogy
allergic
anomaly
pragmatic
catholic
peripheral
adamant
vicarious
exigency
tantamount
hegemony
accolade

1. In the modern world, vocabulary is often _____ to intelligence.
2. This book by its title creates a convenient _____ between verbal and monetary affluence.
3. It is based on _____ evidence that systematic vocabulary study will improve a student's average in all of his subjects.
4. With its depth studies, it offers more than a _____ attack on word analysis.
5. It is a regrettable _____ that a potentially brilliant student may fail because he does not know a few thousand crucial words.
6. Even if one is _____ to the use of big words, a need exists to know what they mean.
7. Each student who gets all of the practice sets right in a unit deserves the _____ of an *A*.
8. Such students are the kind who are _____ in their refusal to give up.
9. With a finer command of English words, one is better able to meet each _____ that may arise.
10. Thus one will have a truly _____ capacity for comprehension and expression.

NOUNS FOR SPECIAL USES

1. accolade   (ăk′ə lād′)   ***award, recognition***

The movie that received the top accolade of the motion picture industry that year was filmed in England.
The Nobel Prize in literature is the most cherished accolade a writer can achieve.
At times an accolade is awarded to a person after death, as in the case of a heroic fire-fighter lost while saving another.

Accolade was once the act of conferring knighthood. The candidate was given a light blow on the neck, later on the shoulder, with the flat side of a sword. The ceremony grew more elaborate during the late Middle Ages.

Modes of recognition:

> *Commendation, citation, encomium, eulogy* (pp. 305, 350), *panegyric, curtsy, salaam, kowtow, genuflection* (pp. 55, 279).

2. amnesty   (ăm′nəs tē′)   ***general pardon (especially for political offenses)***

After the revolt was put down, King Charles II granted amnesty to all of the rebels who would swear allegiance to the Crown.
The government's declaration of amnesty healed many hostilities.

> Amnesty comes from Greek <u>a</u>- (not) and *mnasthai* (to remember).
> *Amnesia* (loss of memory) comes from the same Greek root.

3. analogy   (ə năl′ə jē′)   ***partial similarity, comparison***

The teacher used the analogy of water pressure to explain voltage.
Amperage or current is analogous (ə năl′ə gəs) to the amount of water flowing in a pipe.
The relation between the size of the wire and the size of the water pipe is analogous.
A faucet is an analogue (ăn′ə lŏg′) of the switch in an electric circuit.
Arguing that a nation, like a person, grows old and dies is reasoning by analogy.

Modes of comparison:

> *Similarity, resemblance, correspondence, parallelism, simile* (p. 99), *metaphor* (p. 97), *parable* (illustrative story), *similitude, allegory* (p. 241).

4. anomaly   (ə nŏm′ə lē)   *irregularity, abnormality*

The police were puzzled by an apparent anomaly: the cell was empty and the prisoner gone, but the gate was locked.
It would be anomalous to find United States coins on Mars.

Related words:

> *Erratic* (p. 52, 114) behavior is irregular, uneven, and unpredictable. *Anomalous* is used of a single deviation from normality, *erratic* of a habit or tendency. *Capricious* (p. 114) behavior is intentionally, imaginatively, or playfully irregular.

5. exigency   (ĕk′sə jən sē)   *urgent need, requirement*

Police responded well to the exigencies of the recent disorder.
The steel strike produced an exigent situation overnight.

> An *exigency* may be an emergency or the need arising from an emergency.

6. franchise   (frăn′chīz′)   *the right to vote; a business privilege granted by a government*

The franchise was extended to women after World War I.
The Fifteenth Amendment was an act of enfranchisement (ĕn frăn chiz mənt). Eighteen-year-olds were enfranchised when Congress decided that young people, old enough to be soldiers, were old enough to vote.
The city refused to renew the bus company's franchise.

> Compare *disenfranchisement*. It happens to convicted felons.

7. hegemony   (hə jĕm′ə nē)   *leadership, dominance*

The hegemony of Athens over the neighboring city-states was established before the Peloponnesian wars.
Results of British cultural hegemony are still discernible in the nations which once were British colonies.

> *Hegemony* is used almost wholly of states or nations that maintain leadership over a group or confederation; the hegemony of the U.S.S.R. in eastern Europe is very visible.

8. iconoclasm   (ī kŏn′ə klăz əm)   *attacking of cherished beliefs*

Nudist camping is a primitive form of societal iconoclasm.
Malcolm is a bearded iconoclast (ī kŏn′ə klăst′) who practices yoga.
Belief in flying machines was still iconoclastic in 1900.

> *Iconoclasm* originally meant image breaking. The iconoclasts were those who in the eighth century denounced the use of images or icons in the churches as idolatrous.
> *Iconology* is the study of religious images, pictures, and symbolic representation generally.
> The *iconoscope* is the picture tube (image viewer) of a television set.

9. nepotism   (nĕp′ə tĭz′əm)   *favoritism to relatives (especially in politics or employment)*

The governor was accused of nepotism when he made his son-in-law attorney general.

Nepotism flourished in the city government at one time. The mayor was a notorious nepotist.

> *Nepotism* in government or politics draws criticism, but it is taken for granted in a one-man enterprise like the Hearst newspapers, which became a family industry.

10. therapy   (thĕr′ə pē)   *treatment, healing*

Therapy by drugs is not the only method of combating illness.

Psychotherapy, or mental treatment, is a branch of therapeutics.

Rest and sleep have important therapeutic (thĕr′ə pyo͞o′ tĭk) value.

The nurse who just came in is a radium therapist.

> *Therapeutics* is the medical branch concerned with treatment of disease.
> *Hydrotherapy,* treatment with warm baths and mineral waters, dates back to the ancient Greeks.
> *Radiotherapy* is important in treating cancer.
> Compare *sanative* (curative), *medicinal.*

ADJECTIVE ASPECTS

1. adamant   (ăd′ə mənt)   *unyielding*

Lincoln was adamant on matters of moral principle.

The judge is adamant in his refusal to reduce the sentence.

It took adamantine (ăd′ə măn′tēn) courage to storm Mt. Suribachi on Iwo Jima.

Adamant, once the name of an imaginary stone of extreme hardness, was later applied to the diamond. In time, the word was used to describe any object, feeling, or act of unyielding hardness.

2. allergic   (ə lûr′jĭk)   *abnormally sensitive*

A neighbor says that she is allergic to cat's fur; it causes her skin to become inflamed.
Hay fever is the result of a common allergy (ăl′ər jē) due to pollen in the air.

Allergy is a medical term, but popular usage permits one to be allergic to such annoyances as egotists, billboards, and spoiled children.

3. catholic   (kăth′ə lĭk)   *universal, widely inclusive*

The president of the college is an executive of catholic interests—scientific, cultural, artistic, financial, and political.
Kissinger's catholicity (kăth′ə lĭs′ət ē) was the measure of his usefulness.

Curio: *catholicon* means a panacea or cure-all.

4. halcyon   (hăl′sē ən)   *calmly happy, tranquil*

The halcyon days of autumn passed too swiftly.
Tessie looks back fondly on the halcyon era of her childhood.

This word comes from the Greek word *alkyon* (kingfisher), which was supposed to have a calming influence on the sea during the winter solstice.
Compare *tranquil, pacific, Saturnian* (prosperous and peaceful).

5. histrionic   (hĭs′trē ŏn′ĭk)   *of play acting, theatrical, affected*

The visiting columnist earned undeserved admiration by his histrionic accounts of the dangers a reporter must face.
Mark's histrionics were predictably elaborate when Dad said no.

Thespian means dramatic, with no unfavorable connotations. The word comes from Thespis, a sixth-century Greek poet supposed to have been the innovator of tragedy in the theater.

From Greek drama:

The *protagonist* is the central figure or chief "struggler." The word derives from *protos* (first) and *agonistes* (actor); *agon* means struggle.
The *antagonist* is the figure opposed to the hero and is often the villain.

6. peripheral   (pə rĭf′ər əl)   *of the outer surface or area, external;*
                                            auxiliary, supplementary

The study of the customs and values of that country is peripheral to learning its
language.
Searchers found many bodies around the periphery of the fire area.
The island was explored peripherally, but no one landed.

Surface words:

> A *tangential* incident or allusion barely touches on the subject at hand. See -tang-
> (p. 342).
> A *superficial* view or analysis is very much on the surface of the subject.

7. pragmatic   (prăg măt′ĭk)   *practical, judging an idea*
                                          by its results

"Let's take a pragmatic view of our problems," the president of the firm said
soberly.
The pragmatism (prăg′mə tĭz′əm) of William James was considered an indigenous American philosophy.
The newly elected official admitted to being a pragmatist, a person who could
be expected to have a practical approach to all problems.

Related words:

> An *empirical* approach to a problem, like the pragmatic, is based on observation
> and experiment. In this way Franklin discovered that lightning is electricity.
> The *rational* way of investigating is to construct a theory or hypothesis on the basis
> of what one already knows and then, if possible, to test it. Thus the theory of organic
> evolution is a rational explanation, which rests on limited evidence.
> What is the *inductive* approach?

8. tantamount   (tăn′tə mount′)   *equivalent*

The suspect's account of the crime was tantamount to a confession.
A recommendation to the Naval Academy was tantamount to appointment.

> The word is used for equivalence in value, effect or meaning, not to similarity be-
> tween objects.

9. utopian   (yo͞o tō′pē ən)   *characteristic of an ideal society*

The Oneida Community in New York State began as a utopian project.
New Harmony, Indiana, was social reformer Robert Dale Owen's adventure
in utopianism.
Is there any place in the world idyllic enough to be called a utopia?

> In 1516, Sir Thomas More's book, *Utopia,* was first published. In it he described
> an ideal commonwealth situated on an imaginary island. The name of this perfect
> society, Utopia, was formed from the Greek o̲u̲ (not) and to̲pas (a place).

Other utopias:

> Plato's *Republic,* Francis Bacon's *New Atlantis* (scientific), Campanella's *City of the Sun,* Samuel Butler's *Erewhon,* and the legendary *El Dorado* (rich in gold).

10. vicarious   (vī kâr′ ē əs)   ***experiencing through another,***
taking the place of

Novels, films, and television serials provide many vicarious adventures. Vicariously, the reader or viewer dies a hundred deaths and surmounts every obstacle.

> What is the theological concept of the vicarious atonement?
> The *vicar* in an Anglican church is the rector's deputy or substitute, with the *vicarage* as his residence.
> Compare *vice-president, vice-admiral, vice-regent, viceroy,* etc., from the same root.

First practice set

Which entry word from this unit best replaces each *italicized* word or group of words?

1. The scientific world's *recognition of special merit* is often bestowed on those who are daring in their *attacking of cherished beliefs.*
2. *General pardon* for political offenses after a revolt, armed or parliamentary, is a form of political *healing.*
3. The privilege of the *right to vote* was once merely *characteristic of an ideal society.*
4. The impresario met each *urgent need* or crisis of the concert company with *theatrical* sobs.

5. Because Ned is *abnormally sensitive* to tropical vegetation, he can enjoy Bermuda only *through another person's experience.*
6. One does not need to have *universal* insight to see the *partial similarity* between succeeding in business and climbing a mountain.
7. One *supplementary* benefit from these *tranquil* weeks of vacation is the way your absence makes your employer appreciate what you do.
8. Giving the appointment to a close friend of doubtful ability is *equivalent* to *favoritism to relatives.*
9. The teacher is *unyielding* about not letting Marilyn appear on the program, and her reasons are extremely *practical.*
10. The kindly way the settlers established their *dominance* over the islands was an *abnormality.*

Second practice set

Which word from the list at the left best replaces each *italicized* word or group of words?

tangential
amnesia
Erewhon
allegory
hydrotherapy
City of the Sun
rational
capricious
disenfranchisement
erratic
antagonist
therapeutics
New Atlantis
superficial
iconology
parable
empirical
eulogy
vicar
El Dorado
Republic
kowtow
protagonist

1. The victim of *loss of memory* was moving across the room in a very *unintentionally irregular* way.

2. The science of psychology is necessarily *based on observation and experiment* in a *reasoning* kind of way.

3. A famous legendary utopia is *the one rich in gold,* and another is *a scientific utopia,* which establishes the kind of collaboration that is practiced today.

4. A *deputy for a rector* is the *chief figure* in a well-known play.

5. In her paper Nancy discussed the truth of human existence represented by the *opponent* in the *symbolic story* we were studying.

6. Mr. Hill's remarks, *barely touching on the subject* at best, were supposed to prepare us for reading (the) *Plato's utopia.*

7. The book on *the treatment of disease* tells how the Greeks used *water treatment.*

8. The *speech-of-praise* for the dead patriot proved to be *very much on the surface.*

9. After *losing the voting privilege,* the expatriate lawyer took up *the study of religious pictures.*

10. The narrator was *intentionally irregular* in her use of the *illustrative story.*

Third practice set

Which lettered pair of items comes nearest to having the same relationship as the pair printed in capital letters?

1. TANTAMOUNT:EQUIVALENT:: (a) Thespian:histrionic (b) tranquil: sanative (c) analogous:vicarious (d) pragmatic:empirical

2. ACCOLADE:COMMENDATION:: (a) analogy:parable (b) hegemony: franchise (c) adamant:diamond (d) therapy:therapeutics

3. HALCYON:UTOPIAN:: (a) pragmatic:empirical (b) vicarious:therapeutic (c) tangential:erratic (d) peripheral:analogous

4. ATHENS:HEGEMONY:: (a) nepotism:utopia (b) protagonist:histrionics (c) allergy:therapy (d) analogy:allegory

5. ICON:ICONOSCOPE:: (a) franchise:disenfranchisement (b) analogy: similarity (c) therapy:psychotherapy (d) eulogy:accolade

6. THERAPIST:THERAPY:: (a) pragmatist:analogy (b) amnesiac:amnesty (c) iconoclast:iconoclasm (d) catholic:catholicism

7. ERRATIC:ANOMALOUS:: (a) histrionic:thespian (b) vicarious:therapeutic (c) halcyon:utopian (d) peripheral:tangential

8. AMNESIA:THERAPIST:: (a) amnesty:iconoclast (b) allergy:nepotist (c) exigency:pragmatist (d) utopia:amnesiac

9. EXIGENT:URGENT:: (a) pragmatic:analogous (b) erratic:capricious (c) superficial:tangential (d) utopian:amnesiac

10. GREAT BRITAIN:HEGEMONY:: (a) therapy:allergy (b) New Atlantis: utopia (c) empiricism:pragmatism (d) accolade:eulogy

A word for it

Which word from this unit best replaces each *italicized* word or group of words?

1. A liberal arts college fosters *wide inclusiveness* in one's knowledge and capacities but may actually discourage *attacking of cherished beliefs* and other forms of originality.

2. The study of science should help one make the study of thinking *practical;* the study of English should make easier the presentation of ideas by *comparing by partial similarities.*

3. Good novels often have *healing* value and the reader, even though only *experiencing through another,* can develop an understanding of people through involvement in the lives of fictional characters.

4. Aunt Jennifer's *abnormal sensitivity* to changes in the climate creates an *urgent need* every year in May to travel abroad.
5. *Play-acting* behavior can be *curative* if it relieves one's frustrations and calms one's nerves.

Logophile licks

1. Make a list of <u>ana-</u> words. What are the meanings of <u>ana-</u>?
2. List five words beginning with <u>idio-</u> and explain the effect of the prefix on each.
3. Look up and explain other words connected with Greek drama, such as *skena, proscenium, strophe, antistrophe, peripeteia, choregus, deus ex machina, anagnorisis, hamartia.*
4. Extend the list of <u>-ists</u> and <u>-isms</u> found in this unit. Who can compile the longest list?
5. Devise five to ten synthetic words like "nepolatry" and "icontherapy," using elements in this unit and any others you may need. Offer them to the class to define. Discuss them in committees and decide whether any are needed. Some that you think you have created will probably turn out to be listed already in an unabridged dictionary.

part four

unit one

QUERIES

From the list at the left choose for each blank an exact definition of the underscored prefix or root.

around
before
breath
sticking
across
report
writing
lurking
into
above
toward
moving
bending
through
behind

1. A journalist is called a <u>scribe</u> because the job involves _____ .

2. An odor which <u>per</u>meates a room spreads _____ it.

3. A <u>spiro</u>meter measures one's _____ .

4. <u>Ag</u>gression is the act of _____ (-gress-) vigorously _____ (-<u>ad</u>-) a person or a goal that is difficult to attain.

5. <u>Trans</u>ition is the process of going _____ from one status or condition to another.

6. The <u>pre</u>lude to a gunfight comes _____ the shooting.

7. Ad<u>here</u>nce to a pact means _____ to it.

8. A <u>circum</u>vallation is a wall or trench _____ something.

9. Genu<u>flect</u>ion is the ceremonial act of _____ one's knees.

10. The <u>post</u>erior end of a cow is _____ .

Note: In Part Four, wherever entry words are separated into two parts by use of the ellipsis, the first one is usually of Latin origin, the second one of Greek.

PREFIXES OF DIRECTION

1. ad-   *to, toward, against*

Paint will not <u>ad</u>here to (stick *to*) an oily wall.
A car wreck on the road is sure to <u>at</u>tract attention (draw it *toward* something).
Kay holds an <u>ad</u>verse opinion of foreign cars (is turned *against* them).
A searchlight beam on a store's roof will not always <u>al</u>lure customers (draw them *toward* it).

> The *d* in *ad-* often changes to the first letter of the root to which it is joined. Some-
> times it disappears before *s*, as in *astringent*. Compare *access, accomplish, affix,
> affront, aggregate, aggravate, allude, allocate, announce, applaud, assault,
> attract, attribute.*

2. circum- . . . peri-   *around, about*

We set out to <u>circum</u>navigate the earth (sail *around* it) in a yacht.
<u>Circum</u>locution is a device of diplomats and political candidates (talking *around*
a topic instead of getting to the point).
How does one measure the <u>circum</u>ference of the moon?
The stab wound punctured the <u>peri</u>cardium (sac *around* the heart).
Houses are being built on the <u>peri</u>phery (*around* the edge) of the park.

3. in-   *in or into, to or toward*

Laura forgot to <u>in</u>sert a coin *in* the envelope.
A supercharger <u>in</u>jects fuel (forces it *into* the engine).
A person <u>in</u>clined to drink leans *toward* it as a habit.
Sunbathers <u>im</u>bibe sunshine and fresh air (drink it *in*).

> Compare *inmate, inflame, influx, ingrain, ingrown, invent.*
> <u>In</u>- also means *not*. See examples (p. 295). Note that <u>in</u>- becomes <u>il</u>- before *l*, as in
> *illustrate, illumine;* <u>im</u>- before *m* and *p*, as in *immerse, import;* <u>ir</u>- before *r*, as in
> *irrigate, irradiate.*

4. per-   *through*

A <u>per</u>ceptive person sees *through* your actions readily.
The coffee began to <u>per</u>colate (to filter hot water *through* it).
Smoke <u>per</u>meated the room.
A person must <u>per</u>severe to win (keep going *through* difficulties).

Per- in front of a chemical term means that the compound contains more than the usual amount, or the maximum, of the element named. Thus hydrogen peroxide (H_2O_2) contains twice as much oxygen by volume as water (H_2O).

5. re- *back(ward), again*

The envoy refused to re̲tract the statement (take it *back*).
The article re̲capitulates (states *again*) the arguments for a sales tax.
You re̲deem a bad check or a bond by buying it *back*.

> Compare *react, readjust, reform, regain, reiterate, rejoin, refresh, review, revolve, remake, repeat, respond, resume, retort, review.*

6. trans- *across, beyond*

A tra̲nsatlantic flight takes two hours in a supersonic jetliner.
The tra̲nsverse paths turn *across* each other, forming a crisscross.
The inventor found a way to tra̲nscend each obstacle (climb *beyond* it).
Julius Caesar wrote a famous report of his activities in tra̲nsalpine Gaul.

> Compare *transcend, transfer, translate, transoceanic, transport.*

PREFIXES OF TIME WHEN

1. pre- . . . ante- *before, ahead of time*

Dramamine pre̲cludes seasickness (shuts it out *before* it happens).
The killing of the officer was clearly pre̲meditated.
Leticia had a pre̲monition (warning *beforehand*) of disaster.
Find the ante̲cedent of the pronoun.

> Compare *preplan, preheat, preexist, antedate, anteroom, antechamber, antediluvian* (p. 15).

2. pro-   *forward, before, for or favoring*

Vic found it easy to procrastinate about doing the book report (putting *forward* until later what ought to be done at once).
The prologue was spoken from the balcony.
A proclivity for eating too much (tendency *for* it) may prove fatal.
A pro-Russian diplomat is one *favoring* Russia.

> In *pronoun* and *proconsul*, pro- means "in place of."

3. post-   *after*

Mrs. Jarvis wrote a postdated check because her funds were low.
Stendahl claimed he wrote for posterity (those living *after* him).
Jenny is a posthumous child (born *after* her father's death).
The arts advanced slowly in the postdiluvian world (*after* the Flood).

> Compare *postgraduate, postpone, postscript, post mortem, posterior.*
> Post- in *postmaster, postmark, postpaid, post office* and other *postal* words goes back to the days of stagecoaches. A "post" was a runner or rider on horseback who carried mail from one "post," or station, to the next one. This post thus became a "post office."

ACTION ROOTS FROM LATIN

1. -cede-, -ceed-, -cess- . . . . -gredi-, -gress-   *go, move*

Rose would not accede to her mother's request (*move* toward granting it).
In slippery weather proceed (*move* forward) slowly.
The girl preceded the boy down the aisle.
Watch New York's skyline recede as the ship leaves the harbor.
Grant's aggressiveness (*moving* toward what he wanted) pleased Lincoln because he wanted to get the war over with.
If you do not progress, you may regress.
Schooling is a vital ingredient of a useful life.

> Compare *intercede, intercession, concede, concession, exceed, excess, secede, secession, recession, congress, digress, transgress.*

2. -flect-, -flex-   *bend, turn*

The pond reflects her face (*bends* the image back).
The rules should be flexible (readily *bent* or modified).
The French word *âme* has a circumflex accent (*bent* over a letter).
The people genuflected (*bent* their knees) before entering the pew.
To play basketball well, you must have agility and quick reflexes.

3. -fract- . . . -rupt-   *break, breaking*

The fracture of a vertebra caused intense pain.
Infractions *(breaking)* of traffic rules cause many accidents.
Refracted light *(broken* up into colors) caused the rainbow.
The rupture between father and son was painful to both.
When the volcano erupted, molten lava *broke* forth.
A noisy gang tried to disrupt the meeting.

> A *fracture* usually involves bones or rocks or some hard object; a *rupture* is a muscular, a social, or a figurative break.

4. -fus(e)-   *pour*

The girls tried to infuse new life into the dramatics club.
Jack insulted his employer, but later apologized profusely.
The auctioneer displayed verbal diffuseness *(pouring* out words).
The teacher would always interfuse praise with criticism.

> *Fusion* is a pouring or melting together of persons, qualities, materials, or other ingredients. Thus, the United States is a *fusion* of cultural elements from many nations. The hydrogen bomb gains its power from the *fusion,* or atomic combining, of certain chemical elements.

5. -here-, -hes-   *stick, cling*

Gum will not adhere to a wet surface.
Particles of sand and cement cohere to form concrete.
The young artist's inherent weakness *(clinging* to her) was a fear of failure.
Adhesive tape is painful to remove because it *clings* to the skin.
Love is the cohesive force that binds the family together.

6. -lude- . . . -lus-   *play (i.e., run, lead, perform)*

Boris would not let foolish fears delude him *(lead* him away).
Bandits may elude the police for a while.
The boy did not allude *(lead* or refer) to his recent mishap.
The speech contained many literary allusions (references).
The lively prelude pleased the audience immensely.
The interlude (skit or *play* between the main events) was a farce.

7. -mute-   *change, transform*

The bishop's kindness began to transmute Jean's hate into love.
In that well-publicized case the governor commuted the death sentence to life imprisonment.
Biologic mutations *(changes* of form or nature) are rare.
The numbers 314 and 431 are permutations of 1, 3, and 4.

8. -scribe-, -script- . . . -graph-, -gram-   *write, writing*

Don Quixote inscribed Dulcinea's name on rocks and trees.
Agnes tried to describe the scene in the cave.

The third word of the postscript is the password.
The medicine is sold only by prescription.
Camp rules proscribe smoking (*"write"* it out of permitted activities).
A graph or a diagram is a form of nonverbal *"writing."*
The seismograph made a *record* of the earthquake in Peru.
The epigram (brief piece of *writing*) about Nan was very clever.
The encephalogram (*recording* of brain waves) indicated an abnormal condition.

> -Graph- and -gram- are Greek roots, more formal, more technical, and broader in the kind of records they denote than -scribe- and -script-.

9. -spire-, spirat- . . . -hale-   *breathe, breath*

The singer never failed to inspire her audience (*breathe* life into it).
The old dog, a much-loved family pet, expired quietly.
Hard physical work makes a person perspire (*"breathe"* through the skin).
Do not inhale (*breathe* in) the smoke.
The child who was ill had halitosis (bad or offensive *breath*).
The exhalation of fire and gases from the volcano was terrifying.

> In words like *aspire* the root meaning is elusive: You aspire to a career in aviation. It suggests that you pant for such a career (ad + spire) or that you seek it breathlessly. Compare *transpire*.

First practice set

What is the literal meaning of each <u>underscored</u> prefix and root in the following sentences?

1. The engineers directed that a ditch be dug to de<u>flect</u> or _____ away the stream while the dam was being built.
2. A <u>post</u>humous book is one published _____ the author's death.
3. To <u>pre</u>empt a seat is to "buy" it _____ .
4. A <u>pro</u>posal for peace is an idea you put _____ .
5. The <u>ante</u>chamber lies _____ the main room.
6. To <u>re</u>heat a meal is to warm it _____ .
7. Con<u>spir</u>ators literally _____ together.

8. In a day or two you may <u>proceed</u>: _____ _____ .
9. An <u>adhesion</u> occurs when one tissue or organ _____ _____ another.
10. A football player's re<u>fl</u>exes (automatic muscular _____ or rebounds) must be good.

Second practice set

Supply a word formed from roots and prefixes of this unit to fit each definition in parentheses. Use the list of words at the left only if you must.

aggressive
precede
transpire
antedate
accession
infuse
aspire
cohesive
infraction
disruption
circumscribe
peroxide
transoceanic
respiration
allusion
inflexible
permutation
transfusion
postscript
perspire
prelude
mutation
proscribe
adhesive
interlude

1. A guest should _____ (go before) the hostess or host through a doorway.
2. Did the American Revolution _____ (come on a date before) the French Revolution?
3. "_____ (breathe toward) to lofty goals," the speaker urged.
4. How can we _____ (pour in) new life into the team?
5. How much should one _____ (limit by "writing around") a child's activities?
6. Lindbergh made a _____ (across the ocean) flight in 1927.
7. A reporter has to be quite _____ (going toward vigorously, pushing) to get a story.
8. The _____ (playing before) was a Bach composition.
9. The Queen's _____ (going) to the throne ended the war.
10. A minor _____ (breaking) is not always punished.
11. April brings a _____ (pouring across) of new life into dormant vegetation.
12. _____ (references) to Shakespeare please English teachers.
13. It is necessary to _____ ("write" forth or exclude) the feeding by visitors of certain animals in a zoo.
14. If you pull it off, _____ (stick-to-it) tape will often leave a dirty mark.
15. Many ages had to _____ ("breathe across," *i.e.,* happen) before human beings appeared on earth.
16. The _____ (writing afterward) was longer than the letter.
17. The _____ (skit between main events) was the funniest part of the show.
18. How do space flights affect _____ (breathing)?
19. Algebra includes the study of _____ (changing combinations).
20. Hydrogen _____ contains twice as much oxygen as water.

Third practice set

What is the number of the definition in the right column that goes with each *italicized* word in the left column?

A

1. *Regressive* eye movements
2. *Rupture* of a friendship
3. *Fusion* of four groups
4. *Inherent* fondness
5. Routine *transcription*
6. Pathetic *aspiration*
7. *Proscribed* hobby
8. *Mutable* health
9. Poisonous *inhalation*
10. *Recessive* vitality

1. breaking up
2. enduring
3. ambition, striving toward
4. going back (every so often)
5. decreasing (going backward)
6. inborn
7. changeable
8. merging
9. written attack
10. record in writing or sound
11. breathing in
12. forbidden

B

1. *Access* to a water supply
2. Foxlike *elusiveness*
3. *Profusion* of colors
4. *Diffraction* of light waves
5. A family's *cohesiveness*
6. Pungent *epigram*
7. Inflamed *pericardium*
8. *Adhesiveness* of the paint
9. Normal *precedence*
10. Lengthy *prologue*

1. brief bit of writing
2. privilege of going before someone else
3. means of approach
4. tendency to stick to something
5. clever manipulation
6. visible event
7. pouring forth
8. breaking apart into components
9. ability to keep from getting caught
10. membrane around heart
11. tendency to stick together
12. speech before the main event

Suffixes and such

1. Study Group I, Makers of Nouns, in the Appendix (pp. 376–377). Go over the examples of prefixes and roots in this unit and list others ending in each of the following suffixes:

   -ence-   -ity-   -ness
   -ion (preceded by *s* or *t*, which is usually part of the root or stem)
   Think of two or three, like *visitor,* ending in -or.

2. Look over the Adjective Makers in Group II (pp. 378–379). Survey the adjective examples in this unit and find instances of four or five of the suffixes listed in the Appendix.
3. Write a paragraph using five or six of the ''go-move'' words listed under the -cede- group in this unit.
4. Analyze the words in illustrative sentences which do not have an explanation in parentheses.

unit two

THE RIGHT WORD

Which of the words in the list at the left fits best in each blank?

retract
devolve
infect
corroborate
preclude
immobilize
conjecture
impend
extort
postpone
absolve
protract

1. The doctor's lack of time for golf now does not _____ the possibility that she will have time next year.

2. The trench warfare of World War I tended to _____ an army for weeks or months at a time.

3. When the president of the corporation is out of town, his duties _____ upon the vice-president.

4. The vice-president tends to _____ the business sessions unduly. They go on for hours.

5. Police _____ that the missing girl got lost on the desert and died of thirst.

6. The kidnappers tried to _____ the ransom money from the victim's parents.

7. The doctor had to _____ his unfounded claim that he had discovered a cure for cancer.

8. For those who are careless or foolish, notable misfortunes must surely _____.

9. It is unwise to _____ a decision too long.

10. Do not ask a court to _____ a person who is clearly guilty of the crime as charged.

PREFIXES OF SEPARATION

1. ab-   *from, away from*

Her departure was abrupt (she broke *away* too quickly).
Edward VIII abdicated (declared his separation *from*) the throne.
The boy was abducted for ransom.
Patricia abhors (shrinks *from*) turnips.
The cashier absconded (ran *away*) with the money.

> Sometimes *s* is added, as in *absent* (Latin *ab + s + esse*, to be). The *b* is omitted before *v*, as in *avert* (to turn away). Can you explain these changes?

2. de-   *from, down from, down*

Plague depopulated London in 1665.
During the Reign of Terror in France, hundreds were decapitated (heads cut *off*).
The machine will start when you depress the lever.
Dulcie watched the squirrel descend (climb *down* from) the tree.
A jet plane, upon landing, must decelerate (slow *down*) rapidly.
Henry despises cats (looks *down* on them).

> Does de- always mean *from, down from, down*? See your dictionary.

3. dis-   *away, away from*

The teacher did not dismiss (send *away*) the class in time for me to catch my bus.
Clarice disarmed the bandit with a pole.
Records disprove the culprit's claims.
The collision of two airliners was a strange disaster.
The boys dismantled an old car (took various parts *away from* it).

> Compare *disarrange, disapprove, discharge, discolor, discomfort, disconnect, disbursement, discourtesy, dismissal.*

4. ex-, e-   *out, from*

Munera recited an excerpt from the Koran.
Martin Luther was finally excommunicated from the Church (declared *outside* its fellowship or communion.
An ex-president of the country club died recently.

> The prefix ex- is reduced to e before *d, g, l, m, n, r, v,* and, in rare instances, before *b: edict, educate, egress, elude, elect, emit, enervate, erupt, evaporate.*
> Ex- becomes ef- before *f* as in *efface, effect.* It sometimes becomes es- or ec- as in *escape, escort, ecstasy,* and *eccentric.* See *excoriate, exhume, ex libris, extant, extradite,* and *exodus* if you wish to extract a few additional word secrets.

5. se- *away, apart*

Which was the first state to <u>se</u>cede, or go *apart,* from the Union?

When you are <u>se</u>cure, you live *away from* care.

To <u>se</u>lect a partner is to choose or, literally, to set one *apart.*

If you <u>se</u>clude yourself, you shut yourself *away* from others.

> In *sedition,* the <u>se</u>- becomes <u>sed</u>-. Can you explain why? See your dictionary for the root. What is the first letter of the root?

THREE PREFIXES OF CLOSE RELATIONSHIP

1. con- . . . syn- *together, with*

Thousands attended the society's <u>con</u>vention.

The shooting caused a <u>com</u>motion in the hotel.

Hoyle's <u>com</u>pendium gathers *together* much information about bridge.

The book was a <u>syn</u>thesis (placing *together*) of theories about the origin of the human race.

Connie expended more <u>sym</u>pathy than her friend deserved.

A <u>sym</u>posium (placing different opinions *together*) on morals will be held today in the parish house.

> The prefix <u>con</u>- may appear as <u>col</u>-, <u>com</u>-, <u>co</u>-, and <u>cor</u>-, depending on the first consonant of the root. <u>Syn</u>- may become <u>sym</u>-.
>
> Compare *collect, complex, cooperate, corroborate, correlate, synonym, symphony, symptom.*

2. epi- . . . sur- *on, upon*

Sunburn inflames the <u>epi</u>dermis (layer of skin lying *upon* the dermis.)

Because of her constant singing, Angela earned the <u>epi</u>thet "Sparrow" (title put *upon* her).

"He lies" was a strange <u>epi</u>taph to put on a tombstone.

Gianini was the banker's <u>sur</u>name (placed *upon* the "given" name).

The team will <u>sur</u>mount every crisis that arises—we hope.

3. sub- *under, below*

The subcellar filled up with water.
A subagent stole the entire stock of goods.
The plumbing and electrical work are covered by subcontracts.
Making monkey faces is subhuman behavior.

> The *b* sometimes changes to *c, f, g, m, p, r,* to agree with the first letter of the
> root to which the prefix is attached: *success, suffocate, suggest, summon, sup-*
> *plant, supposition, surreptitious.* The *b* sometimes becomes *s,* as in *susceptible,*
> *suspend, sustain.*

LATIN VERB ROOTS

1. -clude-, -clus- *shut, close*

Would you exclude a dishonest person from your circle of friends?
Fraternities are exclusive, *shutting* out many who wish to join.
Is exclusiveness justifiable if based on common interests and tastes?
A student may seclude herself (*shut* herself apart) just before exams.
A hermit is a recluse who lives in seclusion.

> Compare *cloister* (a place of seclusion, literally a covered walk in a convent,
> monastery, or church): The nuns talked quietly when they met in the cloister.

2. -fact-, -fect- . . . -fict- *make, do*

A spaghetti factory is a place that *makes* spaghetti.
All political parties have factions that dissent from certain party policies.
When bacteria *make* you ill, you've probably acquired an infection.
Paradoxically, fiction is *make-believe*, presenting life as it is interpreted by
the author.
Jane's alleged illness was a fictitious excuse.
What is the effect of the new traffic system?
The loose door in the car is a structural defect.
Pretending to be wealthy is an affectation (a pretense).

> Note the prefix and root meaning of: *fact, factitious, de facto, perfect, prefect,*
> *refectory, confection.*

3. -ject- *cast, hurl, throw*

A book is an inappropriate projectile (object to *hurl* forward.)
Marla felt terribly dejected (*cast* down, discouraged).
Dominic made an abject apology.
The gossip's conjecture (guess, surmise) was right after all.
The club voted to eject its youngest member.
The glowing missile cast its trajectory across the sky.

4. -mit-, -miss-   *send*

Agnes e<u>mit</u>s a scream when scared.
The government sent ten men on a <u>miss</u>ion to Iran.
A <u>miss</u>ionary in South America (e<u>miss</u>ary, person sent on a religious mission
or campaign) was killed in a plane crash.

> Compare *admit, admission, commit, commission, committal, dismiss, permit,*
> *permission, remit, remittance, submit, submission, transmit, transmission.*

5. -move-, -mot-, -mobil-   *move*

What was her <u>mot</u>ive (what *moved* her to action) in refusing the promotion?
The judge showed no e<u>mot</u>ion when sentencing the criminal.
The owner de<u>mot</u>ed the engineer from outdoor to indoor projects.
The new employee's job will be sales pro<u>mot</u>ion.
Many live in <u>mobil</u>e homes.
The governor will <u>mobil</u>ize the National Guard.
A strike im<u>mobil</u>ized the building project.

> Compare *motor, motorize, promote, promotional, remote, remoteness, mobility,*
> *mobilization, demobilize.*

6. -pend-, -pense-   *hang, weigh*

Large ex<u>pend</u>itures (sums "weighed" out) wiped out the surplus.
The im<u>pend</u>ing tornado (*hanging* over the place) roared wildly into the Texas
town.
It is the court's task to dis<u>pense</u> justice ("weigh" it out).
The sus<u>pense</u>ion bridge (*hung* from vertical supports) bends in the wind.
Sherry is a <u>pens</u>ive person (*weighs* her thoughts carefully).
The population tables are in the ap<u>pend</u>ix of the book.

Watch for:

> *Suspense, dispense, dispensation, compensate, compensatory, recompense* (p.
> 95), *propensity* (p. 20), *compendium* (above under <u>con</u>-) (p. 287).

7. -pone-, -pose-, -posit-   *place or put*

The Jensens had to post<u>pone</u> their trip.
Peter bought the com<u>pon</u>ents (units to *put* together) for a stereo system.
A young engineer was the pro<u>pon</u>ent of the plan for the shopping mall.
Donna's <u>pose</u> made her look taller.
Mr. Bortil is a local ex<u>pon</u>ent of art (he sets forth its charms).
We had to write a paragraph of ex<u>posit</u>ion on horses.
Few will op<u>pose</u> the pay raise for police.

Mary, Queen of the Scots, was deposed (*put* down from the throne) and later beheaded.

The *pone* words come from the Latin verb *ponere* (to place or put).
The *pose* words come from the Latin verb *pausare* by way of the French verb *poser* (put down).

8. -solve-, -solu(t)-   *loosen, set free, disunite*

Water is a familiar solvent (liquid to *loosen* or dissolve a solid).
The investigator set out to discover if the company was still solvent (*free* from unpayable debts).
The priest will absolve the penitent sinner.

> Compare *solve, solution, soluble, insoluble, resolve, resolution, absolute, absolution, dissolute, dissolution.*

9. -tort-   *twist*

Blackmail is a way to extort money from a person.
Dee did not distort the facts ("twist" them from the truth).
The clown's contortions amused the children.

> *Torque* is a force that creates a twisting or rotating motion, as in the driveshaft of a car: High torque means much power.

10. -tract-   *draw, drag*

Blimps carry streamers to attract attention.
Television is a distraction which *draws* students away from their work.
The editor writes abstracts of new trade books (*draws* the main ideas from them) *i.e.,* summarizes them.
In a fit of abstraction the professor walked into a pond.
The custodian had a protracted (*drawn* out) argument with one of the tenants.
Jeffrey proved intractable (not easily *drawn* or persuaded) about lending money to his sister.
A contract is a set of promises *drawn* up and legally binding.

11. -volve-, -volu-   *roll, turn*

We watched the plan gradually e<u>volve</u> (*roll* forth).

After the re<u>volu</u>tion, the country's new government sought world recognition.

The task of raising money de<u>volves</u> upon Howard.

Shirley became in<u>volve</u>d in a personal problem.

First practice set

What is the meaning of the <u>underscored</u> prefixes or roots in the following sentences?

1. To <u>dismiss</u> a person is to _____ him _____ .
2. A <u>tract</u>able person is easy to _____ along with you.
3. <u>Defect</u>ion from duty is _____ing an escape _____ it.
4. A <u>pend</u>ulum is a weight to _____ from a ceiling or clock.
5. To <u>distort</u> the truth is to _____ it _____ the facts.
6. Re<u>volv</u>ing mirrors are so called because they _____ .
7. <u>Com</u>ponents of a model plane are its parts; you _____ them _____ .
8. <u>Dissolu</u>tion sometimes means the _____ of the body _____ its physical life.
9. To live in <u>seclus</u>ion is to _____ yourself _____ .
10. <u>Eject</u>ing the dog from the house means _____ him _____ .
11. <u>Retract</u>ion of a claim for damage is _____ it _____ .
12. An <u>absolute</u> statement is one _____ _____ any limits or qualifications.
13. The <u>mobil</u>ity of an army means it can _____ readily.
14. An <u>emiss</u>ary offering peace is a person _____ _____ .
15. <u>Deject</u>ion is a state of being _____ _____ .
16. An <u>*ex post facto*</u> law was objectionable because it was a law made _____ the _____ (facto) for which it prescribed punishment.
17. <u>Remiss</u>ion of fees is literally _____ them _____ .
18. A <u>suspend</u>ed sentence in court means you _____ or live _____ the threat that it will be carried out if you misbehave again.
19. A <u>contract</u>ion of a muscle means it _____ itself _____ .
20. An <u>append</u>age is something that _____ _____ a body, like an arm or leg.

Second practice set

What word in the list at the left, made from roots and prefixes taught thus far, best completes each of the following sentences? The *italicized* word or words will give you the clues.

involvement
disaster
assumption
dissolve
suspension
abstraction
motive
seclusion
pensive
dismissal
missionary
mobilize
distraction
exclusion
compendium
epithet
demotion
impend
dejection
supposition
synthesis
fiction
extortion
conjecture

1. A _____ is that which *moves* one to act.

2. A _____ person *weighs* his thoughts carefully.

3. To *loosen away* a solid substance with a liquid is to _____ it.

4. If disaster *hangs* over, or *against*, one it _____.

5. _____ is *twisting* money *out* of a person.

6. _____, or *shutting out*, of _____ which *drag*

7. *one away* is necessary in studying.

8. A _____ bridge *hangs under* its supports.

9. A _____ is a religious person *sent* to carry out a duty.

10. A _____ is a belief *placed under* one's thinking, and a _____ is a guess, literally *thrown together*.

11. _____ is the condition of being, or .feeling, *cast down*.

12. _____ is a form of *make-believe*.

13. The act of *shutting out* someone is _____.

14. _____al means *sending* one *away* from a job or group.

15. _____ is *moving* a person *down* to a lower place or job.

16. _____ment is the process of being *rolled* up *into* events.

17. A _____ is a *"weighing"* together of much information on a topic.

18. Sometimes the National Guard finds it necessary to _____, or *get into motion*.

19. An _____ is an idea one *takes to* or upon oneself as a basis for action.

20. A fit of mental _____ is a *drawn-away* state of mind.

Third practice set

Write the number of the definition in the right column that goes with each *italicized* word in the left column below.

1. Adequate *compensation*	1. binding by legal agreement
2. *Exponent* of culture	2. irregular, sporadic
3. *Contractual* obligations	3. rearrangement, interchange
4. Brief *appendix*	4. pretense, insincerity
5. *Dissolute* behavior	5. loose, lax, immoral
6. Startling *transposition*	6. encourager, interpreter
7. *De facto* segregation	7. depending on conjectures
8. Ceaseless *affectation*	8. material added at end
9. *Interjectory* remarks	9. reward, gift, bonus
10. *Suppositional* thinking	10. payment
	11. actual, if not intentional
	12. explosive, exclamatory

Suffixes and word building

1. List the different suffixes found in the -<u>mit</u>-, -<u>miss</u>- words and give examples of each. What is the effect of each suffix on the meaning? What other suffixes may be used with one or more of the words?
2. List five words ending in -<u>ix</u>, such as *appendix*. What does the suffix -<u>ix</u> indicate about a word?
3. Complete and extend the following tabulation of words from -<u>pon</u>-, -<u>pos</u>- and -<u>posit</u>-.

component	compose	composition
_____	expose	_____
* * *	_____	reposition
_____	propose	_____

Two in the last column take an -<u>ory</u> ending as well. Which are they? What is the effect of the -<u>ory</u> ending? Which two in the middle column have a -<u>ure</u> form?

unit three

MEANING HUNT

What is the exact meaning of each <u>underscored</u> prefix, root, or word in the sentences below?

1. <u>Non</u>essentials are _____ important.
2. To <u>mis</u>apply a statement is to apply it _____.
3. To <u>ob</u>viate a difficulty is to make headway _____ it.
4. He concealed his <u>anti</u>pathy for us (feeling _____ us).
5. <u>Contra</u>band goods are goods imported _____ the law.
6. To <u>re</u>port the news is to _____ it back to others.
7. To <u>re</u>pel a person is to _____ him _____.
8. <u>Ten</u>acity makes one _____ on to something.
9. To <u>inter</u>vene in a love affair is to _____ in _____ the lovers.
10. A <u>convoca</u>tion of musicians is a _____ _____.

EIGHT NEGATIVE PREFIXES

1. a-   *no, not*

The <u>a</u>nesthetic produced a state of *no* feeling in the broken leg.
Clay is <u>a</u>morphous, having *no* fixed form or shape (<u>-morph</u>-).
With <u>a</u>pathy (no feeling) the stunned survivors of the disaster awaited rescue.
A lion's behavior is <u>a</u>moral because animals have *no* moral sense.
<u>Im</u>moral actions violate the human code of right and wrong.

The prefix a- in this entry is the Greek-derived prefix for *not*. It attaches almost always to the less familiar, more technical, Greek roots. Sometimes it takes an *n* before a word beginning with a vowel: Anhydrous means *without water* (hydr-). The a- in *adrift, awash, awake,* and many everyday words comes from Old English and means *out, up off,* or *of.*

2. anti, ant- against or opposing, opposed to

The nurse quickly gave the victim an antidote for the poison.
Congress passed an antilabor law.
Anti-American riots broke out in several countries.
Most people have a special antipathy to rats.
The antagonist (pitted *against* the hero) in the movie is a creature from another planet.
Living is rigorous in the Antarctic area.
Bad is the antonym of good.
The toothpaste contains an antacid as well as fluoride.

> From what language do many of the ant(a)- words like *antagonist* come? Note that ante- is a prefix meaning *before* (p. 278).

3. counter- . . . contra- against or opposing, opposed to

The defendant in the damage suit entered a counterclaim.
On a seesaw one child counterbalances the other.
The FBI was accused of a counterplot *against* the conspirators.
The cook added lemon juice to the concoction to counteract the sweet taste.
Contraband drugs were smuggled across the border.

> Compare *contradict, counterfeit, counterirritant, counterproposal.* See your dictionary for others.

4. in- not

A convicted felon is ineligible to vote.
A person incapable of hitting a ball should not join the team.
The host's actions were inconsistent with his words.
Illicit actions, like the smuggling of jewels, are *not* lawful.
Marty is sometimes irresponsible.

> The prefix in- becomes im- before *m* and *p,* il- before *l,* ir- before *r:* Compare *immovable, impossible, illogical, irreligious.*
> Sometimes this prefix means *against,* as in *indict.* Often it means *to, into,* or *toward,* as in *increase, inspire* (p. 281).

5. mis- wrong(ly), incorrect(ly)

The child misbehaved by running about and annoying others in the doctor's waiting room.
Joe miscalculated, and the car hit an abutment.
He was later discharged from the Army for misconduct.
Slipping on the smooth concrete was a costly misfortune.
Memorizing the speech was misdirected effort.

6. non-   *not*

Glass, a nonconductor, is used for insulators.
Sit-down strikes are a form of nonviolent resistance.
A closed shop excludes nonunion laborers.
A nonpartisan issue, like daylight time, does *not* involve party politics.

7. ob-   *against, opposing, opposed to*

If you object to howling cats, you hurl out words *against* them.
To obstruct a plan for longer school hours is to "build" (-struct-) *against* it.
Bad manners offend the people one wants to impress favorably.
Theaters oppose a higher tax on tickets.

> The prefix ob- means *to* or *toward* in words like *oblige* and *observe*. It may also
> mean *upon* or *over*, as in *occupy*. The *b* changes to *c*, *f*, or *p*, if the root begins
> with one of these letters.

8. un-   *not*

Rosa's eyes showed unfeigned delight when she won the prize.
The unsought praise for being honest was *not* unwelcome.
The furniture in the mansion was depressingly undistinguished.
Carl made the unwarranted statement that studying is unimportant.

> This prefix comes from Old English. Sometimes it expresses the idea of reversing,
> as in *untwist, untangle,* and *undress.*
> Compare *unconfirmed, ungenerous, ungovernable, unattached, unbearable,
> unceasing, uncompromising, unmanageable.*

TEN LATIN ACTION ROOTS

1. -duce-, -ducat-, -duct-   *lead*

If the Army can induce you to enlist it will then formally induct you into its
ranks.
It will provide you with an education, *leading* to new knowledge and technical
skills that will help you get a job later on.
Once in the Army, you will soon deduce (*lead* out or surmise) that you must
obey orders promptly.
You will learn that copper is a ductile metal, easily "led" or shaped, but that
steel is not.

> Compare *reduce, reduction, conduct, conducive, seduce, seductive, abduct,
> abduction, product, introduce.*

2. -fer-, -late-   *carry or bear, bring*

The con*fer*ence on public health *brought* together hundreds of nurses and doctors.

Opium is a sopori*fer*ous (sleep-*bringing*) drug.

Limburger cheese is notoriously odori*fer*ous.

Stella finds French quite easy to trans*late* into English.

How does thought trans*fer*ence (*carrying* across) from one mind to another take place?

Other -fer- words:

>   *Differ, infer, offer, prefer, refer, suffer.*

>   **Note:** The word *interfere* comes from a different root, *fere,* from Latin *ferire,* meaning to strike.

Other -late- words:

>   *Ablative, oblation, dilate* (p. 88), *prelate, relate, latitude.*

3. -pel-, -pulse-   *drive, push*

Sarah's wit helped to dis*pel* (*drive* away) the winter's gloom.

The principal had to ex*pel* three seniors for misbehavior.

A patrol fought bravely to re*pel* the guerrilla attack.

Signe felt a wild im*pulse* to contradict the pompous lecturer.

Mr. March's im*pulse*iveness led him to give a beggar ten dollars.

A quart of fuel will pro*pel* a scooter a long way.

Jet pro*pulse*ion burns a large amount of fuel per hour.

>   Compare *compel, compulsion, impel, impulsion.*

4. -port-, -portat-   *carry, bring*

A porter will *carry* your suitcase to your room.
The teacher praised the three brothers for their good deportment *(carriage, behavior)*.
Glenda drives an imported car she *brought* home last year.
Deportation of alien criminals to their native country is one way to deal with them.

Other -port- words:

> Comport(ment), disport, importune (p. 5), export(ation), support, purport, report, transport.
> What is the root meaning of *opportunity?*

5. -serve-   *keep, save*

Swimmers learn to conserve their energy and make it last.
Patriotic observances *save* our best national traditions by *keeping* them alive.
The box office will reserve four seats for the ice show.
A subservient person is easy to *keep* under control.
The conservationists want to *save* our forests and parks from misuse.

6. -sist-   *stand, set*

Nick insists *(stands* on the fact) that he will win the speech contest.
We must persist in our efforts to have the amendment passed.
The judge issued a cease-and-desist order against an illegal strike.

> *Consistent* actions *stand* together, *i.e.,* agree with each other in motive and spirit.
> An *inconsistent* person may be pleasant one day and ugly the next.

Stand words:

> Assist(ance), exist(ence), resist(ance), persist(ence).

7. -tain-, -ten(t)-   *hold*

Water is retained *(held* back) in reservoirs by dams.
Agatha has a very retentive memory.
The bulldog's tenacity *(holding* power) prevented Leonard from getting home on time.
The tenements (buildings meeting minimum standards that someone *holds* as owner) belong to a person who lives outside the state.
Quaker tenets (beliefs *held)* include pacifism.

Hold words include:

> Detain, detention, attain, attainment, contain, tenable, tenacious, tenability.

8. -vene-, -vent- *come*

Members of the Rotary Club con<u>vene</u> once a week.
The government may inter<u>vene</u> in the labor dispute.
Inter<u>vent</u>ion is a last resort, however.
How did the ad<u>vent</u> *(coming)* of television change American home life?
In<u>vent</u>ors were able to circum<u>vent</u> the technical problems of constructing spacecraft that could analyze soil samples on Mars.

Come words:

> *Event, eventuate, advent, adventitious, convent, conventicle, prevent, preventive, invent, inventiveness.* What others can you add? Compare *revenant* (ghost).

9. -vert-, -vers- . . . . -verge- *turn*

Xavier swerved just in time to a<u>vert</u> (avoid) an accident.
Pam has an a<u>vers</u>ion to brothers who try to di<u>vert</u> *(turn* away) her attention when she is telephoning.
In the summer it is easy to re<u>vert</u> to the lazy behavior patterns of carefree childhood.
Atmospheric in<u>vers</u>ion *(turning* upside down) causes warm air to rise to the hilltops while cold air takes its place in the valleys.
A fit of <u>vert</u>igo (dizziness) seized two of the hikers as they looked over the edge of a 3,000-foot wall from the top of Mount Whitney.
The two roads con<u>verge</u> near the town.
Eclipses of the moon provide incontro<u>vert</u>ible proof that the earth is round.

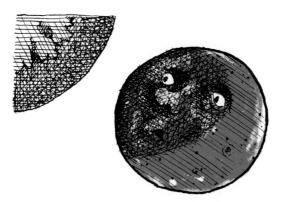

10. -voke-, -vocat- *call*

When Becky criticized the officer, he re<u>vok</u>ed her permit.
The college held a con<u>vocat</u>ion for prospective students.
Church services start with an in<u>vocat</u>ion *calling* in God's presence.
Coin collecting is an expensive a<u>vocat</u>ion (hobby, not one's calling).

Compare *evoke, evocation, provoke, provocation, vocation(al).*

First practice set

What is the literal meaning of each underscored prefix, root, or word in the following sentences?

1. An ob̲stinate person stubbornly stands _____ what others want.
2. A non̲assessable policy is one which is _____ assessable.
3. A counter̲plot is a scheme directed _____ a plot.
4. Anti̲aircraft guns are directed _____ aircraft.
5. A mis̲conception is a _____ interpretation of a problem.
6. Il̲limitable stretches of desert are _____ limited.
7. A duc̲tile substance is easily _____ .
8. A provoca̲tion, like breaking a dish, is capable of _____ing _____ angry words.
9. De̲tention of prisoners is _____ them _____ society.
10. Con̲servation of forests is _____ing them from destruction.
11. To dis̲pel gloom is to _____ it away.
12. Verte̲brae are so called because they _____ .
13. When nations di̲verge from ancient customs, they _____ away.
14. The ad̲vent of spring is the _____ .
15. An un̲tenable belief is one a person can _____ _____ .
16. In̲sistence on courtesy is literally _____ing for it.
17. A coni̲ferous tree _____ cones.
18. Importa̲tion is the process of _____ing goods into a country.
19. The re̲pulsiveness of a murder _____ you back from it.
20. If you ad̲duce your reasons for going to college, you _____ them into the discussion.

Second practice set

Supply or complete the word that fits best in each of the blanks.

1. A spy who spies *against* spies is a _____spy.
2. Resistance which is *not* active is _____violent.
3. Sentiment or feeling *against* something proposed: _____pathy.
4. Feelings *opposed* to war may lead to _____-war demonstrations.
5. Writing which can*not* be read is _____legible.
6. To calculate *incorrectly* is to _____calculate.
7. To *drive* a person *out* of a club or society is to _____ him.
8. A parting of two paths is a _____ence *(turning away)*.
9. A _____ is a rather formal *calling together*, especially in a university.
10. A motive that *leads* one *into* action is an _____ment.
11. To cease, or *stand from,* annoying others is to _____ .
12. Foreigners who misbehave in the U.S.A. are subject to _____tion (penalty of being ''carried'' away from it).
13. Anything *carrying* quite an odor is odori_____ .
14. _____, or *turning upside down,* of air layers sometimes makes hilltops warmer than valleys at night.
15- The process of *leading out* a person's abilities (_____ion) is more than the
16. *holding back* (_____) of facts in one's memory.
17. A person who *stands through* difficulties well is _____ent.
18. A decision which *cannot be called back* is _____able.
19. An argument which *cannot be turned against* is _____ible.
20. The trait *(of)* pushing *(one)* toward *(action)* is _____iveness.

Antonyms

By adding one of the prefixes presented in this unit, change each word below into its opposite:

1. manageable
2. logical
3. septic (poisonous)
4. preventable
5. behavior
6. conductor (of electricity)
7. obtainable
8. existence
9. proposal
10. religious

Suffixing

1. Think up or look up additional examples of each prefix introduced in this unit. How many does your dictionary list for <u>non-</u>? For <u>un-</u>?
2. Make a list of negative forms of adjectives introduced in five of the entries of this unit. Examples: *unreported, unattained, unconverted.*

3. Complete and expand the following table of -<u>duce</u>-, -<u>ducat</u>-, -<u>duct</u>- words, using a dictionary:

reduce	reduction	reducible	irreducible
deduce			undeductible
abduct		* * *	* * *
educate			
conduct		conductive	
induct			
induce		* * *	* * *

4. Compile a class list of -<u>iferous</u> words.
5. List several -<u>vert</u>-, -<u>verse</u>- words formed with suffixes from pp. 376–382. List several -<u>port(at)</u>- words; several -<u>pel</u>-, -<u>pulse</u>- words.
6. List six -<u>sist</u>- verbs, not including *desist,* in a column. Write the -<u>ant</u>, -<u>ent</u> form in a second column and the -<u>ence</u>, -<u>ance</u>, or -<u>ency</u> form in a third. Then insert the negative prefix for those which have familiar negative forms. Note that two have -<u>ance</u> endings and four end in -<u>ence</u>. How can you remember the spellings?

unit four

WORD PRESCRIPTIONS

Select a word from the list at the left which provides the best answer for each of the following.

insomnia
prerogative
conjunction
obstruction
avocation
placebo
Dictaphone
astringent
colloquy
annunciation
mandate
parliament

1. Something to contract the tissues and stop persistent bleeding.
2. Something often caused by fear, grief, or a guilty conscience.
3. Something held for teachers or others so they can discuss their problems.
4. Something set up to hinder traffic.
5. Something a doctor gives to please the patient, not for medical reasons.
6. Something you accept as a special duty to be carried out.
7. Something enjoyable for one's leisure hours.
8. Something that makes many speeches and many laws.
9. Something that remembers everything you say.
10. Something that links words, phrases, and sentences.

MOSTLY FOOTWORK

1. -ambul-, -ambulat-   *walk*

Mr. Schmidt is an <u>ambul</u>atory patient (able to *walk* about).
Lady Macbeth was a somn<u>ambul</u>ist; she *walked* in her sleep.

A per<u>ambula</u>tor is a baby carriage or buggy.

> Compare *amble,* to walk at an easy pace. It comes from an old French word which derives, like -<u>ambulat</u>-, from the Latin verb *ambulare.*

2. -cur(r)- . . . . -curs-, -course   *run, running*

If he is not courteous, Stephen will in<u>cur</u> his teacher's dislike.
A <u>curs</u>ory reading of the assignment is not enough.
The Grand Con<u>course</u> is a boulevard where hundreds of cars *run* daily.
The convict is serving two sentences con<u>curr</u>ently (at the same time).
The re<u>curr</u>ent rumor about the prices of stocks keeps *running* through financial circles.

More run words:

> A *courier,* once a "runner," is today a special messenger.
> A *current* in a stream is "running" water.
> *Current* events are happening now.
> A *course* in school is literally a race to be run, and an *excursion* is a special trip (a *running* out from or forth).
> The *precursor* of an event is the forerunner, like the movement of tectonic plates which foreshadows an earthquake.
> List other forms of *concur, recur, occur.*

3. -migr(a)-   *travel, move (from place to place)*

The Pilgrims decided to leave Leiden and <u>migr</u>ate to America.
<u>Migr</u>atory fruit workers *travel* from place to place harvesting crops.
Im<u>migr</u>ants *travel* into a country to live; e<u>migr</u>ants *travel* out.
Trans<u>migr</u>ation of the soul is a Hindu and Greek belief that the soul after death *moves* to another life in a new body.

> Compare -<u>move</u>- (p. 289).

4. -scend-, -scent-   *climb*

Few visitors prefer to a<u>scend</u> the Washington Monument on foot.
The a<u>scent</u> of Mount Everest takes much preparation and skill.
The heiress conde<u>scend</u>s to wash cars.
The sunset was a scene of tran<u>scend</u>ent beauty ("climbing" beyond the power of words to express.
Our local librarian is a de<u>scend</u>ant of the colonial founder of the town.
The a<u>scend</u>ancy of one political party was an unexpected development.

> The verb *scan* (meaning to mark verse to show metrical structure *or* to examine by point to point observation) comes from the same Latin word, *scandere,* to climb.

MAINLY MOUTHWORK

1. -dict-, -dictat-   *say, command*
    -loqu-, -locu-   *talk, speak*

A Dictaphone records what a person *says* or dictates into it.
The commissioner is very dictatorial *(commanding)*.
The weather report predicts rain tomorrow.
An indictment is a condemnation (charge *spoken* against a culprit).
The manager issues edicts *(commands)* like a king or a dictator.
Children are often loquacious, especially in groups.
The colloquy *(talking* together) lasted three hours.
In elocution Elsie was trained to *speak* clearly.
The interlocutors *(speakers)* on the stage made jokes at the expense of the audience.
Eloquence is effective speaking forth, and grandiloquence is pretentious eloquence.

Talk words:

Contradict, predict, addict, indict, apologue, circumlocution, obloquy.

2. -logue- . . . -logy-   *speaking, speech, science*

The prologue to a tragedy is a *speech* before the play begins.
The dialogue between Romeo and Juliet was amorous.
The Governor delivered a long eulogy *(speech* of praise) of the President.
Katie wants to major in biology, the *science* of life, which has many branches, such as physiology and zoology.

> The Greek root *logos* means *word,* in the sense of spoken knowledge, or simply knowledge. It is used in words like *apology* for knowledge in behalf of, or justifying, someone.

3. -mand-   *order, command*

Banks demand repayment of loans on time.
When the judge remands a suspect, he *orders* the person back to prison.
The supervisor countermanded her order for more supplies.
A senator has a mandate *(command)* to work for the betterment of the nation and the interests of his constituents.
Safety glass is mandatory in all cars *(required* by law).

4. -nounce-, -nunci- . . . -sert-   *declare, state*

The party platform denounces graft and payoffs (*declares* its disapproval of).
Edward VIII renounced the British throne (*declared* it vacant).
The Annunciation was the act of *declaring* to the Virgin Mary that she would
give birth to a Son.
To assert the truth is to *state* it firmly.
Mrs. Szabo will insert a clause in her will designating a new heir.

5. -parl-   *talk, speak*

When Parliament meets, the members will *talk* about new labor laws.
The bullpen is baseball parlance (way of *speaking*) for the area where relief
pitchers practice.
The referees held a parley (conference) between halves.
A parlor was originally a room for conversation.

> The -parl- words go back to Latin by way of Old French. *"Parlez-vous français?"*
> means "Do you speak French?

6. -rog- . . . -quir-, -quisit-   *ask, say, declare*

Detectives will interrogate the suspect (*ask* questions).
The council voted to abrogate the old zoning law (cancel it).
The commentator's derogatory remark about the team (*saying* or expressing a
low opinion) irritated the coach.
It is the loser's prerogative to *ask* for a rematch.
You inquire, or make inquiry, about a friend's health.
The Inquisition was a formal, prolonged investigation.
If you need supplies, you must fill out a requisition listing them.
The scientist's disquisition *(statement)* about the theory was brief.

Seek words:

> Query, quest, acquire, conquest, inquisitive, require, request, conquer,
> conquistador.

COOPERATIVE ACTS

1. -don(a)-, -ded-   *give*

Who will donate $1000 to save a child from starving to death?
The Red Cross has a constant need for blood donors.

We condone the crimes of Robin Hood (make allowances).
Lincoln wanted his hearers to dedicate *(give)* themselves to "the great unfinished" task that lay before the nation.
The dedication of the new church took place yesterday.

2. -junc(t)- . . . -juga   *join*

A golden spike marked the junction *(joining)* in Utah of the two parts of the Union Pacific Railroad.
The court issued an injunction *(enjoining* action) against the strike.
Gilbert and Agnes exchanged conjugal vows at a quiet wedding in the chapel.
The British were never able to subjugate the Irish people *(put* them *under a yoke).*

> What are the conjunctions in this sentence: "Put more space between 'King' and 'and' and 'and' and 'queen'"?

3. -merge-, -mers-   *dip, plunge, sink*

When a diving bell submerges, it *dips* under the surface.
Ulysses was about to emerge from the sea unclad when he saw Nausicaä and her maidens on the shore washing clothes.
The proposed merger of the two firms would "plunge" them into a larger entity.
A factory paints a casting quickly by immersing it in paint.

> Compare *immersible, emergence, emergency.*

4. -plac- . . . -placa-   *please, appease*

Saranac Lake is a placid *(soothing)* body of water in the Adirondacks.
The doctor gave the lady a placebo, an inactive "medicine" designed merely to *please,* or *soothe,* her.
Ben Franklin knew how to placate an enemy with tactfulness and modesty.
Madame Defarge turned out to be Darnay's implacable enemy, whom he could not *appease.*

5. -sequ-, -secut-   *follow*

The sequel to the first book *follows* the fortunes of the family for another thirty years.
The history of science is a long sequence *(series)* of failures, with a few notable successes.
Millions died as a consequence *(result)* of the famine in India.
One, two, three, and four are consecutive numbers.
The English persecuted Joan of Arc *(followed* her to torment her).

> Compare *execute, execution.* An *executive, executor,* and *executioner follow* through to get something done.

6. -somn- . . . -dorm- *sleep*

The <u>somn</u>olent audience applauded when the speech finally ended.
Doctors say that grief is a common cause of in<u>somn</u>ia *(sleeplessness)*.
A <u>dorm</u>itory, not a classroom, is a place for *sleeping*.
A <u>dorm</u>ant bear in a cave is *asleep* for the winter.
A <u>dorm</u>er window is likely to belong to a bedroom.

7. -stringe-, -strict- *draw together, tighten*

Divorce laws are very <u>stringe</u>nt *(tight)* in most of the states.
A styptic pencil is an a<u>stringe</u>nt; it *draws together* the tissues around a cut and
thus reduces bleeding.
Society re<u>strict</u>s the freedom of criminals.
Cancer caused a <u>strict</u>ure of the intestinal wall.

　　　Compare *constrict,* boa *constrictor, district.*

8. -struct- *build*

The World Trade Center in New York encompasses two of the tallest <u>struct</u>ures
on earth.

Enemy guns destroyed the super<u>struct</u>ure of the aircraft carrier.
De<u>struct</u>ive tornadoes raged through Kansas.
What is more inde<u>struct</u>ible than the pyramids of Egypt?
Barbed wire is a device to ob<u>struct</u> intruders.
Does experience in<u>struct</u> (*build* knowledge into) a person better than books do?

9. -sume-, -sump(t)-   *take (upon)*

If you as<u>sume</u> control of a Scout troop, you *take* it *upon* yourself.
A dictator's as<u>sump</u>tion of power puts freedom in great jeopardy.
The station will re<u>sume</u> its broadcasts when it repairs its transmitter.
Many praise the unas<u>sum</u>ing modesty (not *taking on* a sense of importance) of
the new director of the company.

   Compare *consume, consumer, consumption, subsume, presume,* etc.

10. -tend-, -tense-   *stretch*

High-spirited Jeanne <u>tend</u>s to be too generous.
The dress designer will ex<u>tend</u> her exhibition.
Uncle Ron, who eats too much, has a dis<u>tend</u>ed *(stretched)* stomach.
Dis<u>tens</u>ion of the bellows in a pipe organ creates the air pressure needed to pro-
duce music.

   Compare *tense, tension, tenseness, intense, intensive, intention; pretend, pretense,*
   pretension; contend, contentious, contention; retention, retentive, retentivity.

11. -vince-, -vict-   *conquer, overcome*

If you con<u>vince</u> a person that space travel is not dangerous, you *conquer* his
objections.
A person who e<u>vince</u>s surprise, shows it—in the sense that the surprise *over-*
comes the desire to conceal it.
The landlord had to e<u>vict</u> a tenant for not paying the rent.
The <u>vict</u>or at Hastings was William the Conqueror.
For a long time Alexander the Great appeared in<u>vinc</u>ible.

First practice set

What is the meaning of each <u>underscored</u> prefix or root in the following sentences?

1. The wealthy <u>don</u>or (_____) of the building remains unknown.
2. A <u>tend</u>on is a part of the body that _____ .
3. Con<u>secut</u>ive days are those which _____ each other.
4. A dis<u>quis</u>ition on trees is a _____ which may prove quite informative.
5. A con<u>junct</u>ion is a word which _____ together two statements.
6. In<u>somn</u>ia is inability to _____ .
7. Little of good or evil will _____ an incon<u>sequ</u>ential act.

8. To perambulate in the park is to _____ through it.
9. An implacable enemy is one you cannot _____.
10. Elocution is the art of _____ forth clearly and distinctly.
11. A constriction in an artery is a _____ together of its walls.
12. The theory of transmigration states that souls after the death of one body _____ into a new one.
13. The consumption, or _____, of sugar into the body has increased.
14. Incursions of an enemy are _____ in, or inroads.
15. To remand someone to prison is to _____ the person back into custody.
16. Recurrent rumors keep _____ back into circulation.
17. An invincible army is impossible to _____.
18. To pronounce a word is to _____ it correctly.
19. When she condescends, she _____ down to your level.
20. A merger is a _____ together of two or more companies.

Second practice set

Which word from the list at the left best replaces each *italicized* word or group of words?

courier
dedication
transcend
inquisitiveness
cursory
diction
Annunciation
contradict
interrogation
ambulatory
resumption
stringent
placate
construction
immerse
juncture
disquisition
dormitory
extension
migrate
donation
mandatory
victor
somnambulist
invocation

1. When tribes *move* (from place to place) on the desert, they must *climb across* the problems of having enough food and water.
2. The *required* regulations for owning and operating a car have become increasingly *tight*.
3. *Dip* the phosphorus in water before you return to the *place for sleeping*.
4. The inhabitants tried to *appease* the *conquerer*.
5. Answers to the *question-asking* at school are generally in favor of a *taking back again* of fall sports.
6. The *giving* of some rare books to the library brought forth an appreciative *formal statement* from the librarian.
7. The message the diplomatic *runner* brought seems to *say the opposite of* what the cablegram said.
8. The *choice of words* of the speech about the *reaching out* of cancer research at the hospital motivated a number of listeners to donate generously to the project.
9. After a *hasty* reading (as if running) of the contract, the official of the company signed the document authorizing the *building* of the ten-story edifice.
10. Thousands came for the *formal giving* of a priceless old painting showing the angel's *declaration* to Mary.

Third practice set

On a separate sheet write the number of the definition at the right which matches each *italicized* word in the left column.

1. *Abrogation* of a privilege
2. The girl's *prerogative*
3. *Mandatory* insurance
4. A brief *colloquy*
5. Intolerable *strictures*
6. Easy *renunciation*
7. Hasty *eviction*
8. Interesting *discursiveness*
9. Legal *parlance*
10. Youthful *presumption*

1. ordered, required
2. confirmation
3. ejection, expulsion
4. limitations
5. cancellation, abolition
6. taking (too much) upon oneself
7. talking together
8. right or privilege
9. act of making right
10. declaration of giving up
11. way of speaking
12. rambling, runaway quality

Words and their parts

1. Make a list of the suffixes attached to the seven "mouthwork" words in this unit. What is the effect of each?
2. Compare the uses and meanings of -stringe- with those of -tract- (p. 290). To what extent do the meanings overlap?
3. On a sheet of paper complete the following tabulation of -struct- words in columns, as in the example on the first line:

construct	constructive	construction	unconstructive
_____	destructive	_____	* * *
instruct	_____	_____	_____
obstruct	_____	_____	_____

What additional suffix may be attached to each word in the second column? Which one makes a familiar word with -ible at the end and in- in front?
4. List five words in the unit to which -ible or -able is or may be added. Write the resulting word, making sure you spell it correctly. Which root keeps its final *e*? Can you explain why?
5. What is an interlocutory divorce?

unit five

FOUR-SYLLABLE WORDS

From its root, which word in the list at the left is the best answer to each question?

jurisprudence
sororicide
aristocrat
patriarchal
equivalent
maternity
patrimony
gregarious
congenital
dexterity
domination
gratuitous

1. Which word means *motherhood*?
2. Which word describes a condition one is *born with*?
3. Find the word for something one inherits from his *father*.
4. What is the word for anything *given freely*?
5. What is the word for two things *having the same worth or value*?
6. What is the word for a person who *enjoys being with a crowd of other people*?
7. What is a word for the *legal* profession?
8. What is the word for the *act or process of controlling a situation or person*?
9. Which word denotes *unusual skill*?
10. What is the word for *sister killing*?

FAMILY AND HOME

1. -dexter- *skillful (especially with one's hands)*

Canoeing calls for <u>dexterous</u> manipulation of a short paddle.

Rachmaninoff had the finger <u>dexter</u>ity of a great concert pianist.
Thora claims to be ambi<u>dextr</u>ous (*skillful* with both hands).

> In Latin *dexter* meant right (hand) and hence skillful. *Sinister*, meaning left (hand), thus has ominous or evil implications.

2. -dom-   *home, official residence*
-domin-, -domit-   *rule, control*

The hermit established a <u>dom</u>icile high on the side of a steep mountain.
Cheerfulness was only one of Sandra's many <u>dom</u>estic (*home*-type) virtues.
Mr. Woods tried to <u>dom</u>inate (*rule, govern*) his children even after they left home; yet he denies being a <u>dom</u>ineering person.
The <u>dom</u>inant trait of a mule is stubbornness.
In the seventeenth century the British gained <u>dom</u>inion over the seas.
The physicist displayed in<u>dom</u>itable (almost *uncontrollable*) perseverance in carrying out his research.

> What is the relation between -<u>dom</u>-, from Latin *domus* (house) and -<u>domin</u>- (rule)?
> The two meet in *domain*, one's estate, land, or territory.
> The suffix -<u>dom</u> from Old English (*wisdom, kingdom, Christendom,* and *officialdom*) means the land, dominion, or totality of.

3. -frater(n)-, -fratri-   *brother*

Hester's father belonged to a well-known <u>frater</u>nal order.
In his senior year at the university, Douglas resided at his <u>frater</u>nity house.
In wartime one must not <u>frater</u>nize with the enemy.
Cain was guilty of <u>fratr</u>icide (killing a *brother*).

> <u>Soror(i)</u>-, sister, appears in *sorority* and *sororicide*.

4. -mater(n)-, -matr- . . . -metro-   *mother*

Do dolls encourage or merely express a girl's <u>mater</u>nal instincts?
A <u>matr</u>ix, the mold for a casting, is figuratively its *mother*.
Los Angeles is a <u>metro</u>polis, or *mother* city, with a cluster of smaller cities around it.

> *Matrimony,* or marriage, comes from the Latin *mater* (mother).
> *Matriculation* is the act by which one acquires an "Alma Mater." What is the significance of "Mater Dolorosa"?

5. -nasc- . . . -gen-   *born, birth*

Spring offers an annual re<u>nasc</u>ence *(rebirth)* of vegetation and animal life which has been dormant all winter.
<u>Nasc</u>ent oxygen is "fresh" and active because it has just been released.
The <u>gen</u>esis of democracy is traceable to Athens 2,500 years ago.
Milton's blindness was not con<u>gen</u>ital (existing from *birth*).
<u>Gen</u>etics deals with heredity and one's *inborn* traits.

Compare genealogy (the study of family descent or *birth*), genitive (possessive), generate (give *birth* to), regeneration (being renewed or re*born*), primogeniture (inheritance by the first*born*).

Note: -Gen- (birth) is a Greek root. The -gen- in *general, genius, gender,* and *genus* (class, kind, type) is Latin, derived from the same Greek word as -gen- (birth).

6. -(o)nym- . . . -nomin-, -nomen- *name*

Frugal is the antonym of extravagant.

Newspapers will not publish an anonymous letter (no *name* attached).

Mark Twain was the pseudonym (assumed *name*) of Samuel Clemens.

NATO is an acronym (*name* from word tips) for North Atlantic Treaty Organization.

Bill wanted me to nominate him for student president.

Being mayor for a day was a merely nominal honor.

The nomenclature (*naming* system) for plants and animals uses the Latin terms, and is thus the same in every country.

7. -pater(n)-, -patri- *father*

One of the Ten Commandments directs that both maternity and paternity be honored.

The Prodigal Son squandered his patrimony (inheritance from the *father*).

A company treating employees like children is guilty of paternalism.

The choir sang the ''Gloria Patri'' (''Glory to the *Father*'').

Do you believe the United States should repatriate citizens who defect to the enemy?

The American expatriate in Paris celebrated Christmas with her compatriots.

What is a *pater noster*? A *patron* saint?

Compare *patriarch, patriot, patristic, patron(ize), expatriate, patricide, parricide.*

CITIZENSHIP AND SOCIETY

1. -arch- . . . -archeo- *first (oldest), chief, ruler*

Michael, the archangel (*first* or *chief* angel), is named in the Bible.

Abraham, the patriarch of a large family or tribe, chose the barren hill country instead of the well-watered plain in which to live.

Queen Wilhelmina was a much-beloved Dutch matriarch.

Widespread riots create anarchy (no *ruler* or government).

The Catholic hierarchy consists of the church *rulers* or authorities.

The term -arch- may be a prefix, a suffix, or a root. It comes from the Greek *archos* (ruler) and signifies also the *earliest* or *oldest*. Compare -domin-.

The form archeo- means *ancient:* ''Methinks'' is an archaic expression.

Archaeology is the study of life in ancient times, especially by digging up old cities and examining long-buried artifacts.

2. -crat-, -cracy- . . . -pot-   *power(ful), rule(r)*

The rulers were autocratic, for they wanted all the power for themselves.
Democracy is a government which gives the *power* to the people.
Bureaucracy gives much *power* to government offices and agencies.
A person's potential is his or her capacity, or *power,* to perform.
A potential market is the market that a product has the *power* to serve.
The chemical is so potent that a tiny droplet is enough to kill a person.

3. -equ(i)-   *equal, even*

All points on a circle are equidistant from the center.
Equipoise and equilibrium denote *even* or equal balance.
Nothing disturbs the judge's equanimity (*evenness* of temper).
"Liberty, equality, fraternity" was the slogan of the French Revolution.
San Francisco has an equable climate; it does not vary greatly.

4. -grati- . . . -gratu-   *please, pleasing, agreeable, free*

Good grades gratify parents because they bolster their vanity.
Road maps are not always given gratis (*free*).
If you congratulate a friend, you tell how *pleased* you are.
A diplomat not *pleasing,* and therefore not wanted in a country, is declared to be *persona non grata.* (Note that the phrase is in Latin, once the language of diplomacy.)
Why do communist countries forbid gratuities (tips—to show one is *pleased*)?
A gratuitous insult is given *freely;* it is unprovoked.

5. -greg-   *gather, forming a herd or group*

Some members of the family always gather in groups; others are not so gregarious.
Teenagers often congregate in pizza parlors or at hamburger stands.
Hospitals always segregate those patients who have contagious diseases.
Our aggregation (group) of rooters at the game became very boisterous.

6. -juris- . . . -jure-   *law or justice, swear or take oath*

The study of jurisprudence is an old, respectable profession.
Statehood created a new kind of jurisdiction (*law* system) for Alaska.
Jurists (law experts) keep debating the problems of civil rights.
A jury has extra *jurors* in case one gets sick.
To injure someone is to do that person an injustice.
Perjury is *swearing* falsely.
If you abjure a bad habit, you *swear* off or renounce it.
A sorcerer who conjures a spirit *swears* an oath, or invokes a magic charm.

> *Judge, judgment, judicial, judicious* and other -jud- words come from the Latin
> *judex* (judge). Compare *adjudicate* (to give judgment).

7. -liber-   *free*

The governor decided to liberate the eighty-year-old prisoner.
A liberal education (hopefully) *frees* one from ignorance.
The company will liberalize its policy (make it *freer* in providing benefits).
A libertine is a person much too *free* from moral restraints, one that is, there-
fore, dissolute. See -solut- (p. 290).

> Liber- (free) comes from the Latin adjective liber (free). *Library* comes from the
> Latin word *liber* (book).

8. -plen-, -plent- . . . -plete   *full(ness)*

Father replenishes the refrigerator weekly (makes it *full* again).
Parents wish for their children the plenitude (*fullness*) of life's blessings.
The delegates held a plenary session (*full* or complete).

Benjamin Franklin went to France as plenipotentiary ambassador (with *full*
power to act).

Carolyn's skit, "Jim in Gym," is re<u>plete</u> with jokes and quips.
Drought will soon de<u>plete</u> the water supply in the reservoir if rain does not come soon.
A com<u>ple</u>mentary talent, plan, or person *fills* or rounds out a wholeness that neither counterpart could attain alone.
The manager's ex<u>ple</u>tive (exclamation or oath) came from the *full*ness of his angry feelings.

> The -plete- words come from Latin *pletus* (filled), which is the past participle of *plere* (to fill). -<u>Plen</u>- comes from Latin *plenus* (full), which is the source word of *plenitas* (fullness).

9. -polit- . . . -civi-   *citizen*

A telephoto shows the Governor performing her easiest <u>polit</u>ical duty—voting.
Vincent is a <u>polit</u>ic person—prudent, tactful, shrewd—as befits a responsible *citizen*.
Does <u>civi</u>c pride impel you to pick up picnic rubbish?
Before working for the government, one must pass the <u>civi</u>l service exam.

> -<u>Polit</u>- comes from the Greek word *polites* (citizen) with a meaning like that of -civi-, describing the duties of a citizen. *Politics,* the business of citizenship, has come to mean the practical science of government. *Polite,* however, comes from the past participle of the Latin *polire* (to polish).

10. -popul- . . . -demo-   *people*

St. Louis is a very <u>popul</u>ous community.
Even if they were unwise and incompetent, Roman leaders kept the <u>popul</u>ace voting for them by providing free bread and circuses.
<u>Pop</u> art appeals to the *people,* at least it is intended to do so.
A few well-placed hydrogen bombs could de<u>popul</u>ate the earth.
<u>Demo</u>cracy (*people*-rule) needs honest, competent leaders.
A <u>demo</u>gogue (*people*-leader) is a political figure who sways listeners by playing on popular prejudices or by making false promises.

11. -urb- . . . -poli-   *city*

About half the members of our <u>urb</u>anized (*city*-dwelling) society now live in cities.
Sub<u>urb</u>an areas have become cluster cities around a metropolis.
City-bred, our English teacher is <u>urb</u>ane, courteous, gracious, and polished.
New York has become a vast cosmo<u>poli</u>s with people from almost every country in the world.

> Anna<u>poli</u>s is literally the *city* of Anna. What is Minneapolis?

First practice set

What is the meaning of each underscored root or prefix in the following sentences?

1. A fraternal feeling is that of a _____ .
2. An archbishop is the _____ bishop of an area.
3. To ingratiate oneself with John's mother is to make oneself _____ to her.
4. In a sorority each member is a _____ of the others.
5. Ambidexterity is _____ with both hands.
6. A demagogue is a rabble-rouser who is or tries to be a leader of _____ .
7. A patrimony is an inheritance from one's _____ .
8. If you matriculate in a college, you accept it as a kind of _____ .
9. A plenary session of the delegates is a _____ session.
10. A plenipotentiary is an ambassador given full _____ to act.
11. To have dominion over twenty tribes is to _____ them.
12. An interurban bus operates _____ two _____ .
13. In creatures having regenerative powers, a new arm or leg may be _____ .
14. To nominate someone for office is to _____ that person as a candidate.
15. A plutocrat is one whose _____ lies in his wealth.
16. A bachelor juris is a "bachelor of _____ ."
17. To discuss exports in the aggregate is to _____ them together and discuss them as a whole.
18. Parliamentary procedure is mostly _____ .
19. Marcus, a libertine, was much too _____ from moral restraints.
20. Perjury is false _____ or testimony.

Second practice set

Which word from this unit in the list at the left best replaces each *italicized* word or group of words?

demagogue
plenitude
urban
equidistant
genesis
indomitable
maternal
liberal
persona non grata
fraternity
congenital
renascence
equilateral

1. *City* life offers many delights not found in rural areas.
2. Columbus had *almost uncontrollable* courage.
3. Two towns 39 miles from New York are *each the same distance* from the city.
4. Alan decided not to join a college *brotherhood.*
5. A foreign diplomat had to leave when our government declared him *person not pleasing.*
6. Americans enjoy a *fullness* of material comforts.
7. The steam engine signaled the *birth* (beginning) of the industrial era.
8. The boy's deafness is *the kind he was born with.*
9. Television and movies have brought a *rebirth* of interest in Shakespeare's plays.
10. Deborah gave *motherly* care to the orphaned baby.

SORRY, BUT YOU'RE PERSONA NON GRATA IN THAT OUTFIT AND WITHOUT A TOUR TICKET.

Third practice set

On a separate sheet write the numbers of the definition at the right that matches each *italicized* word in the left column.

1. *Domestic* peace
2. *Metropolitan* vastness
3. *Nascent* eagerness
4. *Paternal* severity
5. *Acronymic* brevity
6. *Autocratic* infant
7. An *equable* climate
8. *Replete* with regrets
9. *Demagogic* oratory
10. *Juridical* problems

1. fatherly
2. fortunate, favorable
3. even, with little variation
4. of a very large (mother) city
5. people-rousing
6. of a name made from initial letters of a group of words
7. found in one's home (country)
8. of law or legal procedure
9. plain, homely
10. newborn
11. well filled
12. relating to someone who has or wants supreme power

Suffix series

1. List several additional words ending in -dom and explain the effect of the suffix in each case.
2. Make a list of verbs ending in -ate from this unit and use each in a sentence. Do the same with verbs ending in -ize, adding any you can readily form from illustrative words listed.
3. How many -arch- words can you list using a dictionary? How many ending in -crat or -cracy? What does each mean?
4. Make a list of -nomen- and -nomin- words. Explain the effect of the root in each.

unit six

COUNTDOWN

What is the meaning of the *italicized* prefix in each sentence? In each case it will be a number, whole or fractional.

1. To *bi*sect an angle is to cut it into _____ parts.
2. A *cent*ime is one _____ of a franc.
3. A *nona*genarian is at least _____ years old.
4. An *octo*genarian is at least _____ years old.
5. *Mono*theism is belief in _____ God.
6. A *tetra*hedron is a solid having _____ surfaces.
7. A *cent*enarian is _____ years old or more.
8. A *sex*tet is a musical composition for _____ instruments.
9. Nebraska has a *uni*cameral or _____-chambered legislature.
10. A *sept*ennial is the _____ anniversary.
11. A *dec*ade lasts _____ years.
12. A *mill*ennium is an era lasting _____ years.

NUMBER PREFIXES

1. uni-, unit- . . . mono-   *one*

How does one learn to ride a <u>uni</u>cycle with its one wheel?

The amoeba is <u>uni</u>cellular; its *one* cell must perform all of its life functions.
The grandeur of Yosemite is <u>uni</u>que; there is only *one* such park.
<u>Uni</u>tarians believe that God is *one* being and not three.
The English lord in the play uses a <u>mono</u>cle (*single* eyeglass).
A <u>mono</u>poly exists in business when *one* person or company controls the sale
or use of a product.
News broadcasts are mostly <u>mono</u>logues.
A <u>mono</u>lith is *one* large block of stone or a carving from it, but a <u>mono</u>lithic
mentality is that of a blockhead—as dense as stone.

2. du- . . . bi-   *two*

A <u>du</u>al personality has *two* sides.
If *two* tie for first place, they should receive <u>du</u>plicate prizes.
Humans are <u>bi</u>peds (*two*-footed creatures).
<u>Bi</u>monthly pay checks come every *two* months.
You are <u>bi</u>lingual if you can speak *two* languages readily.
Electronic computers use a <u>bi</u>nary, or base-*two*, number system.

3. tri-   *three*

Newly born <u>tri</u>plets require *three* bassinets.
The celebration is a <u>tri</u>ennial event.
Is there a way to <u>tri</u>sect an angle (cut it into *three* equal parts)?
A <u>tri</u>ad is a "unitary" group of *three* persons, ideas, or musical tones.
A <u>tri</u>dent was the *three*-pronged spear of Neptune, god of the sea.
The French <u>tri</u>color has a red, a white, and a blue stripe.

> The prefix <u>tri</u>- occurs in both Latin and Greek words. Compare *triumvirate,* a
> group of three men or rulers. Caesar, Pompey, and Crassus made up the First
> Triumvirate in Rome.

4. quadr- . . . tetr-   *four*

The college is built around a <u>quadr</u>angle.
A <u>quadr</u>ant is one *fourth* of a circle, or an instrument for measuring the angu-
lar elevation of a star.
Four couples danced an eighteenth-century <u>quadr</u>ille.
Sternutation is a <u>tetr</u>asyllabic word for a spasm called sneezing.
Hiawatha is a poem written in <u>tetr</u>ameter (*four* beats, or feet, per line).
Herod, a Roman <u>tetr</u>arch, ruled one *fourth* of a province.
The use of leaded gasoline, containing lead <u>tetr</u>aethyl (*four* ethyl molecules),
has decreased steadily.

5. quin- . . . pent-   *five*

The Fischer <u>quin</u>tuplets were born in South Dakota.
Five persons make up a <u>quin</u>tet, for basketball or for music.
Sylvia is the <u>quin</u>tessence of brainpower (*fifth* essence, *i.e.,* the finest, most
perfect specimen).

Shakespeare and Milton wrote poetry mostly in iambic pentameter.
A human being, as a pentadactyl, has *five* fingers on each hand and *five* toes on each foot.
Pentecost is literally the *fiftieth* day, but is actually the seventh Sunday after Easter.

6. sex- . . . hex- *six*

Is your grandmother a sexagenarian (person in her *six*ties)?
Do you sing or play in a sextet?
To sextuple a figure is to multiply it by *six*.
The stop sign is a hexagonal figure, having *six* angles and sides.

7. sept- . . . hept- *seven*

September was the *seventh* month of the ancient Roman year.
A septenary is a week of years, or a *seven*-year period.
A septagenarian is at least *seventy* years old.
The shape of Greene County is heptagonal (*seven*-sided).
A heptad is a series or group of *seven*.

8. oct(o)- . . . octa- *eight*

The merchant built an octagonal house near the seashore.
An octave could be a group of *eight* persons, *eight* lines of poetry, or the *eight* notes of the standard musical scale.
Antidemocratically is an octosyllabic word.

Why is an octopus difficult to subdue?

9. nona- . . . nov- . . . ennea-   *nine*

A cake in the shape of a <u>nona</u>gon would be just right for *nine* persons.
Marian's great-grandmother is a <u>nona</u>genarian (in her *nineties*).
<u>Nov</u>ember was the *ninth* month in the Roman calendar.
A <u>nov</u>ena is a *nine*-day act of devotion for Roman Catholics.

> An <u>ennea</u>d is a group of *nine*, especially nine gods. An <u>ennea</u>gon has *nine* sides.
> Do not confuse the root -<u>nov</u>- (new) (p. 348) with the prefix <u>nov</u>-, or <u>non</u>- (not)
> with <u>non(a)</u>- (nine). <u>Ennea</u>- appears in very few words, but is included for
> completeness.

10. dec-, deci- . . . deca-   *ten*

The 1950s are known as the Eisenhower <u>dec</u>ade.
The <u>Dec</u>alogue (*Ten* Commandments) is remarkable for its brevity.
Diseases <u>deci</u>mated the army (killed every *tenth* man, or a very large part) be-
fore it ever fought a battle.
Metric measures use the <u>deci</u>mal system (based on *ten* or *tenths*).

> The form <u>deci</u>- is used with the meaning of a tenth, especially in units of the metric
> system like *decimeter* and *decigram*. The whole of the Latin word *decem* (ten)
> survives in *decimal* and *December*.
> Compare *decasyllable, decathlon* (group of ten events), *decagon*.

11. cent- . . . hect-   *hundred*

The twenty-first <u>cent</u>ury begins in the year 2000.
A <u>cent</u>imeter is *one hundredth* of a meter.
A <u>cent</u>ipede has many legs, but not necessarily *one hundred*.
Water freezes at 0° and boils at 100° on the <u>cent</u>igrade scale, which is divided
into *hundredths*.
Leon can run a <u>hect</u>ometer (*one hundred* meters) in twelve seconds.
A <u>hect</u>ograph was a machine able to print *one hundred* copies.

> In the metric system <u>cent</u>i- is used to mean one hundredth, <u>hect</u>o- to mean one
> hundred. An alternate form of <u>hect</u>o- is <u>hecat</u>-, as in hecatomb, the slaughter of
> one hundred oxen at a time as a religious offering.

12. mill-, milli- . . . kilo-   *one thousand*

Indoor plumbing dates back at least to the second <u>mill</u>ennium (*one thousand*
year period) before Christ.
A <u>milli</u>pede is a worm which appears to have a *thousand* legs.
A <u>milli</u>onaire is a person who has a *thousand* thousands of dollars.
The distance from Chicago to Los Angeles is 3,000 <u>kilo</u>meters.
A <u>kilo</u>gram of ground beef (one *thousand* grams or 2.2 lbs.) costs less in
Spain than in Sweden.
Electric bills are measured in cents per <u>kilo</u>watt hour (*one thousand* watts for
one hour).

In the metric system milli- means one thousandth. A *millimeter* is *one thousandth* of a meter. A *milligram* is *one thousandth* of a gram, and a *milli*ampere is *one thousandth* of an ampere.

13. multi- . . . poly- *many*

The Revoirs built a multipurpose room in their basement.
A multitude of curious people gathered on the hillside.
Multiple sclerosis attacks *numerous* parts of the nervous system.
The multifarious *(varied)* schemes for getting rich devised by the junior partner of the firm all failed.
A person who knows *many* languages is a polyglot.
Africa is polytheistic, with *many* kinds of worship.
Solomon, with *many* wives, practiced polygamy on a large scale.

> Compare *multimillionaire, multicellular, polyhedron, polytechnic.*

14. semi- . . . demi- . . . hemi- *half*

The bank makes semiannual interest payments.
Rescuers found the broker pinned under her car in a semiconscious condition.
Because Florida has a semitropical climate with moderate heat and humidity, it attracts many visitors.
The actor has become a kind of demigod.
Heather can do a demivolt (*half* leap) in horsemanship very adroitly.
Coffee was served as a demitasse (*half* cup) after the dinner.
Air pressure held the Magdeburg hemispheres together.

> Hemi- is Greek, demi- is French-Latin, and semi- is a Latin prefix related to hemi-. Do not confuse it with hema-, hemo- (blood), as in *hematoid* (like blood) and *hemorrhage* (bleeding).

NUMBER-LINKED ROOTS

1. -annu-, enni- *year(s)*

The annual meeting of the Garden Club comes in October.
The semiannual surplus sale takes place next week.
A perennial plant blossoms regularly through the *years*.
The historians hold a quadrennial convention.

2. -gamy- . . . . -nub-, -nupt- *marriage*

Bigamy is *marriage* to two persons at the same time.
Polygamy exists, but not in the United States.
The bride and groom now hope to enjoy connubial bliss.
They took their nuptial vows only this morning.

3. -later-   *side, sidewise*

A lateral pass in the last quarter won the game for us.
A bilateral (two-*sided*) agreement exists between the United States and Canada regarding the St. Lawrence River.
Seizure of Cyprus by a single nation would be a unilateral action.
The two prize-winning stallions have collateral (parallel, *side-by-side*) bloodlines from the same ancestor.

4. -meter-   *measure*

The Outer Drive skirts the perimeter (*measure* around) of the city.
The doctor used a spirometer to *measure* the boy's breathing.
An altimeter *measures* the height a plane is flying above sea level.

> Compare *kilometer, cyclometer, pentameter*. Note the difference between meter- and meteor- (what is in the *air*), as in *meteorology*.

5. -ped-, -pede- . . . . -pod-   *foot*

A pedestrian was arrested for jaywalking.
What animal is first a quadruped, later a biped, and finally a triped?
That was the riddle of the sphinx that Oedipus had to solve.
Enemy snipers tried to impede the roadbuilding (put a *foot* against it).
A camera fan frequently needs a tripod (three *feet*).
Broken arches in one's *foot* require the services of a podiatrist.

> Compare *pedal, pedicure, pedometer* (measures distance by *foot*), *pedestal, impediment, podiatry, podium* (platform for conductor).

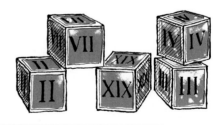

First practice set

What is the meaning of the underscored prefix, root, or (in one case) set of words?

1. A septet is a group of _____ performers.
2. An octosyllable is a word of _____ syllables.
3. Disease decimated the army (killed up to one _____).
4. To quintuple a figure, multiply it by _____.
5. Duplex means _____fold.
6. Triune means _____ in one.
7. A sexpartite object has _____ parts.

8. A tetralogy is a set of _____ related plays.
9. A monotonous voice stays on _____ tone most of the time.
10. Octavo is a book size made by folding large sheets of paper three times to form _____ leaves or sixteen pages.
11. A triumvirate consists of _____ persons.
12. A decathlon is an athletic contest of _____ separate events.
13. A milligram is _____ gram.
14. A _____-watt toaster in an hour uses one kilowatt hour.
15. What device used by photographers has three feet? _____
16. A chronometer _____ time, and is somewhat like a watch.
17. A novena is an act of devotion lasting _____ days.
18. Polyandry is a system in which a woman has _____ husbands.
19. Semiconsciousness is a state of _____ consciousness.
20. A chiropodist deals with the ailments of the _____.

Second practice set

What is the meaning of each underscored prefix or root?

1. A hexarchy is a group of _____ friendly or allied rulers.
2. A quinquepartite arrangement has _____ parts.
3. A septenary celebration occurs once in _____ years.
4. A pentahedron has _____ sides or surfaces.
5. A quadrennial event occurs once in _____ years.
6. A heptad is a series or group of _____ figures.
7. A man married to _____ women at the same time is guilty of bigamy.
8. A tetrarch ruled one _____ of a province.
9. An octangular figure has _____ angles.
10. A decasyllable is a word having _____ syllables.
11. The centigrade thermometer has _____ degrees or steps.
12. A hecatomb was the public sacrifice of _____ oxen.
13. Dual ownership involves _____ persons.
14. A polygon has _____ _____.
15. Pedate is a term in zoology which means _____-like.
16. Pentecost comes approximately _____ days after Easter.
17. It takes _____ novels to make a trilogy.
18. A multilateral surface would have _____ _____.
19. Pre-nuptial events take place before _____.
20. A monochrome is a drawing in various shades of _____ color.

Third practice set

What word from this unit best replaces the *italicized* word or group of words?

1. One does not often meet a *person one hundred years old:* _____
2. The distance *(measure) around* a baseball field: _____

3. The design on the window is a *nine-sided figure:* _____
4. The heavyweight champion is a *half-god* to many children: _____
5. The *five-measure-verse* so widely used in English poetry: _____
6. What Moses presented in the *Ten Commandments:* _____
7. The word for a *one hundred-meter* race: _____
8. Written history goes back only a few *thousand-year periods:* _____
9. Several of the Old Testament patriarchs practiced *marriage to several women at the same time:* _____
10–*Blossoming-through-the-years* bulbs are less work than *seeded-every-year*
11. plants: _____ , _____
12. A music festival held *every three years* is: _____
13. Frank is _____ because he speaks two languages fluently.
14–15. A *half-circle* is not a *half-sphere:* _____ , _____
16– A *many-sided figure* belongs to plane geometry, but a *figure with many faces*
17. to solid geometry: _____ , _____
18. From its name, one would expect _____ to be the *ninth* month.
19. A person who treats disorders of the *feet:* _____
20. *One thousand grams* of butter is a _____ .

What is it?

1. A quadrangle?	11. A decathlon?
2. An ennead?	12. Collateral?
3. Hexameter?	13. A multicellular plant?
4. A centimeter?	14. A pentagon?
5. Polytheism?	15. A nonagenarian?
6. The Trinity?	16. A lateral gesture?
7. A duplex house?	17. Annular rings?
8. A unique vase?	18. A multiplicity of plans?
9. A tercentennial?	19. A millipede?
10. A tetrahedron?	20. A demitasse of coffee?

Curiosity pills

1. What is a *duodecimal* system? What is the *duodenum* and why was it so named? Explain a *binary* number system. Why do computers use such a system?
2. How many <u>mono</u>- words are there in your dictionary? How does this compare with the number of <u>uni</u>- words? Compare the number of <u>pent</u>- words with the number of <u>quint</u>- words.
3. List ten everyday <u>semi</u>- words. Add five additional <u>hemi</u>- words.
4. Look up the article on books in any good encyclopedia. Prepare a report for the class explaining how the signatures are printed, folded, and bound. Demonstrate folio, quarto, octavo, and sixteenmo.
5. New words are created whenever they are really needed. Usually they are constructed from familiar prefixes and roots. Write down what you would expect each of the following words to mean?

unigon	a triologue	biquadrate
a centigon	decuplets	octuplicate

   Which may be found in an unabridged dictionary? How do the actual meanings compare with anticipated meanings? Could a *hemigon* exist? A *sesquicentenarian*? A *polymonocle*? Can you see any objection to the creation of a word like *multigon* or *tetralateral*?

unit seven

RATHER TECHNICAL

Which word from the list at the left is the right word for each of the following?

confluent
superlative
aquamarine
incisive
hyperbolic
introspective
navigable
hypertensive
interspersed
apocalyptic
petulant
supersensitive

1. A trait or quality *beyond* the ordinary, *i.e.,* carried to the highest degree.
2. A person whose thoughts are turned mostly *within*.
3. A dress that is the color of the *sea*.
4. A comparison that goes *beyond* the actual fact, such as calling the sky an inverted bowl.
5. Jokes *scattered* among the main points of the address.
6. A person *too easily* excited or stirred up.
7. A river in which ships are able to *sail* or operate.
8. A *vision* of something hidden.
9. The point where two rivers *flow* together.
10. An *irritated*, annoyed, or mildly angry state.

OUTWARD-INWARD PREFIXES

1. acro-   *tip, end, outer*

An acrostic is a set of words or lines of poetry having *tip,* or *end,* letters that form a word.

The circus acrobat is an expert performer, especially when using the *outer* extremities (hands and feet).

An acronym is a name composed of *tip,* or front, letters of other words: CORE means Congress of Racial Equality.

2. apo-   *from*

The driver's mistake calls for an apology.

The new arrival was an apostle of goodwill, a person sent (Greek *stellein*) *from* an organization or group.

An apocalyptic writer has a view or vision *from* something hidden (Greek *kelyptein,* to cover).

The Apocrypha are books that history hid *from* most of us.

3. extra- *outside, beyond*

The school paper is an extracurricular activity.
Shouting and other extraneous (outside) noises spoiled the recital.
The office manager complained of our extravagance (*beyond* good sense) in buying an excessive amount of stationery.
From past sales, a business analyst can go *beyond* the present to guess what the sales will be next year; this process is called extrapolation.

4. inter- *between, among*

The tailback managed to intercept a forty-yard pass and run for the touchdown.
Pan American World Airways flies intercontinental routes.
An interval is literally the space *between* two walls.
Mary Ann serves as intermediary (go *between*) when her two younger brothers have a disagreement.

5. intro-, intra- *within, inside*

Sandy is an introvert (mind turns *within*) who shrinks from social affairs for she is *inner*-directed, not *outer*-directed or *gregarious* (p. 221).
An introduction leads you *inside* a topic or into another person's acquaintance.
Hamlet was much given to introspection (looking *within* himself).
The introit is music at the opening of the service.
Does interstate traffic in Nevada exceed intrastate traffic?

BEYOND PREFIXES

1. meta- *beyond, besides*

The metamorphosis of a tadpole into a frog gives the tadpole a form *beyond* its present one.
The doctor reported that metastasis had occurred: The malignant tumor had spread *beyond* the original site (-stasis-) in the colon to a lung.

> Meta- is used chiefly in technical words pertaining to chemistry or biology. These include *metabolism, metacenter, metachromatism, metagenesis, metaphysics,* etc.

2. para- *beside, beyond, over, against, contrary to*

The two roads run parallel (*beside* one another) for at least ten miles.
Parapsychology deals with extrasensory perception and other phenomena *beyond* the scope of mere psychology.
The class had to write a paraphrase of the passage.
Parasites are persons who literally eat *beside* you, consuming what rightfully belongs to you.
The truck was loaded with paraphernalia (equipment or furnishings, often *over* or *beyond* what was needed).

Compare *parachute, paradox* (p. 211), *paragon* (p. 211), *paralyze, paranoia,* and *paraplegic.*

Note that *paramount, parapet,* and *paradise* do not come from para-. What is the derivation of each?

3. super-   *beyond, excessive, exceeding*

A superabundance of rain spoiled last year's crops.

The supernal beauty (*beyond* ordinary loveliness) of the far northern sunset can hardly be described.

A miracle is a supernatural happening because it cannot be explained in normal, natural ways.

The British–French Concorde flew the air route at supersonic speeds.

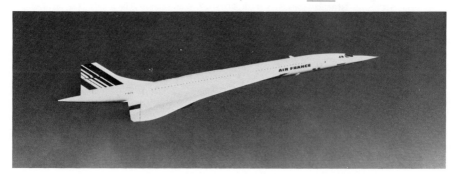

> Words with super- at the beginning are numerous. All imply something over, above, extra, added, higher, or superior, *but not necessarily excessive: superannuted* (beyond working years), *supercharger* (adds extra power). Compare *superficial, superfluous, superhighway, superimpose.*

4. ultra-   *beyond, excessive, extremely*

Aunt Maude is ultraconservative (*extremely* attached to tradition).
Ultraviolet light kills many disease germs.

> Ultra- may imply superiority, as in ultracritical. It has fewer uses than super- and is more likely to be unfavorable.
> Compare ult- (the *last* and often the *best*): The *ultimate* in gems.

5. hyper-   *excessive, beyond*

Hyperacidity (*excessive* acidity) causes a burning sensation.
Teachers often seem hypercritical (*excessively* fault-finding).
In Greek legend, the Hyperboreans lived in everlasting springtime *beyond* the mountains of the North Wind.

> Hyper- is more specific than super- or ultra- in its usage. It occurs in clinical terms like *hypertension* (*excessive* tension). It means *too much* or *beyond* normal, but has a favorable flavor in *hyperbole* (pp. 96, 247), poetic exaggeration, and various chemical terms.
> Hypo- means *below, under, too little:* A hypodermic is applied *under* the skin. Look up the origin and meaning of *hypochondriac.*

SOMEWHAT SINISTER STEMS

1. -cide-, -cis- . . . -sect-   *kill, cut*

Holidays heighten highway homicide.
The referee's decision *cut* the problem off from further consideration.
A surgeon who makes an incision *cuts* into a tissue or organ.
Two of the boy's incisors were knocked out in the game.
A sect, section, or sector is part (a *cutting*) of a larger whole.
Several in our biology class hated to dissect the frog.

> Compare *fratricide, parricide, regicide, genocide, suicide*.
> The suffix -*tomy* denotes a surgical operation: *appendectomy* (cutting out one's appendix), *gastrectomy* (removal of part of stomach), *lobotomy* (operation on a lobe of the brain), *tonsillectomy* (removal of tonsils). Expand the list.

2. necro-   *dead body, death*

Carol came to feel that her home town was a necropolis (city of the *dead*), but the term properly refers to an ancient cemetery.
Gangrene is a form of necrosis (*death* or decay of body tissue).
The group met monthly to read books of necromancy (black magic—literally, communication with the *dead*).

> Compare *necrology, necrophilia, necrophobia*.

3. -pet-   *attack or rush in, force*

Constant nagging is bound to make you petulant (impatient or irritable); you *attack* what annoys you.
Anger gave great impetus (*force*) to Gary's efforts.
Mab was an impetuous person (quick to *rush* in).
A bantamweight fighter cannot compete on equal terms with a heavyweight.

> Compare *impulsive* (p. 221). Pet- comes from the Latin verb *petere* (to seek or attack). From its past participle come *petition, competition, repetition*, and *appetite*. Can you explain the force of the root and prefix in each case?

4. -press-   *squeeze, push, press*

Low grades would depress Sylvia.
Horace could not repress a laugh when the boat overturned.
If you suppress a sneeze, you push, or *squeeze*, it back.

> Consider *impress, express, oppress, compress*, and their variant forms.

5. -sperse-   *scatter*

The dark clouds will disperse sooner or later.
Dispersal of the fishing boats outside the bay was accomplished with dispatch.

When decorating the hall, please inter<u>sperse</u> foliage among the flowers.
Never cast a<u>sperse</u>ions (damaging remarks) on a business rival.

> **Note:** The Latin source of -sperse- words is *spargere* (to scatter). *Sparse* (scattered, thinly spaced) alone retains the *a*. The words *asperity* (roughness, harshness) and *exasperate* come from *asper* (rough).

6. -turb-, -turbat-   *trouble(d), upset*

A stiff wind made the lake <u>turb</u>ulent (*troubled,* stormy).
The teacher will tolerate no dis<u>turb</u>ances.
"Rest, rest, per<u>turb</u>ed spirit!" said Hamlet to the ghost.
A cow is an imper<u>turb</u>able animal.

> Dis<u>turb</u>ances operate mainly from without, but per<u>turb</u>ations take place inside a person. <u>Turb</u>o- (that which whirls) is a prefix related to -turb- in such words as *turbo-generator* (driven by a turbine) and *turbojet* (airplane engine in which the energy of the jet drives a <u>turb</u>ine).

WATER AND THE SEA

1. -flu-, -flux-   *flow*

The town stands at the con<u>flu</u>ence (*flowing* together) of two rivers.
Uncle Ted had a great in<u>flu</u>ence on his fatherless nieces and nephews.
The Tarrants were very conscious of their af<u>flu</u>ence (*flow* of wealth).
The fair will bring an in<u>flux</u> of tourists.

2. -mari-, -marine-   *sea*

The <u>mari</u>time provinces (along the *seacoast*) were invaded first.
The Ancient <u>Mari</u>ner (*sailor*) told a weird tale.
<u>Mari</u>ne biology is the study of plant and animal life in the *sea*.
The inside of the pool was painted aqua<u>marine</u> (color of *sea* water).

3. -naut-   *sailor*

The Arg<u>onaut</u>s (*sailors* from Argos) went to find the Golden Fleece.
Modern astr<u>onaut</u>s are "sailors" in space ships.
Many <u>naut</u>ical terms appear in Virgil's *Aeneid*.

4. -nav-, -navig-   *ship, sail, go by ship*

The St. Lawrence is now <u>navig</u>able for ocean *ships*.
The battle of the Coral Sea was an important <u>nav</u>al engagement of World War II.
Sir Francis Drake was the first Briton to circum<u>navig</u>ate the earth.

First practice set

Write the meaning of the <u>underscored</u> root or prefix in each of the following sentences.

1. A <u>mar</u>ina, a small harbor where boats are kept, is so called because it is located close to the _____ .
2. A <u>necro</u>polis is a city of _____ people.
3. Infanti<u>cide</u> is _____ of a baby.
4. De<u>pression</u> makes one feel very much _____ down.
5. An <u>apo</u>calyptic vision takes the cover _____ something hidden, or something yet to happen.
6. The palm tree is an <u>acro</u>gen because the stem has its growing point at the
    _____ .
7. An <u>inter</u>mezzo is a musical work or movement played _____ larger units.
8. Im<u>pet</u>uosity in a war is quickness to _____ .
9. <u>Ultra</u>nationalism is _____ nationalism.
10. A <u>super</u>natural force is _____ the natural or explainable.
11. <u>Para</u>phernalia is literally what a bride possessed _____ her dowry.
12. <u>Flu</u>ent speech is so called because it _____ readily or rapidly.
13. The Argo<u>naut</u>s were _____ from Argos in Greece.
14. A<u>spers</u>ions about small towns are remarks you _____ about.
15. <u>Turb</u>ulent thoughts such as fears are _____ .
16. The lake is un<u>navig</u>able (not suitable for _____) because it is so shallow.
17. The inter<u>sect</u>ion of Route 18 with Interstate 10 is the point where the two roads
    _____ .
18. "The moon was a ghostly galleon tossed upon cloudy seas" is a <u>meta</u>phor, carrying the moon _____ what it actually is by comparing it to a ship.
19. A fly in the soup is an <u>extra</u>neous object which comes from _____ and does not properly belong to it.
20. <u>Hyper</u>sensitiveness is _____ sensitiveness to criticism.
21. The dentist advised the parents that the child's chipped in<u>cis</u>or (tooth that _____ into) be capped.
22. The question was <u>super</u>fluous because it asked for information _____ what was needed.
23. To dis<u>turb</u> someone is to _____ that person completely.
24. The im<u>pression</u> the visitor made on the students was the reaction that was pressed _____ their minds, senses, or feelings.
25. The affairs of the corporation were in a state of <u>flu</u>x, that is, they were _____ or undergoing constant change.
26. <u>Hypo</u>acidity means the presence of _____ _____ acidity in the body.

Second practice set

What is the word that goes in each blank to define the underscored prefix, root, or word?

1. The superstructure of the building is _____ the ground.
2. Believing the earth is flat is scientific apostasy (standing _____ the truth).
3. A supercharger forces air into an engine in quantities _____ what it would get otherwise.
4. An ultraliberal candidate would be _____ liberal.
5. A meeting of our student council is usually turbulent (_____).
6. The compression, or _____ power, of the engine is low.
7. Wealthy persons are said to be affluent because money _____ to them quite readily.
8. Parapsychology deals with occurrences that go _____ what psychology normally covers.
9. A crusade with little impetus has little _____.
10. Intravenous feeding is injecting nourishment _____ a vein.
11. Extraterritorial rights are the rights of a diplomat _____ those of the country which he serves.
12. Hypertension is _____ nervous excitement.

13. Ultramodern homes and buildings often look odd because they go _____ what most people like.
14. An intermediary is an agent who negotiates _____ two parties.
15. Persons given to introspection are quite intent upon looking _____ themselves.
16. The doctor gave a hypodermic (_____ the skin) injection of penicillin.
17. A meteor is literally _____ what normally exists in the air.
18. Maritime laws pertain to the _____.
19. A hypersensitive (_____ sensitive) person suffers much pain.
20. Interspersion (_____ _____) of dark and light pigments gives a mottled effect.

Replacements

Which word from the list at the left best fills each blank, or best replaces the *italicized* word or group of words?

hypercritical
repression
apocrypha
dispersion
dissecting
nautical
hypodermic
interscholastic
acronym
competitive
extraordinary
marine
interception
superfluous
asperity
impetuous
mariners
homicide
metaphor
necromancy
apostle
incisions
paradox
meteor
confluence

1. A receptionist should avoid conversation that is *flowing beyond what is necessary.*
2. As a boy, Mark Twain learned many *sailing* terms.
3– A medical student learns surgery by *cutting apart*
4. dead bodies and by making *cuts* into tissues or organs.
5. The charge against the accused changed from robbery to *person-killing* when the wounded storekeeper died a few days later in the hospital.
6. _____ contests take place *between schools.*
7. *Excessively critical* friends soon make life unendurable.
8. _____ *(in the sea)* life at great depths is inaccessible.
9– Do *attacking together* sports encourage *quick (to*
10. *rush in)* behavior?
11. St. Louis is located at the *flowing together* of the Mississippi and Missouri rivers.
12. Judith is a character from the _____ *(books hidden from us).*
13. The view from the mountain is truly _____ *(outside the ordinary).*
14. The Argonauts were _____ *(sailors).*
15. A _____ is no longer hovering *beyond* the atmosphere when it is seen.
16. It's the inspector's _____ *(harshness)* which makes him hard to endure.
17. The idea that evil is a form of good is a _____ *(statement beyond, or contrary to, itself).*
18. HEIR is an _____ for Happy Evenings in Rome.
19. A wizard is suspected of practicing _____ (the *black* arts).
20. _____ *(pushing* them *back)* is good treatment for evil impulses.

Change of pace

1. How many <u>inter-</u> words are listed in your dictionary? Select ten using roots with which you are familiar and explain each.
2. Make a list of twenty familiar <u>super-</u> words and five which need to be explained to the class. What is the total number listed in your dictionary?

3. Write the variant forms of each -pet- word presented in this unit and know the significance of each suffix. Explain -petal in *centripetal*.
4. Write an acrostic for your name either in words or lines of poetry.
5. Tabulate the seven -press- words introduced in the study guide with columns for verb, adjective-adverb, and one noun form, thus:
   impress   impressive(ly)   impression
   Explain each. List several prefix opposites like *unimpressive*. Make up a teaser quiz about them.
6. How many -cide- words can you list? What would "aquacide" be? "Astrocide"? Is either word needed or justified? What would an "aquanaut" be? Would one ever need to use such a word?
7. Explain the prefix in each of the following words, define the word, and write an imaginative paragraph containing five or more: *superlative, ultraism, hypertrophy, metabolism, acropolis, supercilious, intermezzo, extralegal, impressionism.*

Matching set

On a separate sheet write the numbers of the definition at the right which matches each *italicized* word in the left column.

1. Grim *apology*
2. Smug *asperity*
3. Guilty *perturbation*
4. *Suppression* of joy
5. Apt *acronym*
6. Gradual *necrosis*
7. Persistent *aspersion*
8. Spirited *introit*
9. Hourly *circumnavigation*
10. Fatal *hypodermic*

1. inner disorder, turmoil
2. excessive warmth
3. name from first letters of a group of words
4. harshness, roughness
5. sailing around
6. damaging comment
7. injection under the skin
8. words of regret (from the offender)
9. dangerous unrest
10. death of bodily tissue
11. squelching, subduing
12. opening music

unit eight

Which of the words in the list at the left fits best in each blank?

spectral
chronological
tangent
psychosis
carnivorous
orthodox
temporal
rectitude
sonic
carnal
corpulence
sentiment
contemporaneous
verification

1. A _____ is a serious mental disorder.

2. _____ beliefs are those generally accepted or approved.

3. A life of notable _____ is marked by unusual moral uprightness.

4. Dogs and cats are classified as _____, or flesh-eating, animals.

5. It is customary to list our Presidents in _____ sequence (the order in which they occurred).

6. _____ is a condition in which one has too much body weight.

7. Monarchs hold sway in _____ affairs (having to do with time and the material world).

8. There was a strong _____ (feeling) for vigorous measures to combat crime.

9. A _____ sight is often ghastly.

10. A _____ boom is a noise like an explosion.

11. In explaining a tangent line to a classmate, the student himself went off on a _____.

12. The _____ at the end of the legal document was signed under oath.

13. _____ events take place at the same time.

TO KNOW AND TO THINK

1. -cog(n)- . . . . -scien- . . . . -gnos-   *knowledge (of), knowing*

Recognition of an old friend in the crowd delighted Lucia.
If you have cognizance of foreign customs, you will get more pleasure from
your trip.
The financier preferred to travel incognito (*unknown, i.e.,* disguised).
Science is systematic, verified *knowledge*.
By some kind of prescience (*knowledge* beforehand), the boy knew which horse
would win.
Conscience is a mysterious way of *knowing* right from wrong.
Greek physicians were skilled in prognosis (predicting the results of a disease),
but not in diagnosis (*knowing* what is wrong).
An agnostic does not *know* whether there is a God or not.

> Compare -logy (*knowledge* of the subject indicated) (p. 305).

2. -doc-, -doctrin- . . . -dox-   *teach, teaching*

Natalie is a docile person (easy to influence or *teach*).
Docility makes her popular with school leaders.
The Monroe Doctrine of 1823 opposed foreign intervention of any kind.
A belief is orthodox if it agrees with the highest authority.
The idea that the sun revolves around the earth is unorthodox.

3. -ment-, -mem(or)- . . . psych-   *mind, mental, memory*

To mention Sue's mistake is to call it to *mind*.
Only a demented person (out of one's *mind*) would eat feathers.
Old friends like to reminisce (call back *memories*) of school days.
The plaque commemorates a battle fought nearby.
Mary's sister wants to major in psychology.
A psychopath (person *mentally* ill) may be very dangerous.

> *Psyche* means soul or spirit as well as mind. *Psychic* phenomena involve mysterious
> powers of the mind, like telepathy and extrasensory perception. *Psychotherapy* is
> mental treatment of various kinds. A *psychosomatic* illness is a physical disorder
> created by a deranged mental state.
> Do not confuse -ment- as a root with the suffix -*ment*.

4. -morph-
form, shape

A protomorphic animal is primitive in *form* or character.
The morphology of a word is a study of its *forms* and syntax.
Sugar is crystalline, but paraffin is amorphous (no *form* or shape).
The Greek gods were thought to be anthropomorphic (having human *form*).

> Compare *metamorphosis* (p. 330).

5. -pli- . . . -plic-
fold, copies

Some people are very pliable (easily influenced, *i.e.*, *folded*).
The father became implicated in his son's crime.
A legal secretary typed the contract in triplicate.
Multiplication is the process of increasing numbers *manyfold*.

> Compare *supplicate, duplicate, quadruplicate, replica* (p. 105).

6. pseudo-
false, seeming

Phrenology is a pseudoscience which relates character traits to shapes and bulges of the skull.
Is *The Wizard of Oz* a pseudoclassic with little value?
"Voltaire" was the pseudonym of François Marie de Arouet.

7. -pute-, -putat-
think, thought

Do not be quick to impute dishonesty to the waiter who overcharges you. Such imputation is unjust until proved.
Glenn's reputation may suffer if he defaults in the match.
A trial is a formal disputation (argument, opposing *thoughts*) in court.
A putative verdict is based on what are *thought* to be the facts.

> Consider *compute, computer, computation, deputy, deputation.*

8. -rect- . . . -ortho-
right, straight

The company will rectify its mistake about the Paris call.
Government service requires rectitude (moral *uprightness*).
Orthography (*right* spelling) is a difficult attainment.
An orthogonal (rectangular) figure has *right* angles.
An orthodontist is a dentist who makes teeth *straight*.

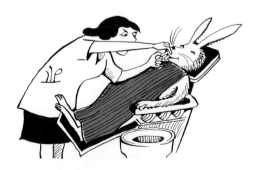

Rect- words include *erect, direct, correct, rector,* and their variants. The Latin source is *regere* (to rule or lead straight), from which we get *regal, regent, region, regimen, regiment.*

Compare *orthodox, orthopedic, orthochromatic.*

9. -temp- . . . -chron-   *time*

Irma's insolvency is temporary.
Contemporary events, like exploration of the planets, are those occurring at the present *time.*
A chronometer measures *time* more accurately than a watch.
A telephone in a movie of the Mexican War would be an anachronism (something contrary to the era involved).

> *Temper, temperament,* and *temperate* come from the Latin *temperare* (to regulate or mix). -Tempt-, in such words as *attempt, contempt, temptation,* comes from the Latin verbs *tentare* (to try) and *tendere* (to stretch). Compare *tempo, temporal, temporize* (p. 196), *chronic* (pp. 89, 116), *chronicle, chronology, chronoscope, synchronous.*

10. -ver-, -verit-   *true, truth*

Police did not verify the report of a disturbance on Main Street (make sure it was *true*).
Her recovery from cancer was a veritable miracle.
What are the verities of human existence (*truths* that few can doubt)?
Shaw's play *Saint Joan* has verisimilitude (*i.e.,* the appearance of *truth*).

11. -vi-, -via-   *way, road*

A devious route is a roundabout *road,* far from being direct.
One must obviate (find a *way* around) each difficulty that emerges.
Dion made a trivial (trifling) excuse and left at once.

> In ancient Greece a place where three roads met was an excellent place to hear or repeat the latest gossip. Thus *trivial,* from tri- (three) and -via- (road) has come to mean trifling or unimportant.
> Do not confuse -vi- (road) with -vi- (life) as in *viable, viands.*

THE FIVE SENSES

1. -aud-, -audit-   *hear, listen to*

Heaving an audible sigh, Holly went to wash the car.
The audition for the operetta comes today.
In college one can audit a course (*listen,* without participating).
The auditory nerve was somehow damaged.

> Compare *audience, auditorium, inaudible, audibility.*

2. -sent- . . . -path-   *feel, feeling*

A strong <u>sent</u>iment for acquittal existed among the jurors.
The captain gave his as<u>sent</u> to the referee's decision.
The rooters expressed dis<u>sent</u> by groaning.
A person in trouble needs sym<u>path</u>y.
It is hard for an audience to achieve em<u>path</u>y (*feeling* as one would in another person's place) with the villain in a play.
Sue could not conceal her anti<u>path</u>y (*feeling* against) for rats.
The plight of war orphans is always <u>path</u>etic.

> <u>Sent</u>iment is *feeling,* but <u>sent</u>imentality is overdone *feeling.*
> <u>Path</u>- means disease or suffering in *pathology* and in many other medical and psychiatric terms.

3. -son- . . . -phone-   *sound*

When the choristers sing in uni<u>son</u>, they sing with one *sound.*
The choir leader has a <u>son</u>orous voice—it *sounds* rich, deep, but unvaried.
A cave is re<u>son</u>ant; its walls echo the *sound* back again.
Dis<u>son</u>ance occurs when *sounds* do not harmonize.
As<u>son</u>ance is a word for *sounds* that recur pleasantly in poetry.
Foreign students study the <u>phon</u>ics (the science of *sounds*) of English.
Poly<u>phon</u>ic music has two or more harmonizing melodies.

> Watch for *phonograph, telephone, euphony* (pleasant sounds), *cacaphony* (harsh, discordant, raucous *sounds*).

4. -spec-, -spect-, -spic-   *see, look (at)*

Two seniors began to <u>spec</u>ulate about the future (*look at* it mentally, *i.e.,* imaginatively).
The color <u>spec</u>trum (something *seen*) is refracted white light spread across a screen like a rainbow.
One class studied the various a<u>spect</u>s of land investment (ways of *looking* at it).
Malcolm is a pro<u>spect</u>ive home owner.
If people re<u>spect</u> you, they *look* at you again in an admiring way.
Was Benedict Arnold a de<u>spic</u>able person?
Samantha is su<u>spic</u>ious of her friends' motives.

> The combining form -scope (view or sight), a Greek root, is found in numerous names for looking devices. These include *microscope, spectroscope, kaleidoscope, periscope, telescope, stereoscope, iconoscope.* What others can you think of?

5. -tang-, -tact-   *touch*

A <u>tang</u>ent *touches* a circle at only one point.
The bloodstains gave <u>tang</u>ible evidence of a crime.
A blind person's <u>tact</u>ile sense becomes more acute.

> *Tact* is literally the sense of touch—a light, considerate touch in dealing with "touchy" people. Consider *contact, tactful, tactless, tangential.*

6. -vide-, -vis-   *look or see, sight*

Parents must provide (*look* out) for their children. To make provision for their future is to *see* ahead, and plan accordingly.

In spite of the stories his sister told him, Jerry just could not visualize a dinosaur.

A vista (*sight* or view) of hills and verdant fields stretched out before the explorers.

> Compare *vision, revision, visible, invisible, visual, visit, visitor, advise.*

BODY AND HANDS

1. -carn- . . . -sarc-   *flesh, body*

A lion is a carnivorous animal; it eats *flesh.*

Teresa is the incarnation of goodness (in *bodily* form).

The carnage on the highways (slaughter, *bodily* harm) continues year after year.

The carnation (*flesh*-colored) is a popular greenhouse flower.

Every year in the spring our school has a carnival (festival).

The laboratory was studying sarcous tissues (*flesh* or muscle).

Among the ruins, no cover was found for the sarcophagus (stone coffin).

> A *carnival* was originally a festival just before Lent began. The word comes from the Latin phrase *carni vale* (farewell to meat).
>
> The word *sarcophagus* (*flesh*-eating) arose because the limestone used in ancient coffins caused rapid disintegration of the body inside.
>
> *Sarcastic* remarks are indeed *flesh*-tearing gibes.
>
> *Sarcoma* is a term for a certain kind of cancerous *flesh.*

2. -corp-   *body*

The corpse was cremated and the ashes scattered.

The Peace Corps, a branch of ACTION, works in many foreign countries.

Henry VIII was a corpulent king; he had too much *body.*

Do children sometimes need corporal punishment?

Many believe that incorporeal beings (not in *bodily* form) exist.

When you incorporate a business, you give it *bodily* form in a legal sense.

3. -man(u)-, -mani- . . . -chiro-   *hand*

The coach wrote a manual (*handbook*) on golf.

She hopes the manuscript will be valuable some day.

Who wants to take up manicuring (care of the *hands*)?

A surgeon is skillful in manipulating (*handling*) small instruments.

The leader's plan soon became manifest (as from an opened *hand*).

If your chirography (*handwriting*) is poor, use a typewriter.

Chiropractic is a method of adjusting the vertebrae by *hand.*

Chiromancy, or palmistry, is fortune-telling by means of the *hand*.

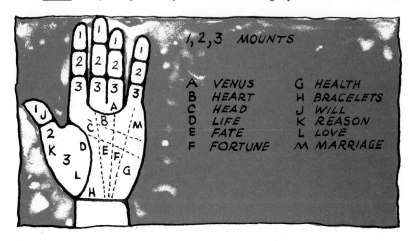

Note: Taste and smell are the neglected senses; they offer few words and no roots that occur in various examples. There is a sixth, or *kinesthetic*, sense of motion and position, but the root kin- is limited to a few technical words and phrases like *kinetic* energy, the energy resulting from the motion of an object or body. *Kinetograph* and *cinematograph* were early terms for motion pictures. From the latter comes the word *cinema*.

First practice set

Write the word which goes into each blank to define the underscored root or word:

1. Hollywood celebrities sometimes travel incognito (_____).
2. Demented persons are out of their _____.
3. Do foreign cars have a good reputation (what people _____ of them)?
4. The ambassador was granted an audition (_____).
5. If two processes are synchronous they keep in _____ with each other.
6. A rectangle has a _____ angle at each corner.
7. Dissonances are jarring _____.
8. Intangible qualities like courage are not traits you can _____.
9. A devious route does not follow the direct _____.
10. Morphology is a biological science dealing with the _____ and structure of plants and animals.
11. Carnage produces many dead _____.
12. Contemporary science deals with what is happening at the present _____.
13. Dissent is _____ not in accord with the prevailing view.
14. A despicable person is one you _____ down on.
15. Incorporation of a business gives it a legal _____.
16. The video section of a television set produces what you _____.

17. To <u>explicate</u> a problem or situation is to un_____ its mysteries.
18. <u>Verisimilitude</u> has to do with the _____ to life of a play.
19. In a <u>retrospective</u> mood one _____ back on previous events.
20. <u>Doctrinaire</u> persons are too positive about _____ which they accept.

Second practice set

Which word from the list at the left best replaces each *italicized* word or group of words?

prognosis
amorphous
implicate
spectacular
incorporeal
incarnation
supersonic
obviate
chronology
erect
audible
sentiment
carnivorous
doctrine
veracity
manual
empathy
orthodox
pseudonyms
resonant
cognizance
antipathy
incorporation
chronic

1. Certain admirers think George looks the *embodiment* of a Greek god.
2. The shouts of the man inside were *capable of being heard*.
3. "Recalling the *exact time order* of the events is almost impossible," the storyteller began.
4. That prolonged sunbathing is beneficial is an opinion definitely not *considered to be right*.
5. A teacher has special *responsibility for and knowledge of* the students in her class.
6. The velocity at which new passenger planes fly is *beyond the speed of sound*.
7. The child's plans for the future are quite *shapeless*.
8. *Inclusion (in the body of the book)* of the newest knowledge is important in preparing a science textbook.
9. Greek physicians had more skill in *knowing beforehand what would happen* than most people realize.
10. The announcer has a *deep (but even-sounding)* voice.
11. Substances that are *not in bodily form* have no weight or substance.
12. His mother has *long-continuing* arthritis.
13. He could not *find a way against or around* the danger.
14. The disappointed office seeker faced the prospect of job-hunting with *a strong negative feeling*.
15. Human beings were made to stand *upright*.
16. The evidence of the witness will *"fold in"* the owner in the crime.
17. The *hand* controls may be used if the power fails.
18. Often a writer will adopt a *seeming name*.
19. The Hardanger Fiord in Norway is as *impressive a sight* as the Grand Canyon.
20. Do you ever question the *truthfulness* of what you read?

Matchmaker

On a separate sheet write the number of the definition at the right which matches each *italicized* word in the left column.

A

1. *Auditory* sensations
2. *Sentimental* behavior
3. An *introspective* mood
4. A *putative* millionaire
5. *Amorphous* as beeswax
6. A *veritable* paradise
7. A *rectilinear* design
8. *Tactile* effects
9. *Sonorous* lecturer
10. *Visual* sharpness

1. having to do with sense of touch
2. thought to be, supposed
3. true, in fact
4. having to do with hearing
5. deep-toned, but unvaried
6. tending to look within oneself
7. gentle, having a kindly manner
8. having no definite form or shape
9. showing excessive feeling
10. unpleasant, harsh, ugly
11. having to do with seeing
12. marked by straight lines

B

1. A new *corporation*
2. Delicate *manipulation*
3. A long *viaduct*
4. Dangerous *prognostication*
5. Experiments in *psychology*
6. Smiling *orthodontist*
7. Tiresome *indoctrination*
8. Temporary *cognizance*
9. Lack of *empathy*
10. Surprising *carnality*

1. roadway, especially a bridge
2. suffering, distress
3. feeling as one would in another person's place
4. process of instilling teachings
5. skillful handling
6. knowledge and responsibility
7. inclination to interfere
8. prediction
9. emphasis on bodily urges alone
10. science of the mind
11. specialist in making teeth straight
12. organization, having a legal "body"

NEITHER WIT NOR WORD

unit nine

CONTRASTS

Find a word from the list at the left to match each phrase.

homogeneous
autopsy
malingerer
panchromatic
neolithic
primeval
neologism
retrogression
apprehensive
omniscient
euphemism
amphibious

1. Film that responds to *all* colors: _____
2. Animals that can live *both* on land and in water are said to be: _____
3. An *operation* to determine why a person died: _____
4. A *new* era when human beings could make good stone implements and pottery, but could not use metal: _____
5. One who seems to know *everything:* _____
6. A person who feigns *illness* to avoid duty: _____
7. Persons who are very much the *same* in habits, appearance, and other ways: _____
8. A *new* word or phrase: _____
9. A person (*seized* with fear) about chaotic conditions: _____
10. The practice of referring to death as "passing," or "eternal rest": _____

MORE PREFIX STUDY

1. alter- . . . hetero-   *other, different*

Marilyn wanted to <u>alter</u> the dress, making it *different*.
<u>Alter</u>ation of a house is costly.

Steve <u>alt</u>ernates, wearing one pair of shoes one day, the *other* the next.
Bess has a <u>heterog</u>eneous collection of coins (a variety, very *different* from each other).
<u>Heterod</u>ox teachings are *different* from the accepted, orthodox views.

2. ambi- . . . amphi-   *both*

An <u>ambi</u>dexterous person has notable skill with *both* hands.
Otto is <u>ambi</u>valent; he *both* loves and at times hates his father.
Lara is an <u>ambi</u>vert; she has *both* introvert and extrovert traits.
''Perhaps'' is an <u>ambi</u>guous answer to the question, ''Would you like to go to the party?''
<u>Amphi</u>bious creatures, like frogs and crocodiles, can live *both* on land and in the water.
An <u>amphi</u>bian plane can alight on land or on water.

> <u>Ambi</u>- and <u>amphi</u>- both mean *around* or *about,* but in compounds signify *both* or *double.*

3. auto-   *self*

Have you read Benjamin Franklin's *Autobiography*?
An <u>auto</u>nomous school system is *self*-governing.
<u>Auto</u>mation is the process by which machinery does most of the work of manufacturing by *itself,* without human operators.

> Why is an automobile so named? An autopsy? What is an *auto da fé*?

4. neo- . . . nov-   *new*

A <u>neo</u>logism is a *new* word, phrase, or way of speaking.
Mr. Gould is a <u>neo</u>phyte in the clothing business—literally a *new* plant (-<u>phyte</u>-) and thus a beginner.
<u>Neo</u>n was so named because, when discovered, it was a *new* gas.
The <u>neo</u>lithic era in human history was the *new* Stone Age.
The <u>nov</u>itiate in a convent is the period of *newness* or probation, while a <u>nov</u>ice is a beginner, or a person admitted to probationary membership in a religious community.

> Compare *novelty, nonce, innovation* (p. 186).

5. omni- . . . pan-, panto-   *all, every*

Larry's father sometimes seems <u>omni</u>scient (*all* knowing).
Why does an <u>omni</u>potent (*all*-powerful) Deity permit evil to exist?
Maxine is an <u>omni</u>vorous reader (reads *all* kinds of books).
<u>Omni</u>vorous animals eat *all* kinds of food.
Many think socialism is a <u>pan</u>acea (cure-*all*) for economic ills.
The <u>Pan</u>theon in Rome was a temple for the worship of *all* the gods.

> What is *panchromatic* film? *Pantheism* in religion? A *pandemic* pestilence? A *panoramic* camera? A *pantomime*?

6. tele-   *at a distance, far away*

Telemetry (measurements *at a great distance*) by means of instruments in satellites has played a major role in space science.
Telepathy is one form of extrasensory perception (ESP).
The teletype machine transcribes news stories on hundreds of typewriters in *faraway* cities.

> **Tele- words:** *telescope, telegraph, telephone, telephotography, television, telecast, telekinesis. Teleology* (the study of creative design in nature) comes from a different Greek root: tel- or telo- (end, purpose).

7. verd-, virid-   *green, grassy*

The verdant hillsides you saw in Vermont are the *Green* Mountains.
Spring rains made the verdure (*green* growth) fresh and luxurious.
On the bronze statue were patches of verdigris (*green* of Greece), a *greenish*-blue corrosion.

8. retro-   *back(ward)*

Retrorockets slowed the spacecraft's reentry into the earth's atmosphere.
After a long advance, the economy began to retrogress (move *backward*).
The wage increase adopted February 10 is retroactive to January 1.
How do last year's triumphs look in retrospect?

> What is *retrograde* motion in a star?
> Compare *retribution* (p. 36, 153).

ANTITHETIC PAIRS

1. bene- . . . eu-   *well or good*

Martin Luther King was a benefactor who did many *good* deeds.
In a beneficent moment, Marge contributed most generously to the Community Chest.

Sister Regina is an especially benevolent teacher.

Eugenics, the science or theory of being *well* born, would seek to improve the human race through control of heredity.

"Passing away" is a euphemism (*pleasant* phrase) for death.

> Compare *eulogy,* a speech of praise, especially for someone who has just died. See -logy- (p. 305).
>
> A *bonus* (Latin word for *good*) is a gift or extra payment. *Bon* (French word for *good*) occurs in a number of expressions in English such as *bonhomie* (*good* nature), *bon mot* (*good, i.e.,* apt saying), *bon vivant* (person who lives and eats *well*), *bon voyage,* and *bonne foi* (*good* faith, *i.e.,* honesty, sincerity).

mal-   *bad, evil, ill*

There was malice in the sailor's eyes as he spoke.

The wretch never ceased to malign (speak *evil* of) his benefactor.

Many died of the strange tropical malady.

The new patient is a malingerer, feigning *illness* to escape duty.

After committing a number of serious offenses against the law, the malefactor (*evil*doer) was finally caught.

The malevolence (*evil* wishes) of the authorities made it difficult for the Peace Corps to help the people.

Most martyrs met maledictions (*evil* accusations) meekly.

2. magna-, magni-   *great, large, big*

The club seeks business magnates (important figures) as members.

An electron microscope can magnify viruses, making them visible.

The Magna Charta of 1215 limited the English king's power.

The Senate appreciates the magnitude of the road-building project.

> Compare *magnificent, magnanimous, magniloquent.* The *magnet* words come from the Greek *Magnetis lithos,* stone of Magnesia. The word *magnesium* comes from the same source.

micro-   *very small*

The new micrometer measures *very small* distances, down to thousandths of a centimeter.

Two graduate students are making a study of microorganisms (*very small* forms of life, such as bacteria and viruses).

> Compare *microscope, microfilm, microprint, microgroove, microcosm, Micronesia, microbiology.*

3. prim-   *first, early*

The primary reason for building the Roman roads was military.

Janice decided that primitive dwellings did not look very comfortable.

English law centuries ago established primogeniture, the inheritance of an estate by the *first*born, or eldest, son.

-termin- . . . -fini(t)-   *end, limit*

The city will terminate its contract with the bus company.
Omaha was the eastern terminus (*end* place) of the Union Pacific.
The company exists to exterminate insect pests.
The lawyer made an interminable *(unending)* speech at the meeting.
Scientists would like to know whether space is finite (having a *limit* or *end*) or infinite.
A definition of a word gives the *limits* of its meaning.

4. -don-   *give*

Goodwill Industries asks you to donate cash, old clothes, and discarded equipment for its work.
The new dormitory is named after its donor.
One cannot condone carelessness (*forgive* by seeming to overlook), especially in the maintenance of aircraft.

-prehend-, -prehens-   *take, seize, grasp*

The police are always eager to apprehend *(seize)* a burglar.
Sam is apprehensive (*taken* with fear) about getting into college.
Joyce finds it easy to comprehend geometry.
The Dilseys worked out a comprehensive plan of action.

Compare *apprehension, incomprehensible, reprehend, prehensile.*

5. -cal(or) . . . -therm-   *heat*

A calorie is a unit for measuring *heat*.
A calorimeter is an instrument that measures *heat* produced.
Mixing the two chemicals caused a thermal *(heat)* reaction.
Thermite, a mixture of powdered metals used in fire bombs, generates intense *heat*.
In a thermonuclear reaction, nuclear fission releases *heat*.

Compare *thermometer, thermos bottle, thermochemistry, thermodynamics.*

-frig- . . . cryo-   *cold*

The Arctic region is frigid, even in summer.
The new refrigerator works well.
What are the uses of cryogen (''freezing'' gas) as a refrigerant?
Hospitals employ cryotherapy (ice packs to lower bodily temperature).
Cryonic societies exist to preserve bodies from decomposition until a cure is available for the disease that caused death.

Compare *cryogenics, cryometer, cryophyte, cryoscopy.*

6. homo- *same*

"Foul" and "fowl" are <u>homo</u>nyms, but "row" (line) and "row" (fight) are <u>homo</u>graphs.
Most milk today is <u>homo</u>genized so that the cream is mixed in.
The results of <u>homo</u>geneous grouping in our classes indicated that students in all groups were profiting from the change.

-misce- *mixed*

A <u>misce</u>llaneous pile of tools had accumulated.
In the hall closet lies a pro<u>misc</u>uous (mixed, chaotic) tangle of clothing.
Pro<u>misc</u>uous study habits are irregular and casual.
At the end of the term the teacher collected the best student essays for publication in a <u>misce</u>llany.

Pro<u>misc</u>uity often means loose and indiscriminate moral behavior.

First practice set

What is the meaning of each <u>underscored</u> root or prefix?

1. The forest <u>prim</u>eval is the _____ forest before it was disturbed by humanity.
2. A <u>micro</u>groove record has _____ grooves.
3. The <u>bene</u>diction is a blessing, an expression of _____ wishes.
4. <u>Retro</u>grade motion is motion _____.
5. An <u>auto</u>mat is a restaurant that offers _____ service.
6. <u>Hetero</u>dox opinions are _____ from the accepted view.
7. <u>Nov</u>ocaine was a _____ form of cocaine.
8. <u>Verd</u>ure is almost sure to be _____.
9. A <u>tele</u>photo lens on a camera takes pictures _____.
10. <u>Cryo</u>surgery uses a jet of extremely _____ air.
11. A <u>mal</u>ingerer pretends _____ to avoid work or duty.
12. A <u>pan</u>acea is a dose or plan to cure _____ ills or evils.
13. In an <u>ambi</u>guous promise, _____ meanings seem valid.
14. A <u>neo</u>plasm is a _____ growth of some kind.
15. Dia<u>therm</u>y produces _____ in certain tissues.
16. Two co<u>termin</u>ous railroad lines have their _____ in the same place.
17. Pro<u>misc</u>uous study habits means an _____ application to one's books.
18. <u>Homo</u>nyms are words pronounced _____ but having different origins, meanings, and spellings (usually).
19. <u>Eu</u>phoria is a state of feeling especially _____.
20. An <u>omni</u>present spirit is present _____ at the same time.

Second practice set

What word or word element from the list at the left best replaces each *italicized* word or group of words?

thermal
miscellaneous
innovation
retroactive
reprehensible
verdure
donation
neolithic
amphibious
benediction
refrigerant
heterogeneous
carnivorous
homogenize
autonomous
malign
interminable
pantheon
omnivorous
homograph
verdigris
apprehend
microscope
magnate
homonym

1. It is easy to *speak evil of* a political opponent.
2. Who invented the *instrument for seeing very small objects*?
3. (Lee) Chang-Kin's collection of fish was *varied and diverse*.
4. The increase in pay will be *effective backwards* to June 1.
5. "Bury" and "berry" are *words of different meaning pronounced alike*.
6. A *greenish-blue coating* may form on exposed bronze surfaces.
7. A heap of *widely assorted* junk does not enhance one's front yard.
8. *New Stone-Age* people lived in primitive dwellings.
9. J. C. Penney was a *great and dominant figure* in merchandising.
10. Horses are not *eaters of both meat and plants*.
11. Methyl chloride has been widely used as a *freezing agent*.
12. Creation of the United Nations in 1945 was a major *new method of operation* in international affairs.
13. The *heat-producing* effects of the process make cooling necessary.
14. When one is tired, a short train ride may seem *without end*.
15. A *temple for all the gods* had been erected in the ancient city.
16. Crocodiles are *able to live both on land and in water*.
17. Luxembourg is a(n) *self-governing* principality.
18. Police were not able to *seize* the suspect.

Third practice set

On a separate sheet write the number of the definition at the right which matches each *italicized* word in the left column.

A

1. Unnecessary *alterations*
2. Reformed *malefactor*
3. Rapid *automation*
4. Prolonged *novitiate*
5. Soothing *panacea*
6. *Magnification* of grievances
7. Unusual *bonhomie*
8. Effects of *primogeniture*
9. *Extermination* of fleas
10. Prolonged *frigidity*

1. mechanization
2. putting an end to the existence
3. cure-all
4. inheritance by the firstborn
5. coldness, lack of warmth
6. evildoer
7. both outgoing and reflective person
8. hopes, dreams
9. time of newness, initiation
10. good nature, pleasant manner
11. enlargement, exaggeration
12. changes

B

1. *Omnipotent* ruler
2. *Amphibian* plane
3. *Verdant* fields
4. *Terminated* agreement
5. *Infinite* resources
6. *Comprehensive* training
7. *Microscopic* energy
8. *Retrospective* mood
9. *Autonomous* islands
10. *Ambivalent* motives

1. endless, unlimited
2. self-governing
3. inclusive
4. thoughtful, pensive
5. very small in amount
6. all powerful
7. fresh, green
8. mixed, both good and bad
9. operating on both land and water
10. tending to look backward
11. religious, devout
12. ended

Family connections

1. Roots and affixes naturally find themselves in easily-associated families, among them the *numerical,* the *scientific,* the *physical,* and the *sensory.* While some of the following word elements are taught in depth later in the book, you may wish to make a stab at placing each under one of the above headings: -pod-, -scien-, -helio-, mono-, -audit-, -man(u)-, -stell(a)-, bi-, -vis-, gust-, -sol-, tri-, ambul-, -tang-, gastro-, -corp-, -ped-, -aud-, -vide-, -mani-, luna-, uni-, du-, gastr-, -aud-.
2. Write two sentences for each of the above families of words, using elements you have listed under each heading.

Literally speaking

On a separate sheet write the number of the literal meaning at the right that matches each *italicized* word in the left column.

1. *corpuscle*	1. "swiftfoot"
2. *velocipede*	2. "to free one caught by the foot"
3. *contingent*	3. "the body of the offense"
4. *corpus delicti*	4. a "little body"
5. *expedite*	5. "touching together"

Bonus

1. From the material in this unit, build as many adjective pairs as you can, such as *alterable* and *unalterable*.
2. Write pairs of opposites based on -diction, -volence, -factor, -geneous, -gression, -spect.
3. What is the opposite of *cryotherapy*?
4. List ten or more pairs of homographs.
5. Explain each illustrative word in the unit that is not defined.

unit ten

WORDS IN ORDER

Supply a word from the list at the left for each of the following purposes.

astral
ephemeral
magnanimity
aquatic
vitality
sacrosanct
concord
geology
lucid
diurnal
pneumatic
acrophobia

1. A word for bigmindedness, especially in dealing with enemies.
2. A word for harmony and agreement among families, nations, or other groups.
3. A word for something very short-lived.
4. The word for the study of the earth and its composition.
5. A word for mental or physical vigor or liveliness.
6. A word with a root relating to air pressure.
7. A word for a particularly clear explanation.
8. A word pertaining to activities in the water.
9. A word for fear of high places.
10. A word for something considered especially holy.

THE COSMOS AND THE CREATION

1. -cosm(o)-   *world, universe*

Is our <u>cosmos</u> (ordered *universe*) the "best of all possible worlds," an "unweeded garden," or a "place of wrath and tears"?

The crusade for peace is a cosmic task.
Should we call space explorers cosmonauts or astronauts?
Paris is cosmopolitan because it draws inhabitants from many countries.

2. -de(o)-, -de(us)- . . . . -theo- *god*

For ancient Egyptians, the sun was the chief deity.
Deification of the sun was a natural, but gradual, process.
Theology, or the knowledge and study of *God,* was once called the "queen of the sciences."
Theodore is a name meaning "gift of *God.*"
Apotheosis is the process of deification. It may be applied to a person, a system, a technique, or any part of the creation.

3. -di(urn)- . . . . -journ- . . . . -ephem- *day*

Do you enjoy your diurnal *(daily)* routine?
Isadora kept a diary of her trip to Africa.
The writer's journal *(daily* record) will not be published this year.
Congressional leaders hope to adjourn early this year.
Fashions and slogans are usually ephemeral; they last but for a day.

> Both -diurn- and -journ- come from the Latin *dies* (day), one directly, the other by way of French. A *journey* was once a day's work or a day's travel. A *journeyman* in the medieval guilds was a worker who had completed an apprenticeship and could then be hired by the day. A *journey* and a *sojourn* (visit) were once thought of as lasting but one day.

4. -helio- . . . . -sol- *sun*

A heliograph sends messages by reflecting *sunlight* from a mirror.
Sunbathing is to some degree a form of heliotherapy.
Heliolatry (*sun* worship) is quite common among primitive peoples.
Astronomers travel far to study a solar eclipse.
The house had a large solarium (a room for *sun*bathing).
During the summer solstice, the *sun* stands at its farthest point north of the equator.

> *Sol* is the Latin word for *sun,* but -sol- has meanings from other sources, as from the Latin word *solus* (alone) in *solitary, solo, soliloquy.*

5. -luc- . . . . -lumen-, -lumin- . . . . -photo- *light*

A lucid explanation of rainbows is as clear as *daylight*.
A translucent pane is not transparent, but it lets *light* pass through.
A lumen is a unit for measuring the flow of *light*.
Many alarm clocks have luminous dials.
A photometer measures the intensity of *light*.
In photosynthesis, *light* creates carbohydrates in plants and trees.

6. -mort- . . . -thanato- *death*

The youth received a mortal wound in battle.
The auto mortality rate is depressingly high.
The court ordered a postmortem (medical examination after *death*) to discover the cause of the man's sudden demise.
Many advocate euthanasia (mercy *death*) for a person incurably ill. (See eu-, p. 349.)
Thanatophobia (abnormal fear of *death*) often keeps people awake.

> Compare necro- (p. 332).

7. -stell(a)- . . . -astro- *star*

Michelle gave a stellar performance in the school play.
The Big Dipper is a familiar constellation (a group or configuration of *stars*).
Stella likes to show off her mother's stelliform table (*star*-shaped).
Hester wants to study astronomy.
Astrology is a pseudoscience about the *stars* and astral influences.

> An *asterisk* is a starlike figure. What does *disaster* mean literally?

8. -vir- . . . -anthropo- *man*

The big-boned barber has a virile (strong) face.
The delegation was a learned triumvirate.
Gertrude likes her course in anthropology, the study of customs, habits, and traditions all over the world.
The chimpanzee is an anthropoid ape from Africa.
Jonathan Swift was accused of misanthropy (hatred of mankind, *i.e.*, the human race) because of his forceful satire.

> **Caution:** Latin has three roots which begin with vir-: *virtue* comes from *virtus* (strength). *Viridity* (greenness) and *virulent* (very hostile or poisonous) comes from *virus* (a poison). *Virus* in English is a submicroscopic infective agent that causes diseases.
>
> **Antonym:** Fem(in)- is not a true antonym because -vir- and -anthropo- words are generic rather than sexist.

9. -vita-, -vi- . . . -bio- *life*

Tina has amazing vitality. She swam all day without getting tired.
Nothing should devitalize the campaign against crime in our cities.
Pine trees are viable (able to *live*) in timberline weather.
Professors of biochemistry (chemistry of *life* processes) are trying to create life in their laboratories.
A graduate student is making a study of symbiosis, in which different kinds of *life* live in close dependent relationship.

> **Note:** Theo-, -photo-, -helio-, -ephem-, -astro-, -bio-, -anthropo-, -cosmo- and -thana- in this group are from Greek; the others are from Latin.

THE FOUR ELEMENTS

1. -aqua-, aque- . . . . -hydr-, -hydro-   *water*

Rhoda has a large aquarium (tank for fish and *water* plants).
Aquaplaning is one of the most popular aquatic sports.
You study subaqueous life (under*water*) in a glass-bottomed boat.
The runaway car uprooted a fire hydrant.
Hikers on the John Muir Trail carry dehydrated food (*water* removed), or else
eat food brought in by pack horses.

Water words:

>*Hydraulic* (relating to water power), *hydrogen* (water gas), *hydrotherapy* (cure
>by water), *hydrology* (study of water), *hydrophobia* (fear of water).

2. -flagr- . . . . -pyr-, pyro-   *fire*

Claiming illness to go hunting was a flagrant (glaring, literally *flaming*) abuse
of sick leave.
Chicago was destroyed by a huge conflagration (destructive *fire*) reputedly
started when a cow kicked over a lantern.
The dead chieftain's body was laid on a funeral pyre (heap of wood for *burning*
corpses).
The pyromaniac was arrested when she returned to the scene.
An expert in pyrotechnics (art of making or using *fireworks*) will speak.

3. -pneumat-   *air*

A car with pneumatic tires literally rides on *air*.
Leslie carried out an experiment in pneumatics.

>Both *pneuma* in Greek and *anima* in Latin mean (1) breath or air, and (2) spirit,
>soul, or the Holy Spirit. Pneumatology is the study of spirits, but pneumat- today
>is used in English chiefly of air or wind, and anima chiefly of soul and spirit. Hence
>*anima* is included in the next section rather than in this.

4. -terr-, -terra- . . . . -geo-   *earth, land*

No new territory remains to be discovered on *earth*.
The swampy terrain (*land* surface) made road building difficult.
Because it was never found, Amelia Earhart's body was never interred (put in
the *earth*) in her homeland.
Geology is a popular science course in college.
The geocentric concept made the *earth* the center of the cosmos.

>Compare *terrace, terra firma, geodesy, geomancy.*

OUR ROLE IN THE COSMOS

1. -ami(c) . . . . -phil(o)-   *friend*

Envoys tried to create amity *(friendship)* between the hostile nations.
Explorers found the Incas amicable people.
Philately (*friendliness* to stamps) has long been a popular hobby.
The American ambassador to London and his family became real Anglophiles
(lovers of the English).
In London, Hester played at a concert given by the Royal Philharmonic Society.

> What is *philogyny*? What does Philadelphia mean literally?

2. -amor- . . . . -amat-   *love*

Romantic fiction contains many amorous speeches.
Paris's amative nature was quickly stirred when he saw Helen of Troy.
T. S. Eliot, enamored with English society, became a British subject.
Cleopatra was Antony's paramour (*lover,* usually illicit).

> **Explain:** *amateur, amour propre, inamorata.*

3. -anim-   *life, spirit*

The tree is an animate object; a locomotive is inanimate.
Barbara is so animated (full of *life* and *spirit*), she attracts many friends.
It was magnanimous (big-hearted) of Lillian to forgive her assailant.
The woodchuck proved pusillanimous (cowardly *spirited*) in its encounter with
the beagles.
What stirred your animosity (hostile *spirit*) in such a memorable way?

4. -cord- . . . . -cardi(o)-   *heart*

Canada and the U.S.A. live in concord.
Meanwhile, peoples in some areas of the world live in restless discord (hearts
apart).
Mr. Parks had to retire because of a cardiac ailment.
Each week the hospital makes a cardiogram of certain patients.

5. -ferv- . . . . -ard-   *glowing, burning*

Paganini played his violin with fervid zeal *(glowing, burning).*
Emily Brontë had a fervent desire to become a writer.

The sophomores play football with great ardor; they are "on fire" with their efforts to win the championship.

Even as a youth, the future playwright was an ardent reader of the classics.

> *Fervid* zeal is more intense than *fervent* zeal.
>
> *Ardor* suggests more fire and less heat than *fervor*. The roots are *fervere* (flow, boil, rage) and *ardens* (burning).

Related words:

> *Effervesce* originally meant to boil. Today it means to fizz, like soda water. An *effervescent* person is sparkling and lively.
>
> A *scintillating* personality is sparkling, if not flashy, with a hint of art and mental brilliance. Stars, diamonds, raindrops scintillate in sunlight.
>
> Flames *coruscate* (glitter, emit flashes of light), as do waves, brilliant minds, and white-hot stars. There is more hint of heat and vibrant energy in *coruscation* than in *scintillation* or *effervescence*.

6. -fid-, -fide-   *trust, faith*

The judge's unswerving fidelity (*faith*fulness) won her much praise.

Iago was guilty of perfidy (breach of *faith*).

Desdemona was not guilty of infidelity to her husband, Othello.

Thomas is a diffident boy; he is shy because he lacks faith in himself.

Carol was grateful for a friend in whom she could confide.

7. -pen- . . . -penit-   *punish(ment), sorrow*

The referee should penalize the team for delaying the game.

A penal colony was a place of *punishment*.

Peter's penitence (*sorrow* for wrongdoing) was deep and prolonged.

The thrill killer spent forty-eight years in a penitentiary.

> Pen- comes from the Latin word *poena* (punishment). Penit-, on the other hand, derives from *poenitere* (to be sorry).

8. -phobia-   *fear*

Worries and various phobias kept Frieda from having much fun.

The burglar with claustrophobia (*fear* of closed spaces) went insane.

A victim of acrophobia (*fear* of high places) should not be a steeplejack.

9. -sanct-   *holy*

St. Francis lived a life of sanctity (saintliness).
Enter the sanctuary (*holy* place) reverently with bowed head.
Mary is a sacrosanct (especially *holy*) church figure.
The suspect had a sanctimonious look (pretended *holiness*) on his face.
Do your parents sanction (approve) your going to camp?

First practice set

What word goes in each blank to define the underscored prefix, root, or word?

1. A pusillanimous person has a cowardly _____.
2. A mortician is a person who works with the _____.
3. To confide in a person is to _____ that person.
4. Aquamarine is the color of sea _____.
5. Symbiosis involves two kinds of interdependent _____.
6. Claustrophobia is a _____ of closed places.
7. A diary is a _____-by-_____ account of one's experiences.
8. An amative nature is _____.
9. A philologist is a _____ of words, individually and collectively.
10. A conflagration is a huge _____.
11. The pericardium is a membrane surrounding the _____.
12. A penitent person is _____ for a misdeed.
13. A stelliform hat would be _____-shaped.
14. A pyromaniac has a compulsion for starting _____.
15. A constellation is a configuration of _____.
16. Deification of a person would make that person a _____.
17. Butterflies are ephemeral. They live but for a _____.
18. To elucidate a problem is to throw _____ on it.
19. The flow of _____ was measured in lumens.
20. A sanctuary is a _____ place.

Surprising interlude

1. What is the root-prefix significance of *amphitheater*? of *cosmetics* and *cosmetology*? of *cryometer*? of *hydrophobia*? of *philander*? of *geopolitics*?
2. With un-, in-, non-, or dis-, cite or form a negative adjective for each of the roots presented in this unit. Check in the dictionary to verify any forms you are not sure about.
3. What is *xenophobia*? *bataphobia*? *phonophobia*? What others can you add? Compile a list of -philes.
4. Look up *anthropology, biogenesis,* and an article about *astronauts.*
5. How many forms of worship can you think of besides *heliolatry*? Compile a list. Some of the words may be your own creations, using the names of screen or television stars or sports "deities." What would *bibliolatry* be? *gyneolatry*? *eugeniolatry*? *anthropolatry*?

Second practice set

Which word from the list at the left best replaces each *italicized* word or group of words?

heliolatry
perfidy
luminous
animosity
cosmos
diffident
mortality
territory
amicable
cardiac
astronomy
acrophobia
misanthrope
flagrant
apotheosis
vital
sanctimonious
philanthropist
vitality
stellar
animated
diary
heliopolis
penitentiary
hydrology

1. *Glaring* violations of the traffic code tend to increase
2. the *death* rate from accidents.
3. It takes unusual *aliveness* to carry out a political campaign.
4. While most of the Rembrandt painting was in shadow, the face of the subject was *light-giving* and expressive.
5. The book is a pseudoclassic written in the form of a *daily record*.
6. The town needs a *friend of humanity* who will build a music hall.
7. One of the oldest primitive religions is *sun worship*.
8. Fear of spending another ten years in a *place of sorrow (for wrongs committed)* kept Bert on the straight and narrow.
9. A *person who dislikes mankind* usually has few friends.
10. Is a life that is *full of pretended holiness* easier than a life of self-sacrifice?
11. The aviator had a *heart* disorder.
12. Alaska, the *land area* bought from Russia, is thinly populated.
13. *Spirited and lively* persons are usually popular.
14. A future scientist needs training in *the study of the stars*.
15. It is hard to believe the virtual *deification* of Lenin in Russia.
16. Political campaigns often produce a strong *hostile spirit*.
17. *Fear of high places* does not trouble a high-wire performer.
18. Whoever told the secret was guilty of *a breach of faith*.
19. We know more about the *world-universe* than our forefathers did.
20. *Friendly* settlement of the strike seems possible.
21. The *study of the waters of the earth* is his chief concern as an environmental scientist.
22. The French singer, whose final song was "Stella by Starlight," was the *star* attraction at the concert.
23. The *City of the Sun* of ancient Egypt was situated at the apex of the Nile delta.
24. No longer *shy,* Fern exuded an air of assurance.

Matching exercise

Write the number of the definition on the right that goes with each *italicized* word in the left column.

1. *Sanctity* of marriage
2. Inflamed *pericardium*
3. *Coruscations* of fireworks
4. Reckless *ardor*
5. Mathematical *infinity*
6. *Amorous* glances
7. Course in *geology*
8. Quiet *fervor*
9. Youthful *pyromaniac*
10. *Geomancy* as a hobby

1. indicative of love
2. study of earth and its makeup
3. changeableness
4. firebug
5. brightly burning zeal
6. determination
7. membrane around the heart
8. divination by handfuls of earth
9. sacredness, holiness
10. endlessness
11. brilliant, sparkling flames
12. warm, glowing eagerness

"*DUMBO ALWAYS HAS TO HAVE THE LAST WORD.*"

SPELLING TRICKS AND TECHNIQUES

Spelling bothers students today more than it once did. It bothers teachers and educators, too, much more than it did, for example, in Shakespeare's day. In that uninhibited era, only a few fortunate young people were able to obtain an education, and spelling was a legitimate indulgence in individuality.

It is probably absurd in the twentieth century to insist that each new generation labor to preserve the linguistic history that is recorded in dictionary spellings. Quite a few persons, among them George Bernard Shaw, have at one time or another recommended that spelling be simplified to the point of plain standard phonography. Thus, the word *through* would be spelled *thru* or *throo,* and *caution* might become *cawshun.* The advocates of simplified spelling have, however, been unable to convince enough editors, educators, and elitists to bring about such a reformation. Each student must, therefore, either accept the mandate of society and spell words as the dictionaries demand or else abandon all claims to literacy.

Meanwhile, all is not lost. A number of principles and rules exist that will help students to get their *p*'s and *q*'s in the right places, to put double or single letters where they belong, and to insert the right mix of vowels in between. The best principle to embrace at the outset is that you, the student, should formulate your own rules from the raw material provided. Then you will remember the rules better and practice more readily what you yourself have discovered.

The problems that follow are arranged somewhat in order of difficulty and cover the subject about as well as it can be covered in practical terms.* If you seldom err in the area of problem 1, you should simply go on to problem 2. Concentrate on the areas where you get the most citations from teachers and other friends.

1. **The Long and Short of It.** In hundreds of short, everyday words from Old English, the pronunciation offers a reliable but not infallible reminder of the spelling. If you study the lists below, you will be able to devise a simple rule about the relation between the pronunciation and spelling where you have a vowel plus a consonant plus a final *e:*

can	cane	sat	sate	. . . . .	create
Dan	Dane	pal	pale	. . . . .	delete
man	mane	not	note	. . . . .	dissipate
plan	plane	pet	Pete	. . . . .	emulate
Sam	same	sit	site	. . . . .	percale
fat	fate	bath	bathe	. . . . .	baste
human	humane	breath	breathe	last	. . . . .
prim	prime	cloth	clothe(s)	past	paste

*The material for these problems is drawn largely from *Word Wealth Junior,* a vocabulary builder that approached the subject more scientifically than most spellers. Such material was based on a careful study of the best that had been written, suspected, or demonstrated about the tricky art of putting the right letters in the right places.

List other examples. What is the principle involved? Does it need to be qualified at all? Look on p. 374. (Your teacher will provide dictation if you need it.) Does the principle apply to words ending in a vowel plus a double consonant plus *e*? (What about the word *caste*?)

2. **"Double, Double, Toil and Trouble."** When do you double the final consonant when adding -<u>ing</u>, -<u>ed</u>, and -<u>er</u> forms? Study the following pairs of words and state the difference in pronunciation that almost always tells you when to double the final consonant:

Sweet corn:	can	canning	canned	canner
Sugarcane:	cane	caning	caned	caner
A hand:	grip	gripping	gripped	gripper
To complain:	gripe	griping	griped	griper
A bunny:	hop	hopping	hopped	hopper
A speller:	hope	hoping	hoped	hoper
For a floor:	mat	matting	matted	matter
Birds:	mate	mating	mated	mater
It pricks:	pin	pinning	pinned	pinner
To grieve:	pine	pining	pined	piner
Will it work?	plan	planning	planned	planner
A tool:	plane	planing	planed	planer
Fighters:	spar	sparring	sparred	sparrer
To save:	spare	sparing	spared	sparer
To do or not?	tip	tipping	tipped	tipper
Blood:	type	typing	typed	typer

How do *toll, roll, coal, doll, fool, moll,* and *poll* fit into this picture? Can you devise a rule that is simple, with few if any exceptions? If not, you will find help on p. 374.

Exercises:

a. Now write a line for each of the following: *begin, bite, chin, dine, gape, grin, hit, mop, pile, rip, rot, sin, sit, slap, top, tube, unite, whine, write.* What part of speech are most of the forms?

b. Now write the -<u>ing</u> form, the -<u>ed</u> form, and, if there is one, the -<u>er</u> form for *combine, commit, complete, determine, dim, line, occur, omit, slide, slip, slope, submit, worship,* and *yoke.* How could you ever misspell one of them again—even though two do not follow the rule?

3. **Plurals Are Persistently Perverse.**

a. Plurals in -<u>es</u>. Try to pronounce each of the following words as if their plural forms were spelled with -<u>s</u> instead of the extra syllable provided by -<u>es</u>:

birch	birches	church	churches	relish	relishes
brush	brushes	coach	coaches	search	searches
bush	bushes	dish	dishes	wish	wishes

What do these words have in common that makes the extra syllable necessary? Why are *strengths* and *lengths* spelled normally? Expand each list and then devise a simple rule that applies to most of the examples you or the class can list. Compare your rule with the one on p. 374.

b. Plurals of words ending in *o*. Most words ending in *o* add -<u>es</u> to form the plural. This fact is helpful in the absence of any definite rule. Here is a partial list of such words:

| cargoes | echoes | mottoes | noes | tomatoes |
| dominoes | mosquitoes | | potatoes | vetoes |

What do a majority of the following exceptions have in common? To what category of things do most of them belong?

| altos | boos | radios | silos | studios | twos |
| banjos | pianos | rodeos | solos | sopranos | zoos |

Do you sense a subtle difference in pronunciation? Use the dictionary when in doubt about spelling. Note that *volcanos* is now permitted, and *banjoes* is no longer incorrect. Can you improve on the rule on p. 374?

c. Plurals of words ending in *y* sometimes give trouble, in case you never discovered or learned the rule. What is the difference between the two kinds below?

baby	babies	lady	ladies	alley	alleys	monkey	monkeys
colony	colonies	library	libraries	boy	boys	turkey	turkeys
company	companies	memory	memories	day	days	valley	valleys
enemy	enemies	story	stories	essay	essays		

Once you notice the difference between the two lists, you will never need to look up one of these words. In case you have not been able to devise or remember the rule, look on p. 374.

4. **Two Words or One?** If you say what you mean and mean what you say, you will distinguish between the pairs of sentences below. What is the difference in meaning in each case and in the way you read them?

1. They were also sorry.	They were all so sorry.
2. We were almost happy.	We were all most happy.
3. You were already outside.	You were all ready outside.
4. Scouts are always prepared.	Scouts are prepared all ways.
5. Come, although you were not invited.	Come all, though you were not invited.
6. We are altogether satisfied.	We are all together satisfied.
7.	Everything is all right.
8. He will maybe be there.	He may be there.

How would you restate each? See p. 374.

5. **Which Word Do You Want?** The following pairs below are sometimes confused. What means can you devise for making certain you write the one you mean? It may be a mnemonic device, a rhyme, mispronunciation, or some other association:

1. angle—a figure formed by lines that meet

   angel—heavenly being

2. carrot—vegetable

   caret—omission mark ($\wedge$)
   carat—unit of weight for gems

3. cease—stop

   seize—grasp

4. cemetery—burial park

   seminary—training school

5. dairy—home for cows

   diary—daily record

6. formerly—in time past

   formally—done in accordance with rules or forms

7. loose—not tight

   lose—suffer loss of

8. quite—really

   quiet—(two syllables) not noisy

9. route—path or road

   rout—drive away (an enemy)

10. sphere—globe

    spear—sharp weapon

It is mostly a matter of pronunciation, but you might associate *loose* with *boot* or *root,* and *lose* with the verb *misuse.* Pronounce each word distinctly and think how it is spelled. Write a mnemonic device, a rhyme, or a short sentence for each one.

6. **These Pairs Sound Alike Because They Are Homonyms.** How can you dissociate the two in each case? Can you think of a way? For example, there is always an ant on a currant, and the school principal is always (hopefully) a pal. *Stationery* contains the *e* of p*e*ns and p*e*ncils, and writing letters is a rite. Dessert has an extra *s* for s-sweet.

1. coarse—rough or unrefined

   course—path, route, or series of studies

2. canvas—cloth

   canvass—sell or solicit

3. compliment—bit of praise

   complement—something that completes

4. council—an assembly for consultation or advice

   counsel—advice or lawyer

5. current—occurring in the present time; general trend; the fastest part of a stream

   currant—red, black, or white berry used for making jelly

6. desert—abandon

   dessert—tasty sweet dish (tsk! tsk!)

7. metal—cold, shiny stuff

   mettle—courage

8. principal—money or chief

   principle—rule or generality

9. stationary—immovable

   stationery—for letter-writing rite

10. troop—large number, groups

    troupe—group, usually of actors

7. Do IE and EI Bother Ye? Three simple rules will help. Try to formulate them and then turn to p. 374.

a. What is the sound of *ie* in each of the following words: *achieve, apiece, belief, believe, brief, chief, field, fiend, grief, grieve, hygiene, mischievous, piece, pier, pierce, priest, relief, relieve, retrieve, shield, siege, thief, tier, yield*? The following words have the same sound for *ei*, but how do they differ? What letter precedes the *ei* in *conceit, conceive, deceit, deceive, perceive, receive*? A few exceptions exist and these are found in this sentence: The weird financier seizes no leisure, neither to stave off the devil nor to worship the Deity.

b. What do all of the following words have in common? How do all differ from the words in *a* above? *chow mein, deign, feign, feint, foreign, forfeit, geisha, height, heir, neighbor, reign, Sinn Fein, skein, sleigh, sovereign, vein, weigh, weight. Sieve* is an exception.

c. In German words, *ei* is regularly pronounced like *i* in *vine; ie* is pronounced *ee: Arbeit* (work), *geist* (ghost or spirit), *Krankheit* (illness), *mein* (my), *meister* (master), *stein* (stone), *zeit* (time); *dien* (serve), *dieser* (this), *liebe* (dear, beloved), *lied* (song and ballad), *liefer* (hand over, give). Compare *diesel engine.*

8. Word Building Helps Spellers. This is especially true in the case of double letters caused by prefixes. Learn to distinguish prefixes. Remember that most double letters near the beginning of a word occur because of a prefix. (See rule on p. 374.) Study the following examples:

To abbreviate a speech.	To transship goods.
A drug addict.	Unnatural behavior.
To connect a wire.	Overripe tomatoes.
To dissect a frog.	To override a veto.

Exercises:

a. Make a list of ab- and ac- words, such as abbatoir, access, accident, addenda, afflict, aggressive, allocate, announce, appoint, arrest, assent, attention, etc.

b. Make a list of con- words, such as collapse, collision, commission, reconnoiter, correlated, etc.

c. Do the same for ex-, in-, sub-, and ob-. Check over the other prefixes, and find out what happens.

9. Silent Letters Demand Recognition. Many short words have a silent *a*, especially words from Old English, because the vowel sound was once greatly prolonged. (See rule on p. 374.)

heard	beacon	deaf	dreary	beagle
dream	health	leaf	weary	eagle
stream	retreat	season	increase	cease
feat	threat	measure	creature	disease
sweat	hoard	treasure	peanut	villain
loan	road	roar(ed)	boast	carriage

How to remember them? Pronounce so as to bring out the silent *a*, imitating however crudely the way they were once articulated. *Beard* apparently sounded something like "bee-ard" or "bay-ard."

Other silent letters include:

a. The *sc*- words: *ascend, conscience* (with *science!*), *conscious, descend, discipline, fascinate, scissors,* etc. Mispronunciation will help. <u>Sci</u>- is a root meaning know(ledge).

b. The *dg*- words: *bridge, budge(t), dodge, hedge, judge, lodge, ridge,* etc. Expand the *d* and try to pronounce each word as spelled, or insert an *i* to help you.

c. Silent *e* words: *bade, determine, pageant, foreign, forfeit, surfeit, vengeance, foretell* and other <u>fore</u>- words, *height, sleight, ninety, luncheon, pigeon, surgeon,* etc.

d. A silent *g* sleeps in a troublesome group of words including:

campaign	deign (to come down to another's level)	benign	gnash
design	feign (pretend)	foreign	gnaw
resign	reign	sovereign	gnome
sign			

e. Remember the silent *h* in such words as:

ghost	anchor	architect	character	chasm
ghoul	shepherd	orchestra	chemistry	chord

f. The silent *gh* craves attention in:

bough	caught	bought	freight	sleight (of hand)
dough	naughty	fought	neigh(bor)	height
through	ought	sought	weigh(t)	straight
thorough	taught	wrought		

g. The silent *p* in certain words pleads for inclusion:

psalm	psychology	pneumatic
psalter	psychic	pneumonia

10. **A Nibble at -<u>Able</u> and -<u>Ible</u>.** Examine the words in the following lists. Can you find any principle or rule that might be helpful in learning to spell the two groups? Expand the lists. Tabulate the words according to the letter preceding the -<u>able</u> or -<u>ible</u>. Does this help? Exaggerated pronunciation will probably do more than anything else to help you spell the words correctly. (See rule on p. 375.)

-<u>Able</u> I	-<u>Able</u> II	-<u>Ible</u> I
agreeable	adorable	contemptible
available	advisable	convertible
commendable	comparable	discernible
considerable	desirable	perceptible
enjoyable	durable	resistible

-Able I	-Able II	-Ible II
estimable	imaginable	audible
explainable	irritable	credible
fashionable	likable	divisible
favorable	miserable	eligible
habitable	pleasurable	forcible
honorable	receivable	gullible
payable	recognizable	horrible
portable	removable	intelligible
preferable	retrievable	legible
profitable	usable	negligible
remarkable	valuable	permissible
respectable	pliable	plausible
suitable	reliable	possible
transferable	variable	sensible
workable	veritable	terrible
	capable	visible
changeable	hospitable	
manageable	probable	
noticeable		
pronounceable		

11. **"Thar She Blows."** Quite a few words end in -ar. One can almost sense the harsh *a* sound or flavor in the normal pronunciation. Exaggerate it if the words prove troublesome. Here are twenty of the most familiar:

beggar	circular	particular	scholar
burglar	collar	peculiar	similar
calendar	familiar	poplar (tree)	singular
cedar	grammar	popular	vinegar
cellar	liar (teller of lies)	regular	vulgar

Which letters most often precede the -ar?

Quite a few words end in -or:

actor	elevator	janitor	radiator
author	emperor	labor	rumor
aviator	error	major	scissors
bachelor	flavor	minor	senator
conductor	honor	mirror	terror
doctor	horror	odor	traitor
editor	humor	pastor	vigor

What part of speech is each one? What letter most often precedes the -or? Stress the ending of any that bother you—and savor the word that the last three letters form in several cases if you add an *e*. The normal ending is -er for most person or agent words and for all comparative forms of longer adjectives.

beaker	doer	filler	lancer	purser	thinker
caterer	faster	go-getter	neater	talker	worker

One could list hundreds. The best spelling strategy is to concentrate on the -<u>ar</u> and -<u>or</u> words, accepting -<u>er</u> as the normal ending. (See p. 375.)

12. Suffixes Sometimes Cause Suffering.
a. What happens to the final silent *e* of a word before any suffix beginning with a vowel? The -<u>able</u> and -<u>ible</u> words above (with some exceptions) offer one example of this rule. (See p. 375.) The following may also be listed:

bake	baking	infer	inference	adverse	adversity
consecrate	consecrating	persevere	perseverance	impure	impurity
debate	debating	rely	reliance	precise	precision
permeate	permeating	revere	reverence	secure	security

If the suffix begins with a consonant, the *e* is retained. Exceptions include *argument, judgment, truly.*
b. A footnote worthy of attention involves the missing *l* in -<u>ful</u>. As a suffix, it is always -<u>ful</u>, even though the word *full* has two *l*'s. Another note has to do with a mysterious *k* that creeps into words ending in -<u>ic</u>. Verbs ending in -<u>ic</u> recover this lost *k* in the past and participial forms. What is the function of this *k* and why is it revived in the inflected forms?

frolic	frolicking	frolicked	antic	sonic
panic(ky)	panicking	panicked	basic	technic(al)
picnic	picnicking	picnicked	manic	terrific
mimic	mimicking	mimicked	public	topic(al)

How do the fourth- and fifth-column words get along without the *k* that creeps in?
c. A cue for you. In English, the letter *q* is always followed by *u: acquire, Quebec, queen, quick, require, requite,* etc.

Spelling principles

In the last analysis, spelling problems may largely be solved by adhering to five simple precepts:
1. *Observe words.* If you look at them carefully enough, the image becomes part of your deeper consciousness. Spelling them will then come naturally.
2. *Pronounce words accurately* and even exaggerate the pronunciation of those that are irregular or that do not behave as expected. The sound image will reinforce the visual image.
3. *Think about the structure of the word and identify the elements that make it up.* Spelling will then begin to make sense, and you will have logical associations that reinforce visual and auditory memory.
4. *Find mnemonic or other devices to help you with words that still bother you.*
5. *Look up words you are not sure about.* Every error complicates and weakens the effect of the other four principles. Remember that good spellers are made, not born. They observe, pronounce, think, look up, and devise artificial ways to remember the words that bother them.

One hundred spelling challengers

1. abbreviate
2. accident(ally)
3. accept
4. accommodate
5. accurate–accuracy
6. alter (a marble alt*a*r)
7. annual(ly)
8. arrange(ment)
9. argument
10. appear(ance)
11. athletics
12. because (it's awful)
13. begin(ning)
14. business (bus and I)
15. calendar (goes far)
16. capital (a domed capit*o*l)
17. cease (seize)
18. certain
19. cloth(es)
20. coarse–of course!
21. college
22. committee
23. conscious
24. crystal
25. curious (curiosity)
26. definite
27. descend
28. dessert (on a desert)
29. dining
30. disappoint
31. dropped (why?)
32. dyeing (cloth)
33. embarrass (double double)
34. enemies (including enema)

35. exaggerate
36. finally (last of all)
37. foreign
38. forfeit
39. freight
40. government
41. grammar (goes *far*)
42. grievous–grievance
43. guarantee
44. harass
45. height
46. humorous
47. illegible
48. immediate(ly)
49. judgment
50. later (than you think) –latter
51. loose–lose (it's lost)
52. mischievous chief
53. misspell (not Ms. Spell)
54. mystery
55. necessary
56. neighbor
57. Niagara
58. niece (the *nice* one)
59. ninety
60. noticeable
61. occasion
62. occurred, occur- rence, occurring (double double)
63. opportunity
64. opposite
65. parallel (la-la-lu)
66. permissible
67. perseverance

68. possess(ion)
69. prejudice
70. principal(ly)– principle
71. privilege
72. probably
73. psychology
74. quite, quiet (only when asleep)
75. receive a receipt (for money paid)
76. recommend
77. resistible–irresistible
78. respect
79. rhythm
80. Satan
81. scissor(s)
82. secretary
83. separate
84. sincere(ly)
85. stationary (hard) stationery (to write on, using *p*ens and *p*encils)
86. stopped
87. straight
88. sovereign
89. sphere
90. success
91. syllable
92. synonym
93. tomorrow
94. tragedy
95. trespass
96. truly truly truly yours
97. usually (use *you*, Allie)
98. villain (in a villa)
99. Wednesday (wed on Wednesday)
100. written–writing

Spelling rules

Rule 1: Words that have a single final consonant at the end preceded by a long vowel sound add a silent *e*. *Bade, musicale,* and a few other words, however, add the silent *e* even though their final consonant is not preceded by a long vowel. And words like *loath* and *sheath* have the long vowel sound even before adding the silent *e* to make *loathe* and *sheathe*.

Rule 2: A verb ending in a single consonant preceded by a short vowel ordinarily doubles this consonant in -<u>ing</u>, -<u>ed</u>, -<u>er</u>, and other forms. If the final consonant is preceded by a long vowel, the consonant is not doubled. Examples: *commit, committed, committee; divide, dividing, divided,* etc. Exceptions: *worshiped, kidnaping, determined. Toll, roll, poll,* and other such words create no problem because the final consonant is already doubled.

Rule 3a: If a word needs an extra syllable to pronounce the plural form, add -<u>es</u> instead of -<u>s</u> to spell it.

Rule 3b: Most words ending in *o* spell the plural by adding -<u>es</u>. Quite a few, especially musical terms, simply add -<u>s</u>.

Rule 3c: Words ending in *y* preceded by a consonant form the plural by changing the *y* to *i* and adding -<u>es</u>. Words ending in *y* preceded by a vowel simply add -<u>s</u> to form the plural.

Rule 4: Think what you are saying and make sure that, by proper pronunciation and emphasis, you relay the desired meaning.

Rule 5: Use the material you have devised to help you distinguish between words with marked similarities.

Rule 6: Use the devices suggested or original ones of your own, as needed, to help you distinguish between homonyms.

Rule 7a: When the sound is *ee,* spell it with *i* before *e,* except after *c.* Exceptions are contained in the sentence given.

Rule 7b: When the sound is not *ee,* the spelling is *e* before *i.* The word *sieve* is an exception.

Rule 7c: Given in text.

Rule 8: Prefixes ending in a consonant usually change the consonant (for the sake of euphony and to avoid awkwardness) to the one with which the root or stem begins.

Rule 9: Double vowels are commonly found in short words of Old English origin. The silent vowel should be sounded in any such words that pose a spelling problem. The same device will help one to remember and to include silent *s, d, e, h, p,* and other letters.

Rule 10: Words ending in *r* appear more likely to be -<u>able</u> words, but no generalization is reliable enough to help much.

Rule 11: -<u>Ar</u> and -<u>or</u> words: *-ar* is more likely to be preceded by *g, l,* or *d; -or* by *t* or *r*.

Rule 12a: The final silent *e* is usually dropped before a suffix beginning with a vowel. Among the exceptions to this rule are the words *changeable, manageable, noticeable,* and *pronounceable* (listed on p. 371) that retain the silent *e* to preserve the "soft" sound of *c* and *g*.

Rule 12b: Given in text.

Rule 12c: Given in text.

appendix

SUFFIXES

Here are five groups of common suffixes with examples of each. They are accompanied by questions and comments and followed by practice exercises.

Group I   Makers of nouns

-al   arrival, betrayal, portrayal, refusal

This suffix is often used to form nouns from verbs.

-ance   connivance, maintenance, nonchalance, obeisance
-ence   acquiescence, deference, iridescence, transference

The two forms of this suffix originally represented two different conjugations in Latin. There is no dependable rule for spelling them in English.

-dom   Christendom, kingdom, officialdom, wisdom
-hood   brotherhood, fatherhood, manhood, motherhood, neighborhood, sisterhood, womanhood

-ship   discipleship, friendship, partisanship

From what language did these three suffixes and most of the roots in the example words originally come? Notice that most of the roots are nouns.

-ee   appointee, devotee, draftee, nominee, repartee, trainee

Which of these words does not denote a person? From what language did the suffix -ee originally come?

-er   abstainer, embezzler, loiterer, transformer, transmitter
-ess   actress, princess

These suffixes denote persons. The suffix -ess when added to person words makes them feminine, although with the preference for nonsexist language this form is falling out of use. What is the source of -ess in words like *duress* and *witness*?

-ice   apprentice, avarice, novice, service

-ism   fetishism, galvanism, pessimism, socialism, truism, witticism

Each of these words denotes a set of beliefs, a saying, or a process. Can you add ten more -isms to the list?

-ist   antagonist, dogmatist, plagiarist, psychiatrist, therapist

Each of these words denotes a person. How many others can you add?

-ity   agility, possibility, reliability, versatility
-ty   fealty, liberty, loyalty, novelty

-ium   auditorium, curium, presidium, radium

-ment   abridgment, chastisement, curtailment, enticement, resentment

Which of the example words varies slightly from the expected spelling? Can you give a very familiar legal noun that is often misspelled because it varies in the same way?

-ness   furtiveness, gruesomeness, hopefulness, pensiveness

From what language did -ness originally come? Notice that each example word is formed by adding this suffix to an adjective.

-or   incisor, innovator, mediator, proprietor, speculator

-(s)ion depression, diversion, obsession, suspension
-(t)ion abolition, coalition, liberation, mediation, sedition

-ure   expenditure, seizure, verdure

-y, -ry empathy, husbandry, irony, rivalry, sympathy
-cy   adjacency, bankruptcy, complacency, consistency, constancy

Group II   Makers of adjectives

-able	consolable, disposable, readable, reconcilable
-ible	contemptible, discernible, irresistible, reducible

-al	abysmal, epochal, fiscal, hexagonal, nocturnal
-ial	connubial, custodial, menial, mercurial, parochial
-ual	casual, gradual, manual, perpetual, visual

> Which words are used both as adjectives and as nouns? What -al, -ial, and -ual words can you name that serve as nouns? What did *individual* originally mean? Note: The suffix -al sometimes serves as a noun suffix: *dispersal, recital, reversal.*

-ese	Balinese, Chinese, Japanese, Portuguese

-ic	nomadic, prosaic, soporific, sporadic, symphonic
-tic	aromatic, dogmatic, pathetic, synthetic, traumatic

> The suffix -ic is often used with -ist nouns, such as *imperialistic* and *futuristic*. Can you think of other examples?

-ine	bovine, equine, labyrinthine, porcine, serpentine
-ile	ductile, infantile, puerile, senile, servile, sterile

> Each of these suffixes has two possible pronunciations. If you are not sure of the pronunciation of the example words, consult a dictionary.

-ive	cursive, festive, pensive, pervasive, regressive, sedative

> Which word has usurped "noundom"? Note: For the use of this suffix in making verbs and nouns, see Group V.

-ish	bookish, fiendish, greenish, peevish, selfish
-ful	delightful, graceful, neglectful, resentful, rueful, sinful
-less	defenseless, graceless, guileless, hapless, relentless
-like	homelike, sylphlike, zephyrlike

> From what language do -ish, -ful, -less, and -like derive? Do most of the roots derive from the same source? Notice that you can add -ness to most of these words and make nouns.

-ous	analogous, rapturous, rigorous, solicitous, tempestuous
-ious	devious, meretricious, sacrilegious, specious, tedious

Group III Makers of verbs

-ate	alleviate, amalgamate, annihilate, compensate, prevaricate

Many words ending in -ate are not verbs. See Group V.

-ify	amplify, deify, gratify, humidify, nullify, pacify
-ize	amortize, burglarize, ostracize, subsidize, temporize

Group IV Makers of adverbs

-ly	adroitly, astutely, complacently, defiantly, warily

This suffix, added to adjectives, produces virtually all of the adverbs in the English language. Occasionally, the suffix makes an adjective: *comely, heavenly, homely, leisurely.*

Group V Versatile suffixes

Certain suffixes may be used to make more than one part of speech. The following suffixes make verbs, nouns, and adjectives, but NOT adverbs.

-ant	assailant, claimant, occupant, savant (nouns) exultant, radiant, self-reliant, valiant (adjectives)

In verbs such as *warrant, decant, recant,* and *supplant,* the -ant is part of the root and not a suffix.

-ary	aviary, functionary, notary (nouns) arbitrary, mercenary, military, subsidiary (adjectives)

What does each word mean? Which of the adjectives are also used as nouns?

-ate   abrogate, deviate, emanate, mediate, perpetrate, terminate (verbs)

See also -ate under Group III.

advocate, candidate, mundate, palatinate, potentate (nouns)

Which of the nouns can also function as a verb?

collegiate, desolate, intermediate, intimate, sedate (adjectives)

Which may be used as a different part of speech without change of form or spelling? What variations in the pronunciation of the suffix do you notice in this list?

-ent   portent, solvent, superintendent (nouns)
evident, insistent, subsequent (adjectives)

Can you define each one? Can you add ten more to the list, with or without the aid of a dictionary of rhymes?

-ite   expedite, ignite, incite, unite (verbs)
Benthamite, Israelite, parasite, satellite (nouns)
exquisite, favorite, finite, tripartite (adjectives)

In chemistry, this suffix has a special meaning in such words as *nitrite, ferrite,* and *fluorite.* Compare *nitrate, ferrate,* and *carbonate.*

-ive   derivative, expletive, substantive (nouns)
affirmative, conclusive, decisive, excessive, restive (adjectives)

The ending -ive in verbs such as *arrive, survive, contrive,* and *derive* belongs to the root and is not a suffix.

-ory   directory, factory, oratory, purgatory (nouns)
advisory, auditory, commendatory, dilatory, inflammatory (adjectives)

-(r)ior   exterior, interior, posterior
anterior, inferior, ulterior

Which one serves as either adjectives or nouns? The ending -(r)ior is the comparative form of Latin adjectives. It provides a pattern for comparative adjectives in English, such as *prettier, happier, merrier.*

Suffix exercises

Most of the words in these exercises are entry words. The addition of suffixes will often produce variant forms you have studied in the units.

1. Give a noun form that corresponds to each of the following verb forms:

   1. abate
   2. abolish
   3. acquiesce
   4. acquit
   5. bereave
   6. connive
   7. defer
   8. disburse
   9. indict
   10. infer

2. What is the noun form that corresponds to each of the following adjective forms?

   1. avaricious
   2. arrogant
   3. authentic
   4. complacent
   5. despotic
   6. grotesque
   7. partisan
   8. ribald
   9. sovereign
   10. versatile

3. Cite a noun—person or agent form—for each of the following words:

   1. abet
   2. appoint
   3. assail
   4. counsel
   5. custody
   6. imperial
   7. loiter
   8. optimistic
   9. skeptical
   10. tyrannical

4. What is the adjective, other than an -ing form, for each of the following verb forms?

   1. congratulate
   2. console
   3. discern
   4. err
   5. indulge
   6. pervade
   7. relent
   8. reproach
   9. reverse
   10. surmount

5. Cite a familiar adjective form that corresponds to each of the following noun forms. Which of these adjectives may be changed into an adverb form?

   1. amenity
   2. chaos
   3. coquette
   4. guile
   5. hypocrisy
   6. libel
   7. mercury
   8. puerility
   9. rigor
   10. sacrilege

6. What is the verb form of each of the following noun forms?

   1. alien
   2. antagonist
   3. brevity (with prefix)
   4. hybrid
   6. proximity (with prefix)
   7. reciprocity
   8. satire
   9. subsidy

    5. indemnity   10. vigor (with prefix)

7. What is the verb form that corresponds to each of the following adjective forms?

    1. domestic   6. luminous (with prefix)

    2. fatuous (with prefix)   7. mobile

    3. galvanic   8. recuperative

    4. immune   9. synthetic

    5. iterative   10. tolerant

index

WORDS, STEMS, AND PREFIXES

All words set in **boldface** *appear as main entry words in the text.*

Pronunciation Key

ā   as in fate, age
ă   as in fat, map
â   as in dare, air
ä   as in father, pa, barn
ē   as in be, equal
ĕ   as in bet, ebb
ê   as in mere, near
ī   as in bite, ice, ride
ĭ   as in bit, if
ō   as in note, boat, low

ŏ   as in hot, box
ȯ   as in dog, law, fought
ô   as in more, roar, door, four
oi as in oil, boy
ou as in out, loud
o͞o as in too, rule
o͝o as in book, put
ŭ   as in fun, up
û   as in fur, term

ə stands for the sound of: **a** in ago, Senate; **e** in open, hopeless, fairness; **i** in peril, trellis; **o** in lemon; **u** in minus, argument; **ou** in famous; **ai** in mountain; **oi** in tortoise.

b   as in bed (bĕd), tub (tŭb)

ch as in chill (chĭl), batch (băch)

d   as in deed (dēd)

f   as in fate (fāt), huff (hŭf)

g   as in get (gĕt), leg (lĕg)

h   as in hop (hŏp)

hw for "wh" as in what (hwŏt), wheel (hwēl)

j   as in jam (jăm), job (jŏb); and for "g" in gentle (jĕn′təl) and range (rānj)

k   as in kin (kĭn), smoke (smōk); for "c" in coal (kōl); and for "ck" in rack (răk)

l   as in let (lĕt), bell (bĕl)

m   as in men (mĕn), him (hĭm)

n   as in not (nŏt), ran (răn)

ng as in song (sȯng); and for "n" in think (thĭngk)

p   as in pup (pŭp)

r   as in ride (rīd), very (vĕr′ē)

r   as in fur (fûr), tar (tär) (This r is not pronounced in some sections of the country.)

s   as in sod (sŏd), must (mŭst); and for "c" in cent (sĕnt), price (prīs)

sh as in she (shē), rush (rŭsh)

t   as in tea (tē), hot (hŏt)

th as in thin (thĭn), bath (băth), breath (brĕth)

th̶ as in then (th̶ĕn), bathe (bāth̶), breathe (brēth̶)

v   as in vat (văt), dove (dŭv); and for "f" in of (ŏv)

w   as in we (wē)

y   as in yet (yĕt)

z   as in zero (zêr′ō), buzz (bŭz); and for "s" in wise (wīz)

zh for "s" as in usual (yo͞o′zho͞o-əl), vision (vĭzh′ən); also for some "g's" as in mirage (mə räzh′)